D1450599

SOCIAL
SCIENCE
and
SOCIAL
POLICY

SOCIAL
SCIENCE
and
SOCIAL
POLICY

Edited by

R. Lance Shotland
Melvin M. Mark

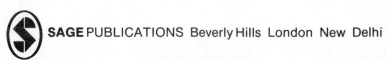

SAGE PUBLICATIONS Beverly Hills London New Delhi

For information address:

SAGE Publications, Inc.
275 South Beverly Drive
Beverly Hills, California 90212

SAGE Publications India Pvt. Ltd.
C-236 Defence Colony
New Delhi 110 024, India

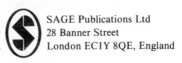

SAGE Publications Ltd
28 Banner Street
London EC1Y 8QE, England

Printed in the United States of America

Library of Congress Cataloging in Publication Data

Main entry under title:

Social science and social policy.

1. Policy sciences--Addresses, essays, lectures.
2. Social sciences--Addresses, essays, lectures.
I. Shotland, R. Lance. II. Mark, Melvin M.
H97.S635   1984   361.6′1   84-18196
ISBN 0-8039-2160-8

FIRST PRINTING

Contents

In memory of
CAROLYN WOOD SHERIF,
who was firmly committed to the use of the
social sciences to improve the human
condition and to further social justice

Carolyn Wood Sherif:
A Memorial Note

LEIGH S. SHAFFER
STEPHANIE A. SHIELDS

Carolyn Wood was born on June 26, 1922, in Loogootee, Indiana. She attended Purdue University and graduated with highest distinction in 1943 with a B.S. degree in General Science. She went directly to graduate school at the State University of Iowa, and within a year had completed work for her Master's Degree in Psychology. During her studies at Iowa, she read Muzafer Sherif's book, *The Psychology of Social Norms,* and years later recalled, "I went around telling anyone— that is the kind of social psychologist I want to be." Upon graduation she moved to Princeton, New Jersey, to work at a survey research firm, but soon found that she was disenchanted with commercial research. A letter of inquiry to Hadley Cantril about further graduate study led to an offer of a research position with Muzafer Sherif. Not surprisingly, she was eager to work with Sherif who had already become an important intellectual model for her. Their collaboration became a partnership when they married in 1945.

The first decade of their marriage was an extraordinarily productive period in which Carolyn managed to integrate the demanding roles of student, research collaborator, wife, and mother. She took graduate coursework at Columbia University with Clifford Morgan and Fred Keller while collaborating with Muzafer on studies of attitude formation and their first joint work on intergroup relations. In 1947, Sue, the first of three daughters, was born, followed by Joan in 1950 and Ann in 1955. *Groups in Harmony and Tension*, a summary of their first experiments on intergroup relations, was published in 1953 and was quickly followed in 1954 by the study for which their collaboration is best known: The Robber's Cave experiment. Published in 1961 in the volume *Intergroup Conflict and Cooperation* (with O. J. Harvey, B. J. White, and W. R. Hood), the Robber's Cave experiment examined the origins of intergroup conflict in competition for limited resources and demonstrated the superiority of superordinate goals as a means for reducing such conflict. By this time it was clear that a distinctive Sherifian approach to social psychology was emerging. They always studied significant human and scientific problems without succumbing to the faddishness of research topics that has often opened social psychology to criticism. They always sought to rigorously apply find-ings from basic research to the study of social behavior; one example is the application of research in psychophysics to the study of social judgment. Finally, they studied all facets of a problem irrespective of traditional divisional boundaries; they not only eschewed the ar-bitrary schism between "psychological" and "sociological" social psychology, but were interdisciplinary in their approach before that term became fashionable.

Shortly after Sue's birth, the Sherifs relocated in Oklahoma and became affiliated with the Institute of Group Relations. In 1958, at Muzafer's urging, Carolyn Sherif, already the author or coauthor of several papers and one book, returned to graduate school at the Univer-sity of Texas to complete her Ph.D. under Wayne Holtzman. She com-pleted the degree requirements in a compressed effort that was not without its ironies. *Intergroup Conflict and Cooperation* was published while she was in graduate school, and Carolyn later recalled that as she left a statistics exam, a fellow student stopped her and asked her to autograph a copy of the book! Upon completion of her degree, the Sherifs returned to a more normal lifestyle in Oklahoma, but they were looking for an institution in which they could both hold tenure track positions. The Sherifs accepted visiting appointments at the Pennsylvania State University in 1965 and assumed regular academic appointments the following year. Carolyn held her position until her untimely death, having been promoted to a Full Professor in 1970.

The 1960s had been a time of scholarly growth and maturation. With Muzafer she published *Reference Groups* in 1964, a study of natural adolescent groups in five American cities. Her continuing in-terest in adolescence as a period epitomizing the problems of the individual as a group member led to the publication of *Problems in Youth* in 1965—again with Muzafer Sherif. In addition to her concern for social problems, she was also concerned with developing appropriate methods for scientific measurement. In this area she will be best remembered for a third book, *Attitude and Attitude Change* (published in 1965 with Muzafer Sherif and Roger Nebergall). Already listed by *Current Contents* as a "citation classic," this volume summarized the highly influential social judgment-involvement approach to attitudes. This approach was the only theory of attitudes that attempted to integrate the study of specific attitudes with the overall structure of the individual's self-system. Two additional books were published in the 1960s: *Attitude, Ego-Involvement and Change* (published in 1967) that further explored the social judgment-involvement theory and *Social Psychology,* the third revised edition of a textbook (published in 1969).

Through the 1970s, Carolyn Sherif continued research in the areas of the self-system, intergroup conflict and cooperation, and social judgment, but she also assumed a leadership role in psychology both nationally and internationally. As the quality and quantity of her work gained wider recognition, she was asked to contribute to areas of research and scholarship outside of her own field. For example, her work on the Robber's Cave study and subsequent studies of adolescent groups had made ingenious use of children's and adolescents' sports activities in the study of natural group processes. This expertise in groups and the competitive process led her to contribute to the emerging field of sport psychology. She was the only woman speaker at the plenary session of the Scientific Congress held before the 1972 Olympic Games in Munich and was a participant in several other sports-oriented conferences. The 1970s also saw her professional and scientific concerns for women's status come to the forefront of her activities. Following her involvement with a student-initiated graduate seminar on the Psychology of Women at The Pennsylvania State University in 1972, she devoted a considerable amount of her research and professional efforts to the issue of gender and psychology. She became very active in Division 35 (Psychology of Women) of the American Psychological Association (APA), serving in various capacities including Division President in 1979-1980. Two of her best known articles include "What Every Intelligent Person Should Know About Psychology and Women," published in 1979, and "Bias in Psychology," which received the Distinguished Publication Award of the Association for Women in Psychology in 1980.

Recently her efforts received many of the highest distinctions offered by her peers. Her long-standing concern for social policy and social justice was recognized when she was named editor of the *Journal of Social Issues,* a post she never assumed. Her concern for students' welfare, reflected in the number of students' papers she encouraged, sponsored, and coauthored and in her 1976 textbook *Orientation in Social Psychology,* was recognized when she received APA's Distinguished Contribution to Education Award in Psychology for 1982. She was also a contributor to the Nebraska Symposium on Motivation (published in 1980), was a Sigma Xi Lecturer for 1981 and 1982, and was a G. Stanley Hall Lecturer at the 1981 APA Convention in Los Angeles. After a brief illness, and at the brink of a new period of productivity, Carolyn Wood Sherif died on July 23, 1982.

Carolyn once wrote that "psychology today is not a developed science, but a series of brews prepared by different cooks and served cafeteria style." We cannot help but believe that she would have savored the menu for this volume. She never let her students forget that social behavior is always located in some real world context; individuals' lives represent a small slice of human history, and the broad dramas of national politics and world events are not irrelevant to the actions of any individual. The result was that she encouraged us to reach out to other disciplines to understand that context and avoid projecting our own ethnocentrisms onto false accounts of human behavior. But above all, it was her nature to be interested in people, the quality of their lives, and the role she could play in bettering their lives. The topics of this volume honor her memory: She believed in applying scientific knowledge to formulating social policy and that scientific knowledge, stripped of bias and stereotype, served the interests of social justice.

Introduction

Research designed to inform policymaking processes has become commonplace. Indeed, such research is often sponsored by policymakers or mandated by law. For example, Chelimsky (1983) reports that the Government Accounting Office (GAO) found that in the 1980 fiscal year there were approximately 2,400 nondefense evaluations in progress in the Executive Branch of the U.S. Government, with a combined budget of about $180 million. Although a proportion of these evaluations were not social science research, the total number and the funding level for social science-based evaluations in the Executive Branch is clearly large.

Social science evidence is considered, in varying degrees, at virtually all levels of government. Federally, the Executive Branch is a major sponsor of research, as Chelimsky's (1983) data from GAO suggest.[1] The Legislative Branch also sponsors and evaluates social science research, as evidenced by the conduct and synthesis of such research by the GAO and other congressional offices (e.g., Chelimsky, 1981; Saxe & Koretz, 1982). Judicial use of social science data is also apparent, at least since the 1954 Supreme Court decision in Brown vs. Topeka (Saks, 1980). Further, the consideration of social science data in policymaking processes is not restricted to the federal level. State and local use of evaluation data, although limited, appears to be increasing. In addition, nonprofit organizations (e.g., the Ford Foundation, the Center for the Prevention of Handgun Violence) often conduct, contract, or review social science reseach for use in attempts to affect policy.

Policy relevant research, then, is pervasive. Yet dramatically conflicting opinions exist about how successful the social sciences are in contributing to policy (e.g., Berns et al., 1981). It therefore seems appropriate to critically evaluate the role of the social sciences in shaping and evaluating social policy. This volume attempts to do so: It examines the past, present, and potential of the social sciences in policy creation, implementation, and evaluation processes.

There is a considerable range of opinions presented in this book about the ability of the social sciences to provide useful information, varying from stark pessimism to confident optimism. The most common view, we believe, is: The social sciences *can* contribute to policymaking processes, but these contributions are likely to be modest in many if not most cases; social science contributions involve not only empirical answers to particular policy questions, but are as likely to involve raising or clarifying questions or changing conceptualizations; and there are ways of making the social sciences more useful to policy.

The possibility of improvement constitutes a central goal of the volume: To consider ways of making the social sciences more useful for social policy processes. All of the chapters examine obstacles to more effective social science contributions. Further, many of the chapters include explicit recommendations for improvements, and those chapters without explicit recommendations point the way toward improvements by identifying current shortcomings in policy relevant research. Taken as a whole, the chapters point clearly to certain methods for improving social science research on policy issues, and we highlight some of these possible improvements in our concluding chapter.

ORIGIN OF THIS VOLUME

Carolyn Wood Sherif, an extremely influential social psychologist, died suddenly after a short illness in July, 1982. Her colleagues at the Pennsylvania State University wanted to commemorate her memory.

Carolyn's scholarly interests were quite varied; her illustrious career included several phases focusing on a number of different research topics. This volume is not a *Festschrift;* it does not attempt to touch upon the various research interests Carolyn had. Rather we sought to identify the broader themes underlying all of Carolyn's work: (1) A concern for the use of the social sciences to better the human condition; (2) a desire to further social justice; and (3) an interest in interdisciplinary social science collaboration. Many of the chapters in this volume therefore address policy issues related to Carolyn's interest in social justice in the areas of race, gender, and human development; these include affirmative action, comparable worth, school desegregation, rape legislation, compensatory education, and day care.

ORGANIZATION OF THE VOLUME

The authors of the four chapters in Part I were asked to address particular factors that affect the usability of social science research in a wide range of policy areas. These four chapters deal respectively with: Methodology, and particularly multiplism as a strategy in research methods; measurement and the characteristics of social science numbers; program implementation and the lessons of implementation for evaluation; and the role of the social scientist as an actor in the policymaking arena. These chapters focus largely on existing obstacles to social science contributions to policy and on strategies for making the social sciences more useful.

Part II of the book includes nine chapters, each of which focuses on the role the social sciences have played and could play in a particular policy area. These nine chapters are divided into three sections of three chapters each. The chapters in each section share a focus on a broad policy domain. The three policy domains represented are: The economy and interventions in the workplace, educational policy and child care, and criminal justice policy. The chapters in Part II focus largely on assessing the nature of social science contributions; that is, they evaluate how well we have done in the past. In addition, most of these chapters identify obstacles to making greater contributions, and several recommend means of increasing the usefulness of the social sciences.

To a degree, the chapters in Parts I and II overlap like the threads in a weaver's loom. The chapters in Part I that concern general factors are the "warp threads" of the book. The chapters in Part II, which examine specific policy areas in which the general factors considered in Part I arise, are the "weft threads." Together these sections create the "cloth" of the book. This is not to say that the cloth is whole, that stitches are not missing, or that the woven pattern is perfectly clear. Nevertheless, we hope the end product will be helpful in clarifying the roles of social science in social policy processes and in suggesting strategies for increasing the usefulness of the social sciences in policy. To that end, the final part of the volume consists of a concluding chapter by the editors in which we try to review, clarify, and extend some of the themes of the book.

PREPRATION OF THE VOLUME

Edited volumes are often characterized by a lack of cohesion, particularly when they include the number of diverse topics the present volume does. In an attempt to create a coherent volume, two steps were taken. First, each author was asked to consider a list of possible obstacles to the more successful application of the social sciences to policy. This list included such possible problems as shortcomings of methods, measurement, problem definition, theory, implementation, and politics. Authors were also asked to consider whether some apparent failures of social science occur because we are sometimes faced with an intractable problem. This list was not meant as a framework around which authors would organize their chapters; rather, its purpose was to encourage all the authors to consider the range of factors that may affect the relationship between social science and social policy. Nor was the list meant to lead authors to particular conclusions. Indeed, authors were asked to judge the relevance of the potential obstacles and to draw their own conclusions about how successfully the social sciences were being applied in policymaking.

As a second step toward cohesion, the authors were asked to present preliminary drafts of their papers at a conference entitled *Social Science, Social Policy, and Social Justice* at the University Park campus of The Pennsylvania State University on April 22-24, 1983. We believed that an opportunity for face-to-face exchanges among the authors, and between the authors and editors, would make the book more cohesive. Nearly all of the contributors to the volume attended the conference and presented preliminary versions of their chapters.

We did not suggest to the authors a particular definition of "policymaking" or of what constitutes a successful "use" of the social sciences. Our preference was to allow authors to employ their own interpretations of these constructs. It is worth noting that (1) different authors employ somewhat different notions of use and policymaking (that are often implicit rather than explicitly stated), and (2) on the whole, a contemporary, complex conception of both "policymaking" and "use" emerges from the volume. In the final chapter of the book, we return to the question of the alternative uses of social science data and the conceptualization of policymaking.

ACKNOWLEDGMENTS

We would like to thank the Department of Psychology, that with additional financial help from the Departments of Sociology, Economics, the Colleges of Human Development and Education, and the Keller Conference Center, supported the conference *Social Science, Social Policy, and Social Justice*. Without their help this important link in the production of this volume could not have been undertaken. We specifically would like to thank Robert Stern, the Head of the Psychology

Department, for his encouragement, cooperation, and moral support. We are also grateful to Robert Sinclair and Mark Miller, two of our graduate students, for their able assistance during the conference. We wish to thank Esther Strause and Ellen Trumbo for their fine clerical assistance. We thank our wives and colleagues, Lynne Goodstein, and Mary Beth Crowe, for their suggestions, comments, and help on various phases of the project. We are also grateful to Fred Bryant of the Loyola University of Chicago for his helpful comments on the concluding chapter. Mitch Allen, the editor at Sage who worked with us initially; Terry Hendrix, the editor who saw the project through to completion; and the Sage staff were courteous, professional, and a pleasure to work with in producing the book. Our acknowledgments would not be complete without thanking the authors who made our work interesting and fun. Obviously, without their contributions, the book would be rather empty!

—*R. Lance Shotland*
Melvin M. Mark

NOTE

1. Federal funding of social science research has declined during the Reagan Administration. The impact of this decline on utilization is yet unclear. Nevertheless, the overall level of policy-relevant research and the potential use of such research remain socially significant.

REFERENCES

Berns, W., Horowitz, I. L., Kristol, I., Nisbet, R., Prewitt, K., Riesman, D., Rossi, A., & Wilson, J. Q. (1981). Is social science a god that failed? *Public Opinion, 4,* 10-15.
Chelimsky, E. (1981). *Designing backward from the end-use.* Presidential address to the Evaluation Research Society, October 1981.
Chelimsky, E. (1983). Standards for federal program evaluation. *ERS (Evaluation Research Society) Newsletter, 7*(2), 1, 4-5.
Saks, M. J. (1980). The utilization of evaluation research in litigation. In L. A. Braskamp & R. D. Brown (Eds.), *Utilization of evaluative information.* San Francisco, CA: Jossey-Bass.
Saxe, L., & Koretz, D. (Eds.). (1982). *Making evaluation research useful to Congress.* San Francisco, CA: Jossey-Bass.

PART I

General Issues

The four chapters in this part address factors that affect the utility of social science research in a wide range of policy areas. We might also note that several of the chapters have important implications for more basic social science research as well. In Chapter 1, Tom Cook focuses on "multiplism" as a strategy for enhancing social science policy research; by multiplism Cook essentially means the use of multiple methodologies, the investigation of multiple research questions, and the representation of multiple constituencies in defining research goals. Multiplism, in these many forms, recurs throughout the book as a strategy for increasing the usefulness of social science research. Cook suggests that multiplism has arisen in the social sciences from the erosion of authority given particular methods and particular questions; this erosion has arisen primarily for two reasons: (1) The attacks on the positivistic logic of science underlying previous research practices, and (2) the lessons from applied social science research of the Great Society. In considering these sources of multiplism, Cook provides a brief history of the philosophy and practice of research methodology in applied social sciences. Cook concludes his chapter by discussing the limits of multiplism and pointing out the importance of a critical, thoughtful use of multiplism.

Chapter 2 concerns measurement in policy relevant research. Lee Sechrest begins this chapter by describing a set of criteria for evaluating measures that go beyond the familiar standards of reliability and validity. Sechrest then describes and illustrates a variety of problems that may plague measurement efforts in social policy research. Sechrest also provides suggestions for "renumbering"; that is, for making our numbers more useful. In concluding, Sechrest points out that we should acknowledge that in some cases our numbers are not useful or important in social policy processes. This is a point that will arise again in later chapters.

Milbrey McLaughlin addresses the issue of program implementation in Chapter 3. After too-frequent experiences in attempting to evaluate a program that was not in place as intended—and even in some cases, when there was no program at all—program evaluators have become increasingly interested in assessing implementation. McLaughlin reviews some important lessons from the literature on implementation and discusses their implications for policy research. Among the many points McLaughlin makes are the importance of studying *process,* and—reminiscent of Cook—the need for multiplism in our evaluation questions and methodologies. These points arise frequently, in various forms, in the chapters that follow. McLaughlin also calls our attention to the form of conclusion that evaluators should make in light of the possibility of higher order interactions on which program effectiveness may depend. She further notes the importance of alternative evaluation models that seek to provide regular feedback to "street-level bureaucrats."

Tom Pettigrew, in the fourth and final chapter of Part I, addresses the ability of social scientists to be effective actors in the policy area. Pettigrew first provides a brief historical review of social science activities in policy, complementing Cook's earlier historical review. His discussion highlights that the use of social science in policy deliberations depends not only on the quality of the social science research but also on a number of mediating influences, such as the press, and on the receptiveness of the policy-makers. This view of social science influences as indirect and mediated, which Pettigrew discusses, implicitly underlies nearly every other chapter in the book.

1

Postpositivist Critical Multiplism

THOMAS D. COOK

This chapter is concerned with what I think is the most pressing methodological problem of our day: How can scientific practice be justified in light of the cogent criticisms of its most basic premises by philosophers, historians, and sociologists of science? This difficulty is felt more acutely within the social than the natural sciences, and perhaps most acutely by those who have worked at the interface between social science and social policy. This is because social science theory and method were used in the 1960s and 1970s to help design and evaluate social programs aimed at ameliorating social problems, but the results from these programs were disappointing. Was this because social science is an inappropriate source of input into social policy and cannot produce effective programs or clear-cut evaluations? If so, the reasoning goes, might social policy benefit no more from social *science* knowledge than from other forms of knowledge about society and human nature?

Commentators have responded to the doubts about science in general and about the role of social science in policy analysis by attempting to justify science in what I call a multiplist mode. Among other things, multiplism is associated with the call for (1) *multiple* operationalism (e.g., Webb, Campbell, Schwartz & Sechrest 1966); (2) *multimethod* research (e.g., Campbell & Fiske, 1959); (3) planned research programs based on *multiple* interconnected studies (e.g., Lakatos & Musgrave, 1970); (4) the synthesis of *multiple* studies related to each other in haphazard fashion (e.g., Glass, McGaw, & Smith, 1981); (5) the construction of complex *multivariate* causal models instead of simple univariate ones (e.g., Simon, 1957; Blalock, 1961); (6) the competitive testing of *multiple* rival hypotheses rather than testing a single hypothesis (e.g., Popper, 1972); (7) the use of *multiple* stakeholders to formulate research questions (e.g., Cronbach et al., 1980); (8) the use of *multiple* theoretical and value frameworks to interpret research questions and findings (e.g., Cronbach, 1982; Dunn, 1982); (9) the advocacy that *multiple* analysts examine important data sets (e.g., Mosteller & Moynihan, 1972); and (10) the desirability of *multitargeted* research that seeks to probe many different types of issue within a single study (e.g., Chen & Rossi, 1980; 1983).

The purpose of this chapter is to examine how well a multiplist approach meets the total set of challenges that come from the philosophy, history, and sociology of science and from experiences using social science during the social reform years of the 1960s and 1970s.

THE ORIGINS OF MULTIPLISM

In a world where one way of conducting research was universally considered to be "correct," scientific practice would be easy. Researchers would simply do what is correct. It is the current absence of total certainty about what constitutes correct practice that leads to the advocacy of multiplism in perspectives and methods. The current uncertainty arises, I think, from two principle sources. The first is the systematic attack on the theory of knowledge that was dominant until 20 years ago in most philosophy of science; the second is the move social scientists made toward causal research in field settings. This meant a move away from the laboratory and the traditions of causal research it represents based on control over stimulus materials and external events, and also a move away from the descriptive theory and cross-sectional research methods then prevalent among sociologists and political scientists. Given these moves, lessons had to be learned from experience about what happens when control is reduced while the ambition to infer is simultaneously increased—the state of affairs during the Great Society years.

A. The Attack on Positivism

An amusing incident took place in 1961 in Tubingen during a special symposium held on epistemological issues in the social sciences. Popper was the first speaker, and Adorno was the second. It was widely expected that Popper would defend epistemological positions believed to be "positivist" and that Adorno would challenge these positions. However, because Popper unequivocably denounced positivism, the anticipated confrontation did not materialize. It was then left to Dahrendorf, the rapporteur, to reveal why. He noted that Popper defined positivism in terms of the "empty bucket" theory of induction. This assumes that some associations repeatedly occur in nature that can be validly observed by senses that bring no prior knowledge to bear, and from these observations general laws can be induced. This conception of positivism is quite different from the more hypothetico-deductive version that Adorno attacked. The latter assumes that totally explicit theories are possible from which hypotheses can be deduced that can subsequently be confronted with empirical data that will confirm or reject the theory from which the hypotheses were derived.

The difficulties Popper and Adorno had in agreeing on a definition of positivism incline me not to offer my own. Because many varieties of positivism can be constructed, I will outline the ontological, epistemological, and methodological assumptions that characterize the scientific beliefs and practices that are today more likely to be labeled "positivist," irrespective of their links to past theories of positivism. I do not want to suggest that any social (or natural) scientist has ever subscribed to all these assumptions, or that they adequately describe scientific practice as it occurs, or that practice has evolved only from positivism or from any other single philosophy of science for that matter. Scientific practice has multiple origins that include the trial-and-error behavior of practitioners, selective adaptations from prior philosophies, and research on research. Nonetheless, the assumptions I call positivist were widely disseminated after 1930 and were used to justify a particular set of scientific practices. These assumptions were partly based on logic and partly on how philosophers thought physicists went about the business of doing research and constructing theories.

1. Ontological assumptions Positivists are realists and assume the existence of the world outside of the mind. They further assume that this world is lawfully ordered and that the major task of science is to describe this order. The order is assumed to be deterministic in its manifestations (rather than probabilistic) so that once the laws of nature are known, perfect prediction will result. Indeed, only when perfect prediction has been achieved do positivists want to speak of having discovered a law. Laws are preferred if they are general and apply to many phenomena, if they are functional in form and specify how observable forces are related to each other, and if they are parsimonious because few forces need to be invoked. Einstein's $e = mc^2$

meets these criteria. It applies to all motion and subsumes all prior theories of motion; it specifies the form of a relationship; and because one parameter is a constant only one other needs to be estimated. Most positivists further assume that the terms in their laws will be ahistorical, based on forces that are permanent fixtures of the external world, and nonmentalistic, devoid of conceptions based on intentions and wishes.

All these ontological assumptions have come under attack. Some are probably false. For instance, to assume determinism flies in the face of discoveries from particle physics and molecular biology suggests that the most basic elements of the universe are related probabilistically. The assumptions have come under attack in the social sciences because of their dubious relevance to human nature, social organization, and the current status of social theory. Practicing social scientists know that perfect prediction (i.e., $R^2 = 1$) is impossible with current theories. They also realize that to increase prediction nearly always entails adding more constructs to a theoretical system. But this jeopardizes parsimony. They also believe that most research areas are circumscribed in coverage (i.e., they apply only to, say, attitude change or intergroup cooperation) and that making them more general would probably lead to highly abstract verbal theories with little predictive power for particular instances. To take perfect prediction as a criterion for inferring laws and generalities seems inordinately unrealistic to many of those who criticize the relevance of physics to the social sciences.

Positivists gravitate to prediction because it depends on observing the correlation between variables; they want to avoid constructs like "causation" that cannot be directly observed. But prediction does not necessarily lead to causal or explanatory knowledge (Bhaskar, 1979; Scriven, 1971) and does not guarantee control over events (Collingwood, 1940). For instance, we can almost perfectly predict the length of any day from the length of prior days and the length of the same day one year ago. But that hardly helps either to explain the length of a day or to modify its length. Because prediction, whether in a deterministic or probabilistic mode, does not necessarily entail explanation or manipulation, some critics of positivism reject it as the sole, or even major, criterion for judging the adequacy of theories. Most want to replace it with causal explanation.

But in the social sciences such explanation is not likely to take the simple form of the laws of physics. Most social phenomena are multiply determined; each unique cause may be related to other causes in complex ways; and each cause may itself be complexly and multiply determined by other forces that are not themselves direct causes of what is being explained. To practicing social scientists, causal explana-

tion is not likely—in the near term, at least—to involve simple relationships that look like parsimonious laws. Instead, multiple causal determinants, multiple causal paths, and multiple causal contingencies have
to be assumed, making human nature and social relationships seem
more like pretzels than single-headed arrows from A to B or simple
functional equations—more like convoluted multivariate statistical interactions than simple main effects (e.g., Cronbach & Snow, 1976; House,
1980; McGuire, 1984).

It is difficult to assume that the circumscribed level of prediction
that social scientists now attain will remain stable over settings and
times. To exemplify this, replace the analogy of physics with that of
macrobiology. Unlike the case with physical objects, animals (including
man) seek to control their environments, and the knowledge they achieve
is often stored as genetic mutations or as the teachings of priests,
grandmothers, law books, and even methodology texts. The past lives
on in the behavioral and cognitive present, influencing how we define
problems, select possible solutions, and envisage future opportunities.
Because it is rare that only one response will be adequate for meeting
individual or species' "needs," a macrobiological perspective suggests
that the same set of external contingencies can result in a wide variety
of apparently adaptive responses, with the form of the response depending on what unfolds from within, what has transpired in the
past, and what is available in the present, including chance and present
plans for the future. The argument is, then, that laws about human
nature and social life cannot be inferred using the physicists' assumptions of ahistoricity and nonmentalism.

The preceding arguments are about how human nature and social
relationships are organized in the real world. They are not about whether
there is an external world. However, even this fundamental assumption
has come under attack from scholars who contend that humans have
a compulsion to understand their world, and, in so doing, construct
meanings in their minds. Because people respond to such constructions
rather than to the external world itself, critics like Habermas (1972)
or Harré and Secord (1972) contend that it is mind that determines
behavior and not the world outside of the mind, if there is one. Note
that this denial of realism is not based on a direct refutation. Rather,
it postulates that we do not need to assume an external world if we
can never prove that one exists and if we believe that humans react
anyway to mental constructions of the world rather than to the world itself.

2. Epistemological assumptions Crucial to positivism is the assumption that "objective" knowledge is possible—that theory-neutral obser-

vations can be made that tap directly into nature and are not affected
by the wishes, hopes, expectations, category systems, etc. of observers.
So pervasive is the role of observation that positivists espouse a definitional operationalism that makes an entity no more or less than its
measure. From this belief follows the dictum that "IQ is what IQ
tests measure"; IQ is not seen to be a hypothetical entity defining
the cognitive skills that are considered most useful for manipulating
abstract knowledge.

Attacks on the neutrality or objectivity of observation have come
from many quarters, largely on the grounds that science is conducted
by people, and people cannot divorce themselves from their prior
knowledge and expectations. The subjective components in observation
may come from many sources—the social class biases stressed by Marxists,
the paradigmatic biases emphasized by Kuhn (1962), or the investigator
expectancies stressed by Merton (1957) and Rosenthal (Rosenthal &
Jacobson, 1968). To those who crave certain knowledge from the senses
no consolation is offered from modern developments in epistemology,
metascience, or human perception (Campbell, 1974). And to those
who believe that individuals may be biased but multiple observers
may not be in the aggregate, it must be pointed out that Kuhn's work
(1962) became so salient because his thesis was that *all* the scientists
in a particular field at a particular time may share the same set of
fallacious and unacknowledged assumptions that enter into all observations of nature.

Critics have also taken issue with according a special status to observables. Science has often progressed because bold thinkers were
willing to postulate the unobservable, and, in some cases, were eventually proven correct. We still today cannot see the core of the earth,
and yet geologists and mineralogists do research on how it might be
composed. Moreover, some theories have only improved explanatory
power by invoking constructs that cannot be directly observed, as
with recent shifts by behaviorists to incorporate cognitive and affective
phenomena (e.g., Bandura, 1977; Bower, 1981). The pragmatic case,
then, is that neither prediction or explanation is enhanced by restricting
oneself to observables.

The epistemological basis of positivism goes beyond postulating
the possibility of observation that is both theory-neutral and comprehensive. Logic is also involved. Inductivist versions of positivism rely on
abstracting general statements from observed regularities. To achieve
this requires a defensible theory of induction, but none is yet available
(Popper, 1959). Although attempts have been made to construct

defenses of induction, it is not clear that they can deal with the logical problem inherent in inferring from past regularities that the same regularity will continue into the future. Among social scientists, a hypothetico-deductive version of positivism has had more adherents than a pure inductivist version. Accepting this critique of induction, hypothetico-deductivists recommend that scientists should strive to deduce unique observable hypotheses from a theory and they should then confront these hypotheses with observational data that will definitively confirm or disconfirm the hypotheses and their parent theory.

One of the many assumptions behind the hypothetico-deductive approach is that the theory being scrutinized is totally explicit in the constructs and patterns of relationship it specifies and in the ways it specifies how each construct should be measured. If a theory is not specific on these matters, disconfirming observations can be used, not to reject the theory—as is required in positivism—but rather to add novel theoretical contingencies that encompass the disconfirmations by specifying when a particular relationship should and should not be found or how a construct should and should not be measured. Unfortunately, nearly all of the social science theories of today are so "squishy" or "incommensurable" that little ingenuity is required to accommodate disconfirming results. Moreover, the passion that leads individuals to develop theories may often incline them to reject deviant findings in preference to accepting them as the new "truth." And when many of the major scholars in a field are proponents of a particular theory, disconfirmations will have an even more difficult battle because they then need to prevail against a powerful "invisible college" of scientific opinion-makers.

3. Methodological assumptions The primacy of indentifying functional relationships between observables means that observation and quantitative measurement play large roles in positivism. Without such data one cannot sensitively test the specific equations that predict an outcome. From the importance of quantified observation follow several important methodological consequences. The first is a stress on developing better techniques of measurement, e.g., more powerful telescopes, microscopes, x-rays, attitude scales, physiological measures, etc. The second is a move toward experimentation and laboratory sciences. Measurement is easier when the objects of study do not change in unknown ways, as occurs in much physics in which inert objects are studied and all the external sources of change in these objects have been earlier identified and can either be kept out of the explanatory system by such means as lead-lined walls or can be directly measured in credible ways.

However, the objects of study are not inert in the human sciences. They mature. They react to historical events. Moreover, we do not know all of the factors to which people react, and many of those we do know about are not measurable. From this arises the rationale for laboratory research, with its goal of isolation and control over extraneous variables. However, humans are adaptable and can construct beliefs and behaviors that help them adapt to the unique ecology of the laboratory. For instance, we know that humans often react to the suspicion they are being observed. But sometimes they react negatively, sometimes with resignation, and sometimes even with a misguided sense of helpfulness (Weber & Cook, 1972). Unfortunately, we do not know when they react each way; and even if we did we could not easily quantify how much the knowledge of being observed influenced particular responses. Because these theoretical irrelevancies cannot be totally specified, some scholars believe that it is preferable to prevent them from occurring at all. This means leaving the lab and conducting field research with unobtrusive measurement.

The concern with perfect prediction leads positivists to methods based on analytic reductionism—breaking an observed relationship down into the components that are necessary and sufficient for a relationship to occur. Positivists would not be satisfied with establishing that X is sometimes related to Y. They would like to discover what it is about X that is invariably related to some particular aspect of Y. To do this they decompose X and Y into their constituent elements, each of which will eventually be studied in its own right. But decomposing X into its causally efficacious components (say X') and Y into its causally impacted elements (say Y') may still not be enough. Perfect prediction may further depend on relating X' and Y' to "third variables" that codetermine their relationship, especially the more microscopically specified variables that occur after X' has changed and before Y' has been influenced. The upshot of the urge to improve prediction through decomposition and the discovery of substantively relevant mediating variables is a science that slowly gravitates to a more reductionist level of analysis, relatively closed systems as testing sites (e.g., the laboratory), and a form of research in which the control afforded by experimentation is valued more than the holism faciliated by naturalism.

Positivism is also associated with the belief that a single "crucial experiment" can definitively test a theory (or the difference in viability between one or more theories). Brute empiricism of the kind, "what will happen if I do X?" is not prized; nor is descriptive research that is devoid of hypothesis testing or willful intrusions into nature. The emphasis on the crucial experiment also leaves out of science phenomena that cannot be easily quantified or controlled, thereby running the risk that substantive importance may play less of a role in selecting research topics than the degree to which quanitification, control, prediction, experimentation, and theory testing are possible. We can see in the attack on positivist methods a rejection of the primacy of observation over introspection, quantification over understanding, micro-level over macro-level analysis, control over naturalism, theory testing over discovery, and crucial experiments conducted on select parts of nature over more tentative probing of all of nature.

4. The consequences of such attacks When scientists share a common set of assumptions it is presumably easier to decide how to proceed with the practice of science. One simply selects the kinds of problems and methods commensurate with the guiding assumptions. But when—as today—foundations are under attack, question and method choice become more problematic. It is now not easy to assume one is trying to describe a social world that is lawfully fixed, deterministically ordered, and can be perfectly described with elegant and simple functional relationships; it is not now easy to assume that everything of importance can be measured, that value-free measurement is possible, and that our theories are perfectly specified. It is not now easy to assume that closed-system methods generalize to open-system contexts, that crucial experiments are possible that provide definitive tests of theories, and that little value should be accorded to methods of discovery as opposed to methods of testing. Multiplism arose partly in response to such questioning of old certainties about question and method choice. But that was not its only origin, at least not in policy-related research.

B. Social Reform in the 1960s and 1970s

The Kennedy, Johnson, and Nixon presidencies were associated with social reforms in many sectors of the social welfare system. By and large, these proved to be disappointing in their effects. The major reasons for this were probably (1) inadequacies in the knowledge of society undergirding the design and implementation of social programs; (2) inadequacies of the social science methods used to evaluate these programs; and (3) limitations in the range of values and interests incorporated into both the definition of social problems and the selection of approaches designed to ameliorate these problems. Because these diagnoses overlap with the critique of positivism and disappointment with the gains of the Great Society and its offshoots occurred at about the same time positivism came under attack, it is difficult—if not impossible—to distinguish which parts of the advocacy of multiplism followed from the attack on positivism and which from the intellectual inquests on the Great Society.

We turn now to a discussion of *how* disappointment with social reform attempts influenced practice among social scientists. We argue that uncertainty was created about the degree of authority warranted by substantive social theory, by the research techniques then most widely accepted, and by the use of formal decisionmakers as the sole source for generating policy-relevant research questions.

1. The decrease in authority experienced by substantive theory Every social program is implicitly or explicitly undergirded by theoretical postulates about factors that will ameliorate a social problem, whether it is poor academic achievement, underemployment, or prison recidivism. Not surprisingly, social planners and program developers looked to social scientists for some of the knowledge they needed to design into specific practices that might ameliorate these problems. In retrospect, we can see that such expectations were inappropriate.

One difficulty that quickly became obvious was that most of the hypotheses used were internally inadequate. That is, doubts quickly became clear about the validity of such hypotheses as better food promotes learning in poor children; more police visibility reduces crime; rehabilitation lowers prison recidivism, largely because the relevant theories failed to specify the types of conditions under which a given relationship did and did not hold. The contact hypothesis in race relations is an instructive example in this regard because some contingencies were specified from its earliest days in the 1930s (Allport, 1935), but these were inadequate and new contingencies were added (Amir, 1969). But these, in their turn, did not turn out to be comprehensive enough, and we still cannot structure interracial contact that reliably decreases prejudice except in certain very controlled settings in schools.

A second problem with the substantive theories was that they were not comprehensive enough to use as action blueprints. In order to tell service deliverers about the specific acts they should perform under various sets of circumstances much improvisation had to take place on the part of program developers and local personnel. They were forced to build some forms of knowledge into program design that were not contained in the substantive theories of social scientists. Instead, they came from practitioner knowledge or from trial and error learning.

Finally, a new awareness emerged of how problematic it was to implement well in practice those relatively few activities about which substantive theories were indeed explicit. Pressman and Wildavsky (1979) stressed the implementation problems stemming from chaotic events that occur at the site of service delivery where the activities of multiple actors have to be coordinated; Williams (1980) stressed the problems of communication, commitment, and capacity that occur in trying to implement changes in multilevel organizational hierarchies; Fullan (1982) stressed practitioners' reluctance to accede to changes that were asked of them by superiors or outsiders who did not seem to understand or appreciate the pressures on service deliverers; and, finally, Berman (1980) and Bardach (1977) stressed how much implementation depends on system-level considerations of power, language, and history that bind or separate different groups in organizational contexts.

By the middle of the 1970s the authority of substantive social science theory for girding program design was under heavy attack, and alternatives and supplements were sought. Thus, the decrement in authority attributed to theory was accompanied by a corresponding increase in the authority attributed to other forms of knowledge, particularly practitioner wisdom. The claims on its behalf went beyond stressing how it was needed to fill in the gaps in social science knowlege. Claims were also heard that the practices advocated by social service professionals might be just as legitimate as scientific knowledge. The rationale offered was that in a vast nation like the United States, practice is likely to invent many variants, most of which never enter into the "permanent" stock of professional wisdom because they do not seem to be effective or only seem effective in restricted contexts. This suggests that the practices remaining in the permanent stock should include many that have repeatedly withstood unsystematic tests of their adequacy. The implication is that practice should be treated more like a legitimate, alternative form of relevant knowledge than as an ugly stepsister to science.

During the same period, a new value was accorded to observing closely what goes on in programs as they are first implemented. The expectation was that such observational studies would help improve the internal operations of programs and would also lay down a body of general knowledge from which principles about the design, implementation, and revision of social programs could be induced. Implicit in the advocacy of grounded observation was the critique that substantive social theory is often too abstract, too little tested in multiple action contexts, and too rarely formulated with implementation in mind. Consequently it fails to reflect, or be responsive to, the contextual density in which clients and practitioners actually operate and on which the effectiveness of programs depends. The growing pessimism about substantive theory was leavened, then, by growing optimism about the validity and utility of practitioner wisdom and about the roles that grounded observation can play when it is not guided by preordained theoretical concepts.

2. The decrease in authority experienced by particular social science methods In positivist science decision rules were clear and justified "authoritative" statements about scientific practice. As applied to the social sciences, most of the rules were about which methods to use in pursuing particular types of question; thus, to probe causal questions, randomized experiments were advocated; to probe descriptive questions about populations, sample surveys were proposed; and to probe descriptive issues about system relationships, participant observation was proposed. Rules were further formulated about how to do experiments, surveys, and observational studies and about the types of invalid inference that would result if inappropriate methods were chosen. In the 1950s and 1960s it was not difficult to know what were the proper things to do in the social sciences. But experience in the evaluation of social programs led to a weakening of the old links between research functions and methods. Previously advocated methods came to be seen as less deserving of hegemony for the tasks for which they were originally designed; other methods came to be seen as deserving more merit than had previously been allotted to them.

Perhaps the most famous example of this concerns methods for probing the causal effects of programs. Pessimism arose about the efficacy of randomized experiments for this purpose because so many experiments proved to be difficult to mount or to maintain in the desired form over time, especially because of the frequency of treatment-correlated attrition from the study. Moreover, the findings of most experiments were greeted, not with universal approval, but with cacophonous discord about what had really been discovered (Lindblom & Cohen, 1979). Although some of the criticisms were not relevant to random assignment per se, others were. One criticism stressed how random assignment exacerbated invidious comparisons between groups receiving treatments of different value; another stressed the differential attrition that can arise when treatments differ in desirability; and yet another mentioned how random assignment often led to undesirable restrictions to the external validity of studies. Thus, the crucible of experience forced out many of the problems inherent in conducting randomized experiments in open-system contexts. The same identification of weaknesses through experience happened with other forms of experimentation. The authority of many quasi-experimental designs came to suffer from an enhanced realization of the difficulty of specifying all the relevant ways in which treatment groups were nonequivalent and perfectly measuring all the constructs specified in models of such initial nonequivalence.

As might be expected, the identification of problems with particular methods also led to attempts to improve them. Thus arose the advocacy of randomized experiments in which all irrelevant sources of desirability between treatments were reduced; in which the units receiving one treatment could not communicate with those receiving another; and in which the implementation of the experimental design was monitored so as to detect differential attrition early in order to deal with it before it became too late (Cook and Campbell, 1979). (It was also hoped that such monitoring would improve the chances of detecting side effects and of specifying the different populations and settings in which a treatment might have an impact.) In the quasi-experimental domain, the identification of problems led to more self-consciousness about the need for explicit and defensible selection models and to attempts to circumvent the nonequivalence problem in other ways than through measurement and subsequent statistical manipulation; e.g., by means of dry-run experiments in which pretest measurement occurs on two separate occasions; by means of switching replication experiments in which treatments are eventually given to controls; or by means of nonequivalent dependent variables, only one of which is supposed to be affected by a treatment but each of which should be affected by the most plausible alternative interpretations of a treatment effect (Cook & Campbell, 1979). But although experimental methods were improved because of the knowledge generated from the problems identified during the course of social reform attempts, perfection did not result. Experimental methods were still stigmatized.

Some critics of the experiment argued that it was not enough to "band-aid" marginal improvements onto methods that, in their opinion, were fundamentally flawed. The most radical critics of the experiment wanted to search for truly novel methods of causal inference. In particular, a variety of qualitative alternatives were espoused. They were espoused not only on grounds that they facilitated inferences about simple causal relationships, but it was also stressed that they made it easier to assess the quality of treatment implementation, to detect unanticipated side effects, and to provide contextual understanding

(Patton, 1978). Supporting this advocacy were theories that explicitly set out to create a logical basis for inference based on qualitative data (e.g., Scriven's 1976 *modus operandi* approach and Campbell's apparent renunciation of the monolithic supremacy of experiments in Cook & Reichardt, 1979). With qualitative techniques added to the list of possible causal methods and with doubts being so public about the efficacy of randomized experiments, the authority of experiments shrank and method choice became all the more difficult for those who wanted to answer causal questions.

It would be wrong to believe that a decrement in authority was only experienced with experimental methods. As a means for describing populations, survey research methods have been much advocated and are regularly employed. However, recent critiques have stressed the practical difficulties that sometimes occur when trying to implement them; e.g., when resources permit mounting a demonstration project at only a few sites but generalization to the nation at large is desired (Cook, Leviton, & Shadish, in press). Also, ethical and political pressures demand that social research be increasingly conducted with groups and organizations that are fully informed about the research and can opt not to participate. Volunteer biases arise, and need adding to those associated with telephone ownership, being away from the home by day, etc.

As with experiments, the absolute decrement in authority attributed to survey methods was accompanied by an increase in the authority attributed to alternative means of generalization. Cook and Campbell (1979) proposed basing inferences about generalizability in terms of the degree to which relationships were dependably replicated across purposive but heterogeneous samples of respondents and settings, or on the degree to which the samples studied were impressionistically modal of a desired target population (see also St. Pierre & Cook, in press). The popularity of meta-analysis seems also to have added credibility to the idea that generalized statements are often warranted when findings have been multiply replicated across heterogeneous samples of respondents, settings, and times, none of which were chosen with known probability from a designated population. Although inferences based on continuities across heterogeneous instances do not have the same logical warrant as inferences based on samples in which the probability of selection is known, they are nonetheless not completely without worth. This being so, we can see that the authority of the sample survey was squeezed from two ends: Increased doubts arose about its absolute adequacy, and an enhanced justification was offered for some alternatives that are more easily implemented. This double squeeze is exactly what occurred with experiments.

The experiences gained in designing and evaluating social reforms in the 1960s and 1970s led to another important insight about method choice. Such choice is made all the more difficult, not only because many methods exist for fulfilling any one research function, but also because multiple functions have to be met in most individual research studies. To be more specific, in the 1960s and 1970s applied social scientists with backgrounds in psychology became increasingly aware that experimental design was only a part of research design, and that the latter involved choices about sampling, measurement, data collection, data analysis, and strategies for disseminating results. Correspondingly, researchers with backgrounds in sociology and economics became more aware of causal concerns and experimental design.

More important than the realization of more decision points and more alternatives at each point was the realization that the methods chosen for one research function might constrain the range of methods available for fulfilling another function. Thus, when a particular experimental design was chosen, this constrained sampling options, and vice versa. Likewise, if a particular data collection procedure was chosen, the choice of data analysis was constrained, and vice versa. Research design came to be seen more as the art of reconciling conflicting demands imposed by the constraints that followed once a particular method was chosen for fulfilling a particular research function. Scholars even came to realize that one may sometimes choose a generally inferior method on the dual grounds that it provides valid "enough" results about, say, causal connections *and* also makes it easier to select a different method for fulfilling a different research function; say, generalization. Methods have to be selected not only for their logical adequacy, but also for their fit to the rest of an overall research design and to the priorities built into that design. Because of this realization method choice became even more difficult.

3. The decrease in authority experienced by formal decisionmakers

Most social scientists in the 1960s seem to have been willing to work within a system for defining and solving social problems that was set by formal decisionmakers from the executive and legislative branches of government. Social scientists were widely seen to be the servants of such persons, helping them to plan policy and programs and test how efficacious they were. So long as this source of policy-relevant questions remained unproblematic, it was not especially difficult for researchers interested in social policy to formulate the issues and questions they sought to investigate.

But experience in the 1960s and 1970s made it clear that in the world of social policy it is rare to find clear definitions of problems, potential solutions, and research questions, for a lack of specificity helps create the political consensus required for obtaining agreements about action from a group of heterogeneous and powerful interests. Moreover, decisionmakers do not operate in a void. They are open to multiple sources of influence and to many conflicting values. In deciding what to support, decisionmakers consider many points of view—national ideology, personal preference, political survival, and personal advantage. They also sometimes consider social science evidence. But this is only one of many inputs into decisionmaking and will rarely be of sufficient centrality to determine decisions (Weiss & Weiss, 1981). The political system is a world where many statements are deliberately unclear and do not reflect what is intended, many conflicting forces operate, many different forms of knowledge are respected, and action is multiply determined. But although the political system is open and includes many actors representing many points of view, formal decisionmakers may themselves be relatively homogeneous in some respects. They may be especially inclined, for instance, to blame social groups and individuals in need for their plight, to propose solutions that are marginally ameliorist and not radical, to favor solutions that directly or indirectly favor the interests of business, and to press for actions that promise seemingly dramatic results in a short period. Given the growing evidence about how the political system operates, it is not surprising that a decrement occurred among some social scientists in the authority they were prepared to attribute to formal decisionmakers as the sole, or even the major, source of problem definitions, potential solutions, and information needs.

As with theories and methods, the decline of formal decisionmakers as the major source of priorities and values was associated with the rise of other alternatives. Foremost among these was a pluralist conception based on conducting policy research whose assumptions and questions reflect the values and information needs of multiple stakeholders. Researchers were no longer encouraged to see themselves as servants of powerful, formal decisionmakers. Instead, they were urged to consider and consult with all interested parties. In the health system, this meant not only federal agencies and congressional committees and their staffs, but also hospital administrators and the professional associations representing them; physicians and nurses and the associations representing them; insurance companies; hospital patients; and health policy researchers. These groups have different interests concerning health matters and different information needs about particular health programs. Formal decisionmakers can only imperfectly represent these multiple interests, each of which could probably represent itself much better. Consequently, pluralists emphasize that researchers should avoid building the restricted set of assumptions of the powerful into their research; they want researchers to consult with all the relevant stakeholder groups in the sector under study.

Some theorists advocate pluralism in the formulation of policy questions, not only because this reflects the form of democracy in which they believe, but also because they believe that consulting with multiple stakeholders is more likely to lead to research results being used in policy debates. This is because the results should be relevant to more groups, and more groups should then know of them (Leviton & Hughes, 1981). Other theorists see pluralism as a means of raising the researcher's consciousness about the social values latent in how formal decisionmakers interpret problems and questions. However, stakeholder analysis is not the only means of forcing out hidden assumptions and values. Other means to this end include procedures such as the Science Court and substantive standing committees in the manner of the National Research Council (briefly reviewed in Hennigan, Flay, & Cook, 1980), as well as textual analysis in the manner of hermeneutics and the Delphi technique. However, the major point is not that techniques exist to make assumptions explicit; rather, it is that in the last 20 years a decline in the authority of formal decisionmakers has taken place that required the development or use of such techniques. It is not now easy to see formal decisionmakers as the major, legitimate source of research priorities and of the values built into the design of research or the interpretations of findings. Related to this decline is an increase in the authority of alternative sources of questions and values, particularly pluralist sources or sources based on some form of critical analysis.

4. Declines are not disappearances With theory, methods, and values I have described a decrease in the authority of established choice alternatives and a growth in the authority of other alternatives, some of them previously discredited. It is important in this respect to note that the decreases in authority were not to a level that made the dominant alternatives lose all their authority. Substantive theory is still useful for program design; certain methods are still useful for generating particular forms of knowledge; and formal decisionmakers are still useful for producing research that gets used. Indeed, in all three cases it is probably still possible to argue that, of all the possible alternatives, the old one is the best. In the last 20 years we have witnessed the overthrow of the hegemony previously attributed to particular choices and a consequent increase in the difficulties of choice for practicing social scientists. It is within this context of old certainties unthroned, but not abolished, that the call for multiplism arose.

MULTIPLISM

1. The theory The fundamental postulate of multiplism is that when it is not clear which of several options for question generation or method choice is "correct," all of them should be selected so as to "triangulate" on the most useful or the most likely to be true. If practical constraints prevent the use of multiple alternatives, then at least more than one should be chosen, preferrably as many as span the full range of plausible alternative interpretations of what constitutes a useful question or a true answer. To make this concrete, consider one of the oldest explicit rationales for multiplism—that offered for multiple operationalism (Campbell & Fiske, 1959; Webb, Campbell, Schwartz, & Sechrest, 1966).

Once the notion has been rejected that an entity is equivalent to its measure, four major difficulties arise in deciding how to measure entities or constructs. Deciding on a clear definition is crucial to measurement. Yet in every scholarly field or policy domain there is active disagreement about definitions. Even after one or more conceptual definitions has been selected, each still has to be operationally specified in terms of manipulable or measurable procedures. The second difficulty is that each operational definition will inevitably include components not in the conceptual definition. These components can be of many kinds. One that often occurs is when a measure is made in a particular mode but the mode is not part of the definition; e.g., aggression is measured in a paper-and-pencil mode (Campbell & Fiske, 1959). Another is when a measure is made at one time, but the situational factors that might have influenced responding at that one time are not part of the definition. The third problem is that operational measures will sometimes fail to include necessary components of the conceptual definition; e.g., the "intent to harm" that is crucial in some definitions of aggression. Finally, with multidimensional constructs, the weights implicitly assigned to dimensions in the operational measure may correspond imperfectly to the weights implicit or explicit in conceptual definitions. Thus, a mathematics test might be designed to measure knowledge of algebra, trigonometry, and arithmetic equally, but, in practice, may assign more weight to algebra than the other two components. In this case, all the substantive components are present, but their weights deviate from what has been defined. For these four reasons, a single measure will inevitably be inadequate.

Because it is not clear what a "correct" measure is, it is desirable to measure or manipulate a construct in several ways. From a multiple operationalist perspective, the choice of operations is constrained by several requirements. First, each representation should by itself be a "reasonable" measure of the target construct. Second, the various measures should differ in the dimensions they contain that are irrelevant to the target construct but might influence how it is measured. This implies that across all the instances there should be a "heterogeneity of irrelevancies" so that the same irrelevancies are not present with all the representations of a construct, as would happen if we had several measures of X but all were collected in a face-to-face interview. Third, at least one measure should contain all of the dimensions considered necessary to the target construct so that the full definition of a construct is present in at least one of its representations, even though other irrelevancies are also likely to be present with that representation.

The purpose of multiple operationalism is to examine whether comparable results are obtained with each measure or manipulation. If they are, researchers can conclude that a triangulation of results is achieved across measures that are similar to each other in theoretically relevant sources of shared variance but differ from each other in the theoretically irrelevant sources of variance each contains that might have influenced the relationships obtained with any one of the measures. The multiple measures are meant to converge on a single interpretation by fulfilling two functions: (1) Demonstrating replication; and (2) ruling out all alternative interpretations of the measures because no single alternative is present across all the heterogeneous instances in which a particular construct-defining empirical relationship was obtained.

When the obtained results do not converge across different measures of the same construct, an empirical puzzle results. In synthesizing many causal studies, for example, the implication would be that X and Y are only related under some conditions, and the need arises to specify these conditions. If an irrelevancy in one of the measures were eventually isolated as the crucial causal contingency, one would then specify that X and Y are related, when, say, direct observation occurs but not when paper-and-pencil measures are used. In this particular case, the contingency is of minor theoretical importance. However, other controlling contingencies can be of greater theoretical or practical utility, as when one specifies that a particular substantive component of construct X is crucial for bringing about the observed X-Y relationship.

One can then specify that Y is related to X' but not X", e.g., mandatory desegregation is related to minority achievement gains but voluntary desegregation is not. Whatever the outcome, multiple operationalism is always useful. Empirical convergences increase confidence about dependability; and failures to converge present empirical puzzles whose solution will often specify the particular operational formulations on which a relationship depends.

2. The forms of multiplism Although I outlined the theory of multiplism as it was developed to circumvent the problems inherent in definitional operationalism, a similar conceptualization based on multiple verification and the falsification of identified alternative interpretations undergirds all forms of multiplism. Because, in my construction, multiplism was a response to the attacks on positivism and to the experiences gained in studying the social reforms of the 1960s and 1970s, we might expect the forms multiplism takes to correspond to the specifics of these attacks and experiences. In general, they do.

One form multiplism takes is in the search to discover systems of causal determination that are more complex than the predictive equations of positivism or the simple bivariate causal connections of most laboratory research. Following leads from population biology, social scientists have increasingly turned to path analysis or structural equation modeling. This technique is based on using theory to identify the hypothesized—and usually multiple—determinants of a particular phenomenon, including the ways in which these determinants are linked to each other and are themselves determined by outside forces. Such causal modeling assumes a social world whose structure is more "multivariate-complex" than the physical world, and the links in this structure are thought to be probabilistic rather than deterministic, for the coefficients that link constructs in path analysis are expressed as probability statements. The world that social scientists seek to describe is also assumed to be influenced by many types of constructs, not just the physical and immediate. Indeed, sociological models of status attainment include historical constructs (e.g., mother's education), motivational constructs (e.g., need for achievement), cognitive constructs (e.g., achievement level), and observable structural constructs (e.g., the number of positions available at each level in an organizational pyramid). Although realist, the operational ontology of most social scientists differs from the positivists' world of parsimonious, deterministic, ahistorical, and nonmentalist observable forces.

Many social scientists now assume a highly contingent world in which few relationships are so dependable that they hold across a wide variety of persons, settings, and times. Statistical main effects will not describe this world as well as higher-order statistical interactions. But to isolate these interactions requires, at a minimum, sampling across multiple groups, settings, and times. This necessarily entails probing how generalizable particular relationships are. Postpositivist social science cares more than its predecessors for heterogeneous sampling and data analyses that examine the degree of dependability achieved across subpopulations.

But because of obvious resource constraints, this preference cannot always be well addressed in the design and analysis of individual studies. This helps explain the higher status recently accorded to literature reviews, for they can be used to probe the degree of dependability achieved across the range of populations, settings, and times sampled in the multiple studies conducted in the past. As a reflection of this renewed interest in reviews, Cronbach (1982) has sought to raise evaluators' awareness of the gains to be made by fitting one's findings into the existing literature without necessarily doing any new data analyses. However, novel methods of quantitative syntheses have recently become available thanks largely to the work of Glass, Rosenthal, and Light, recently summarized by Light and Pillemer (in press). The hope is that through syntheses of multiple studies one will be able to identify relationships of such stability that they hold across a wide range of populations, settings, and times, as well as across a wide range of operational representations and previously unexamined threats to internal validity. The value of single studies is reduced in the postpositivist world, especially the value of studies that claim to be crucial experiments.

It is perhaps in the epistemological domain that multiplism is most obvious in recent practice. I have previously outlined the general move from definitional to multiple operationalism. Within the context of causal modeling, multiple operationalism is best exemplified by maximum likelihood factor analytic models such as LISREL (Joreskog & Sorbum, 1978), which require researchers to make theoretical models as explicit as possible and to specify the nature of the links between theoretical constructs and the multiple imperfect measures that have been made of each construct. This form of causal modeling makes it more difficult than heretofore to squirm away from disconfirming data by arguing that hypothesis tests were inadequate because the substantive theory was poorly specified, the constructs were poorly measured, or the links between measures and latent constructs were not clear. Do not get me wrong. Even with causal modeling done by LISREL, one can still argue that the quality of measurement was too low to provide a convincing test. The present argument is only that sustaining such a case is more difficult when multiple measures have been collected that obviously triangulate on a construct than when a single measure has been used to represent each of the theoretical constructs.

In postpositivist multiplism, researchers do not aspire to the single perfect test that will confirm or falsify a hypothesis. Indeed, they may even reject single tests altogether. Statisticians like Tukey (1977) consider all inferential data analyses as exploratory and they note that inferences are better based on multiple probes of a relationship than single tests. In quasi-experimental research, multiple data analyses will particularly raise the quality of interpretations because many different and plausible models of selection can be invoked to describe pretest group differences. The aspiration is to triangulate on the same inference despite any presumed differences in bias built into the various selection models used as part of a data analysis strategy. With causal explanatory models, the advocacy is to pit multiple models in competition with each other rather than to test the goodness of fit of a single model. The problem with testing a single model is that, even if the obtained data are consistent with the model, they might be even more consistent with other models. When multiple explanatory models are explicitly pitted against each other, the aim is to see which one is superior rather than which one is necessarily "true." Notice at this point the many levels at which multiplism is possible. First, multiple causal models should be placed in competition with each other; second, each of the models should include multiple constructs; third, each construct should be multiply measured; and fourth, the constructs can be of multiple types—mentalist, historical, or whatever. Finally, multiple probes of the relative fit of the models may be needed if ambiguities of interpretation should occur after the first analysis.

In policy research that follows a social science model we have recently witnessed a growing advocacy of studies with a multitask focus (Chen & Rossi, 1980, 1983). The 1960s were dominated by a social experimentation model that explicitly assumed the priority of research tasks designed to probe questions about how program-related variables affected outcomes that seemed to be related to the amelioration of social problems. No one was more associated with this position than Campbell (e.g., 1969). But at the same time in econometrics, and later in both sociology and evaluation, the priority shifted from exploring bivariate causal relations to exploring multivariate explanatory models that specify why something causes something else. This entails investigating within the programmatic black box so as to probe what there is in it that might make a program effective. But because most programs were less effective than hoped, opening up the black box was most important for determining why the effects obtained were so modest in size and range. Of the many reasons for disappointment, one was that program services sometimes failed to reach their target beneficiaries; another was that even when they did, the services were not implemented as often or as well as had been hoped. These hypotheses helped put onto the research agenda the study of how services were targeted and implemented.

Policy studies were thus expected to fulfill multiple descriptive and explanatory tasks simultaneously. At a minimum, they were supposed to provide descriptions of program clients, service implementation, and program effects. It was also expected they would explain why some clients were reached and not others, why some patterns of implementation were obtained and not others, and why some effects came about and not others. As the popularity of hermeneutics increased, policy studies came increasingly under pressure to include analyses of the implicit value assumptions in how a social program was formulated and in how the results might be interpreted. Also, calls were increasingly heard to expand the researcher's role so that he or she was made increasingly responsible, not only for producing relevant and valid results, but also for acting to bring the results to the attention of relevant parties and to help them interpret the results in terms of their interests (Cronbach et al., 1980).

The multiplicity of tasks is inevitably associated with a multiplicity of methods. But multiple methods were not now advocated for making heterogeneous the method variance associated with a single test of a single research question. Now multiple methods were espoused because it seemed more important to answer a wider range of questions than those concerned with describing the causal effects of social programs. The hegemony of causal questions justified the near-exclusive advocacy of experimental methods. But once questions about populations, service delivery, the range of effects, the nature of causal contingency variables, the use of research results, and their value assumptions became more important, so too did issues of sampling, measurement, data collection, data analysis, and textual criticism. The primacy of quantification also seemed less obvious, and qualitative methods came to be more openly espoused and made relevant to more research tasks. Indeed, the rationale for them subtly shifted. No longer were they promoted to describe implementation, to discover unplanned side effects, and to give grounded and firsthand understanding. They also came to be promoted because they can sometimes facilitate inferences about causal relationships and causal explanations. The legitimization of a wider range of tasks in policy research meant not only that multiple questions and issues were raised, but also that multiple methods were increasingly used in individual studies.

The advocacy of qualitative data collection methods goes beyond their flexibility and potential for describing, discovering, explaining, and communicating. Also involved is their potential for prioritizing research issues. If researchers take seriously their own firsthand experiences in the field and those of the managers, service providers, clients, and experts with whom they come into contact, then grounded knowledge may emerge from which it may be possible to infer new research priorities. This suggests a new source of research questions over and above derivations from substantive theory or catering to the presumed information needs of formal policymakers. Indeed, in a democracy with pretensions to pluralism, formal policymakers should probably not be the only group whose information needs, and hence whose political interests, evaluators should meet. Every policy decision has the potential to impact on multiple stakeholder groups, and discussions with these groups often teach us that they want to learn different things. For instance, although formal policymakers in the federal or state capitals might want to know how school desegregation influences white flight, the academic achievement of black children, and classroom discipline, judges and school districts facing desegregation decisions may want to know how different desegregation plans influence public acceptance of desegregation. They want to identify the options they should choose, and the label "desegregation" is far too global to be helpful in their planning. On the other hand, officials in school districts that have already desegregated may want to identify classroom practices that prevent resegregation within classrooms or that enhance cross-race contact; parents in those districts may want to know how desegregation has influenced academic achievement and discipline; local political officials may want to know how desegregation affects taxpayer identification with the school district and approval of the school board; and local business leaders may want to know how desegregation influences property values, sales tax revenues, and the type of families moving into the district. A respect for direct experience and for the experiences and wishes of multiple stakeholders means that multiple sources and types of research questions become legitimate. This, in turn, creates more sources of uncertainty for the social researcher interested in policy. Where should he or she look for guidance about which research issues are worth tackling and about how these issues should be phrased?

Once it was realized that social science is concerned, not with guaranteeing truth or utility, but with offering defensible interpretations of what is in the outside world, the problem arose as to who should offer such interpretations. In a culture that claims to be libertarian and pluralist, it is not surprising that the answer was that multiple interpretations and values should be offered that cover a broad spectrum of individual and group interests. This went beyond the call for multiple stakeholders research; it also included the call for secondary analysis in which multiple researchers have the chance to criticize others' formulations of issues, choice of methods, and interpretations of results. The purposes of multiple competing analyses are to estimate the degree of correspondence between investigators who differ in their value and method preferences and to use any differences in findings to discover the nature of the analysts' implicit assumptions. The important point is that investigators who actively seek to reexamine another's work are likely to be especially motivated to detect errors or limitations in the assumptions made (Cook, 1974). The presumption is that no one is better able to identify factors that restrict interpretations than one's professional "enemies." Without their motivated criticism, plausible alternative interpretations are less likely to be identified and probed, and knowledge claims are all the more likely to turn out to be false in the long run.

The advantages of heterogeneous review were also associated with the call to have policy research be actively monitored by advisory boards composed both of scholars with substantive or methodological expertise and members of heterogeneous interest groups. Also heard were calls to provide funding for multiple, simultaneously conducted studies on the same issue from different value perspectives. To this end, the National Institute of Education recently asked six experts to conduct meta-analyses of the school desegregation literature. Two of the scholars had publicly claimed that desegregation increases the achievement of minority children; two others had claimed that desegregation does not influence achievement; and the other two seemed more value-neutral judging by what they had published on the issue. But perhaps the most salient response to the value-ladenness of science has been the call to use a variety of different iterative techniques to discover all the hidden assumptions in research, whether this be in a science court context, through hermeneutic textual analysis, or through invited debates involving publicly identified proponents of multiple value positions. In all of these suggestions is the assumption that parochial value perspectives can be easily slipped into that run throughout all the research on a topic. By making multiple and heterogeneous the preferences and values of investigators, the aim is to infuse research with multiple value perspectives and to analyze completed research from a variety of different value positions. In all cases, the concern is the same: To identify commonalities of finding and interpretation through processes that vigorously attempt to falsify all the claims made about knowledge and utility.

3. *The advantages of multiplism* Multiplism is meant to raise consciousness about what should be learned to help increase the likelihood that knowledge claims are true. It aims to do the former by discovering as wide a range of perspectives on utility as is possible, probing for correspondence and differences, and using the differences to analyze why they occur so as to achieve a better understanding of the reasons to prefer some formulations of what is useful over others. Multiplism aims to foster truth by establishing correspondences across many different, but conceptually related, ways of posing a question and by ruling out whether any obtained correspondences are artifacts of any epiphenomena of value, substantive theory, or method choice that have been inadvertently incorporated into individual tests.

Multiplism is attractive inferentially because the greater the heterogeneity of irrelevancies across which a relationship holds, the greater is the likelihood that threats to any kind of validity can be ruled out. Thus, when results are demonstrably stable across populations, settings, and times, external validity is enhanced. When results are stable across many ways of assessing covariation (and not just a single statistical test), statistical conclusion validity is enhanced. When results are stable across multiple potential threats to causal inference, internal validity is enhanced. And when interpretation of the meaning of relationships in theoretical and value terms is common across a wide variety of perspectives, objectivity—defined as intersubjective verifiability—is enhanced. Multiplism does not guarantee that all the threats to each of these kinds of validity are ruled out, but it does increase the likelihood. Moreover, the gain in validity should be associated with a gain in credibility. This may, in turn, increase the likelihood that results based on a multiplist approach will be used as part of the total input into decisions about social action. Multiplism promises payoffs, then, for generalization, theoretical meaning, dependability of associations, the validity of causal knowledge, and the social utility of research knowledge. This is a considerable potential.

But multiplism also promises greater specificity. When data patterns do not converge across multiple measures, methods, populations, settings, times, and the like, the search begins to identify the contingencies controlling the relationship. Being able to specify such contingencies helps avoid misinterpretations about generality. This is especially important if X and Y are related positively under some conditions but negatively or not at all under others, as opposed to the case in which X and Y are related by the same sign but the magnitude of the relationship varies. Being able to specify causal contingencies also helps create a specificity about domains of relevance, as when one learns that *Sesame Street* increases knowledge of the alphabet but not problem solving. Even when resources or ingenuity have not allowed all the relevant theoretical and value interpretations to be directly examined empirically, a multiplist frame of mind is still useful. It identifies more of the still untested assumptions on which provisionally identified knowledge depends, thus creating an environment in which the consumers of research are invited to make up their own minds about the explicitly acknowledged assumptions on which their acceptance of findings should depend.

Multiplism also promises to provide us with more comprehensive pictures of how policies impact on the social world than those to which we are used. It teaches us that question formulation benefits from considering multiple sources, such as competing theoretical models, the information needs of multiple stakeholder groups, and the use of one's own and others' grounded experience to trust novel issues to the fore. If all of these sources are used to identify research issues, the latter will be framed at a higher level of consciousness. Moreover, it is highly likely that they will eventually create a more comprehensive understanding of which policy changes are needed, of what the changes implemented to date have achieved, and of why they have achieved what they have. From a multiplist perspective it would be well-nigh impossible to have learned how school desegregation influences white flight without also having probed how it affects property values, black achievement, school discipline, racial prejudice, or parental cooperation in the PTA; it would be almost impossible to have learned something about such a global and variable entity as school desegregation while remaining ignorant of the effects of various forms it takes, e.g., magnet schools, metropolitan desegregation plans, etc. Multiplism breeds knowledge about a broad universe of effects, a large set of contingency conditions, and differentiated conceptions of the social policy or social program under analysis.

Finally, multiplism promises to make policy research more intellectual, value conscious, and debate-centered. This promise follows from the frank recognition that social science research, although it strives to minimize the intrusion of values or deliberately tries to make them heterogeneous, can never totally rule them out. From this arises the multiplist's impulsion to explicate latent value and interest assumptions. Multiplists hope that primary authors will do this in a self-conscious fashion. But they know that it is best achieved through critical commentary by scholars, practitioners, and other interested parties who hold different values and methodological preferences from those of primary authors. Although some persons may deplore the social and possibly contentious nature of the knowledge so achieved and still aspire to nuggets of truth revealed by some divine methodological hand, these nuggets will not be forthcoming. Multiplism has the potential to breed honesty rather than self-delusion and to force out assumptions for more enlightened public debate. But in such debates it is important to realize that although points of disagreement may generate the most heat, there will often be some points of convergence. These promise to be sources of light and so deserve special scrutiny in case they have attained their special status by withstanding all attempts to refute them, and so reflect more than an underexamined social consensus.

THE LIMITATIONS OF MULTIPLISM

Despite its real and potential advantages, multiplism is no panacea. Among its limitations, I want to discuss two: The problem of constant bias across heterogeneous instances; and the absence of an algorithm for specifying what should be made heterogeneous in a single study granted that for practical reasons not everything that should be made heterogeneous can be. In discussing this last point we shall discuss the danger of falling into a flabby relativism about question and method preferences that makes all sources equally legitimate and equates truth with social consensus.

1. Constant bias: The single source The old story according to which Tycho Brahe and all before him saw the sun move to set behind the stationary earth illustrates that some biases—in this case a perceptual, geocentric one—are so widely shared socially that they cannot be made heterogeneous. No one can conceive of the bias being a bias. Kuhn (1962) has discussed the same issue in more recent times. In the more mundane setting of current survey research we are mindful of the constant biases potentially produced when, despite multiple versions of a question, all the interviewers are middle class and ask questions face-to-face. While question-wording is heterogeneous in this case, the mode of data collection is not. Similarly, if parental reports, peer reports, and playground observation each indicate increased children's aggression, this makes heterogeneous the observer and the mode of data collection. But if for each measure the response categories are limited to verbal aggression, pushing, and shoving many laymen might want to label the tests as measuring boisterousness or incivility rather than aggression, for none of the measures is explicitly based on intending to do harm or on leaving the other person in physical pain. In the previously discussed meta-analyses of school desegregation (National Institute of Education, 1984), the 19 school districts studied were from all parts of the United States, the studies covered a 20-year period, and the desegregation plans varied considerably. But still, the latest study was published in 1971; nearly all the school districts desegregated voluntarily rather than as a result of court mandates; achievement gains were assessed after one or two years of desegregation; and no reasonable estimates could be made of the gains of children who had never attended segregated schools before transferring to desegregated ones. Once again we see that, despite considerable heterogeneity, a number of different biases were constant throughout the studies. As a final example of constant bias consider Director's (1979) research on job training programs. He surveyed many studies that differed in many ways, all of which concluded that the programs in question failed to benefit graduates. However, in all cases, the persons receiving training had poorer employment histories than the control groups, resulting in what Campbell and Boruch (1975) would call a constant underadjustment of the initial differences between people in job programs and their controls. If it occurred, this source of constant bias would underestimate the effects of job training.

When many sources of potential bias have been made heterogeneous in a study or across a set of studies, the danger always is that the obviousness of the heterogeneity so achieved may lull researchers out of a critical frame of mind. They may be less likely to ask whether any other sources of bias-inducing homogeneity might still be operating that produce repeated convergence on the wrong answer! The origins of this danger go beyond the human preference to attribute a law-like status to multiple repeated instances of a relationship (Tversky & Kahnemann, 1977). They also stem from the fact that, *ceteris paribus,* even mindless multiplism entails a wider range of demonstrated convergences and the ruling out of more threats to validity. Thus, a review of job corps studies is likely to include centers with different operating philosophies and different populations of job seekers; the centers are likely to be located in many different parts of the country;

seen as a whole, the evaluations are likely to have many different measures of job preparation, earnings, and job performance; and, finally, some of them are likely to have been set up quasi-experimentally and others (post-Director!) as randomized experiments. In light of such achieved heterogeneity it would indeed be tempting to claim that the obtained results hold for job corps centers in general (and not just for those with particular philsophies), for job seekers of all backgrounds (and not those of a certain ethnic group or education level), for all parts of the country (rather than certain regions), for all measures of earnings (and not just self-reports), and for studies in which the various treatment groups were initially constituted in a similar or dissimilar fashion. However, the relationship between the degree of multiplism and the likelihood of more valid inferences is governed by a *ceteris paribus* clause. What multiplism makes more likely, it does not necessarily guarantee. It does not follow from multiple heterogeneous replication that all sources of constant bias have been identified and ruled out.

   2. *Constant bias: Multiple sources operating in the same direction* It is important to differentiate between a constant source of bias (as illustrated in the examples above) and a constant direction of bias. The two are related; all things being equal, a constant source of bias will result in a constant direction of bias. Note, though, that a constant direction of bias can also result when all the individual sources of identified doubt have been made heterogeneous across all of the tests examined. To exemplify this, consider the literature on the effects of television violence, recently reviewed by Huesmann as part of the NIMH Report on *Television and Behavior* and studied meta-analytically by Hearold (1979). Only a minor part of Huesmann's chapter deals with whether television violence increases aggression; for like most others, he believes that the issue is closed. His belief rests on the consistency of past findings from laboratory and field experiments, cross-sectional surveys, and panel studies. To accept such consistency as a basis for believing that television causes aggression, one must logically accept that the different methods do not share biases operating in the same direction and the past studies using unbiased methods have been accurately reviewed.

   It is obvious why laboratory experiments may exaggerate any link between television violence and aggression for normal children in everyday settings. Experiments have to produce aggression to discriminate between the outcomes of different treatments. Yet aggression is a relatively rare event. So, experiments are designed to minimize inhibitions against aggression, to minimize external cues sanctioning aggression, and to maximize the clarity and intensity of short-term experimental treatments that have been deliberately chosen because they are likely to foster aggression. Although appropriate for discriminating between treatments, this strategy is not obviously relevant to drawing conclusions about regular television programming in the home, in which internal cues against aggression may operate more powerfully, situational cues sanction aggression, and television aggressors are punished, usually by characters with prosocial qualities that are themselves presumably worthy of emulation. Also, the violent scenes on television are interspersed with many different types of activity, and viewers are free to watch intermittently or with low levels of involvement.

Positive bias is also likely in cross-sectional surveys in which the amount of exposure to violence is correlated with aggression scores, holding constant background variables that are thought to correlate with viewing and aggression. The adequacy of this approach depends on how completely selection differences between heavier and lighter viewers are modeled and how well the constructs in the model are measured. Usually, the selection models are primitive, involving demographic variables such as age, sex, race, etc. that are presumably proxies for the true (and unknown) psychological and social factors that cause differences in exposure to violence. Campbell and Boruch (1975) have argued that "underadjustment" is likely to occur in this situation so that although some of the true selection differences will be removed; not all of them will. The synchronous correlation between viewing and aggression is positive, although usually small: In the .15 to .25 range. If Campbell and Boruch are correct, some of the background differences between heavier and lighter viewers will not have been removed, and estimates of the relationship between television and aggression will be somewhat inflated. Not everyone agrees with Campbell and Boruch. Cronbach, Rogosa, Floden, & Price (1977) believe that overadjustment can sometimes occur, as can perfect adjustment. However, in the last case we do not yet know when it will be! The point is *not* that underadjustment bias has occurred in all past cross-sectional studies of television and aggression; it is only that a plausible case can be made that the bias might have operated.

Huesmann mentions six reports of field experiments involving random assignment in nonlaboratory settings. Four were said to have yielded evidence of a positive relation between violence viewing and aggression, the exceptions being Feshbach and Singer (1971) and Wells (1973). However, the study of Loye, Gorney, and Steele (1977) is also an exception because the data show that the group assigned to a television diet of high violence was no more likely to commit hurtful behaviors than the controls. Moreover, the experiment of Stein and Friedrich (1972) showed weak effects confined to a subgroup of initially more aggressive children, and, according to Parke, Berkowitz, Legens, West, and Sebastian (1977), this result failed to replicate it (Sawin, 1973). Thus, four of the six studies are problematic. Of the two others, the work of Loye et al. is also included as one of three experiments reported in Parke et al. (1977) that therefore emerges as the crucial report claiming to find effects of television violence. However, these field experiments deal with institutionalized children; regular television viewing was forbidden, possibly creating frustration; and in two studies the boys assigned to view aggressive films were intially more aggressive. In our view, the field experiments on television violence produce little consistent evidence of effects despite claims to the contrary and the instances in which an effect is claimed involve populations that seem to be initially more aggressive.

It is widely agreed that the best method for studying television effects involves longitudinal panel studies. Unfortunately, the state of the analytic art has recently changed. The formerly advocated analysis based on cross-lagged panel correlations is misleading when test-retest correlations differ between variables. Then, the less reliable measure will spuriously appear to be causal (Cook & Campbell, 1979; Rogosa, 1980). Television viewing is nearly always less stable than aggressiveness, as in the study by Lefkowitz, Eron, Walder, and Huesmann (1972) in the Surgeon-General's report and in the original data that Huesmann includes in his chapter in the NIMH report. It may also be the case with Singer and Singer (1980), who used cross-lagged panel analysis. Thus, a bias may also have operated in past panel studies to produce a spurious relationship between television viewing and aggression. Indeed, two recent panel studies that used more appropriate analytic models resulted in one case that concluded that no relationship exists between television violence and aggression (Milavsky, Kessler, Stipp, & Rubens, 1982) and in another case that concluded that at most only a very modest relationship might exist (Huesmann, Lagerspetz, & Eron, 1982).

Like most summaries of television violence and its effects, the NIMH Report is somewhat uncritical in its claim that the question has been answered and in its implication that the effect is widespread. The reliance on evidence from multiple methods is admirable—in the abstract. But the viability of such a strategy depends on the absence of biases operating in the same direction across all of the methods. However, this absence cannot be assumed. Although it is indeed the case that what was problematic with the laboratory experiments was made

heterogeneous across the other kinds of research and what was problematic with the surveys was made heterogeneous across some of
the other forms of research, there is nonetheless presumptive evidence
that in each form of research a unique form of bias operated to
overestimate the effects of television. We do not, then, have a constant
source of bias; but we do have a constant direction of bias despite
demonstrated heterogeneity in every currently conceived source of bias.

3. Constant bias: Identifying plausible sources of constant bias The
likelihood of avoiding a constant direction of bias depends on identifying all the plausible source of such bias. There are by now enough
lists of threats about enough kinds of validity that one would think
it unlikely that any sources of bias remain undiscovered. But they
may, particularly if some sources are unique to particular topics.
Besides, human ingenuity is restricted, and sources of spuriousness that
cannot be imagined at this time will seem self-evident to future
generations. Hence, even the best means of discovering sources of
constant bias are fallible. Nonetheless, they are useful because they at
least sensitize us to many viable contending interpretations.

After examining the published list of validity threats, it is desirable
to consult with a wide variety of persons with very different
methodological and value preferences and to induce them to be as
critical as possible in conceptualizing alternative interpretations to those
that primary analysts first prefer. This is undoubtedly a social process;
and those who labored to produce particular results may not always
be too keen to have their work and themselves be critically scrutinized
in public. Yet some form of public commentary is probably the best
technique available for generating a comprehensive list of plausible
alternative interpretations of a piece of research, even research conceived in a multiplist mode. Although such scrutiny is needed at
all stages of a research project, it is perhaps most needed when a
study is initially planned and when preliminary results have been extracted.

It is one thing to claim that research should be offered for public
critical scrutiny, and quite another thing to achieve such a diversity
of conflicting and even antagonistic points of view that all the plausible
threats to valid interpretation will emerge. It is only because of personal
hostilities between scholars, the passions engendered by ideology and
personal intellectual commitments, and the ambitions of young scholars
and outsiders who want to overthrow the conventional wisdom that
science and critical reason can flourish. Without these forces, conventional wisdom will restrict the range of alternative interpretations and
"paradigm dominance" is likely to continue. Science belongs in an
open society committed to respect for one's intellectual enemies; it

requires the passion to pursue one's ideas, the courage to welcome criticism, and the openness to take it very seriously. Although the spirit of dispute does not, and cannot, guarantee that the ineffable truth will emerge, it does increase the likelihood that the knowledge achieved will approximate the truth because all the relevant heterogeneous parties have reflected on the research at a high level of consciousness and have agreed that no alternative interpretation of a particular relationship is plausible right now. This is a consensus; but it is a consensus that no viable alternatives exist to a knowledge claim after a process of open criticism from multiple, conflicting perspectives. Consensus about alternatives to a relationship count more in science than consensus about a relationship. It is this process of encouraging heterogeneity in world views and beliefs about method and of encouraging the critical and even skeptical application of all these sources of heterogeneity to knowledge claims that characterizes science and best discriminates tentative and critically achieved truth from social consensus.

2. *The absence of an algorithm for choosing what to make heterogeneous* Once sensitivity has been raised to the necessity of avoiding a constant direction of bias, the problem then confronting everyone who designs a single study is in deciding what to make heterogeneous. If a conceptually important factor sometimes remains homogeneous even though scores of studies have been conducted on the topic—as with television violence and its effects on children—how can the individual researcher hope to have the insight and resources to make heterogeneous within a single study all the factors that should be made so? After all, a study that is truly multiplist requires the capacity not only to answer multiple research questions but also to uncover novel questions and issues. It also requires multiple constructs; multiple measures of each construct; and multiple populations of persons, settings, and times. Also needed are multiple mechanisms for triangulating on inferences about cause; multiple data analyses for every important substantive issue; and commentary by many people who have unique values and method preferences that relate to research questions and procedures. Who has the resources to do all these things? And even if one did, might not the logistics of so much probing compromise the quality of the answers provided? Guidelines are needed in any practical theory of multiplism to help individual researchers decide what to make heterogeneous, given that not everything can be.

But specifying in cookbook form the aspects of research that should be made hetereogeneous smacks of rigidly codifying what scientific practice should be. Critics have always held it against positivism that its tenets were so easily codified into slogans for practice (e.g., science requires hypothesis testing; all knowledge depends on observation) or into lists of recommendations (as with the lists of threats to validity of Campbell & Stanley, 1966, and Cook & Campbell, 1979). Nonetheless, because scientists often look to theorists of methods for help in deciding what to do (just as practitioners look to substantive theorists in other fields), so theorists of methodology have some responsibility to enlighten though not to try to force behavior into specific channels. As part of this responsibility it is not difficult to suggest some modest general guidelines to consider in deciding what can and should be made heterogeneous within the resource constraints of a single study.

The decision should depend in part on factors that have been left homogeneous in past studies and that can be easily defended as important. Thus, if school desegregation research were exclusively based on studies of voluntary desegregation, it would be useful to conduct the next study in districts with both voluntary and court-mandated desegregation because most of the districts now desegregating are doing so in response to legal pressure. If only a single district could be studied, this would be a district where the courts have forced desegregation. Although this involves sampling districts homogeneously when seen from the perspective of the single study, it would also entail sampling with some heterogeneity when seen from the perspective of the whole research tradition. The strategy of creating a single case that goes contrary to an undesirable source of past homogeneity is apparent among meta-analysts. In order to examine whether an average effect size is due to a methodological artifact or is restricted in generality, meta-analysts often compute average effect sizes for the majority of studies and contrast them with the effect sizes from the one or two studies in which there has been random assignment (e.g., Zdep, 1967; Crain & Mahard, 1983), from the few studies in which respondents are in placebo control groups as opposed to no-treatment controls (Devine & Cook, 1983), or from the few school districts that desegregated under court mandate (Cook, 1984). In all such cases the comparisons are suspect, not only because of low sample sizes and nonindependent errors when some studies provide more than one effect size estimate, but also because the few studies are inevitably different from the main body of studies in many ways other than the form of the treatment assignment, the nature of the control group, or who authorized school desegregation. Nonetheless, multiplism suggests a new rationale for the single study: To create heterogeneity where formerly homogeneity reigned.

But one has to be careful, for not all sources of homogeneity are equally important in their implications. One has to look for homogeneities discussed by informed commentators from different value perspectives;

further, these informed discussions should lead the researcher to conclude that the homogeneities in question reduce the interpretability
or relevance of what is known. For instance, many commentators on
school desegregation believe that kindergarten and the first grade are
important ages to study. Children who enter desegregated schools at
this level have usually not previously experienced segregated schooling
and are unlike their older cohorts who moved to desegregated schools
from previously segregated ones. If it is seen as particularly crucial
to get good estimates from the younger grades, this might lead to
a preference for sampling these grades at the cost of gathering little
or no information on later grades. But even so, it should not be forgotten
that multiple features of the research can be made heterogeneous even
when working with a single grade. Because multiplism is a multilevel
concept, more outcomes can be measured; particularly important outcomes like academic achievement can be measured with a new set
of tests, the tests can be given under different (but still relevant) social
conditions, etc. The art is to make heterogeneous on a priority basis
while always bearing in mind the difficulties inherent when one person
or group decides what these priorities should be.

It should not be forgotten that the costs of multiplism are partly
related to what is being made heterogeneous. In general, it costs considerably more to add sites to a single study design than to opera-
tionalize constructs in multiple ways. It costs much more to make
heterogeneous the times of study and measurement than to add a
measure of, say, gender to the measurement plan. It costs more to
add face-to-face commentary on a design plan from a wide variety
of people with different value and methodology preferences than it
does to, say, conduct multiple analyses of the same quasi-experimental
data set in order to vary the selection models employed to control
for initial group nonequivalence. These cost differentials mean that
some forms of multiplism should verge on the routine, especially those
relating to more measurement on the same persons. I am not trying
to argue that this is universally possible, for obvious limits of time
and energy constrain what can be measured and many scholars have
a preference to measure more constructs rather than to measure fewer
constructs in more ways. Nonetheless, measurement involves one of
the least expensive ways of facilitating multiplism. In this context,
it should not be forgotten that multiple options exist for answering
some questions, and they vary in expense. Using the past literature
to provide additional sites is less costly than sampling new sites and
collecting data in them, whereas puzzling over one's findings from
the personally imagined perspectives of managers, practitioners, and
clients, or from libertarian, elitist, pluralist, socialist, and Marxist perspec-

tives, will be less costly than holding a Science Court or doing multi-attribute utility analyses with multiple stakeholder groups. I am not trying to argue that all the alternative techniques produce equally valid findings—only that they are available, each helps, and they vary considerably in the resources they require.

A final point to consider is that multiplism can degenerate into the mindless relativism implicit in assuming that no question is more justified than any other and no method is more justified than any other for a particular purpose. The decreases in authority mentioned earlier for substantive theory, particular methods, and formal decision-makers did not involve either total losses or decreases to a point at which all the available options for question generation and method choice are equally appropriate. Some methods are still superior to others for particular purposes when judged from a variety of logical perspectives; moreover, some types of questions promise better payoffs than others. But because their superiority does not involve hegemony and is not universally acknowledged, it seems to us to be both politic and logically necessary for all social scientists interested in policy to point out and publicly defend their decisions about the features of research they have left homogeneous because they believe that the gains expected from making them heterogeneous would be minimal. Presumably a greater likelihood exists of persuasive rationales for those sources of homogeneity that are deliberately allowed to remain if researchers do not rely exclusively on their own judgment about what is the "best" single version of a question or method, but instead subject their initial beliefs to active scrutiny from multiple perspectives. Thus, even the decision not to act heterogeneously should be based on multiplist principles.

CONCLUSION

In response to attacks on a more positivist conception of science in general and of social science in particular, a new and more tentative approach to knowledge growth has taken place. It stresses multiplism: Approximating the ultimately unknowable truth through the use of processes that critically triangulate from a variety of perspectives on what is worth knowing and what is known. Triangulation requires generating multiple instances of some entity and then testing whether the instances converge on the same theoretical meaning despite the irrelevant sources of uniqueness that any one instance may contain. Such multiplism can be seen in the advocacy of multiple stakeholder research, multiple competing data analyses and interpretations, multiple definitionalism, multimethod research, multitask research, multivariate causal modeling, putting multiple plausible hypotheses into competition with each other, and assessing the generality of relationships across multiple populations, settings, and times.

The problems with a multiplist approach are largely practical. Multiplism calls for judgment based on knowledge of the assumptions behind the choice of particular methods, and knowledge of how to reconcile the various methods that might be used for each of the ends that usually have to be represented within a single study. Although we might like to triangulate on many things and take account of the perspectives of all stakeholder groups, this is manifestly not possible in most single studies. Nor is multiplism invariably desirable, given what is already known about a particular substantive issue or the characteristics of a particular feature of research design. After all, decades of research on research have identified some research procedures that are superior to others, e.g., when survey interviewers and interviewees are of a similar race. But because so much still is unknown, sensitivity to multiplism is a crucial adjunct to research design so as to reduce the chances of parochial question formulation and of generating research findings that are unnecessarily method-specific.

However, multiplism is no panacea, for we can multiply replicate the same mistake or the same parochial set of assumptions. At issue is a critical multiplism that never gives up being self-questioning and never abandons the search to discover hidden sources of inadvertent, constant biases in past work. And to ensure that hidden assumptions are likely to emerge, it is crucial for multiplists to cultivate intellectual and interest "opponents" who hold different value and method preferences and to elicit from them commentary on what has been done and any knowledge claims that have been made. Such criticism is most likely in open societies that thrive on differences, encourage idiosyncracies of perspective, and allow the young and ambitious to challenge the established. From a multiplist point of view, truth is provisionally attained when a powerful consensus of many disparate parties agrees that no alternative interpretations are plausible other than those offered publicly. Such knowledge claims deserve more of a status as facts than do consensual interpretations that have not been critically probed at a high level of consciousness from all the currently identified perspectives of relevance, however "wild" they may seem to be.

Many of the more fervent critics of positivism will reject all the foregoing remarks and will interpret them as an ad hoc attempt to save positivism by improving it at the margin while retaining many of its most fundamental and flawed assumptions. Their criticism may be that we have recreated in this chapter the process whereby substantive theorists add contingencies to their theories to preserve them from disconfirming observations. They would probably acknowledge that we are postpositivist in some of our beliefs, but would refuse to accept two assumptions that buttress multiplism: That there is a real world, and that we can know it to be a useful, but imperfect, degree through observation based on multiplist procedures that have been critically selected after considering multiple perspectives about what the purposes of the research should be, what prior research indicates is known, and what the preferred methods of study might be.

We are happy to retain these assumptions. To reject them would probably mean rejecting nearly all of the achievements of the social sciences to date. Although it is debatable how fundamental or extensive they have been, it is hardly debatable that some progress has been made. Moreover, the current generation of researchers is not likely to reject all they have learned and practiced for which they have also often been rewarded. They will not begin their careers again under a radically different set of assumptions about knowledge and its growth, especially in the absence of well-articulated *practical* alternatives for conducting research. Perhaps they should, but they won't. What multiplism offers is indeed incrementalist, for it builds on past theory and practice in methodology as well as on critiques of these same theories and practices. Multiplism is not as revolutionary as other alternatives to pure positivism. However, this should not blind us to how difficult it is to implement multiplism in research practice and how it subtly undermines the motivation of researchers who hope for more from single studies than multiplism leads us to believe can realistically be achieved. The long-term payoff of multiplism, though, should be more incisive and comprehensive research questions as well as results that are more dependable. These are not trivial expected gains, and will only be hard-won. They will not come easily or quickly, but they will come.

REFERENCES

Allport, G. W. (1935). Attitudes. In C. M. Murchison (Ed.), *Handbook of Social Psychology.* Worcester, MA: Clark University Press.

Amir, Y. (1969). Contact hypothesis in ethnic relations. *Psychological Bulletin, 71,* 319-342.

Bandura, A. (1977). Toward a unifying theory of behavioral change. *Psychological Review, 84,* 191-215.

Bardach, E. (1977). *The implementation game.* Cambridge, MA: MIT Press.

Berman, P. (1980). Thinking about programmed and adaptive implementation: Matching strategies to situations. In H. M. Ingram & D. E. Mann (Eds.), *Why policies succeed or fail.* (pp. 205-227). Beverly Hills, CA: Sage.

Bhaskar, R. (1979). *The possibility of naturalism.* Sussex: Harvester.

Blalock, H. M., Jr. (1961). *Causal inferences in nonexperimental research.* Chapel Hill, NC: University of North Carolina Press.

Bower, G. H. (1981). Emotional mood and memory. *American Psychologist, 36,* 129-148.

Campbell, D. T. (1969). Reforms as experiments. *American Psychologist, 24,* 409-429.

Campbell, D. T. (1974). Evolutionary epistemology. In P. A. Schlipp (Ed.), *The philosophy of Karl Popper. The library of living philosophers.* (Vol. 14, 1). LaSalle, IL: Open Court Publishing.

Campbell, D. T., & Boruch, R. F. (1975). Making the case for randomized assignment to treatments by considering the alternatives: Six ways in which quasi-experimental evaluations tend to underestimate effects. In C. A. Bennett & A. A. Lumsdaine (Ed.), *Evaluation and experience: Some critical issues in assessing social programs.* New York: Academic Press.

Campbell, D. T., & Fiske, D. W. (1959). Convergent and discriminant validation by the multitrait-multimethod matrix. *Psychological Bulletin, 56,* 81-105.

Campbell, D. T., & Stanley, J. C. (1963). Experimental and quasi-experimental designs for research on teaching. In N. L. Gage (Ed.), *Handbook of research on teaching.* Chicago: Rand McNally.

Chen, H. T., & Rossi, P. H. (1980). The multi-goal, theory-driven approach to evaluation: A model linking basic and applied social science. *Social Forces, 59,* 106-122.

Chen, H. T., & Rossi, P. H. (1983). Evaluating with sense: The theory-driven approach. *Evaluation Review, 7,* 283-302.

Collingwood, R. G. (1940). *An essay on metaphysics.* Oxford, England: Clarendon Press.

Cook, T. D. (1974). The potential and limitations of secondary evaluations. In M. W. Apple, M. J. Subkoviak, & H. S. Lufler, Jr. (Eds.), *Educational evaluation: Analysis and responsibity* (pp. 155-235). Berkeley: McCutchan.

Cook, T. D. (1984). What have black children gained academically from school desegregation? A review of the meta-analytic evidence. Special volume to commemorate *Brown v. School of Education.* In *School desegregation.* Washington, DC: National Institute of Education.

Cook, T. D., & Campbell, D. T. (1979). *Quasi-experimentation: Design and analysis issues for social research in field settings.* Boston: Houghton Mifflin.

Cook, T. D., Leviton, L. L., & Shadish, W. (in press). Program evaluation. In G. Lindsey & E. Aronson (Eds.), *Handbook of social psychology,* (3rd ed.). Boston: Addison-Wesley.

Cook, T. D., & Reichardt, C. S. (Eds.). (1979). *Qualitative and quantitative methods in evaluation.* Beverly Hills, CA: Sage.

Crain, R. L., & Mahard, R. E. (1983). Minority achievement: Policy implications of research. In W. D. Hawley (Ed.), *Effective school desegregation: Equity, quality and feasibility.* Beverly Hills, CA: Sage.

Cronbach, L. J. (1982). *Designing evaluations of educational and social programs.* San Francisco: Jossey-Bass.

Cronbach, L. J., Rogosa, D. R., Floden, R. E., & Price, G. G. (1977). *Analysis of covariance in nonrandomized experiments: Parameters affecting bias.* Occasional paper, Stanford University, Stanford Evaluation Consortium.

Cronbach, L. J. et al. (1980). *Toward reform of program evaluation: Aims, methods, and institutional arrangements.* San Francisco: Jossey-Bass.

Cronbach, L. J., & Snow, R. E. (1976). *Aptitudes and instructional methods.* New York: Irvington.

Devine, E. C., & Cook, T. D. (1983). Effects of psyco-educational interventions on length of hospital stay: A meta-analytic review of 34 studies. In R. J. Light (Ed.), *Evaluation studies review annual* (Vol. 8). Beverly Hills, CA: Sage.

Director, S. M. (1979). Underadjustment bias in the evaluation of manpower training. *Evaluation Quarterly, 3,* 190-218.

Dunn, W. (1982). Reforms as arguments. *Knowledge: Creation, Diffusion, Utilization, 3,* 293-326.

Feshbach, S., & Singer, R. D. (1971). *Television and aggression: An experimental field study.* San Francisco: Jossey-Bass.

Fullan, M. (1982). *The meaning of educational change.* New York: Teachers College Press.

Glass, G. V., McGaw, B., & Smith, M. I. (1981). *Meta-analysis in social research.* Beverly Hills, CA: Sage.

Habermas, J. (1972). *Knowledge and human interests.* London: Heinemann.

Harré, R., & Secord, P. (1972). *The explanation of social behaviour.* Oxford: Basil Blackwell.

Hearold, S. L. (1979). *Meta-analysis of the effects of television on social behavior.* Unpublished doctoral dissertation. University of Colorado.

Hennigan, K. M., Flay, B. R., & Cook, T. D. (1980). "Give me the facts!": The use of social science evidence in formulating national policy. In R. F. Kidd & M. J. Saks (Eds.), *Advances in applied social psychology* (Vol. 1) (pp. 113-148). Hillsdale, NJ: Erlbaum.

House, E. R. (1980). *Evaluating with validity.* Beverly Hills, CA: Sage.

Huesmann, L. R., Lagerspetz, K., & Eron, L. D. (1982). *Intervening variables in the television violence-aggression relation: A binational study.* Unpublished manuscript, University of Illinois at Chicago.

Joreskög, K. G., & Sörbom, D. (1978). *LISREL IV, analysis of linear structural equation systems by the method of maximum likelihood: User's guide.* Chicago: International Educational Services.

Kuhn, T. S. (1962). *The structure of scientific revolutions.* Chicago: University of Chicago Press.

Lakatos, I., & Musgrave, A. (Eds.). (1970). *Criticism and the growth of knowledge.* Cambridge, England: Cambridge University Press.

Lefkowitz, M., Eron, L. Walder, L., & Huesmann, L. (1972). Television violence and child aggression: A follow-up study. In *National Institute of Mental Health Television and Social Behavior Reports and Papers,* (Technical report to Surgeon General's Scientific Advisory Committee on Television and Social Behavior, Vol. III). Washington, DC: Government Printing Office.

Leviton, L. C., & Hughes, E. F. (1981). Research in the utilization of evaluations: Review and snytheses. *Evaluation Review, 5,* 525-548.

Light, R. J., & Pillemer, D. B. (1984). Summing up. Research synthesis. Cambridge, MA: Harvard University Press.

Lindblom, C. E., & Cohen, D. K. (1979). *Usable Knowledge.* New Haven, CT: Yale University Press.

Loye, D., Gorney, R., & Steele, G. (1977). Effects of television: An experimental field study. *Journal of Communication, 27,* 206-216.

McGuire, W. J. (1984). Contextualism. In L. Berkowitz (Ed.), *Advances in experimental social psychology.* New York: Academic Press.

Merton, R. K. (1957). Bureaucratic structure and personality. In *Social theory and social structure.* New York: Free Press.

Milavsky, J. R., Kessler, R. C., Stipp, H., & Rubens, W. S. (1982). *Television and aggression: The results of a panel study.* New York: Academic Press.

Mosteller, F., & Moynihan D. P. (1972). *On equality of educational opportunity.* New York: Vintage Books.

National Institute of Education. (1984). *The effects of school desegregation on the achievement of black children.* Washington, D.C.

Parke, R. D., Berkowitz, L., Leyens, J. P. West, S., & Sebastian, R. J. (1977). Some effects of violent and nonviolent movies on the behavior of juvenile delinquents. In L. Berkowitz (Ed.), *Advances in experimental and social psychology* (Vol. 10). New York: Academic Press.

Patton, M. Q. (1978). *Utilization-focused evaluation.* Beverly Hills, CA: Sage.

Popper, K. R. (1959). *The logic of scientific discovery.* New York: Basic Books.

Popper, K. R. (1972). *Objective knowledge: An evolutionary approach.* Oxford, England: Clarendon Press.

Pressman, J., & Wildavsky, A. (1979). *Implementation: How great expectations in Washington are dashed in Oakland* (2nd ed.). Berkeley: University of California Press.

Rogosa, D. (1980). A critique of cross-lagged correlation. *Psychological Bulletin, 88,* 245-258.

Rosenthal, R., & Jacobson, L. (1968). *Pygmalion in the classroom.* New York: Holt, Rinehart and Winston.

Sawn, D. B. (1973). *Aggressive behavior among children in small polygroup settings with violent television.* Unpublished doctoral dissertation, University of Minnesota.

Scriven, M. (1971). The logic of cause. *Theory and Decision, 2,* 3-16.

Scriven, M. (1976). Maximizing the power of causal investigation: The modus operandi method. In G. V. Glass (Ed.), *Evaluation studies review annual* (Vol. 1). Beverly Hills, CA: Sage.

Simon, H. A. (1957). *Models of man.* New York: John Wiley.

St. Pierre, R., & Cook, T. D. (in press). Sampling strategies in program evaluation. In R. Conner (Ed.), *Evaluation studies review annual* (Vol. 9). Beverly Hills, CA: Sage.

Singer, J. L., & Singer, D. G. (1980). *Television, imagination and aggression: A study of preschoolers' play.* Hillsdale, NJ: Erlbaum.

Stein, A. H., & Friedrich, L. K. (1972). Television content and young children's behavior. In J. P. Murray, E. A. Rubenstein, & G. A. Comstock (Eds.), *Television and social behavior* Vol. 2: *Television and social learning,* Washington, DC: Government Printing Office.

Tukey, J. W. (1977). *Exploratory data analysis.* Reading, MA: Addison-Wesley.

Tversky, A., & Kahneman, D. (1977). Judgment under uncertainty: Heuristics and biases. *Science, 185,* 1124-1131.

Webb, E. J., Campbell, D. T., Schwartz, R. D., & Sechrest, L. (1966). *Unobtrusive measures.* Skokie, IL: Rand McNally.

Weber, S. J., & Cook, T. D. (1972). Subject effects in laboratory research: An examination of subject roles, demand characteristics, and valid inferences. *Psychological Bulletin, 77,* 273-295.

Weiss, J. A., & Weiss, C. H. (1981). Social scientists and decision makers look at the usefulness of mental health research. *American Psychologist, 36,* 837-847.

Wells, W. D. (1973). *Television aggression: Replication of an experimental field study.* Unpublished manuscript, University of Chicago.

Williams, W. (1980). *The implementation perspective.* Berkeley: University of California Press.

2

Social Science and Social Policy
Will Our Numbers Ever Be Good Enough?

LEE SECHREST

As social scientists we want to believe that our research findings have reasonably direct relevance for social policy. It is likely that many policymakers, under pressure to rationalize their decisions, would like to believe the same. There are many reasons why the proper relationship between social science findings and social policy might be attenuated. I want to direct my comments to a limited set of issues having to do with the characteristics of the numbers we produce and whether those numbers provide an adequate basis for social policy recommendations and decisions.

A distinction is drawn here between recommendations and decisions. That is because I consider recommendations to be tentative and based on narrow premises of the *ceteris paribus* variety. Recommendations may be made on an "if you had to guess" basis with somewhat lower standards of truth than would be expected in the enactment of social policy. Moreover, recommendations may be made from a limited perspective, whereas the decisions often require the simultaneous consideration of several perspectives. For example, there is good evidence that increasing the legal age for drinking from 18 to 19 or 21 results in a decrease in alcohol-related traffic fatalities (Wagenaar, 1982). A social scientist

AUTHOR'S NOTE: Preparation of this chapter was supported in part by research grant No. HS 0702 from the National Center for Health Services Research and ONR Contract N000114-78-C-0469.

may, on the basis of that evidence, recommend a change in drinking age. The decision actually to do so, however, has to take into account considerations of civil liberties, losses of revenue to business persons, enforceability of the change, and so on. But these data are sufficiently compelling to tempt a decisionmaker to override the other factors. By contrast, there is also some evidence that a curfew on 16-year-old drivers at 11 p.m. or so would decrease motor vehicle crashes and injuries (Preusser, Blomberg, Williams, & Zador, 1983). And a conscientious social scientist may, based on the data, recommend a curfew. But the existing data are not so strong as those for drinking age, and other considerations might preclude adoption of a curfew until the evidence for its effects is much stronger.

For the most part, my remarks have reference to social statistics and large-scale analyses of secondary data sources and, to a lesser extent, to the outcomes of program evaluations. Some of the comments are quite relevant to other types of social science data, e.g., smaller scale experiments and laboratory studies, but I shall concentrate on larger pictures.

I am concerned about the nature and the quality of the numbers we produce. Perhaps I do not even need to warn that I am skeptical about many of our numbers and their utilities. I do not want to leave the impression that social science is a shambles, that we have nothing to offer but to fold our tents and steal away. But I am concerned that exaggerated claims for what social science has done, is doing, can do, and will do are constantly being put forth—sometimes by social scientists. I would like us to be appropriately cautious. We ought to be bold when we are sure of ourselves, but that boldness ought to reflect large measures of wisdom and very little hubris. Harry Truman used to say, "it's what you learn after you know it all that counts."

THE QUALITY OF OUR
NUMBERS IN SOCIAL SCIENCE

Our numbers must have several critical characteristics if they are to be useful in relation to public policy: Dependability, evaluability, validity, interpretability, and communicability. These characteristics will be implicitly relevant in the discussion that follows, but I will comment briefly on each of them.

Dependability refers among other things to what is usually called reliability. By dependability, I mean being relatively free from error, trustworthy, and so on. Some of our numbers may not be dependable indicators of what is really going on in society because the phenomena they reflect are themselves unstable. For example, in any given locale, burglary rates may fluctuate widely as gangs become active, are arrested, move on to other areas, and so on. These fluctuations may easily be misread as more fundamental social changes. Other numbers may be undependable because they present opportunities for substantial error; e.g., estimates of the money supply (M1, M2, M3) may contain large errors because there is no very good way of knowing what the money supply is at any given time (Washington Post, National Weekly Edition, 1984). Still other numbers may be undependable because they are susceptible to falsification or distortion; e.g., crime rates in a city may be made to go up or down by changes in reporting practices. A recent story out of Chicago (Newsweek, 1983) revealed that for the past 20 years the police there have been concealing crime reports to keep the statistics down. About 25 years ago they went up precipitously when a new police commissioner demanded more honest reporting.

Evaluability is the term I employ to refer to our ability to assess our numbers for dependability. We may be able to determine the degree to which crime rates for a municipality are dependable; we may not be able to assess the dependability of a statement concerning the number of persons living on incomes below the poverty level at a given point in time. Evaluability of numbers requires that we have available the kinds of information and resources that are required to estimate dependability. The Panel on Statistics for Family Assistance and Related Programs of the Committee on National Statistics (1983) noted the great need for better ways of estimating error rates in state data on welfare programs. Some numbers may not be evaluable because they are put together in such complex ways that we cannot check them; e.g., few persons have the capability of evaluating estimates of the Gross National Product, and the rest of us just have to assume that the numbers are reasonably good. Other numbers may not be evaluable because the information necessary to do so is not available to us. When we are told, for example, how many missiles with what kinds of warheads are possessed by the United States and the U.S.S.R., we have to take the figures for whatever we think they are worth; even though the missiles are enumerable, none of us could count them.

Validity is used here in its usual sense; i.e., the degree to which our numbers reflect what we think they reflect. If we think that police records of rapes in two cities reflect the occurrence of rape in each, and, in fact, the difference is attributable to systematic differences in the ways in which rapes are recorded and reported in the two cities, the number is invalid for the purpose for which it is used. A number may be invalid because it is undependable or because it is used inappropriately. Thus, infant mortality rates may be reasonably dependable numbers for many countries, but those rates may not be very good indexes of the health of populations or for the adequacy of medical care available.

Interpretability refers to our ability to make sense out of the numbers we obtain. Numbers may be difficult to interpret because they are inherently complex; rate of economic growth is a good example. Numbers may be difficult to interpret because they are in a metric or a form that is hard to understand. If we were told that a variable had a canonical weight of .25 on a variate, most of us would not know what to make of that. Gerbing and Hunter (1982), for example, have called attention to the lack of meaning of the metric involved in expressing latent variables in LISREL. Numbers may also be difficult to interpret because we really do not know what they mean. For example, an observed difference in surgical death rates in two hospitals may mean almost anything and cannot be considered as any more than a simple "fact" without further information that would permit interpretation. Differences in death rates may reflect different case-mixes, differences in surgical skill, differences in surgical aftercare, or differences between populations being served (e.g., see Hebel, Kessler, Mabuchi, & McCarter, 1982).

Communicability has to do with our ability to explain our numbers to other persons; e.g., lay audiences, policymakers. Ideally we should like our audience to have the same understanding of and feelings about our numbers as we have. If we are 40 percent tentative in accepting a number as accurate, we ought to want our audience to be 40 percent tentative. If we think a finding is important even though small, we would like our audience to think the same thing. No more, no less. We often lack skills in communicating our findings, and some numbers are easier to communicate about than others. I recently attended a presentation to the press of some findings on the causal effects of watching TV violence on behavioral aggressiveness in children (Milavsky, Kessler, Stipp, & Rubens, 1982). The results were fairly uniform in indicating that the effect, if there is one, must be exceedingly small. Yet another analysis (Cook, Kendzierski, & Thomas, 1983) suggested at least the slight possibility that there is an effect that increases over time. The findings were all subtlety and nuance. I am not sure that the panel that presented and discussed the findings for the press was successful in conveying just the right amount of confidence that there is no effect, shaded by the nuance that there just may still be a small effect that could be enhanced over time. The cost-of-living index, for another example, is easily communicated to ordinary persons even if the methods of constructing it are far from simple. By contrast, various estimates of risk may be derived in simple ways, but we probably do not know how to communicate risk assessments very well. Perhaps for that reason people regularly behave as if they underestimate some risks and overestimate others (Kahneman, Slovic, & Tversky, 1982).

Our number problems appear to me to be of various natures and to have various origins. Some of the problems are not under the direct control of social scientists; some are. We ought to do what we can to improve matters with respect to our use of numbers whose production we cannot control and to go to great lengths to improve the numbers we produce directly.

THE NATURE OF NUMBERS
IN SOCIAL SCIENCE

Our number problems in social science often begin with the numbers available to us. We often use numbers that are generated outside the limits of our direct control; e.g., many economic statistics. In some instances, e.g., opinion polls, social science may exercise some indirect control, but any individual investigator may lack control altogether.

Problems Inherent in Problems We Study

Some difficulties we have in obtaining good, useful numbers are inherent in the problems we try to address. There are two difficulties I want to discuss here, although there are surely many others. The two are processes that are sensitive and difficult to control, and rare events.

There are many processes about which we would like to have information that are sensitive or difficult to control or both. For example, the process of arresting a citizen is a sensitive process, for arrest is fraught with consequences, both for the citizen arrested and for the police who make the arrest. Moreover, it is difficult to control arrest as a process because arrests are stochastic with respect to a wide range of variables and, hence, are difficult to monitor. Additional problems arise because arrests are outcomes of interactions between police officers and citizens, and officer contributions to the process are often subtle and always difficult to manage. When we have an opportunity to deal with sensitive processes not easily controlled, it is likely that the situation is special in many respects. It is also likely that the scope of our investigations will be quite limited. To study arrest as a process, it is necessary to get substantial cooperation from a hypersensitive public service unit, to train field workers carefully, and so on. That almost guarantees that the study can be carried out in only one site, or in at most a few sites; that data collection will be expensive with the consequence that samples will be small; and that the study will be of short duration so that it can be completed before anything "bad" happens. All of these factors also virtually guarantee that our numbers will be of limited interpretability. Put another way, sensitive problems are likely to be studied only under such special conditions in which the external validity of findings is sure to be limited.

A notable instance is provided by the recently completed Police Foundation study of the effects of arrests on subsequent occurrence of domestic violence (Sherman & Berk, in press). The study was remarkable in conception, for it called for police dealing with domestic violence to follow a random pattern of arresting offenders, ordering them off the premises for a cooling off period, or counseling and advising the couple involved, probably including a warning to improve their behavior at risk of later arrest. Police are not accustomed to arresting people randomly—nor in any other way not reflecting their judgments of the immediate situation. Astonishingly, however, the Police Foundation was able to sell the Police Department in Minneapolis on the idea of doing a randomized study of arrests in domestic disputes. To do so, it was necessary to negotiate with individual officers to secure their participation. Ultimately, 30 to 35 officers participated, but even after nearly a year only 328 cases of domestic violence fit the criteria for the study, and other considerations reduced the analysis to 252 cases. It was also necessary to limit the follow-up period to six months. The results did show that only 10 percent of those offenders arrested were involved in a new, officially reported incidence of domestic violence within six months, whereas 16 percent of those given advice and 22 percent of those ordered off the premises were involved in new violent incidents.

Those numbers cause, or ought to cause, us difficulties. Even if statistically significant, the results are a slim peg on which to hang any policy decisions, especially in cities other than Minneapolis. Replication of the experiment is not likely soon, but the extant study, however intriguing, is not a very persuasive argument for encouraging policies leading to increasing frequency of arrest of participants in domestic violence. The authors of the Police Foundation report are properly cautious in their inferences, but that does not help policymakers.

Some of the phenomena with which we, as social scientists interested in public policy, would like to deal are important but rare. Consequently, we find it difficult to accumulate enough cases to make studying them worthwhile from a policy standpoint. Moreover, the cases may occur under such circumstances that it is even difficult to estimate the size of the population from which our adventitiously encountered cases are drawn. It may be tempting to make a few simplifying assumptions and apply a bit of arithmetic in order to bolster the case for policy, but the consequences can be ridiculous. As an example, an estimate was once made from the census that there were at the time 20,000 "latchkey" children nationally; i.e., preschool children left home alone all day by their working mothers. That estimate apparently was made by extrapolating nationally from a total of probably 12 actual known cases (Bruce-Briggs, 1977)! I have been told that a similar extrapolation was used to estimate the number of welfare cheats in the country from a handful of known cases in Milwaukee (R. Berk, personal communication, November, 1982). Another report (see Barnard, 1979) used 12 cases of cheating in a medical benefits program (out of total sample of 67 cases) to estimate that national losses might total $12 million. Infrequent phenomena tend to result in undependable numbers, especially when they are extrapolated. Hard cases are said to make bad law; similarly, rare cases may make bad social science.

Limitations of Original Data Sources

Some of the important limitations we face in using social statistics and other data lie in the inadequacies of the original data sources. Many years ago, Morgenstern (1950), in a book entitled *On the Accuracy of Economic Observations,* detailed the shortcomings of many types of social statistics, including those of an economic nature. Morgenstern published the second edition of his book in 1963 without being able to remark on any widespread improvement in economic and other social observations. His book is well worth reading even today, for most of the same, and perhaps even some new, problems prevail.

Morgenstern discusses ten sources of errors in economic and other social statistics. These sources are:

(1) Lack of designed experiments.
(2) Hiding of information and lies.
(3) Reliance on untrained observers.

(4) Poorly constructed questionnaires.

(5) Mass (aggregated) observations. (It often happens that in aggregating observations errors are cumulative, many different systems of observation of varying accuracy have to be relied upon, and so on).

(6) Poorly defined phenomena and misclassification. (Definitions of "unemployed" may differ from place to place, or a manufacturing firm may be misclassified because its name is misleading with respect to its products.)

(7) Fallible instruments.

(8) The factor of time. (If crime data are recorded by calendar months, problems will arise not only because some months are longer than others, but some months will also have more weekend days than others, and crime tends to peak on Friday and Saturday nights.)

(9) Observations of unique phenomena.

(10) Interdependent and stable errors.

These sources of error are highly relevant to the discussion that follows in this chapter.

Unstable observations over time In perhaps his most notable example of a problematic data series, Morgenstern observed that data pertaining to that hallowed economic indicator, the *Gross National Product* (GNP), continue to come in long after any policy decisions based on the GNP would be relevant and that, in fact, it is about 15 years before the final figure is arrived at. In the meantime, however, the variability in the GNP over the 15 years is likely to be considerably greater than the variability between GNP figures for adjacent years. Thus, attempts to adjust national economic policy to the fact that last year's GNP was up or down border on the absurd because no one will know for quite some time whether the GNP was up or down and by even approximately how much. At a recent national training conference on health psychology, data were presented (Matarazzo, 1982) showing the proportion of GNP spent on health care over a period of several years. The proportion may be increasing, but given the problems with the estimate of GNP, not to say of health care expenditures, the claim that health care went from 9.4 percent of the GNP in 1980 to 10.5 percent in 1982 is suspect, to say the least.

The Federal Reserve Board publishes three estimates, M1, M2, and M3, of the quantity of money in circulation. In 1981 the Board had to reconsider its policy of publishing weekly figures because of the overreaction to them by the financial community (Berry, 1981). Again, the problem lies in the instability of the numbers. On one occasion the estimates had ultimately to be revised by $1.6 billion dollars after many decisions had already been made.

Currently our politicians, our business community, and just ordinary "we" pay close attention to monthly figures on unemployment rates, interest rates, inflation rates, and so on. Moreover, we pay attention to these statistics down to the third decimal. Thus, a change from 10.6 (actually .106) to 10.5 unemployment is regarded as good. That tenth of one percent represents fewer than 100,000 workers. Perhaps that seems like a lot of workers, but when one considers the vagaries of defining "employed," the necessity of some arbitrary procedure for counting workers, and the numbers of separate reporting units across which data have to be aggregated, 100,000 workers more or less can easily get lost or found in the shuffle. A recent concern about unemployment figures arose because of the fear that an improvement in the economy would attract more potential job seekers and actually increase apparent unemployment. Once I was talking to a Captain in the Bureau of Personnel of the U.S. Navy, and he told me that on any given day, the Navy does not know where approximately 25 percent of its personnel are. That is to say, about 25 percent of U.S. Navy personnel are on leave, being transferred, traveling, AWOL, or maybe just plain lost on any given day.

Forced reliance on estimates Some of the numbers we deal with are likely to have to be estimated; they cannot be obtained directly. For example, there has been controversy about the number of Americans with arrest records. One investigator (Miller, 1979) has surmised that the only possible way anyone could determine the number from FBI files, the best such records available, would be to sample file drawers to see about how many records there are per drawer, count the number of drawers per file and use that as a multiplier, then multiply again by an estimate of measures of the linear feet of file cabinets. There appeared in 1979 to have been about 45,000,000 arrest records, but estimates have ranged as low as about half of that number.

One group, certainly not distinterested in the outcome (Main, 1983), sought to estimate the number of "homeless" people in the city of New York. They began with an estimate by an agency serving such persons that with their caseload of about 9000 persons they were serving only one-third of the total. Because the agency whose figures were being used served only males, they also used another estimate of the possible number of homeless females and finally concluded that there were 36,000 homeless persons in the city. However, even with a fairly intensive shelter program, there were never more than 4500 persons or so being cared for on any given night. The agency making the original estimate was inclined to take the discrepancy in figures as an indication of the shameful inadequacy of the shelter program, claiming that many homeless persons preferred the streets. Other persons believed that the original estimates were wrong.

As another example, there is no direct measure at the macroeconomic level of personal savings in the United States. Savings is a residual number, currently estimated in two ways: First, as earnings minus consumption, and, alternatively, as an increase in assets minus an increase in liabilities. These two ways of estimating savings have recently varied by as much as 100 percent. Note also that in recent years it has been alleged that Americans save less than do the Japanese or Germans. It is well when contemplaing social statistics to remember the words of Sir Joseph Stamp, who, although speaking of the bureaucracy in India, speaks to us all:

> The government is very keen on amassing statistics. They collect them, add them, raise them to the *nth* power, take the cube root and prepare wonderful diagrams. But what you must never forget is that every one of these figures comes in the first instance from the *chowty dar* (village watchman), who just puts down what he damn pleases. (Stamp, 1929, pp. 258-259)

Inconstancy of meaning of observations The adequacy of our social statistics is also impaired by the fact that they lack constancy of meaning over time and circumstances. This lack of constancy is attributable to deliberate changes in indexes or the elements that go into them; shifts in implications of indexes or their elements over time or place; and temporal or spatial variations in circumstances that bear on the interpretation of indexes. The Dow-Jones stock index, for example, has increased so greatly in absolute magnitude that comparisons of changes over time may be meaningless; what was a large percentage change in the Dow when it was down around 200 is now a very small change when it is around 1000. Cost-of-living indexes may change in meaning over time if the market-basket is not regularly adjusted, e.g., to take account of changes in type and cost of housing, but every adjustment in the market-basket creates the possibility of non-comparability over time. Mechanic has noted that estimates of the prevalence rates of untreated mental illness yield a median rate seven times as high for studies done after 1950 when compared to those done before. Box and Hale (1983) have shown that supposed changes in female participation in crime are quite difficult to assess because of changing male patterns, changing definitions, and other factors. Unemployment rates may also change because as unemployment persists over time, many persons may give up looking for jobs altogether.

A recent article in the New York *Times* (Williams, 1983) called into question the Federal Reserve Board's estimate of the percentage of the nation's industrial capacity now being used. The steel industry, for example, is said to be running at 55 percent of its capacity. These figures are thought to be important because as they climb higher, i.e., more of the capacity is being used, businessmen will become increasingly willing to build new plants. The problem stems from the fact that many industrial plants have been abandoned altogether and will never be reopened, but they are counted in the denominator of the index. Some economists and business persons think that the denominator should reflect only those plants likely to be used again, in which case the index would be higher and the outlook for business would be better.

Cost-of-living and per capita income indexes need to be interpreted in light of characteristics or populations to which they apply. Thus, for example, per capita income figures will seriously overestimate the relative poverty of societies or geographic areas characterized by subsistence agriculture or populations with large proportions of juveniles (Petersen, 1982). Various indexes involving economic activity, health, homicide, suicide, accident rates, and so on can be properly interpreted only if a variety of relevant population variables is taken into account.

In some cases our social statistics or other numbers may change in meaning over time because of more general societal changes. For example, the social meaning of "born out of wedlock" is certainly far different today from, say, 40 or 50 years ago. Are movies today any more shocking than they were in 1943? Well, they are different; words are used freely that were once strictly proscribed, and partial nudity is commonplace. But one gets the feeling that audiences are not any more shocked than ever. It is just that standards have changed.

Results of overreliance on numbers Of course, changes do not occur simply as a result of the passage of time; it is what happens during that time that counts. One thing that can happen to our numbers is that they can become too impressive, so that they get to be used not widely but too much. When numbers are well accepted, they often become criteria or goals against which performance is judged, and when that happens, there is virtually inexorable progression toward corruption of the measures. That often results in activities directed toward producing good numbers even if some more fundamental outcome is sacrificed. Thus, police units are often judged, or at least they think they are judged, on the basis of clearances of crimes. Because, then, it is in the interests of the police to clear up crimes, or appear to do so, they may be particularly well disposed toward apprehended criminals who clear up a lot of crimes by confessing. That led in at least one jurisdiction (Skolnick, 1966) to the anomalous result that the more burglaries an apprehended burglar confessed to, the lighter his sentence! At the other end of some scale, corporate officers are often judged by the profits they turn. That aparently led some corporate executives to opt for certain tax situations in which, although they were able to show higher profits, they actually paid more taxes and had a worse bottom line (Business Week, June 1, 1981).

Biased reporting As Morgenstern (and many others) noted, one has to be aware that social statistics are often provided by persons or agencies with less than a disinterested outlook on them. In some cases, social statistics may represent outright lies. A newspaper report (Seattle Post-Intelligencer, August 16, 1974) indicated, for example, that a widely cited estimate that 70 percent of homicides by gunfire are committed with "Saturday Night Specials" was actually a fabrication promoted by gun interests. Apparently a much higher proportion of homicides than gun interests would like us to believe are committed with high quality handguns.

Phony statistics may be a special problem in cross-national comparisons of many kinds because many governments have a particular interest in the image they may present through their statistics. It is said (Wallis & Roberts, 1956) that a census was once conducted in an area of China to determine the population for purposes of taxes and military conscription. The population was 28 million. Only a few years later, another census was taken to determine the population for purposes of famine relief; the population was 105 million! I was in the Philippines during a time when the number of communist insurgents was said to be negligible (the army was doing a good job), and only a few months later the number was large and growing (the army needed a larger budget). One wonders about the objectivity of estimates of the need for mental health professionals when those estimates are produced by the professions. Estimates of the prevalence of untreated mental disorder range from less than one percent to more than 60 percent (Dohrenwend & Dorhenwend, 1968).

But even without lying, many satistical series are highly susceptible to bias resulting from reporting pressures (Cochran, 1978). Crime statistics, for example, are known to vary greatly simply because of changes in reporting practices (Nagin, 1978). If there is pressure on to "do something about crime," police officers may lack diligence in taking reports, downgrade crimes in seriousness, persuade victims that no offense took place, and so on. Sherman and Langworthy (1979) compare newspaper clippings with death certificates from 36 cities over a ten-year period and discovered that death certificates probably underestimate the number of people killed by the police by about 50 percent. Sherman and Langworthy (1979) believe that rather than the 250 to 300 deaths per year officially attributed to police action by the National Center for Health Statistics, the true figure is about 600, which is almost 4 percent of homicides nationally. The discrepancy may be partially explainable by pressures, perhaps implicit, not to put the onus on police for a death if it is avoidable. Police acquaintances of mine have told me that police may often underestimate the value of goods stolen in burglaries (police are keeping burglary down) and overestimate the value of goods recovered when crimes are solved (police are effective in solving burglaries).

Variations in definitions Additional problems with many statistical series may arise out of variations in definitions across reporting units. It may surprise many persons, for example, as it did me when I learned from Barry Glick of the Police Foundation, that there is no uniform defintion of "arrest" across police jurisdictions (Glick, personal communication, 1982). Thus, in some places a person may be considered to have been arrested and thus will have become a statistic if informed by the officer that he/she is under arrest and if a report of any kind is taken. In other jurisdictions, a person may be considered arrested only if taken into a station and booked. If a suspect is arrested, released, and rearrested, in some places that may appear as two arrests for statistical purposes; in other places, it would be only one arrest. In some cases, if a person is pursued across a jurisdictional line, such as a city limit, and arrested, that person may appear as an arrestee on the books of both the jurisdiction from which the officers chased him and to which he was returned, and the jurisdiction in which the actual apprehension occurred. The United States often compares somewhat unfavorably with other industrialized countries in satistics on infant mortality, but at least part of the difference is attributable to definitions. In Norway, an infant who dies soon after birth may be counted as stillborn, with the consequent effect of lowering apparent infant mortality rates (Erickson & Bjerkedal, 1982).

Inadequate recording systems Still other problems may arise because of the way in which information is recorded or kept; i.e., the numbers are undependable. In some instances serious biases may occur as a result of the instruments or forms used to collect information. A study

of 104 randomly selected motor vehicle accidents (Brown, 1971) identified 668 contributory factors and resulted in the conclusion that
50 percent of the factors involved are vehicle related, 31 percent are
environmental, and only 19 percent are attributable to the driver. That
conclusion is in stark contrast to the repeated conclusion of the National Safety Council that 85 percent of motor vehicle accidents are
the result of driver errors. But the standard form on which auto accidents are reported to the National Safety Council (NSC) allows for
noting ten contributory factors related to the driver, two related to
the vehicle, and none for the roadway. NSC reports on the 104 accidents
would have reduced the 668 contributory factors to only 140, and
125 of those would have been driver-related. Death certificates are
often examined as sources of information, but they are probably poor
sources of information because they are rarely audited and the cause
of death (medical diagnosis) is irrelevant to the two major purposes
of the certificate: to permit burial and to collect insurance. A study
of deaths from pancreatic cancer recorded on death certificates in
two counties indicated the almost certain probability that no more
than 52 percent of the deaths in one county and 81 percent in the
other could be attributed to pancreatic cancer (Holmes, Baker, Hearne,
& Wilcox, 1981).

Frazier (1983) has shown how quite misleading findings about a
juvenile diversion program resulted from biases in record keeping. Logistic
regression models indicated that some variables having to do with
the process of diversion and services offered were actually positively
related to recidivism. Specifically, it appeared that receiving help from
more than one volunteer worker and a high number of hours of service
increased the likelihood of recidivisim. Similarly, intervention by project staff and volunteers with help in school and with justice system
advocacy seemed to increase recidivism. Detailed study of the record
keeping system showed, however, that a second volunteer tended to
assist because the first one failed or quit, and that extra service hours
tended to be recorded with difficult clients because staff believed that
they had worked harder on such cases and wanted credit for it. School
intervention and justice advocacy tended to be recorded only after
a youth had recidivated partly because recidivism led to interventions
at that point. Obviously, the manner in which records come to be
kept is always a phenomenon worth looking into.

Problems Stemming from Foreshortened Time Perspective

It is now widely accepted that important segments of American
industry are dominated by an outlook and an accompanying strategy

that favors the short-run performance. In contrast, Japanese and West German industries are thought to have a longer time perspective that favors research and developments, long-range investment planning, and the like. It is possible, then, to be misled by numbers that reflect immediate or imminent states of affairs while obscuring longer range possibilities. The distinction that St. Pierre (in this volume) makes between proximate and distal measures is relevant here. Two New York newspapers once headlined the exact same state of affairs as "Douglas Aircraft clears $2,000,000" and "Douglas Aircraft loses $2,000,000" (Wallis & Roberts, 1956, p. 74)! Actually one paper was reporting on operating losses; the other was reporting on net income resulting from refunded taxes paid in previous years.

Depending on just what is reported and how, short-run prospects (proximal measures) may look either better or worse than would be justified by long-term considerations (distal measures). That statement may be made of individuals, companies, cities, nations, or any other entities. Money may be saved by deferring maintenance or it may be invested in research and development with a payoff deferred to some relatively remote time.

As a society, we do in fact need measures that, like telescopes, can peer into the distance. The particular government or other social agencies that actually produce many of the numbers we need may, however, have little interest in the quality of those numbers whose significance recedes so far into the future.

Problems Arising from Irrelevant Metrics

Some of our problems arise from the fact that the metrics in terms of which data are available and in which we express our findings or information are not directly relevant, and maybe not relevant at all, to those who need to use them. For example, many statistics are produced by political units—states, counties, cities—that do not at all correspond to the social units in which we are interested. Thus, attempts to develop an index of the degrees to which areas of the country are medically underserved have been less than satisfactory (Kvis & Flaskerud, 1980). The number of physicians per county may be largely irrelevant if residents of counties do not do their business in relation to county boundaries. The safety of various modes of transportation is often couched in terms of deaths per passenger mile. In that case, space travel is the safest of all forms of travel because each astronaut may log a half million miles or so of travel for each day in space. What we want is a number that expresses our likelihood of returning from any particular trip.

NUMBER PROBLEMS UNDER
CONTROL OF THE SCIENTIST

The preceding paragraphs refer to problems that are inherent in the data available to us. There are other problems that are more nearly under the control of the social scientist or the social science community. For these problems we bear a direct responsibility for their avoidance or solution.

Errors in Data Collection and Analysis

Regrettably, social science is not free of error. I doubt that the errors we make are unusually frequent or frequently important in any immediate sense. Errors may be important, however, in the shadow they cast. Mark Twain is reported once to have said that the thirteenth chime of a clock is not only suspicious in and of itself, but it tends to cast doubt on the preceding twelve.

There is growing alarm about outright dishonesty in science, particularly in the biomedical sciences (e.g., Fisher, 1982a), hardhit by several well-publicized examples. As yet the social sciences have not been plagued with uncovered chicanery, but the Cyril Burt case (Dorfman, 1978) was widely covered by the printed media, and the recent controversy over the legitimacy of the conclusions about controlled drinking by alcoholics (Fisher, 1982b) received both print and television coverage. Undoubtedly there will be similar cases in the future. These cases are not of great consequence in and of themselves, but, as Mr. Twain saw so clearly, they are important because they tend to cast a more general doubt on the trustworthiness of social science. They also provide a handy platform from which to attack any social science findings that a critic wishes to dismiss.

There can be outright error. Given the large numbers of scientific projects and their multitudes of findings, it may seem that error is unavoidable. But that does not make error less damaging. When it was first published, the Kinsey Report on sexual behavior of males (Kinsey, Pomeroy, & Martin, 1948) created a considerable sensation— probably a bit difficult to understand now. Immediately the report was attacked, and, aside from easy aspersions on the methods employed in the study, the attack was facilitated by the early discovery of numerous arithmetic, statistical, and other errors (Wallis, 1949). The Coleman report (Coleman et al., 1966) was similarly sensational, and was similarly found to contain important statistical errors and, therefore, was quite open to attack (Smith, 1978). If we want our numbers to be taken seriously, we must take them seriously themselves. A few careless errors resulting from saving hours of careful thought and checking can destroy the impact of years of work.

Uninterpretable Metrics

Isaac Ehrlich (1975) wished to state his conclusion about the deterrent effects of capital punishment on homicide. He concluded that every execution resulted in eight fewer homicides. Ehrlich also stated that:

$$\Delta^*Q/N = -3.176 - 1.553\Delta^*\hat{P}_a^\circ - 0.455\Delta^*\hat{P}_{c/a}^\circ - 0.039\Delta^*PXQ$$
$$- 1.336\Delta^*L + 0.630\Delta^*A + 1.481\Delta^*Yp + 0.067\Delta^*U - 0.047\Delta^*T$$

The advantage of the first statement by Ehrlich is that it is at least immediately clear what his findings mean in terms of potential policy. It is not at all clear what the equation means. Ehrlich's verbal conclusion may or may not be right; that is beside the point. It is expressed in a metric that is intuitively clear to those who want to think about it. Communicability of numbers is important.

Recently Ihilevich and Gleser (1982) have reported on the development of the *Progress Evaluation Scales* for evaluating mental health programs. The scales assess functioning in seven areas: Family interaction, occupation (school-job-homemaking), getting along with others, feelings and mood, use of free time, problems, and attitude toward self. Each scale has five levels. In one study involving 50 male children in treatment, there had been significant improvement of five of the seven scales in Table 2.1. What might we make of these findings? My colleague, Yeaton, and I have argued that almost nothing can be made of them (Sechrest & Yeaton, 1982). The problem is that the metric tells us nothing that would be helpful in deciding whether treatment is useful for the kinds of boys in question (aside from design problems involving lack of any comparision group). The numbers do make more sense, i.e., are interpretable, when we know, however, that a change of about 2.0 scale points is required if it is to be clinically noticeable; i.e., if parents, therapists, etc. are to notice the change in the child's behavior (Ihilevich, personal communication, April 15, 1983).

We social scientists tend, understandably, to choose measures that are convenient and that conform to the requirements of the data analyses we plan. It is easy to forget that the numbers we work with have no inherent, intuitive meaning to those with whom we try to com-

TABLE 2.1

	Mean Improvement	R
Family interaction	.42	<.01
Getting along with others	.46	<.01
Feelings and mood	.48	<.01
Problems	.56	<.01
Attitude toward self	.72	<.01

municate and who need to understand the full meaning of our numbers if they are to make wise policy decisions. We tend to produce coefficients, indexes, corrected values, derived numbers. Even as social scientists we are often hard-pressed to say exactly what we have found beyond the statement that it is or is not statistically significant. For example, what is to be made of a statistically significant regression coefficient of .113 for prediction of peer ratings of aggressiveness by amount of TV watched for 12 year-old boys (Milavsky, Kessler, Stipp, & Rubens, 1982)? Or, so as to be impartial, citing from my own work (Riccio, Sechrest, Glick, & Mabe, 1983), what should one communicate to chiefs of police about a statistically significant beta coefficient of .09 between a police officer's attention to physical evidence at a crime scene and the occurrence of arrest? (Actually, not much because it turns out that officers pay attention to physical evidence only if an arrest is likely.) A beta coefficient of .09, however significant, is no guide to a police manager about how to deal with attention to physical evidence. The contrast with such assertions as that a particular class of workers must, on the average, work from January 1 until April 4 to earn the taxes they will owe is revealing.

We social scientists need to expend much more effort toward the conversion of our research numbers, the tools of our trade, into practical products for the consumers of our research (Sechrest & Yeaton, 1981).

Opaque Statistics

Social science is characterized by increasingly powerful and sophisticated quantitative techniques: Multiple regression, path analysis, multivariate analysis of variance, discriminant functions, structural equations with latent variables, and canonical correlation. This increasing power is coming at a price, however, for it is more and more difficult to comprehend the relationship between the data we begin with and the results that flow from our statistical analyses. I refer to this problem as one of *opaque* statistics, but it is related to the problem of uninterpretability. Years ago, one had only simple statistical tests: *t* tests, one-way ANOVAs and, correlations. Analysis of covariance and simple multiple regressions were about as fancy as one could get. Even factor analysis was fairly simple because the manageable size of problems was limited to a small number of variables, and rotations were done by hand, so that one could see just what happened to solutions as different rotations were tried. These statistics were "transparent" in the sense that one could look at the original data and the outcome of the analysis and have an intuitive feel for what it all meant. One could also intuit the reasonableness of the outcome and the likelihood of serious errors along the way. Our new, and admittedly powerful, opaque statistics do not permit that intuitive sense of what happens during an analysis (Kraemer, 1981, 1982).

It may help to take a simple example. Magidson (1977) was concerned that the original estimates of the effects of Head Start programs that had shown that participants were worse off were biased because of initial differences in socioeconomic status of participants and controls. Magidson, therefore, undertook an analysis that would try to correct for those differences. I will present here just a snippet of Magidson's analysis. On a measure of verbal ability, the Head Start children had a mean score after the program of 19.7, and the comparison children had a mean score of 20.4. Thus, the Head Start children appeared worse off. The correlation between a dummy variable for the program and outcome was -.10, also reflecting the higher scores of the comparison group. Magidson introduced four SES indicators into his analysis: Mother's education, father's education, father's occupation, and family income. He used these variables in a structural equations analysis designed to estimate the "true scores" of the two groups of children. The four SES variables all had negative correlations with the dummy treatment variable, ranging from -.08 (father's occupation) to -.22 (family income). These and other values were used to estimate path coefficients between treatment and outcome variables after allowing for all the intervening relationships. Ultimately the path from the dummy treatment variable to outcome on the verbal measure was estimated to be .12, i.e., rather than Head Start children being worse off for program participation, they were estimated to have been better off. The data were then used to provide new estimates of means that resulted in adjusted values of 20.5 and 19.8 respectively for the Head Start and comparison groups. This was an impressive and elegant result because it so nearly did nothing more than switch initial values for the two groups. But it takes considerable thought and work to determine just exactly what happened as a result of Magidson's analysis. One *can* construct a small set of illustrative values and follow them through Magidson's analysis to see what happens at every point, but it is by no means simple, and probably few readers of his or similar articles can be expected to perform such a task. Magidson's results seem nice, but it requires an element of faith for most readers to accept that they are also correct and dependable. His analysis is actually relatively simple to follow.

There are other analyses that are, I contend, impenetrable for all but the most sophisticated statisticians, and I have questions about even them. For example, canonical correlations may be impenetrable altogether (but see Muller, 1982). Even factor analysis, by now used thousands of times and commonplace, may be more opaque than we would like to think. Overall (1964), in a particularly compelling example, has shown that factor analysis of a data set based on measures derived from the three dimensions of books—height, depth, and thickness—does not yield the expected three factors but instead results in very complex factors whose intuitive meaning is not clear. Gottfredson (1979) did a path analysis of variables associated with school violence, and then, out of curiosity, used the path coefficients in analyses with other dependent variables such as rates of heart attack and venereal disease in the same communities and found that the path coefficients were preserved (significant) remarkably well. To his consternation, he found that even when he substituted random numbers for the dependent variable, the path coefficients were often still significant. Berk (1977) has reported a similar phenomenon for Automatic Interaction Detection that, along with random numbers for variables, "accounted" for 14 percent of the variance in the dependent variable. Apparently analyses such as these allow for such flexible options and permit capitalizing on chance to such a degree that they may not be trustworthy. Such findings call into serious question the uses and interpretations we make of some of our common but opaque statistical analyses.

When economists do cost-effectiveness studies, they often test them by doing sensitivity analyses designed to show the effects of possible errors in estimating critical values. A sensitivity analysis is done by inserting different estimates for values of variables in equations, usually employing estimates that are assumed to bracket the likely true values. Thus, for example, Weinstein and Stason (1982) did an analysis of the cost-effectiveness of coronary artery bypass draft (CABG) surgery. They obtained estimates of the costs involved in such surgery, the effects on life expectancy, the extent of side effects of treatment, and so on, and used these to estimate the cost of an index they call "quality adjusted year of life" (QAYL). For two-vessel disease, their estimate was that CABG surgery cost $47,000 per QAYL. Weinstein and Stason realized, however, that some of their estimates were not completely dependable, so they redid their analysis with a range of seemingly reasonable values inserted in the equations for variables that seemed shaky. The result of the sensitivity analyses was that estimates of the cost of a QAYL ranged from $11,000 to $280,000!

Perhaps social scientists should become accustomed to the methods of sensitivity analyses, especially in light of the widespread availability of large and powerful computers with canned programs that produce even complex analyses quite inexpensively once the basic files have been constructed. The results might be instructive at the very least. Beaton, Rubin, and Barone (1976), to give an example, analyzed a set of economic data in which six variables were used to predict employment. These investigtors did no more than "perturb" the data by introducing randomly selected values within the rounding errors of the independent variables. Thus, for example, a variable that had an observed value of 83.0 was assumed to have a possible range of values between 82.5 and 83.499. Beaton et al. did 1000 multiple regression analyses with independent variables randomly perturbed within rounding limits. In comparison with the unperturbed solution, they found that the values they obtained for beta weights differed widely, sometimes even in direction. For example, one variable that had a regression coefficient of $+15.0619$ in the unperturbed solution had a *mean* value of -26.4404 in the 1000 perturbed analyses. The range of values for that variable was from -232.2792 to $+237.0467$! Analysis of the values of the squared multiple R showed that the mean value for the perturbed series of calculations was 65 standard errors away from the unperturbed squared multiple R. Beaton et al. conclude that for the data set they analyzed, and probably for many other data sets, the precision of the analysis far outstrips the precision of the data. Their work is merely illustrative, but it does suggest the potential desirability of perturbed analyses as a way of estimating dependability of findings.

Although the generality of the conclusions reached by Beaton et al. might be challenged on the grounds that their data set involved severe problems of multicollinearity, I believe that the need for caution is great. Many of our data sets in macrolevel analyses do involve multicollinearity, and I have seen many other data sets in which relatively small changes stemming from decisions about missing data, elimination of outliers, and corrections of coding errors produced substantial changes in outcomes, including reversals of signs on coefficients, let alone marked changes in significance levels (Wainer, 1976, 1978). Simple tests for robustness of data sets, such as data perturbations, ought to become a feature of our analyses. Attention ought also to be paid to the possibility of more direct, supplementary, if simpler, analyses of our complex data sets (e.g., Goldstein, 1982; Tukey, 1977).

Inscrutable Computers

IN 1977, two mathematicians at the University of Illinois (Appel & Haken, 1977) published a solution to a mathematical problem that was then 125 years old, the four-color map problem. Basically, the question is whether it is possible to color a map using only four colors and not use the same color on any two adjacent countries. Although the problem seems simple, it is not. Appel and Haken solved the problem (the answer is "yes") through the brute force of an extraordinarily complex computer program involving many, many algorithms that required 1200 hours of time (equal to 24 hours per day for 50 days!) on three high-speed computers. The two mathematicians noted that there was little hope that the two of them, or even dozens like them, could ever examine the entire proof.

Then in early 1979, an article by a philosopher, Thomas Tymoczko, appeared in the *Journal of Philosophy* (Tymoczko, 1979). In his article, Tymoczko suggested that it appears that a new standard of proof has been admitted into mathematics. He suggests that the new standard of proof is, in effect, "the computer told me so."

I would like to suggest that we have a very similar situation in social science. We often work with very large data sets (I have recently worked on regression analyses with more than 40,000 observations). We also analyze our data by very complicated statistical methods that require even more complicated computer programs. When we are finished, there is often little possibility that our results could be checked and verified and no possibility that they will be. The results are significant— because the computer told me so! There is, obviously, a compounding here of the problem of opaque statistics with the inscrutability of our computers. Dare we hope that our computers are always right?

Aside from the somewhat sobering (I think) results obtained by Beaton et al. (1976) as reported above, there are other reports that suggest that we ought to be cautious in accepting whatever our computers tell us (Boehm, Menkhaus, & Penn, 1976; Gondek, 1981). For one thing, as Beaton et al. suggest, the data we enter into computers are far from perfect, and small errors may get magnified as they are processed through the complex computer routines that are used, for example, in MANOVA or LISREL programs. We may not even be as confident as we ought to be that we know for sure what goes into our computers. I recently had occasion to check the procedures that had been used in constructing a large data set and discovered that key entry had never been verified and that only "data cleaning" methods had been employed. Such methods leave much room for error, and not all errors cancel each other out. It is worth remembering that even when we work with large data sets, we often break down variables in such a way that we are actually working with small numbers.

During the past year I was on a review panel that was excited about a finding in a proposal suggesting a very strong and important relationship between a nursing variable and infant mortality in intensive care units. The investigator was encouraged to rewrite the proposal and did so, but the revisions included a scatter plot of the critical variables. One glance made it evident that the exciting relationship was attributable almost entirely to one outlying value in the small sample. Without the scatter plot—and who ever sees them any more?—the study panel may have continued to be misled.

We are encountering disturbing hints both in our own work and that of others (e.g., Games, 1983; Strahan, 1982) that computers are not infallible, even at what they do. The work of Beaton et al. (1976) was instigated by a previous report on the same data set by Longley (1976), who had found that there were important differences in results obtained by different least squares analyses by computers. These appeared to result in part from differences in rounding routines or failure to consider truncation. With large data sets, even very large computers can run into problems resulting from excessively large numbers obtained by squaring values. Some analyses we have seen recently indicate that problems with the use of personal and other microcomputers may be severe (Sechrest & Kelly, 1983). A recent article speculated that some instances of startling computer failures may be akin to "convulsions" (Peterson, 1983a). It has also been suggested (Ziegler & Lanford, 1979) that computers may be susceptible to random errors resulting from cosmic radiation; even if a data set is clean, it may not stay that way. If these "glitches" occur in computer programs, havoc may result. The Department of Defense has found software errors to be an especially difficult, persistent, and dangerous problem (Peterson, 1983b).

It may be thought that my concern over computer errors attributable to rounding and other errors is inconsistent with the notion that the precision of our analyses outstrips the precision of our data. I do not believe there is any inconsistency. In the first place, two wrongs do not make a right, and compounding all the problems we seem to have in obtaining accurate data by allowing the introduction of calculating errors is the wrong way to go. The errors may be multiplicative rather than canceling. Also, calculating errors may be truly large under some circumstances, and the results may not even be good ball park estimates. It is the intended precision of our analyses that is particularly likely to exceed the precision in our data.

The problem of inscrutable computers results from the complexity of the tasks they perform and the difficulty of mere humans in keeping track of it. When we have no independent basis on which to judge the outcomes we get, either because of magnitude of the data set or opacity of the analysis, we can easily fall into error. A major error in thinking about economic policy (Feldstein, 1974; Feldstein & Pellechio, 1979) appears to have resulted from an error in computer programing (Lesnoy & Leimer, 1981). In a pile of computer printout 12 inches high, it may be difficult to keep track of everything the computer has done. A more interesting note (Kraft, 1981) is that the same computer analysis that showed that the book of Genesis was 82 percent likely to have been written by one person also showed that the works of Emanuel Kant were only 7 percent likely to have had a single author! That the first result was taken quite seriously is probably attributable to the fact that it was so difficult for any humans to interrogate the computer about how it arrived at its answer.

RENUMBERING

Perhaps my paramount concern is with data quality and ways of assessing it. I am concerned for our standards of evidence. I would like to see those standards more explicit and be applied more even-handedly. I have elsewhere called for the "principle of symmetry in interpretation of data" (Goldstein, Heller, & Sechrest, 1967), which states that factors that rule out the use of data on one side of an argument rule out the use of similar data on the other side. I am made quite uncomfortable by the seemingly careless but determined way our social science findings are invoked in the name of some policy or another. Too often I know that the numbers do not warrant the weight put on them.

Because at least some of the sources of our number problems are outside social science, what are we to do? I do not believe we are without influence and impact, and would like to suggest that the social science community devote a reasonable portion of its attention to the quality of numbers problem. We may be able to improve on the state of affairs that now exists.

First, we need more systematic assessments of the quality of social statistics and other numbers with which we deal. The quality of the numbers being produced by governmental and other social agencies should be under continual scrutiny, and problems should be brought to light. Wohlstetter and Boruch (1981) have prepared an exemplary critique of *Condition of Education,* an annual report mandated by Congress from the National Center for Educational Statistics. The report of the American Statistical Association Committee on Methods of Assessing Survey Practices (Bailar & Lamphier, 1978) is also exemplary. Limitations of data series should be made evident and then pressures exerted to improve them. When agencies propose to change the ways in which they calculate or report statistics, social scientists should exert what pressure they are capable of to forestall the change if it is undesirable, propose statistical conversions to maintain comparability when that is possible, and do studies of the likely impact on data series when all else fails. Social scientists and their organizations should bring and keep pressure on the executive branch and the legislature to provide funding and support for production of high quality government statistics. Social scientists should also attempt to develop standards for reporting statistics and methods for assessing the errors in those that exist.

There are, of course, more obvious actions with more dependable outcomes that social scientists may take with respect to the numbers they themselves produce. I would begin with the suggestion that social science should begin immediately to develop methods for quality assurance with respect to the conduct of data and the production of numbers (see also Feinstein, 1982, regarding biomedical research). I will not detail here the variety of quality assurance mechanisms that may be employed, but I think they are numerous, that various mechanisms serve different purposes, and that a system of quality assurance is needed (Sechrest, 1983). One possibility is that research institutes might establish internal audit committes that would be charged with conducting regular audits of randomly selected projects in order to check on the quality and accuracy of records, the construction and documentation of data files, the accuracy of statistical analyses, and so on. National associations that publish journals might set up procedures that would require randomly selected authors of papers to document the procedures reported, data quality, and so on. One senses that under present circumstances authors are implicitly discouraged from admitting mistakes. That could be changed; perhaps the detection and reporting of errors in procedure, analysis, etc. should be a badge of probity rather than of blame.

Social science needs to protect itself against fraud—most definitely. But it needs also to protect itself against carelessness. I have been astonished at some of the incredibly careless errors I have encountered in the work of well-known investigators in well-known institutions. There is no particular excuse that can be offered for careless errors in science. I am not sure just how the frequency of such errors could be decreased, but at the very least our senior and distinguished investigators and our best institutions could be exhorted to be exemplars of carefulness. If, as was suggested in the case of the Coleman report, some errors likely result from haste in putting together reports (Smith, 1978), then it should also be suggested that time pressure should be a signal for extra careful checking. Some errors, one supposes, are unavoidable. We should, however, attempt to detect errors as soon as possible and do what we can to correct them.

I do not think that the penalties exacted from our disciplines for fraudulent and careless social science are trivial, and I do not think we can afford to be cavalier, even in our attitudes toward the margins of social science. When the tar brush starts swinging, we are all likely to be splattered. It is remarkable almost beyond belief that our sports statistics are kept to incredible degrees of accuracy while we tolerate so much inaccuracy in data of far more than recreational importance. We ought at the very least to follow Morgenstern's (1963) suggestions about developing ways of assessing the quality of our numbers.

We need to give much more thought to the ways in which we measure our variables and to the development of better ways of presenting our data. We seem to know very little about how to communicate scientific information to the public so that it will be understood as we understand it. Stipak (1979) has shown that we social scientists need to be careful to ensure that our indicators have the meaning we intend. Tukey's (1977) methods of Exploratory Data Analysis may be helpful, but I know of no research on their effectiveness in communicating. Wainer (e.g., 1974) has done some research on graphic methods of presenting data that seem promising, and his recent suggestions on graphic display of data are most helpful (Wainer, 1982). I have found the suggestions of Ehrenberg (1977, 1981) concerning "numeracy," by which term he refers to the proper and effective presentation of quantitative data, to be excellent advice. A number of colleagues whom I have provided with copies of Ehrenberg's work have thanked me with some fervor. Kaye (1982) has also written a useful article with suggestions about how data ought to be presented in legal cases involving charges of discrimination.

But I still think we need to pay more attention to the "mundane realism" (to use a term from social psychology) of our indexes and other numbers; that is, our numbers should be interpretable in terms of the everyday world or experiences of the persons who are to be using them. The closer we can get to expressing our numbers in terms of what people can expect to see, hear, or feel happen, the better we will communicate. We may, ourselves, come to understand the numbers better. If instead of saying "the path coefficient for the effects of X and Y is significant at the .05 level," we say, "for every ten units of change in X, we can expect one unit of change in Y," we may have an improved comprehension of what our numbers actually mean. And if instead of thinking about the number of points of decrease in hostile attitude scores achieved in a community, we can translate that into the number of hostile encounters avoided or the increase in voting for a minority political candidate, we will have a better grasp on what we are doing. I am persuaded that we need to do more work relating our abstract measures and numbers to real events.

Some of my colleagues recently have told me that they are trying to get back to basics with respect to statistical analysis; e.g., they are trying to get back to simple, transparent statistics. Admittedly there are risks involved. For example, a series of univariate significance tests, often quite transparent, runs the risk of capitalizing on chance and finding things that are not there. But a more complex multivariate analysis may incur at least a compensating risk of concealing rather too much. It is probably very often the case that we capitalize on error, or reify error, in unrecognized ways. We report and use too many digits, we refine small variability that is really error, we interpolate between values, extrapolate beyond them, and so on. A recent article (Diaconis & Efron, 1983) of distinct interest describes a computer-based system of "bootstrapping" data that is, in effect, an iterative procedure for smoothing large data sets to reduce a variety of likely errors. The bootstrapping procedure has not been applied as yet to mainstream social science data sets, but it may have considerable ultimate value. Although bootstrapping may appear to increase the opacity of statistical analyses, the process itself is conceptually simple and straightforward. It may compensate for any apparent opacity by smoothing the data in such a way as to increase our ability to make intuitive judgments about the reasonableness of the findings.

I am not pleading here for any form of statistical illiteracy. I have no objections to complex statistical analyses carried out by researchers who have a profound understanding of them and who can then communicate the findings effectively so that their audience comes to the same understanding that they have. I simply wonder how many researchers can meet those specifications. I certainly know many researchers who are regularly using highly sophisticated canned programs who have no more than the vaguest idea of what is in the black can into which they dump their numbers. I am confident, therefore, that they have no more than a vague idea of what the numbers really mean when they exit the can. I conclude, therefore, that they are probably not capable of truly effective communication to nonsophisticated audiences. Those problems may be laid at the feet of social science and the general inadequacy of its methodological and quantitative training, coupled with the inculcation of the naively optimistic view that it does not make much difference.

Probably we cannot rely less on computers. Probably it would be foolish to try. But we can become more cautious and less foolishly trusting. We can devise ways of testing our computers and the solutions with which they provide us. We will need to do something to avoid the inevitable day when we will have to say, "the computer told me so, and it lied." The use of computers may require faith, but that faith should have some limits.

I do not think we can solve all our problems, and we will simply have to be honest about the limitations of some of our numbers. That honesty may occasionally have to take the form of humility, and even to the extent of denying that we can really help much in answering some questions. We may now and then have to admit that under the circumstances that prevail we cannot produce very useful numbers. If resources are limited, if conditions are special, if control is difficult, it may be better to forego the opportunity to do a research project than to do it and run the highly probable risk that the data will be misinterpreted or misused.

We social scientists should probably also forego what appears to be the pleasure we take in reporting our numbers to specious levels of accuracy. I have a fear that in reporting so many "significant" digits that are spurious we not only mislead our readers but run the risk of misleading ourselves. Morgenstern (1963) has many excellent examples of specious accuracy, but I offer one of my own. One book on mental health (Mechanic, 1969) states that there were approximately 195,000 social workers in the U.S. in 1974 and approximately 50,000 psychiatric nurses. Those are good round numbers, and the implication is that they are right to within a thousand or so. Then the author cites an *estimate* that there were 8,377 clinical psychologists at the doctoral level in 1973.

Finally, we ought now and again to recognize that what we are doing probably has no implications for public policy, however fascinating it might be for us as social scientists. For example, I have no interest from a public policy standpoint in research on the bad effects of child abuse. Child abuse is an evil and should be dealt with as effectively as possible. I do not care whether child abuses later become bad citizens, become themselves child abusers, or whatever. How could that be relevant? I have very little policy interest in the question whether unemployment is related to mental disorder, poor health, crime, or anything else bad. There are many important reasons for wanting high levels of employment, and there are many reasons for regarding unemployment as bad. Our public policy ought to be directed toward reducing unemployment, period. Our numbers do not and should not always count. But when they may count, we ought to concentrate our efforts on producing good ones.

NOTE

1. This book contains many wonderful examples of statistical and other numerical anomalies.

REFERENCES

Appel, K., & Haken, W. (1977). Every planar map is four colorable. *Illinois Journal of Mathematics, 21.*

Bailar, B. A., Lanphier, C. M. (1978). *Development of survey methods to assess survey practices.* Washington, DC: American Statistical Association.

Barnard, R. C. (1979, February 12). CHAMPUS benefits cheats may collect $12 million. *Army Times.*

Beaton, A. E., Rubin, D. B., & Barone, J. L. (1976). The acceptability of regression solutions: Another look at computational accuracy. *Journal of the American Statistical Association, 71,* 158-168.

Berk, R. (1977). The vagaries and vulgarities of "scientific" jury selection. *Evaluation Quarterly, 1,* 143-158.

Berk, R. (1982). Personal communication.

Berry, J. M. (1981, May 3). May change money data, Fed reveals. *Washington Post.*

Boehm, W. T., Menkhaus, D. J., & Penn., J. B. (1976). Accuracy of least squares computer programs: Another reminder. *American Journal of Agricultural Economics, 58,* 757-760.

Box, S., & Hale, C. (1983). Liberation and female criminality in England and Wales. British Journal of Criminology, 23, 35-49.

Brown, G. W. (1971). Analysis of 104 Eastern Iowa motor vehicle casualty accidents. *Proceedings of Third Triennial Congress on Medical and Related Aspects of Motor Vehicle Accidents. International Association for Accident and Traffic Medicine. 1969.* Ann Arbor, MI: University of Michigan Highway Safety Research Institute.

Bruce-Briggs, B. (1977). "Child care": The fiscal time bomb. *The Public Interest, 49,* 87-102.

Cochran, N. (1978). Grandma Moses and the "corruption" of data. *Evaluation Quarterly,* 2, 363-373.

Cohn, V. (1979, November 18). Glitches from space. *The Washington Post,* p. C8.

Coleman, J. S. et al. (1966). *Equality of educational opportunity.* Washington, DC: U.S. Government Printing Office.

Cook, T. D., Kendzierski, D. A., & Thomas, S. V. (1983). The implicit assumptions of television research: An analysis of the 1982 NIMH report on television and behavior. *Public Opinion Quarterly, 47,* 161-201.

Diaconis, P., & Efron, B. (1983). Computer-intensive methods in statistics. *Scientific American, 248,* 116-130.

Dohrenwend, B., & Dohrenwend, B. (1968). The problem of validity in field studies of psychological disorder. In H. Wechsler et al. (Eds.), *Readings in social psychological approaches to mental illness.* New York: John Wiley.

Dorfman, D. D. (1978). The Cyril Burt question: New findings. *Science, 201,* 1177-1186.

Ehrenberg, A. S. C. (1977). Rudiments of numeracy. *Journal of the Royal Statistical Society, 140*(Part 3), 277-297.

Ehrenberg, A. S. C. (1981). The problem of numeracy. *The American Statistician. 35,* 67-71.

Ehrlich, I. (1975). The deterrent effect of capital punishment: A question of life and death. *American Economic Review, 65,* 397-417.

Erickson, J. D., & Bjerkedal, T. (1982). Fetal and infant mortality in Norway and the United States. *Journal of the American Medical Association, 247,* 987-991.

Feinstein, A. R. (1982). An additional basic science for clinical medicine: I-IV. *Annals of Internal Medicine, 99,*(3-6), 393-397, 544-550, 705-712,843-848.

Feldstein, M. (1974). Social Security, induced retirement, and aggregate capital accumulation. *Journal of Political Economy, 82,* 905-926.

Feldstein, M., & Pellechio, A. (1979). Social security and household wealth accumulation: New microeconomic evidence. *The Review of Economics and Statistics, 61,* 361-368.

Fisher, K. (1982). The spreading stain of fraud. *APA Monitor, 13*(11), 1, 7-8.

Fisher, K. (1982). Debate rages on 1973 Sobell study. *APA Monitor, 13*(11), 8-9.

Frazier, C. E. (1983). Evaluation of youth services programs: Problems and prospects from a case study. *Youth and Society, 14,* 335-362.

Games, P. A. (1983). Computer packages revisited: A comment on Strahan and Hamer. *American Psychologist, 38,* 861-862.

Gerbing, D. W., & Hunter, J. E. (1982). The metric of latent variables in a LISREL IV analysis. *Educational and Psychological Measurement, 42,* 423-427.

Glick, B. (1982). Personal communication.

Goldstein, A. P., Heller, K. S., & Sechrest, L. (1967). *Psychotherapy and the psychology of behavior change.* New York: John Wiley.

Goldstein, M. (1982). Preliminary inspection of multivariate data. *The American Statistician, 36,* 358-362.

Gondek, P. C. (1981). What you see may not be what you think you get: Discriminant analysis in statistical packages. *Educational and Psychological Measurement, 41,* 267-281.

Gottfredson, G. D. (1979). Models and muddles: An ecological examination of high school crime rates. *Journal of Research in Crime and Delinquency, 16,* 307-331.

Hebel, J. R., Kessler, I. I., Mabuchi, K., & McCarter, R. J. (1982). Assessment of hospital performance by use of death rates: A recent case history. *Journal of the American Medical Association, 248,* 3131-3135.

Hoaglin, D. C., & Andrews, D. F. (1975). The reporting of computation-based results in statistics. *The American Statistician, 29,* 122-126.

Holmes, F. F., Baker, L. H., Hearne, E. M., III, & Wilcox, D. E. (1981). More on reliability of death certificates. *New England Journal of Medicine, 304,* 737.

Ihilevich, D. (1983, April 15). Personal communication.

Ihilevich, D., & Gleser, G. C. (1982). *Evaluating mental-health programs: The Progress Evaluation Scales.* Lexington, MA: Lexington Books.

Kahn, D. (1983, April 29). If Hitler diaries are not authentic, what would be the motivation for forgery? *Ann Arbor News,* p. A8.

Kahneman, D., Slovic, P., & Tversky, A. (1982). *Judgment under uncertainty: Heuristics and biases.* Cambridge, England: Cambridge University Press.

Kaye, D. (1982). Statistical evidence of discrimination. *Journal of the American Statistical Association, 77,* 773-792.

Kinsey, A. B., Pomeroy, W. B., Martin, C. E. (1948). *Sexual behavior in the human male.* Philadelphia: W. B. Saunders.

Kraemer, H. C. (1981). Coping strategies in psychiatric research. *Journal of Consulting and Clinical Psychology, 49,* 309-319.

Kraemer, H. C. (1982). Reply to Peterson and Berenbaum. *Journal of Consulting and Clinical Psychology, 50,* 585-587.

Kraft, J. (1981, November 15). Computer fundamentalism. *Washington Post.*

Kviz, F. J., & Flaskerud, J. H. (1980). *An evaluation of the index of medical underservice: Results from a consumer survey.* Executive summary of the Final Report for Grant R01 HS 02778, National Center for Health Services Research, Department of Health and Human Services. Washington, DC: Government Printing Office.

Lesnoy, S. D., & Leimer, D. R. (1981). *Social Security and private saving: New time series evidence with alternative specifications.* Working paper No. 22, U.S. Department of Health and Human Services, Social Security Administration, Office of Research and Statistics, Washington, DC.

Lichtenstein, S., Slovic, P., Fischoff, B., Layman, M., & Combs, B. (1978). Judged frequency of lethal events. *Journal of Experimental Psychology: Human Learning and Memory, 4,* 551-578.

Longley, J. W. (1967). An appraisal of least squares programs for the electronic computer from the point of view of the user. *American Statistical Association Journal, 62,* 819-829.

Magidson, J. (1977). Toward a causal model approach for adjusting for preexisting differences in the nonequivalent control group situation. *Evaluation Quarterly, 1,* 399-420.

Main, T. J. (1983). The homeless of New York. *The Public Interest, 72,* 3-28.

Matarazzo, J. (1982). Behavioral health's challenge to academic, scientific and professional psychology. *American Psychologist, 37,* 1-14.

Mechanic, D. (1969). *Mental health and social policy.* Englewood Cliffs, NJ: Prentice-Hall.

Mechanic, D. (1980). *Mental health and social policy* (2nd ed.). Englewood Cliffs, NJ: Prentice-Hall.

Milavsky, J. R., Kessler, R. C., Stipp, H. H., & Rubens, W. S. (1982). *Television and aggression: A panel study.* New York: Academic Press.

Miller, N. (1979). *A study of the number of persons with records of arrest or conviction in the labor force.* Springfield, VA: National Technical Information Service.

Morgenstern, O. (1963). *On the accuracy of economic observations.* Princeton, NJ: Princeton University Press.

Muller, K. E. (1982). Understanding canonical correlation through the general linear model and principal components. *The American Statistician, 36,* 342-354.

Nagin, D. (1978). General deterrence: A review of the empirical evidence. In A. Blumstein, J. Cohen, & D. Nagin (Eds.), *Deterrence and incapacitation: Estimating the effects of criminal sanctions on crime rates.* Washington, DC: National Academy of Sciences.

National Commission for Employment Policy (1980). *Sixth Annual Report to the President and the Congress.* Washington, DC: Government Printing Office.

New Times (1977, June 24). The ripoff society, p. 21.

Newsweek (1983, May 16). Burying crime in Chicago, p. 63.

Overall, J. E. (1964). Note on the scientific status of factors. *Psychological Bulletin, 64,* 270-276.

Panel on Statistics for Family Assistance and Related Programs, Committee on National Statistics (1983). *Family assistance and poverty: an assessment of statistical needs.* Washington, DC: National Academy of Sciences.

Peterson, I. (1983a). Pathways to chaos. *Science News, 124,* 76-77.

Peterson, I. (1983b). Superweapon software woes. *Science News, 123,* 312-313.

Peterson, W. (1982). Social roots of hunger and overpopulation. *Public Interest, 68,* 37-52.

Preusser, D. F., Blomberg, R. D., Williams, A. F., & Zador, P. L. (1983). The effects of curfew laws on motor vehicle crashes. *Third symposium on traffic safety effectiveness (impact) evaluation projects.* Chicago: National Safety Council.

Riccio, L., Sechrest, L., Glick, B., & Mabe, P. A. (1983). *Police arrest productivity: The San Jose Study.* Unpublished report, Washington, DC: The Police Foundation.

Roark, A. C. (1979, February 20). Solution to a 124-year-old problem creates a controversy among scholars. *Chronicle of Higher Education.*

Sechrest, L. (1983). *Quality assurance mechanisms and their applicability in the production of scientific data.* Unpublished manuscript, University of Michigan.

Sechrest, L., & Kelly, P. (1983). *Opaque statistics and inscrutable computers: Some Warnings.* Unpublished manuscript, University of Michigan.

Sechrest, L., & Yeaton, W. H. (1981). Empirical bases for estimating effect size. In R. F. Boruch, P. M. Wortman, & D. S. Cordray (Eds.), *Reanalyzing program evaluations.* San Francisco: Jossey-Bass.

Sechrest, L., & Yeaton, W. H. (1982). Magnitudes of experimental effects in social science research. *Evaluation Review, 6,* 579-600.

Sherman, L., & Berk, R. (in press). The special deterrent effect of arrest for domestic violence. *American Sociological Review.*

Sherman, L. W., & Langworthy, R. (1979). Measuring homicide by police officers. *Journal of Criminal Law and Criminology 70,* 546-560.

Skolnick, J. H. (1966). *Justice without trial: Law enforcement in democratic society.* New York: John Wiley.

Smith, M. S. (1978). Equality of educational opportunity: The basic findings reconsidered. In H. Aaron (Ed.), *Politics and the professors.* Washington, DC: Brookings Institute.

Stamp, (1929). *Some economic factors in modern life.* London: P. S. King & Son, Ltd.

Stipak, B. (1979, January/February). Citizen satisfaction with urban services: Potential misuse as a performance indicator. *Public Administration Review,* pp. 46-52.

Strahan, R. F. (1982). On computer program packages: Not all things to all people. *American Psychologist, 37,* 339.

Tukey, J. W. (1977). *Exploratory data analysis.* Reading, MA: Addision-Wesley.

Turnbull, R. (1983, September 15). Agricultural exports to China drop. *Four County Farm and Ranch,* p. 1F.

Tymoczko, T. (1979). The four-color problem and its philosophical significance. *Journal of Philosophy, 76,* 57-83.

Wagenaar, A. C. (1982). Traffic safety effects of legal restrictions on access to alcoholic beverages: A multi-level time series evaluation. *Second Symposium on Traffic Safety Effectiveness (impact) Evaluation Projects.* Washington, DC: National Highway Traffic Safety.

Wainer, H. (1974). the suspended rootogram and other visual displays: An empirical validation. *The American Statistician, 28,*(4), 143-145.

Wainer, H. (1976). Estimating coefficients in linear models: It don't make no nevermind. *Psychological Bulletin, 83,* 213-217.

Wainer, H. (1978). On the sensitivity of regression and regressors. *Psychological Bulletin, 85,* 267-273.

Wainer, H. (1982). *How to display data badly* (Technical Report #82-33). Princeton, NJ: Educational Testing Service.

Wallis, W. A. (1949). The statistics of the Kinsey report. *Journal of the American Statistical Association, 44,* 463-484.

Wallis, W. A., & Roberts, H. V. (1956). *Statistics: A new approach.* Glencoe, IL: The Free Press.

Washington Post (1979, November 18). Glitches from space, p. C8.

Washington Post (1981, August, 7). A "rosy view" of safety, P. A15.

Washington Post National Weekly Edition (1984, January 2). PP. 18-19.

Weinstein, M. C., & Stason, W. B. (1982). Cost-Effectiveness of coronary artery bypass surgery. *Circulation, 66,* 56.

Williams, W. (1983, June 28). Charting industry's capacity. Fed's figures on utilization questioned. *New York Times,* p. D1.

Wohlstetter, P., & Boruch, R. F. (1981). Numbers, prose, and pictures: A review of the "Condition of Education." *Proceedings of the National Academy of Education, 1980.* Washington, DC: National Academy of Education.

Ziegler, J. F., & Lanford, W. A. (1979, November 18). Cited in V. Conn, Glitches from space, *Washington Post,* p. C8.

3

Implementation Realities and Evaluation Design

MILBREY WALLIN McLAUGHLIN

In most planning, policy, and evaluation agencies, the received view of evaluation is the rational, hypotheticodeductive or "impact" model (Rossi & Freeman, 1982; Boruch & Cordray, 1980.) This approach to evaluation has several defining characteristics. It assumes clear, operationally specified goals, stable program parameters, and specific criteria for success. It rests on a correlational model in which "inputs" generally are considered in the static terms of the experimental paradigm and "outputs" typically are presented as estimates of treatment effect. Both inputs and outputs are framed in unidimensional, constant terms that reference program features but seldom incorporate contextual or process factors. This evaluation paradigm assumes a simple environment with single component goal structures, a hierarchical authority structure, few complex interactions, and a rational reward structure. Concomitant assumptions describe a 1:1 relationship between what can be learned about social settings and what can be affected in them. Natural science provides the intellectual reference for this dominant evaluation paradigm; its rules of evidence, accordingly, are rooted in canons of the classic scientific method.

The hypotheticodeductive model for evaluating programs and policies has strong conceptual appeal. It has refined methods, clear rules of evidence, and agreed-upon strategies of proof. Criteria of an evalua-

AUTHOR'S NOTE: Thanks go to Melvin M. Mark and R. Lance Shotland of Pennsylvania State University for organizing this volume and playing an unusually active editorial role in bringing it to completion. Their comments and those of my Stanford colleague, Henry M. Levin, substantially improved this chapter; I am grateful for their review.

tion's acceptability are grounded in methodological codes that are well-developed and known to the field. Armed with this expertise, an evaluator can be confident of doing a "good job."

However, experience with social programs gained over the past decade or so suggests that reality is much more complex than this dominant evaluation model acknowledges and that our trust in the efficacy of these methods is exaggerated. Efforts to understand and evaluate the spate of special programs generated by the Great Society's social policies and their legislative descendants have shown that traditional correlational or experimental models too often misrepresent the nature of treatment, the notion of program effects, and the relationship between inputs and outputs. Experience gained largely in the 1970s underscores the importance of program implementation and the context in which project efforts are carried out. Yet these issues are seldom treated beyond *ceteris paribus* assumptions or randomization strategies in traditional evaluation models. But the implementation realities that characterize social programs mean that these process and contextual issues are more than academic curiosities or "externalities." They are central to the conduct and effects of special project efforts. To ignore them results in evaluations of limited use to practitioners and assessments that risk misspecification of both treatment and effect.

This chapter draws on experience with program implementation to consider questions of program evaluation. The first section reviews major lessons for evaluation from the past decade's experience with program implementation. The second section discusses implications for evaluation and guidelines for rethinking approaches to social program evaluation. Section three presents a summary and conclusions.

IMPLEMENTATION REALITIES

Implementation is the process whereby programs or policies are carried out; it denotes the translation of plans into practice. Less than a decade ago, there was little research or theory about implementation. Indeed, implementation was not even considered an issue requiring an evaluator's attention. Instead, analysts embraced the "black box" metaphor. The black box represented a reality that accepted program inputs and produced program outputs but whose supposedly idiosyncratic content defied systematic attention from analysts. Further it was also assumed that the black box process whereby inputs were transformed into outputs was not of great significance because of the strong and direct relationship posited between treatment and effects.

However, the avalanche of federal social policy activities associated with Great Society programs and their concomitant evaluation mandates forced analysts to look inside the black box. They sought to explain the frequent and disappointing findings of "no significant difference" associated with these special program efforts. This look at the actuality of how programs were defined and carried out raised fundamental questions about learning from social programs and assessing their effects. Five lessons from experience with social program implementation appear especially central to thinking about evaluation research:

(1) treatment effects are indirect;
(2) implementation choices dominate program outcomes;
(3) implementation is a multistage, developmental process;
(4) implementors pursue multiple and often competing goals; and
(5) decisions made closest to the delivery level are most influential.

Treatment Effects Are Indirect

Correlational or impact designs assume a direct relationship between treatment or program inputs and program effects. However, this relationship seldom exists in reality. "Treatment effects," be they improved student achievement scores, enhanced teacher capacity, or lowered dropout rates, are the result of complex and multiple interactions between program inputs, e.g., technology, training, materials, money, technical assistance, and factors in the program's institutional setting. Social programs are carried out *within* and *through* their institutional setting.

At the local level, factors such as staff background and training, administrator commitment, competing or conflicting system demands, or constituent support are primary determinants of how and how well a program is carried out (Berman & McLaughlin, 1978; Fullan, 1982). Given the central influence of these local institutional factors, the common finding that similar programs have different effects in different settings—or even in the same setting over time—is not at all surprising. Education technologies are, in this sense, "soft"; specific outcomes are people-dependent and context-bound. Direct (or main) effects are institutional or contextual. Programs or policies influence local practices only indirectly and at the margins. Thus as Gilbert, Light, and Mosteller (1975) remark, education treatments (or other social program interventions) cannot provide the "slam-bang" effect many planners, policymakers, and evaluators hoped for.

This implementation reality also means that what is delivered—the "treatment"—varies by setting. This fact generates what can be called the "label fallacy." Programs ostensibly operating under the same level, e.g., the Bank Street model of early education; the Southwest Regional Laboratory reading program, cannot be assumed to be the same program in practice. The factors associated with each institutional setting can result in treatments that are substantively and significantly different even though they may operate under the same manner. Treatment as provided may depart in crucial ways from treatment as planned or designed. Indeed, treatment as experienced by the recipient may have little or nothing to do with project plans.

Implementation Choices Dominate Outcomes

What a program is, research tells us consistently, matters less to program outcomes than how it is carried out (Bardach, 1977; Berman & McLaughlin, 1978; Fullan, 1982; Nakamura & Smallwood, 1980; Sabatier & Mazmanian, 1979). Local choices about how to put a project into practice determine the extent to which a new program, technology, or curriculum fulfills its promise, whether the benefits reach the intended target group, or in fact whether a new policy is implemented at all. Project success is as much an issue of procedure as of substance.

Features of the local institutional environment clearly influence implementation choices; available technical expertise, for example, will affect training choices; staff experience and sophistication can influence project choices; labor disputes can attenuate planning time for a new project. But there are also implementation decisions to be taken that represent discretionary choices for local staff. Examples of such choices are the type and amount of staff participation in planning, the role of building principals in teacher training activities, the distribution of project resources across schools, the frequency of staff meetings to discuss project activities (rather than school or district administrative matters), strategies for evaluating project activities, and strategies for mobilizing support.

Differences in these local implementation decisions can mean that similar (or indeed identical) project designs will be carried out very differently and with substantially different results in various settings. Although a good idea or a promising technology is important to the quality of a planned change effort, local choices about how to put the idea or technology into practice ultimately play a major role in determining how an effort fares in a particular institutional setting. In practice, the relationship between "treatment" and strategy is elastic because any given treatment can be supported by a number of different strategic arrangements.

Implementation Is a Multistage Developmental Process

In general, implementation is a multistage developmental process. Except when policies or program objectives contain all of the information necessary to carry them out, e.g., distributional formulas, or when adoption of a new technology or procedure constitutes implementation, e.g., installation of a more sophisticated electronic communication system within a building, implementation is a complex, multistage process of institutional and individual learning. Policies that direct the allocation of funds among targeted interests are essentially different from policies that direct state or local officials to provide more effective services for particular categories of students. The former tells officials all that they need to know to "succeed"; the latter suggests broad objectives but do not specify the necessary knowledge or processes.

In one sense the process of implementation is heuristic; it is a process of learning and adjusting rather than a process of installation. Further, two and sometimes three substantively disparate kinds of learning are necessary to carry out many program and policy objectives. Policies often require not only new practices or means for service provision but also new organizational processes of targeting, allocating, evaluating, and accounting. One kind of learning necessary to program implementation, then, is learning to comply; that is, learning to administer the program efficiently and within its regulatory framework.

A second kind of learning assumed by those programs or policies that seek change in institutional routines is learning to provide the practices consistent with program goals; for example, classroom activities that are effective for educationally disadvantaged youngsters. This kind of learning involves the development of new activities, the acquisition of new skills, and integration of new practices and expertise into ongoing routines.

When programs or policies represent a normative position, for example, bilingual education or school desegregation, effective implementation can require yet a third kind of learning: The acquisition of new norms and beliefs about appropriate activities and system priorities. For example, federal policies addressing bilingual education, education of handicapped children, and racial balance in the public schools all intend a reordering of state and local priorities for allocating resources and educational service provisions. This kind of learning involves more than marginal adjustment in system routines; it comprises a fundamental change in the normative assumptions that structure system action.

These quite different kinds of learning usually do not and cannot occur simultaneously. In most cases, institutions need to learn the rules of the game before substantial and confident attention can be devoted to learning how to make practice more effective. For example, disappointing program outcomes were common during the early years of programs sponsored by Title I of the 1965 Elementary and Secondary Education Act, the federal government's massive compensatory education program (McLaughlin, 1975). However, evaluations were mistaken to conclude on the basis of these outcomes that Title I "did not work." Practitioners were engaged in determining accounting, delivery, and oversight strategies that were consistent with the program's regulatory framework. It was not until broad compliance issues generally were resolved that effective program activities began to be developed (Kirst & Jung, 1980). Developmental activities of this nature generally require implementor confidence that administrative or regulatory issues have been resolved. Doing it right usually takes precedence over doing it better. The third kind of learning—change in the value structure directing organizational choices—is necessary to the sustained presence of an initiative based on a normative position different from that of the implementing system. Yet for programs of this type, it is a process that takes a long time in most settings and indeed may never transpire.[2]

Substantively different activities accompany these different types of learning. For example, compliance is associated with allocation of funds to activities and stewardship in accounting for expenditures to constituents and others. Learning how to provide effective practice requires program development that translates regulatory requirements into program activities. All three kinds of institutional learning are enhanced by the mobilization of effective political and professional incentives and by the establishment of norms of good practice to guide program activities.

The further one moves through these stages and activities, the more complex is the learning required and the less susceptible is performance to command and control types of decisions and assessment practices. The problems and issues that dominate the process also change as the process evolves. The question central to a newly adopted program or policy are quite different from those associated with a mature, well-established practice. In the early stages of implementation, for example, problems are likely to be technical, procedural, and political. What are the technical requirements of the project and how can they be met? How can support for the project be generated? How can resistance be overcome? How can new practices be integrated with ongoing routines? Subsequent problems tend to be defined primarily as developmental issues: How can practices be refined? Modified?

The process of implementation, in short, is complex and multistaged. At each stage, it involves somewhat different activities and problems of learning, and different actors dominate. Further, at each stage, the "treatment" may be modified as emphases shift, corrections are made, goals and strategies are clarified, or unanticipated demands change the priorities that guide practice.

Implementors Pursue Multiple and Often Competing Goals

Although most evaluations describe a one-dimensional focus on delivery goals—increased student achievement scores, integration of handicapped youngsters into mainstream classrooms, decreased drop-out rates and vandalism, for example—implementors throughout the system in fact pursue multiple goals. In addition to the delivery (or the formal) program goals, implementors also must attend to political and bureaucratic interests. Implementation certainly will be shaped by the extent to which program (or delivery) goals are compatible with or eclipsed by bureaucratic and political objectives.

For example, I visited one midwestern elementary school in which a principal was about to terminate an apparently successful follow-through program. In his view, the high level of parent involvement achieved by the program made it extraordinarily difficult for him to run his school. His bureaucratic interests, in other words, conflicted with and superseded the delivery objectives of the follow-through effort. Similarly, studies of local allocation decisions under the deregulated Model Cities program show that municipal administrators were unable to continue targeting funds to disadvantaged neighborhoods under the new federal policies. Political pressures from more powerful (and advantaged) constituencies meant that funds were expended instead for more general municipal purposes such as parks and recreation facilities or on maintenance in middle-income areas (U.S. Advisory Commission on Intergovernmental Relations, 1981).

The question of relevant goals is complicated by additional factors: Policies have multiple dimensions and categories. A single policy, for example, can have a number of simultaneous purposes. For example, a single policy can seek to redistribute resources, to remedy a specific concern, and provide support for general maintenance. Title I of the 1965 Elementary and Secondary Education Act (now Chapter 1 of the 1981 Education Consolidation and Improvement Act), which provides federal support to state and local agencies for programs targeted at educationally disadvantaged youngsters, is an example. The act supports state level activities such as technical assistance and evaluation, distributes funds according to a formula based on a measure of economic disadvantage, and assumes the development of special programs for educationally disadvantaged youngsters. State and local response to this legislation has been shaped by the priorities assigned particular goals by state and local staff (McDonnell & McLaughlin, 1982).

To complicate matters further, policies also use multiple strategies, or policy implements. Bardach (1980), for example, outlines three categories of public policy implements: Enforcement, inducement, and benefaction. Enforcement involves standard-setting, oversight, and the invocation of sanctions. Inducement uses various means to motivate people to behave in ways consistent with policy objectives such as rewards for performance, competitive awards, tax incentives, and matching grants. Benefaction employs technologies such as transfer payments, technical assistance, and entitlement grants. Most policies typically employ a strategic mix of the three that can shift dramatically depending on particular implementors and actual program focus (Elmore & McLaughlin, 1982).

This multiplicity of goals and policy dimensions molds implementation. Participants in the policy system select and emphasize certain dimensions of a program or policy (Steinberger, 1981). This selection, which occurs as programs are defined, implemented, evaluated, and institutionalized, reflects the constellation of system goals shaping activities at a given point in time (i.e., bureaucratic, political, and delivery concerns) as well as perceptions about the central goals, importance, relevance, utility, and feasibility of the policy to be implemented.

Seen in this way, the illusion of a holistic notion of program or policy goals is apparent. The goals and concerns that drive policy and program decisions will reflect an individual actor's perceptions of the policy and priorities operating in the institutional context. And because multiple actors are involved at different levels of the policy system, a program or policy can be transformed in multiple or inconsistent ways as it moves through the policy system and even at the same level of the system over time. The interaction between implementing system priorities and perceptions about policy objectives means that in reality there are as many "goals" driving implementation as there are implementation points in the policy process.[3]

Decisions Made Closest to the Delivery Level Are Most Influential

In a complex policy system, a policy must pass through many organizational levels and multiple decision points. At each, someone makes a decision (by commission or omission) about policy goals and how they are to be addressed. In this way policy is further developed by the implementation process. Predetermined policy is not simply put into practice. Instead, policy is clarified, specified, and modified as it moves through the policy system. The final decision point, and the one that typically has the most impact on the way programs or policies are carried out, is at the "bottom" of the delivery system; it rests with the "street-level bureaucrat" who interprets policies and programs adopted by the larger system and translates them into services.[4]

For example, in education it is axiomatic that in schools it is the classroom teachers who have the most effect on how students are treated and the services they receive. But the evidence on policy implementation takes this truism one step further. Weatherley, for example, demonstrates in his analysis of Massachusetts special education reform that one effect of imposing a new policy on an already crowded system is to force teachers, principals, and diagnostic personnel to simplify, adapt, adjust, and, in some cases, distort policy just to get their jobs done. Weatherley's (1979) conclusions are consistent with studies of PL 94-142, the Education of All Handicapped Children Act (Hargrove et al., 1981), and with research that portrays the strategic autonomy of teachers in the privacy of their classrooms (Lortie, 1975; Jackson, 1968; Goodlad, Klein, & Associates, 1974). There is, in short, no necessary or 1:1 relationship between what administrators say, or regulations mandate, and what teachers do. The success or failure of a policy or program ultimately depends on what teachers or street-level bureaucrats think and do. Planners and policymakers at higher levels of the system must rely on individuals at the bottom to understand their intent, to endorse it, and to be willing and able to carry it out.

Summary

Implementation realities, in summary, comprise a complex, multistage process in which the phenomenon typically of interest to an evaluator—the relationship between program inputs and system outputs—is indirect and achieved against a noisy and constantly changing institutional setting. Further, the target for an evaluation—a program or policy—is in flux as well. It is created and recreated at various levels of the policy system in ways that are consistent with the interests, goals, skills, and perceptions of various actors. The unitary and apparently fixed "policy" or "program" as defined by an evaluation instrument or report has questionable basis in reality.

IMPLICATIONS FOR EVALUATION

These features of the implementation process raise fundamental questions about the conduct and use of evaluation. Implementation realities have important implications for evaluation both as a mode of inquiry and as a strategy to promote organizational learning, program improvement, or even accountability. Experience with the process of change and social program implementation suggests fundamental rethinking of evaluation design and conduct in five major areas:

(1) evaluation objectives,
(2) unit of analysis,
(3) outcome measures,
(4) differentiation of evaluation strategies, and
(5) concepts of use.

Evaluation Objectives

Contrary to the canons of traditional evaluation design, the effects of social programs cannot be "proven" with certainty or truth in the way that a principle of physics or a geometric theorem can be proven. Proof in this sense requires satisfying a number of conditions, among them that all sources of variance be controlled and that specific program or policy effects can be estimated against the clamor and complexity of the institutional setting.

But satisfying these and other conditions necessary for "proof" is no easy task. For example, the effect of a new reading program on student achievement will represent the combined effect of factors such as student characteristics, teacher expertise, teacher commitment to the curriculum, other responsibilities demanding teacher attention, the emphasis placed on successful implementation by district administrators, and previous reading programs in the students' experience. The list of factors that influence so-called treatment effects is extensive indeed:

> Once we attend to interactions, we enter a hall of mirrors that extends to infinity. However far we carry out analysis—to third order or fifth order or any order—untested interactions of a still higher order can be envisioned. (Cronbach, 1975, p. 119)

In theory, random assignment can control for such situational interactions, thereby isolating treatment effects. However, given the potential significance of third- and fourth-order interactions for program outcomes, vast amounts of data are required to identify and specify higher-order interactions. Consequently, control through randomized assignment would be practically (if not absolutely) impossible. The sample size required by such a strategy would far exceed the budgets or the sites available to evaluators (Cronbach, 1975, p. 124). Nonetheless, higher order interactions cannot be simply dismissed as "noise" or as "externalities." Nature, Cronbach reminds us, does not distinguish between main effects and interactions or between orders of interactions (Cronbach, 1982, pp. 152-153) in terms of the consequences for program effectiveness. However, main effects and higher-order interactions may have considerably different implications for policy, and the possibility of higher-order interactions should therefore not be overlooked.

The importance of site-specific interactions also means that evaluators labor under the burden of "cultural relativism." The factors affecting program outcomes will behave differently and will combine differently in various settings. Thus beyond broad categories of influences (such as the importance of concrete in-service education for new program implementation), the causal and conditional statements associated with an evaluation in one setting are likely to have questionable relevance to program operations in another setting.

The *ceteris paribus* conditions assumed by traditional evaluation design, in short, do not exist. In the fluid, complex, and often random complex reality of the social program setting, scientific proof is not possible. And even if it were possible to "prove" program effects and confidently assign causality, the relevance of this accomplishment would be short-lived from both a scientific and a practical perspective. Social systems are not "self-sealing."[5] They are dynamic—open to their environment, random internal fluctuation, unanticipated pressures, and exogeneous pressures beyond their control. The "effects" demonstrated by last year's evaluation, as well as their "causes," then, may well be ephemeral.

The now classic tale of the *It Works* series illustrates dramatically the erosion of conclusions and generalizations (Hawkridge, Compeau & Roberts, 1969). In the late 1960s, Congress was anxious to hear good news about local programs supported by the massive federal compensatory education effort, Title I of the 1965 Elementary and Secondary Education Act. The American Institutes for Research was awarded a contract to identify and describe a series of exemplary federally funded compensatory education programs. The results were published under the upbeat title, *It Works*. But when evalautors returned to these sites a year or two later they found that these successful projects were no longer "working" (McLaughlin, 1975). Evaluators discovered that the essential contextual components of success, and so the outcomes themselves, had shifted with time. Because main effects are associated with the contextual and institutional factors that determine how a program is carried out, generalizations and findings based in this fluid reality break down over time. As Cronbach put it: "We tend to speak of a scientific conclusion as if it were eternal, but in every field emprical relations change. . .[and] generalizations decay" (Cronbach, 1975, p. 122).

The reality of social program implementation means that evaluations limited to goals traditionally associated with the hypotheticodeductive model, that is, estimates of effect and specification of causality, face substantial obstacles. Social program evaluation cannot control all of the things that "matter" to outcomes; evaluation cannot lead to final statements about causal relationships between program inputs and outputs; evaluation cannot result in detailed prescriptions relevant to other social settings; and social program evaluation rarely can furnish scientific proof.

But this does not mean that evaluation cannot serve its assigned function in the policy system: Support for learning and control. Rather than search for proof about program effects and fine-tuned outcome estimates, a more realistic and useful goal for evaluation would incorporate assessments about the value of a practice relative to other practices in the system and to practices that it replaced. For example, on dimensions such as efficiency, ease of implementation, support for program objectives, to what extent and how is the practice under examination better than former or present practices? Moving away from standards of proof and toward notions of "better than," evaluation can reduce the uncertainty about such relationships and inform practitioners about the conditional nature of social program choices.

Such an approach would reflect more accurately the problems of *learning* about social programs as well as the problems of *effecting* social settings. The changeable nature of social settings means that it is not possible to solve problems—they can be moved, transformed, and hopefully improved, but not forevermore "fixed" (Majone, 1981). Evaluations designed to examine a program's stature vis-á-vis its environment, rather than to generate scientific estimates of effect, can provide valuable procedural advice. (Of course, these two functions may not be mutually exclusive.) Because they stress the relative outcomes of various program choices and outcomes, evaluations of this type support understanding of the conditions under which alternative program or policy choices seem more or less desirable.

These suggestions for reassessing evaluation objectives leave unaddressed the question of "acceptability." If criteria associated with methods of scientific proof largely are inappropriate to evaluation research, what other criteria of acceptability can be applied? Several philosophers of science and social analysts have suggested that the criteria of "goodness" associated with research in the natural sciences be replaced with something no more exotic than common sense. In this view (which is expressed by a number of analysts and philosophers, in particular, Lindblom & Cohen, 1979; Majone, 1981; Kaplan, 1964; Ziman, 1978), criteria of acceptability in evaluation would be derived from craft knowledge and experience. Do the results of evaluation square with common knowledge about policy and practice? Do they incorporate the complexity of relevant decision-making settings? Do evaluations frame recommendations in terms of the actions and choices actually available to practitioners? In considering this view, it is important to recognize that although "acceptability" is grounded in craft knowledge and experience, it is capable of modifying such common sense by force of persuasion.

Majone extends this homely notion of acceptability to methods and data as colleagues make judgments about the quality of one another's work. Generally accepted criteria of adequacy in the domain of policy studies and social program evaluations should reflect the actuality in which programs as well as evaluations must be carried out.

> Such criteria are derived not from abstract logical canons but from craft experience, depending as they do on the special features of the problem, on the quality of data and limitations of available tools, on the time constraints imposed on the analyst, and on the requirements of the client. (Majone, 1981, p. 17)

Unit of Analysis

Almost all evaluations adopt what can be called a "project model" of research in which the project is taken as the unit of analysis without reference to its institutional setting. Most of the history of evaluation is written in such project-specific terms. Yet as we have seen, "treatment" and outcome are the result of complex interactions between project factors and the implementing system. This implementation reality raises questions about the appropriate unit of analysis for an evaluation. Clearly an evaluation that looks at a project in isolation from its institutional setting misspecifies the nature of the process: So-called treatment effects consequently will be misestimated to an unknown degree. This "project model" approach also risks wrong conclusions or advice because of the false dichotomy implicit in its partitioning of reality into problem/nonproblem and treatment/nontreatment. The complex interactions that define treatment make a treatment/nontreatment distinction spurious at best. Similarly, the multiple goals that shape actions and choices within an implementation make project-specific notions of "the problem" meaningless. Advice resulting from a evaluation that draws effectively arbitrary boundaries in terms of the "project" or treatment, then, is bound to be limited and misleading.

Instead of the isolated project, the appropriate unit of analysis for evaluation is what has been variously termed the "implementing system" (McLaughlin 1980), the "policy environment" (Nakamura & Smallwood, 1980) or the "policy space" (Majone, 1981). The reality of program implementation not only requires evaluators to cast a wide net around the project in order to capture important main- and lower-order influences; it also "requires evaluators to attend to the related sequence of decisions and actions together with their behavioral, cognitive, and ideological supports" rather than discrete decisions and actions" (Majone, 1981, p. 20).

This broader view also captures unanticipated consequences or spin-off effects associated with program implementation. These associated effects are often of more than academic interest. They can have major import for an evaluation's conclusions. For example, imagine an instance in which evaluators judged the development and implementation of an arts magnet school highly successful on multiple measures—the quality of the curriculum in place, student achievement in the area of art history and art criticism, as well as the making of art, parent support for the program, and teacher satisfaction. Yet a look at the project within the broader system context may show that the resources, energy, and attention devoted to the art magnet drained and demoralized art education in the regular district program. From this perspective, then, the arts magnet would represent a net loss in the quality of the district's art program.

Outcome Measures

The so-called "goal model" dominates evaluation theory and practice. Majone (1981) calls this strategy "evaluation by results"; Deutscher (1977) warns of the "goal trap." Implementation realities define a number of problems with this time-honored evaluation approach. First, implementors and implementing systems pursue multiple goals, and program or policy goals may be interpreted differently by different actors in various parts of the system. Most evaluations, however, address only a single goal: The ostensible delivery goal of the program being assessed. There are risks in failing to attend to other goals that influence program-related decisions and other system goals or interests (e.g., political and bureaucratic concerns): The relationship between program activities and program effects can be misunderstood, and the evaluation can provide information of only limited utility to policymakers and practitioners. A policy could be effective in terms of a single goal (e.g., delivery), but fail in terms of other system objectives. In a social policy setting, effectiveness is a complex, heterogeneous concept that must incorporate the variegated character of the implementing system as well as differences in perceptions about policy relevance and objectives. Acknowledging the existence and import of multiple goals, important questions arise:

- How does an evaluator determine and decide which "impact" to assess?
- How can multiple and competing policy definitions and emphases be identified and reconciled?
- Given the multiplicity of perceptions about the intent of a program or policy and the dominant system priorities, whose perception "carries the day?" Whose is most important to program or policy outcomes?
- How can shifts and modifications over time and across the implementing system be recognized and estimated? (Maynard-Moody, 1983)

Second, a goal-focused evaluation often pays only minimal attention to the procedures and the implementation choices that shape program outcomes. Goal-focused evaluations typically ask questions of "how much" without examining organizational questions of how and why. Consequently, it shifts attention away from the factors that matter to an important user group: Individuals charged with improving practice. Not only do implementation decisions fix program outcomes, they often are among the most powerful policy variables an evaluator might consider. Ironically, "treatment" may be among the least manipulable of factors now that fiscal retrenchment severely constrains administrator ability to initiate new programs or introduce new materials. For the foreseeable future, administrators are unlikely to be debating whether or not to adopt a new curriculum (that choice may be prohibited by budgetary stringency), but will be instead deliberating about how to get better performance out of existing investments in people, materials, and technologies. This, at its root, is an implementation question.

Third, a goal-focused evaluation typically assumes a well-developed theory of relationship between ends and means—project inputs and program outcomes—as well as agreement on goals among planners, policymakers, evaluators, and implementors. However, such well-developed theories about means and ends generally do not exist. But more importantly, experience with social program implementation shows that policies and programs are transformed in the process of implementation and that agreement on goals cannot be assumed to exist at all or to endure over time. Thus the specificity of most goal-focused evaluations effectively *constructs* a reality that does not necessarily exist in practice. It risks imposing casual models on projects or programs that have only scant resemblance to the "models" upon which staff base program activities.

Differentiated Evaluation Strategies

The realities of program implementation make it clear that a unidimensional evaluation design can neither accurately portray all evaluation situations nor adequately respond to the needs of different evaluation consumers. For example, the methodologies and questions appropriate to the later or mature stages of a program effort are likely to misrepresent activities and accomplishments during the early stages. The presence of disagreement about preferred program practices when a program has been in operation for some time can signal distress. However, this same observation in early stages of implementation can mean something quite different: The beginning of the "unfreezing" of ongoing practices necessary to the learning of new routines. (A California observer of planned change efforts in education dubbed this necessary stage the "thermal period.")

Similarly, the "outcomes" of each stage differ. Assessment of project effects on student achievement is inappropriate to a project still struggling to get off the ground. However, assessment of factors such as the political support available for the project, teacher commitment to carrying out project plans, and administrator support for the project is relevant to this stage of program operation. Actors and organizational locations most important to project activities and outcomes also change through the process of development and implementation; central staff typically are most central in the early stages whereas individuals with direct implementation responsibility have the most influence during later stages.

An examination of art education practices sponsored by the Getty Trust used an analytical scheme that differentiates actors and outcomes by stage of the change process (McLaughlin & Thomas, 1984). At the initiation or adoption stage, relevant outcomes were defined as successful marshaling of the multiple resources necessary to carry out the program and the generation of support for the program throughout the district. For the implementation stage of the change process, outcomes were conceptualized as teacher confidence in carrying out the new practices and demonstrated ability to do so, a high quality of practice across participating schools and classrooms, and activities that are consistent with program goals. Institutionalization is the final stage of the planned change process. At this point, special project status must be replaced by routinized support and activity. Outcomes of interest here include teacher commitment, central office support for the project, provision for the program's continuing developmental needs, and the incorporation of program activities into ongoing district routines. The multiple goals and interests relevant to programs or policies also call for a differentiated evaluation strategy. It is difficult to envision an evaluation that could address all salient goals with the same rigor and scope. Although any evaluation must attend to the several objectives relevant to decision makers, a number of different outcomes could shape the major focus of an evaluation effort including program delivery goals, political support, efficiency, user satisfaction, and the like (Maynard-Moody, 1983).

Mode of analysis and instrumentation is another area in which differentiation would enhance the validity and utility of program evaluation. The dominant evaluation model is quantitative, representing "hard" data and notions of statistical proof. For example, Bernstein and Freeman's 1975 assessment of the "quality" of evaluation research developed a quality index with which to assess more than 200 evaluation research projects (Bernstein & Freeman, 1975). Their major ratings (with the higher numbers indicating higher quality evaluation) underscore the dominance of this quantitative model. Three indicators were assigned for data analysis:

Quantitative (2)

Qualitative and quantitative (1)

Qualitative (0)

Ratings for statistical procedures reflected the same paradign (Patton, 1978, p. 206):

Multivariate (4)

Descriptive (3)

Ratings from qualitative data (2).

Narrative data only (1)

No systematic material (0)

By this rating scheme, qualitative evaluations are judged to have no value and mixed method studies to be seriously flawed. Yet experience with social program implementation shows that quantitative methods pursued alone cannot capture the complex processes, indeterminate factors, and often subtle influences that shape program outcomes. The institutional reality of social program implementation defeats attempts to apply unilaterally the abstract formalism represented by mathematics and the logic of numbers.

First, statistical differences and substantive significance do not always coincide. Statistical significance simply refers to whether an observed difference is likely to be due to chance. Substantive significance refers to the *consequence* of differences in a social setting. How meaningful, for example, is it to know that the level of parent participation has increased significantly unless one also knows who the new participants are (i.e., is the configuration of parent participation changed) and how they participate (i.e., pro forma attendance at meetings or involvement in decisions about school activities)? What practical meaning do significant statistical differences among students have if they represent only a single item difference on a standarized achievement test?

Second, determinant tools often are incompatible with central features of the process of program implementation. Policies and practices change over time as a practice is carried out. Determinant tools, such as a fixed coefficient model, risk misrepresenting transformation in key variables. Relationships and effects that held at time 1 often do not obtain at time 2. Early teacher resistance, for example, may have been overcome by an effective in-service education program. An early and unamended estimate of the level of teacher resistance to a new program and its effect on program outcomes would, in this case, lead to wrong conclusions. Or, particular factors—principal support—may be more or less important at different points in the process of carrying out a new practice. A one-shot, fixed determinant model would miss the shifting "weight" of this important factor. (More complex, time-dependent models could be constructed but are rare in practice and difficult to institute.) The search for simplification implicit in such models may in fact be counterproductive because it ignores differences, interactions, and complexities that are crucially important to effective performance.

Three, the things that matter to program outcomes may be difficult to quantify. For example, the quality of teacher involvement in school decision making or the values and beliefs associated with particular program choices often elude quantification. For any evaluation, there will be information that can be best gotten through quantitative methods, distributions and frequencies, for example. But the state of the art and the realities of social setting defies comprehensive learning with a single method. Evaluation involves more than the logic of numbers and the enumeration and scaling central to quantitative models; it involves the logic of classes that characterizes qualitative research. For example, understanding the institutional norms, statuses, and goals as well as the individual beliefs and values that shape program activities and results requires largely qualitative methods of interviewing and observation.

A unitary evaluation model, in short, is ill-equipped to capture the emergence and resolution (or lack of resolution) of the factors, issues, and quandaries associated with implementation. An evaluation that differentiates methodological choice by the type of information required and the nature of the problem to be addressed is more likely to represent reality accurately and to serve the needs of evaluation users.

Concepts of Use

Evaluations have many purposes ranging from the political to the practical (Goldenberg, 1983). Leaving aside patently political interests, the multiple specific purposes of evaluation can be described by two broad goals: Learning and control (Elmore, 1980). Evaluations are undertaken (1) to learn about program activities and outcomes so practices can be improved and (2) to control the behavior of those responsible for implementation. However, evaluators agree that neither purpose generally has been well served (Pincus, 1980; Wholey, 1979; David, 1982; Patton, 1978).

Implementation realities suggest reasons for this assessment and thus pose fundamental questions about the concepts of use that underlie most evaluations. For example, the typical impact model is designed by higher-ups in the policy system (or even outside the system) with little involvement on the part of those responsible for program implementation. Further, evaluation findings are delivered only to system managers; little effort is made to communicate or explain results to those whose performance was examined. This approach to evaluation ignores the role of the street-level bureaucrat and misunderstands the conditions under which the learning and control assumed by evaluation take place. The concept of use implicit in this model disregards how learning relevant to improved outcomes takes place as well as the nature of effective control in most social policy settings (Elmore, 1980).

To learn, individuals need to reflect on action; to learn how to do better, individuals need regular feedback about their performance (Schon, 1983; Good, 1983). Most evaluations provide little information to support reflection on action; instead evaluations report on the extent to which formal goals have been met. Most evaluations provide summative, one-shot assessments rather than intermittent information about performance.

But even if evaluations addressed these concerns, they would still fall short of their goals because, in the main, they do not direct information to those individuals whose "learning" and performance is of most import to program outcomes: The individuals responsible for service delivery. Most evaluations are built on a command-and-control view of the social system that assumes an effective hierarchy of authority and closely linked operating units. As experience shows, the facts of institutional life in most social policy settings diverge substantially from this platonic notion of concentrated power and responsibility. Yet evaluations seldom leave the management and supervisory units; little effort is made to convey evaluation findings to those charged directly with implementation (David, 1982). Nor, interestingly, does it appear that the people who receive evaluation have the authority to act on their findings (Kennedy, 1980, p. 47). Primary decision makers at the "top" of the system, who are important to changing conditions of support or sanction for implementers, usually are bypassed as well.

In most cases, however, if evaluations were shared with street-level bureaucrats, they would find them questionably relevant. Typically, goals are defined and expressed in the evaluator's terms, not the deliverer's terms. Few evaluators ask individuals responsible for delivery what they intend and what they would like to learn about program operations. In many cases, the evaluator's questions hold limited import for the street-level bureaucrat. Relevance is confounded by format. The language evaluators use to talk to each other usually is practically meaningless to deliverers. For the street-level bureaucrats, meaningful evaluation must be based in the craft knowledge, language, and experience of their professional world (Kennedy, 1980; Lindblom & Cohen, 1980).

Most evaluations, in short, do not collect or target the information that could promote the learning most directly related to program outcomes. In the final analysis, learning acquired at the top of the system requires concomitant learning at the bottom in order for evaluation findings to translate into meaningful program improvement. Evaluation seldom can fulfill its intended purpose if a single decision maker or a solitary center of influence describes its focus. And exclusion of the street-level bureaucrat excludes those most influential in determining program outcomes.

The command-and-control view of authority also misunderstands what effective control means in many social policy systems. As the preceding section argued, there is no necessary and direct correspondence between what administrators (or legislators) mandate and what actors responsible for implementation actually do. Evaluations rooted exclusively in a formal oversight model miss opportunities to exercise the most effective kind of control—control based in professional incentives and motivation. Most people want to do better. Evaluations that provide information to deliverers about the quality of their performance in a way that is relevant and comprehensible are among the most effective mechanisms for control available to an organization.[6] Evaluations that support rational calculation to the exclusion of learning from experience miss significant opportunities to support institutional growth and development.

SUMMARY AND CONCLUSIONS

Since its inception, evaluation research has aimed to describe "lawful relations" between program inputs and outcomes (Cronbach, 1975, p. 121). This standard has been used to identify "good" evaluation questions as well as "good" evaluation methods. Experience with social program implementation, however, points to serious if not insurmountable obstacles to such aspirations. Assumptions essential to the dominant evaluation model, the hypotheticodeductive paradigm, find little support in reality. Whereas traditional evaluation designs generally assume that project treatment or inputs have main effects on program outcomes, these project factors in fact have only indirect and marginal effects because they must operate through the implementing system.

The essentially static notions of treatment found in most evaluation designs seriously misrepresent the variable and changing nature of social programs as they are transformed by implementation choices at different levels of the policy system. Further, these implementation choices are affected by more than just features of the implementing system such as resources, expertise, and relative need. They also are molded by the multiple goals that shape implementer priorities, rather than only by the single delivery goal most evaluations address. For all of these reasons, the classic models for estimating effects and specifying causality as well as scientific standards of proof are largely inappropriate to learning about social programs and assessing their effects.

The concepts of use and usefulness implicit in most evaluations also misrepresent reality. Rather than the hierarchical authority structure assumed by most evaluation and reporting schemes, social settings have multiple sources of power and influence. And the ultimate influence lies with the street-level bureaucrats, individuals who are responsible for carrying out policy, programs, and mandates but who seldom are consulted in the design of evaluations and specification of items to be assessed or involved in the presentation of findings. Implementation realities suggest that notions of learning and control found in most evaluations misunderstand both how learning occurs in social systems and the nature of effective authority.

Finally, in contrast to the search for universals and axioms associated with the dominant evaluation model, evaluation findings are not ageless. The institutional context in which social programs are implemented is fluid, unstable, complex, and often unpredictable. As a result, findings, conclusions, and generalizations break down over time. Social scientists are bound to be disappointed if they hope to emulate the timeless relations of natural science.

What are reasonable expectations, then, for evaluation? What kind of evaluation makes sense? What will be most useful to policymakers and practitioners? The fundamental lack of fit between traditional evaluation paradigms and implementation realities means that it is not a question of "fixing" our old way of doing evaluation business. Experience with social program implementation suggests that different questions and methods are in order. A focus on process questions, for example, clearly is an important evaluation task and one that is largely ignored by most goal-driven evaluation designs. But, because implementation choices dominate project outcomes, advice to policymakers and practitioners needs to specify the nature of these choices, the trade-offs surrounding them, and the process whereby they are carried out. This argues for evaluation that attends as much to *how* something is done and *why* it is done as it does to *what* is done.

Because generalizations decay, and because few social programs are undertaken in the go/no-go spirit of experimentation, evaluation profitably could move from a focus on conclusionary statements of effect toward goals of short-term control and correction. Evaluations could address issues of targeting and implementation, for example, as ways to assist practitioners and policymakers in achieving various program goals. Regular feedback about performance, evidence of success, and suggestions for improvement are crucial to implementer improvement and effectiveness. This provides short-run control of the highest order. It also suggests an approach to evaluation that adopts a regularized strategy for information collection and analysis and abandons the evaluation-as-event, as a once a year way of learning about program activities.

Experience with social program implementation also suggests that evaluations should move from notions of "proof" and static conclusions toward judgments of "better than" and an emphasis on the conditional knowledge to be gained from a special program effort. Among the questions to be asked are: What institutional factors (e.g., existing knowledge base, resource constraints) shaped program choices? What factors impeded or supported implementation? What was the interaction between existing staff capacity and program expectations?

What ancillary effects are associated with program operations? Are some program participants affected differently than others by program activities? This kind of information about program processes and the institutional effects of various program and implementation choices provides practitioners with information they need to make sense of the alternatives before them. It also can furnish the information policymakers need to consider issues central to the crafting of policy, for example, the policy mechanisms most appropriate to particular policy objectives; strategies for differentiation of resources; incentives or sanctions; reasonable expectations; and standards for program operations.

At the very least, experience with social program implementation underscores the fact that traditional evaluation models are only one, and an inherently limited, way of conceiving of the evaluation task and the role of evaluation in social settings. This experience makes it evident that new ways of thinking about evaluation are necessary for generating and integrating new insights and, indeed, for learning from experience.

NOTES

1. This section draws heavily on an earlier essay by Richard F. Elmore and Milbrey W. McLaughlin, "The Federal Role in Education: Learning From Experience," *Education and Urban Society, 15,*3, 1983, 309-330.

2. This fact provides a major rationale for a continued and vigorous federal role in areas that are seen as national priorities but which have uneven support at state and local levels.

3. This is the thesis of J. Pressman and A. Wildavky's landmark study, *Implementation* (1973).

4. "Street-level bureaucrat" is the very apt term used by R. Weatherley and M. Lipsky, "Street-Level Bureaucrats and Institutional Innovation: Implementing Special Education Reform," *Harvard Educational Review, 47,*2, 171-197, 1977.

5. C. Argyris and D. Shon (1978) use this very descriptive phase in *Organizational Learning: A Theory of Action Perspective* (1978) to underline the permeability of organizational boundaries.

6. This conclusion is prominently displayed in T. Peters and R. Waterman, *In Search of Excellence,* New York: Harper & Row, 1982.

REFERENCES

Argyris, C., & Shon, D. A. (1978). *Organizational learning: A theory of action perspective.* Reading, MA: Addison-Wesley.

Bardach, E. (1977). *The implementation game.* Cambridge, MA: MIT Press.

Bardach, E. (1980). *Implementation studies and the study of implements.* Paper presented at the Annual Meeting of the American Political Science Association, Washington, DC.

Berman, P., & McLaughlin, M. W. (1978). *Federal programs supporting educational change: Vol. 8, implementing and sustaining innovations.* Santa Monica, CA: The Rand Corporation.

Bernstein, I., & Freeman, H. (1975). *Academic and entrepreneurial research: The consequences of diversity in federal evaluation studies.* New York: Russell Sage.

Boruch, R. F., & Cordray, D. S. (1980). An appraisal of educational program evaluations: Federal, state and local agencies. Evanston, IL: Northwestern University.

Cronbach, L. J. (1975). Beyond the two disciplines of scientific psychology. *American Psychologist,* 116-127.

Cronbach, L. J. (1982). *Designing evaluations of educational and social programs.* San Francisco: Jossey-Bass.

David, J. L. (1982). Local uses of Title I evaluations. In E. R. House et al. (Eds.), *Evaluation Studies Review Annual* (Vol. 7). Beverly Hills, CA: Sage.

Deutscher, I. (1977). Toward avoiding the goal-trap in evaluation. In F. Carol (Ed.), *The evaluation of social action programs.* New York: Russell Sage.

Elmore, R. F. (1980). *Evaluation, control and learning in organizations.* Paper presented at the Western Political Science Association Meetings, San Francisco, CA.

Elmore, R. F., & McLaughlin, M. W. (1982). Strategic choice in federal education policy: The compliance-assistance trade-off. In A. Lieberman & M. W. McLaughlin (Eds.), *Policy making in education: The 81st Yearbook of the National Society for the Study of Education.* Chicago, IL: University of Chicago Press.

Elmore, R. F. & McLaughlin, M. W. (1983). The federal role in education: Learning from experience. *Education and Urban Society, 15,* 309-333.

Fullan, M. (1982). *The meaning of educational change.* New York: Teachers College Press.

Gilbert, J. P., Light, R. J., Mosteller, F. (1975). Assessing social innovations: An empirical base for policy. In C. A. Bennett & A. A. Lumsdaine (Eds.) *Evaluation and experiment.* New York: Academic Press.

Goldenberg, E. N. The three faces of evaluation. *Journal of Policy Analysis and Management, 2* (4), 515-525.

Good, T. (1983). Research on classroom teaching. In L. Shulman & G. Sykes (Eds.), *Handbook of teaching and policy.* New York: Longman.

Goodlad, J., Klein, M. F., & Associates (1974). *Looking behind the classroom door.* Worthington, OH: Charles A. Jones.

Hargrove, E., et al. (1981). *Regulations and schools: The implementation of equal education for handicapped children.* Nashville, TN: Institute for Public Policy Studies, Vanderbilt University.

Hawkridge, D. G., Campeau, P., & Roberts, A. O. H. (1969). *A study of exemplary programs for education of disadvantaged children.* Palo Alto, CA: American Institutes for Research.

Jackson, P. W. (1968). *Life in classrooms.* New York: Holt, Rinehart & Winston.

Kaplan, A. (1964). *The conduct of inquiry.* San Francisco: Chandler.

Kennedy, M. (1980). *The role of evaluation and test information in the public schools.* Cambridge, MA: Huron Institute.

Kirst, M., & Jung, R. (1980). The utility of the longitudinal approach in assessing implementation: A thirteen-year view of Title I, ESEA. *Educational Evaluation and Policy Analysis, 2,* 17-33.

Lindblom, C. E., & Cohen, D. K. (1980). *Usable knowledge.* New Haven, CT: Yale University Press.

Lortie, D. C. (1975). *Schoolteacher.* Chicago, IL: University of Chicago Press.

Majone, G. (1981). Policies as theories. In I. L. Horowitz (Ed.), *Policy studies review annual* (Vol. 5). Beverly Hills, CA: Sage.

Maynard-Moody, S. (1983). Program evaluation and administrative control. *Policy Studies Review, 2,* 371-390.

McDonnell, L. M., & McLaughlin, M. W. (1982). *Education policy and the rule of the states.* Santa Monica, CA: The Rand Corporation.

McLaughlin, M. W. (1975). *Evaluation and reform: The case of ESEA Title I.* Cambridge, MA: Ballinger.

McLaughlin, M. W. (1980). Evaluation and alchemy. In J. Pincus (Ed.), *Educational evaluation and the public policy setting.* Santa Monica, CA: The Rand Corporation.

McLaughlin, M. W., & Thomas, M. (1984). *History, criticism and production: An examination of the process of art education in selected school districts, Vol. 1: Comparing the process of change across school districts.* Santa Monica, CA: The Rand Corporation.

Nakamura, R. T., & Smallwood, F. (1980). *The politics of policy implementation.* New York: Saint Martin's Press.

Patton, M. Q. (1978). *Utilization focused evaluation.* Beverly Hills, CA: Sage.

Peters, T. J., & Waterman, R. H., Jr. (1982). *In search of excellence.* Cambridge, MA: Harper & Row.

Pincus, J. (Ed.). (1980). *Educational evaluation in the public policy setting.* Santa Monica, CA: The Rand Corporation.

Pressman, J., & Wildavsky, A. (1973). *Implementation.* Berkeley: University of California Press.

Raizen, S. A. & Rossi, P. H. (1982). Summary of program evaluation in education: When? How? To what ends? In E. R. House et al. (Eds.), *Evaluation studies review annual* (Vol. 7). Beverly Hills, CA: Sage.

Rossi, P. H. (1982). Some dissenting comments on Stake's review. In E. R. House et al. (Eds.), *Evaluation studies review annual* (Vol. 7). Beverly Hills, CA: Sage.

Rossi, P. H., & Freeman, H. E. (1982). *Evaluation.* Beverly Hills, CA: Sage.

Sabatier, P., & Mazmanian, D. (1979). The conditions of effective implementation: A guide to accomplishing policy objectives. *Policy Analysis, 5,* 481-504.

Schon, D. A. (1983). *The reflective practitioner: How professionals think in action.* New York: Basic Books.

Stake, R. E. (1982). A peer response. In E. R. House et al. (Eds.), *Evaluation studies review annual* (Vol. 7). Beverly Hills, CA: Sage.

Steinberger, P. J. (1981). Typologies of public policy: Meaning construction and the policy process. In I. L. Horowitz (Ed.), *Policy studies review annual* (Vol. 5). Beverly Hills, CA: Sage.

U.S. Advisory Commission on Intergovernmental Relations (1981). *The future of federalism in the 1980s: Reports and papers from the conference on the future of federalism.* Washington, DC: ACIR.

Weatherley, R. (1979). *Reforming special education: Policy implementation from state to street level.* Cambridge, MA: MIT Press.

Wholey, J. S. (1979). *Evaluation: Promise and performance.* Washington, DC: The Urban Institute.

Ziman, J. (1978). *Reliable knowledge.* London: Cambridge University Press.

4

Can Social Scientists Be Effective Actors in the Policy Arena?

THOMAS F. PETTIGREW

The headlines tell the story. Economic arguments about supply curves and the meaning of a trillion-dollar national debt receive broad coverage. Psychologists debate why recent Scholastic Aptitude Test scores have not continued their downward decline; this crude indicator of school efficiency attracts extensive mass media attention. Voting analyses by political scientists are routinely reported.

These and other stories show how social science is now taken seriously by the mass media, the public, and policymakers. No longer are social science findings and theories of interest only to those in the discipline. Such work now has the potential to affect our lives. And the woman we honor with this volume was enthusiastic about this trend. Although acutely aware of its limitations, Carolyn Sherif wanted social science to aid in the development of a better world. Her career offers a model of how to work for such a goal.

Under certain conditions, then, social scientists are effective actors in the policy arena. But these conditions are limited. The connection between social science and social policy is new, fragile, and selective. This chapter explores this developing relationship between social science and policy by discussing five points:

(1) The link between social science and policy is relatively recent. Thus, it is still evolving; and social science has had the time neither to accustom

itself to this new role nor to establish effective ethical guidelines for policy-related research.

(2) Social science seldom shapes policy directly. Other institutions, such as funding agencies and the mass media, mediate its influence.

(3) There are sharp differences among the social sciences that condition their acceptance into policy. Deductive models from economics, for example, are more readily adopted than inductive models of sociology.

(4) Likewise, there are sharp differences among policy institutions and different levels of government that condition their acceptance of social science contributions.

(5) Finally, ethical guidelines for policy research are urgently needed. Such guidelines are more necessary for policy-related than for "purely academic" work.

THE RECENCY OF THE RELATIONSHIP

Policymakers did not totally disregard social science, of course, before the 1960s. There was an "atmospheric, wisdom-of-the-times" effect of social science ideas throughout the first half of this century. Popularized notions of Freud, Piaget, Keynes, and others percolated through Western society and had a pervasive indirect influence on governmental decisions. One political scientist, Woodrow Wilson, even became President. And there were examples of more direct effects on public policy. The U.S. Census has been a social science instrument of government since the early days of the republic. Rural sociologists have long helped to shape farm programs. Economists were an important part of President Franklin Roosevelt's "brain trust." Anthropologists provided expert cultural analyses during World War II. Social psychologists were witnesses in the early school desegregation cases. And though it caused extreme criticism from the white South, the U.S. Supreme Court cited social science sources in its famous footnote 11 of its landmark public school desegregation opinion in 1954.

But it was not until the mid-1960s that social research began to be relied on routinely in the policy process. Two publicized events mark the transition. In 1965, President Lyndon Johnson cited the expert advice of Walter Heller, the University of Minnesota economist, in advocating a major income tax cut. In 1966, the U.S. Office of Education released the *Equality of Educational Opportunity* study, i.e., "The Coleman Report" (Coleman et al., 1966). Congress mandated this massive national study of 640,000 public school children in the 1964 Civil Rights Act.

The skeptical acceptance of these social science contributions highlights their novelty at that point. President Johnson is said to have growled ominously to Heller just before seeking congressional approval of the tax cut, "Professor, it better damn well work!" And less than a half-dozen reporters came to the release of the "Coleman Report." Only when the Report's relevance for educational policy became controversial did the mass media focus attention on it.

Soon, however, certain types of social science research became a regular arm of the policy process. Congress specified evaluation studies as an intrinsic part of social programs and established its own budget analysis office, headed by Alice Rivlin, an economist. Comparable evaluation efforts were often mounted for social programs in developing countries as well. Federal agencies shifted monies from university-based grant research to more specified, policy-oriented contract research increasingly conducted by large contract research firms (e.g., Abt Associates, Stanford Research Institute, System Development Corporation, The Rand Corporation). And politicians learned to cite social research and data as never before.

This sweeping alteration in the relationship between social research and policy raises an array of new issues, problems, and opportunities. Yet the swiftness of this change has left little time for either social science or government to evolve a comfortable, ethically responsible relationship. Two decades later, the link between social science and public policy remains at best an uneasy alliance.

There can be no better demonstration of this uneasy alliance than the ambivalent actions of the Reagan Administration toward social science. One side of the administration's view of social science is marked by unremitting hostility. Many social science programs were summarily abolished. Others, such as the behavioral science budget within the National Science Foundation, were recommended to be slashed 70 percent or more compared to modest increases in physical science budgets. Even line item appropriations for evaluation research in a variety of agency programs have been totally removed. Perceiving social science in general as an arm of the hated political left, the Reagan Administration made no secret of its intention to cut off federal monies for it. So blatantly ideological were these moves that even a conservative Congress restored many of the budget cuts.

Yet there is another side to the Reagan Administration's response to the social sciences. Reflecting the institutionalization of particular varieties of social science contributions to social policy in recent years, President Reagan and his staff felt compelled to cite social science evidence and ideas that appear to support their political positions.

Indeed, they are conspicuous among recent administrations in this regard. "Supply side economics" were endlessly explained to reporters; Laffer curves, however little modern economics may regard them, were repeatedly leaned on as support for taxation policies; and a pantheon of social science "experts" from Milton Friedman to Thomas Sowell were cited as definitive. It appears that social science work consistent with Reagan policies was needed for legitimization, but most of the field's work was not to be trusted or aided. Broadcast it when it fits; damn it when it does not fit. To be sure, the Reagan Administration is not unique among policymakers in this selective approach to social science contributions—another reason for the uneasy alliance between social science and policy.

THE MEDIATED INFLUENCE OF SOCIAL SCIENCE ON PUBLIC POLICY

Many critics of the policy role of social science, including those in the Reagan Administration, assume that social research not only has a generally pernicious, but a direct and unmediated, effect on policy. They advance, in short, a hypodermic needle model of how social research affects policy. But everything we know suggests instead that an array of mechanisms and institutions mediate the effects. These mediated effects of social research are thus necessarily less pernicious than its detractors fear and less effective than its supporters hope. Let me illustrate this process, and the distortions it can render, by considering the role of federal funding agencies and the mass media as examples of institutions that mediate the influence of social research on public policy.

Federal Funding Agencies

Most large federal educational studies have employed varieties of just one of many possible research designs. The sponsoring funding agencies have repeatedly preferred massive, nationwide surveys as exemplified by the Coleman Report on equal educational opportunity. They have consistently eschewed "the cottage industry model" of local, detailed social experimentation using a variety of measures and methods by different investigators (Campbell, 1975; Pettigrew, 1978). In addition, these same agencies over the past 15 years have shaped these large educational surveys to answer one simple, dichotomous question: Did the program "work?" Yes or no? But more differentiated questions are required. Where did the program work? Where did it not work? And what are the differences between these sites? Such a differentiated approach does more justice to the variegated nature of most federal educational programs. And it provides policymakers with more useful information.

Moreover, program evaluation research techniques are better able to supply accurate answers to these specified questions than to the global query of whether the program worked or not. This differential accuracy is a function of several considerations, the most important of which involves specification. The "success" of a program is generally more of a political than a scientific determination. And it often requires a far from obvious weighting of contrasting dependent variables such as various changes among clients, financial efficiency, job satisfaction of program staff, and the avoidance of political problems. Aggregated studies across multiple sites, each with its own particular mix of goals, clients, procedures, staff, and political context, exaggerate these problems and make refined specification more difficult.

Why, then, have federal funding agencies persisted in these limiting research preferences? Part of the answer lies in the structure of bureaucratic organizations. As Michele Crozier (1964) points out, bureaucracies enhance their power through informational monopolies. And both the selection of single massive research designs and the work-or-not-work conclusions further informational monopolies, and hence the power, of these funding agencies.

The Mass Media

The mass media provide another prime example of how mediating institutions shape the influence of social science on policy. I can illustrate media distortions by posing a three-item quiz about research findings in the race and education field. Is each of the following statements true or false?

(1) "Busing" has failed, for there have been few positive gains for black children resulting from school desegregation.
(2) Court-ordered school desegregation inevitably leads to massive "white flight" from the affected school district.
(3) Children learn more in private than in public schools.

Each of these statements has become a media truism, yet each is an incorrect description of research findings. Thus, most desegregation investigations show modest achievement and extensive career gains for desegregated, as compared with similar segregated, black children. This conclusion is especially true for desegregation in the early grades and for the most rigorously conducted studies (Crain & Mahard, 1978, 1983; McPartland & Crain, 1980).

Likewise, many desegregated school systems have experienced only modest loss of white students, particularly in countywide districts such as Tampa, Miami, Charlotte, and Nashville (see, e.g., Pettigrew & Green, 1976; Sly & Pol, 1978, for entry into the voluminous critical work on the so-called "white flight" research). And major examples of so-called "white flight" have occurred in segregated school districts (e.g., Philadelphia, New York, Cincinnati, Chicago, and St. Louis). There is considerable confusion between the natural demographic loss of white children and school desegregation effects. Often "white flight" involves only "a hastening up" of these long-term demographic trends (Pettigrew & Green, 1976).

Finally, claims of private school superiority are based on research that did not adequately control for social class differences between private and public school pupils. (The media furor over this point was originated by Coleman, Hoffer, & Kilgore, 1981; the control problem was pointed out by Campbell, 1981, and Goldberger, 1981). Because private schools typically enroll higher-status children, this could account for the differences in tested achievement.

Why are these more differentiated, policy-relevant results of social research not better communicated? Clearly, there is a dangerous lack of fit between the mass media and social science. On the media side, social science has yet to be elevated to the status of a specialized "beat." Television networks and a few newspapers and magazines now have economics reporters; but a "science writer" still describes the specialist in physical science or medicine. Only a few work the general social science beat.

All too often general reporters force their social science stories into "human interest" formats that highlight *ad hominem* attacks by opponents in a debate while they ignore the central issues of scientific and policy relevance. In other words, they treat social science as if it were an adversarial contest. Nonspecialized reporters are also responsible for "the first splash effect." The opening salvo of a racial intelligence claim, for example, is given wide coverage typically without critique or rebuttal. Later refutations are not seen as newsworthy. Even if scholarly criticisms are subsequently reported, the initial, now invalidated claim lives on in public memory. Only balanced, sophisticated first-story reporting by those regularly on a social science beat can prevent this "first splash" phenomenon.

On the academic side, few social scientists have experience in dealing with the media. And lecturing to captive audiences of students is not relevant training. Media attention often flatters social scientists

who then express expansive opinions in marked contrast to their typically cautious professional style (Cronbach, 1975).

Both institutions require structural changes. The media should provide regular coverage of the social sciences, a beat that many talented
journalists are eager to acquire. Social scientists, in turn, should develop
a more professional dialogue with specialized reporters. For instance,
they could offer noncredit courses specifically designed for interested
media personnel that emphasize methods, conceptualization, and the
structure of social science as a discipline. Foundations could further
this process, much as the Russell Sage Foundation has done already,
by providing fellowships to journalists who wish to acquire this expertise.

Unless such alterations are made in both the media and academia,
and each learns to regard the other more seriously, inadequate reporting
of policy-relevant social science work will continue. In time, the public
may understandably conclude from the seemingly endless "conflicting
research results" and *ad hominem* attacks that social scientists have
nothing to contribute to policy debates save their own politicized opinions.

THE DIFFERENTIAL ACCEPTANCE
OF THE SOCIAL SCIENCES

Descriptive data and projected forecasts, such as census counts and
estimates, were traditionally the most readily understood and accepted
forms of social research by policymakers. But the recent growth of
policy interest in social research has taken a different direction. Large-
scale econometric models have become popular. Hence, Congress hired
an economist to head its analysis unit; the Reagan Administration
cites economists almost exclusively. Note, too, that there is a Council
of Economic Advisors in the White House but no equivalent Council
of Social Advisors (as proposed long ago by Walter Mondale).

From the perspective of those devising new legislation and regulations in complex domains, elaborate econometric models possess many
advantages. First, they can be impressive, even elegant, in their apparent
mathematical precision. Second, though their assumptions and inner
structure are not readily apparent, econometric models typically offer
straightforward, easily understood outputs. Indeed, this feature relates
to these models' third and most beguiling attribute. Because they are
deductive models that usually draw their data from already existing
files, econometric models can be specially shaped to the policymaker's
immediate needs.

Contrast these advantages with the disadvantages of *inductive*,
sociological and psychological models developed from fresh research

data. Inductive models are less likely to appear elegant and more likely to contain perplexing complexities. They take considerable time to build; hence, they are not likely to be custom-styled to the policy problems of the moment. Faced with the choice, policymakers understandably favor deductive econometric models.

But such made-to-order models have major problems. Unstated, simplifying assumptions that bear little resemblance to "the real world" often drive econometric systems. Especially worrisome to social psychologists are the many fundamental assumptions about individual behavior that are demonstrably wrong. Just as worrisome to the political left, conservative biases often underlie econometric model assumptions. Many of these biases are unwitting. They flow naturally from the market model and the greater accessibility of financial data than cultural, social, and psychological data. Thus, the apparent mathematical elegance, understandable output, and immediate policy relevance of econometric models are sometimes bought at the cost of unrealistic and conservative simplifying assumptions.

Basic remedies for this problem involve more interdisciplinary work within social science. Work that merges inductive with deductive methods is especially needed. Indeed, advanced econometric methods are now receiving wide attention among young sociologists. Better yet, we need ongoing, long-term interdisciplinary work on major social issues that is ready when policymakers will listen. The social sciences, as well as the policy domain, would benefit from such cross-fertilization. Econometricians could learn to employ more inductively derived data instead of rough assumptions that "seem reasonable." Other social scientists could learn how to specify more precisely their often loose formulations and how to design leaner models for maximum applicability for social policy.

THE DIFFERENTIAL ACCEPTANCE AMONG POLICY INSTITUTIONS

Various components of government differ widely in their acceptance of social research. Some actively seek social science. The U.S. Commission on Civil Rights, for which I long consulted, not only values social science but has established an in-house social research staff. And, until the Reagan Administration, such Federal Departments as Human Services, Education, and Housing and Urban Development welcomed policy-relevant social research. Other Federal Departments, such as Justice and Energy, have been typically cool to social science input. State governments have not used social research extensively, though

Wisconsin, Minnesota, and California are notable exceptions. Local government remains the most resistant of all.

The larger problem of the use of social science by agencies of government, however, extends beyond initial acceptance or rejection. It also involves the compatibility of social science perspectives with those of government. A conspicuous example of this problem arises between social science and the law, an example with which I am familiar from serving as an expert witness in school desegregation cases. One study found that 90 percent of over 50 social scientists who had testified in these cases report some incompatibility between their scholarly and witness roles (Chesler, Sanders, & Kalmuss, 1981). The barriers between the law and social science center on two general areas: Conflicting cognitive styles and conflicting operational environments (Pettigrew, 1979a).

Conflicting Cognitive Styles

Distinct cognitive differences occur at all levels. To begin with, the two fields apply contrasting definitions to such key concepts as "expert" and "evidence." More important, they "map" their domains differently; and it is often difficult to obtain a close "fit" between their conceptual schemes. Law and social science also differ in their preferred scope. Law is case-oriented, specific and detailed; by definition, social science is interested in generalization. This can lead to interesting conflicts over evidence, as Wolfgang (1974, p. 244) found when the probability sample of his Arkansas rape and death penalty study did not include the case's particular county, leading the prosecuting attorney to doubt whether the results of Wolfgang's probability sample applied to the county in question. Finally, the two disciplines reason within contrasting frameworks. In desegregation cases, the courts have shown little interest in social class, a central sociological concern. And social scientists find the critical legal distinction between *de jure* and *de facto* segregation to be without empirical foundation (Pettigrew, 1975). These cognitive barriers can be overcome by the early participation of an expert witness in the case, starting at the brief-writing stage. But social scientists usually require considerable experience to accommodate to the law's adversary process.

Conflicting Operational Environments

Participation in a given case is, after all, done on legal turf under the rules of the court. And adversarial procedures conflict with those of science at many points. For instance, the adversary process requires each side to put forth its best argument; and this entails the suppression of any evidence thought to hurt the case. For a social scientist, this practice raises serious ethical concerns. Indeed, the role of witness in a dispute raises an array of role conflicts. Do you testify for "your side," or do you let the chips fall where they may? Do you specify all the usual reservations about your work, or do you respond to adversarial pressures and vigorously advance your data? Each expert witness has to make these decisions. Understandably, social science testimony in desegregation cases has been more effective at the remedy stage, in which these conflicts are less acute.

THE NEED FOR ETHICAL GUIDELINES
FOR POLICY RESEARCH

These ethical conflicts in the courtroom are typical of the ethical issues evoked by the uneasy alliance between social science and public policy. We have noted how the recency of this alliance has not allowed the development of ethical guidelines for policy-relevant social research. But the necessity for such guidelines has become blatantly apparent (Pettigrew, 1979b; Warwick & Pettigrew, 1983). In virtually every major policy area in which social research has entered, the work and its implications has occasioned intense debate. The most publicized cases involve public education, as with achievement testing, the Coleman Report, school desegregation, and the Head Start Program. But bitter exchanges have occurred in other realms, too. Project Camelot, a U.S. Army attempt to use social science to measure and forecast revolutions and insurgency, was abruptly canceled once it received heated opposition from around the world (Horowitz, 1965). Although "politics" is the usual charge, at root these controversies focus on the proper posture that social scientists *should* take in the policy arena—an ethical question.

Natural science has learned that ethical problems mount rapidly as policy decisions are increasingly based on its theory and research, as in DNA work, nuclear plant safety, definitions of life and death, and even earthquake predictions.[1] Social science is learning the same harsh lesson. Social policy research raises special ethical concerns in two directions (Warwick & Pettigrew, 1983). First, policy research heightens the standard ethical problems of all research. There is typically a shorter time span involved, so there is less time for the usual leisurely pace of corrective work to redress any imbalance. There is also more centralization of funding; and we have seen how this leads to a more limited set of methods, investigators, and problem formulations. Policy research has less technical consumers, that is, policymakers and the public rather than disciplinary colleagues. Hence, greater candor about research limitations is required. Finally, the greater emphasis placed on *causal* inferences in policy-related research adds further ethical complications. Unusually intractable epistemological and technical issues surrounding causation lead to especially troublesome ethical concerns.

Second, policy-related research presents unique ethical problems of its own. These problems arise in the final stages of the process involving publication, publicity, and public debate on the policy implications of social reseach. Here there is the least consensus within social science about the appropriate ethical standards. And here the most glaring problems have emerged. Consider the sociologist who conducted an intense national media campaign against interracial schools ostensibly as a scientist reporting on his study of so-called "white flight" (see Pettigrew & Green, 1976). He talked of the motivations of white parents to avoid "busing," although his research involved no interviews with white parents and had no measure of school transportation. Worse, no copies of his report—much less his data—were available for four months following the initial public announcement of the study upon which the campaign was based. In response to such episodes, the American Sociological Association and others have proposed an ethical guideline for policy-related social research that requires that the relevant data be immediately available for reanalysis by other social scientists (Ethics Committee of the American Sociological Association, 1981; Warwick & Pettigrew, 1983).

But most ethical problems in this realm are not so blatant. Subtle problems are created, for instance, when the most powerful research designs available and a wide range of dependent variables are not used. The magnitude and direction of the bias, of course, is determined by the particular type of research weakness involved. If such flaws were roughly randomly distributed within a given field, they would in time be counterbalanced and exert no consistent effect on the field's central conclusions. However, such is not generally the case. Traditions of particular varieties of weak designs develop within specific areas and exert a largely constant, rather than variable, error on the central conclusions drawn. Thus, in pharmacology, the more rigorous research designs show the least favorable effects of antidepressant drugs (Smith, Targanza, & Harrison, 1969). And in school desegregation and compensatory education studies, the more rigorous designs uncover the most significant gains on cognitive measures (Crain & Mahard, 1983; McDill, McDill, & Sprehe, 1969). The policy implications likely to be drawn from these clusters of similarly weak research designs in these areas, then, are too favorable to antidepressant drugs and too unfavorable to educational interventions intended to benefit the children of minorities and the poor.

Striking examples abound of how the selection of outcome measures determines policy conclusions. One form of this problem involves using "soft," easy-to-change attitudinal dependent variables instead of "hard," resistant-to-change behavioral dependent variables. Energy conservation programs appear successful when judged by survey data that show how Americans are becoming increasingly concerned about energy. But their effectiveness is often called into question when the outcome measure is actual use of energy. This difference is caused by the fact that concerns over energy have little direct relation to energy usage (Olsen, 1981), a slippage between attitudes and behavior often noted in social psychology (Hill, 1981).

The tough ethical question is to what extent does the social scientist have an obligation to use the most powerful research design available and the widest range of outcome measures? At the least, social scientists have a professional duty to adopt a design and outcome variables that permit alternatives to be explored and to make clear the rationale and limitations of these choices. Furthermore, policy-oriented researchers have stronger obligations along these lines than other researchers. Although some efforts have been made to develop guidelines for policy research (e.g., ERS Standards Committee, 1982), many ethical issues remain unsolved.

A FINAL WORD

To sum up, the alliance between social science and public policy is an uneasy one for many reasons. The systematic use of social science in policy determination is recent. It is typically mediated and often distorted by funding agencies, the mass media, and other institutions. Policymakers use only a limited range of the potential contributions of the social sciences. Many governmental agencies, especially at the state and local levels, do not use social science at all. Finally, ethical problems abound, but appropriate ethical guidelines are only starting to evolve.

This chapter has dwelled on problems, but I wish to close on a positive note. Like Carolyn Sherif, I ascribe as firmly as ever to the nineteenth-century liberal ideal of applying organized intelligence to human affairs. And I believe we have inched closer toward that ideal in recent decades. I also judge that, on balance, the social science contribution to human welfare has been at least generally positive. Although fraught with problems, the comparison for this judgment is a modest one—the selectively informed speculations of decision makers. But to be fully effective actors in the policy arena, social scientists must address directly the problems that still constrain their uneasy alliance with social policy.

NOTE

1. Consider seismology and the sweeping earthquake predictions of Brian Brady, a mathematician with the U.S. Bureau of Mines. With unusual specificity, Brady predicted that a quake of 8.0 Richter magnitude would hit near Lima, Peru, on or about June 28, 1981, followed by a 9.2 quake on or about August 10th, and culminating in a massive 9.9 disaster on September 16th. This third earthquake would constitute the largest ever recorded by modern instruments. At first, these forecasts were supported by William Spence, a geophysicist of the U.S. Geological Survey. But as understandable concern arose in Peru and a special Evaluation Council rejected the predictions, Spence and others withdrew their support and sharp controversy ensued ("Quake Prediction," 1981).

REFERENCES

Campbell, D. T. (1975). Assessing the impact of planned social change. In G. M. Lyons (Ed.), *Social research and public policies.* Hanover, NH: The Public Affairs Center, Dartmouth College.

Campbell, D. T. (1981). *Public and private schools.* Unpublished manuscript, University of Syracuse.

Chesler, M. A., Sanders, J., & Kalmuss, D. (1981). *Interaction among scientists, attorneys and judges in school desegregation litigation.* Ann Arbor: Center for Research on Social Organization, University of Michigan, Working Paper No. 230.

Coleman, J. S., Campbell, E. Q., Hobson, C. J., McPartland, J., Mood, A. M., Weinfeld, D., & York, R. L. (1966). *Equality of educational opportunity.* Washington, DC: U.S. Government Printing Office.

Coleman, J. S., Hoffer, T, & Kilgore, S. (1981). *Public and private schools.* Chicago, IL: National Opinion Research Center.

Crain, R. L., & Mahard, R. E. (1978). School racial composition and black college attendance and achievement test performance. *Sociology of Education, 51,* 81-110.

Crain, R. L., & Mahard, R. E. (1983). The effect of research methodology on desegregation-achievement studies: A meta-analysis. *American Journal of Sociology, 88,* 839-854.

Cronbach, L. J., (1975). Five decades of public controversy over mental testing. *American Psychologist, 30,* 1-14.

Crozier, M. (1964). *The Bureaucratic Phenomenon.* Chicago, IL: University of Chicago Press.

ERS Standards Committee (1982). Evaluation Research Society standards for program evaluation. In P. H. Rossi (Ed.), *Standards for evaluation practice.* San Francisco, CA: Jossey-Bass.

Ethics Committee of the American Sociological Association (1981). *Code of ethics: May 1981 revision for consideration by the ASA Council.* Washington, DC: American Sociological Association.

Goldberger, A. S. (1981). *Coleman goes private (in public).* Unpublished manuscript, University of Wisconsin, Madison.

Hill, R. J. (1981). Attitudes and behavior. In M. Rosenberg & R. H. Turner (Eds.), *Social psychology: Sociological perspectives.* New York: Basic Books.

Horowitz, I. L. (1965). Life and death of Project Camelot. *Trans-Actions, 3,* 3-7, 44-47.

McDill, E. L., McDill, M. S., & Sprehe, J. (1969). *Strategies for success in compensatory education: An appraisal of evaluation research.* Baltimore, MD: Johns-Hopkins University Press.

McPartland, J. M., & Crain, R. L. (1980). Racial discrimination, segregation, and processes of social mobility. In V. T. Covello (Ed.), *Poverty and public policy: An evaluation of social science research.* Boston, MA: G. K. Hall.

Olsen, M. E. (1981). Consumers' attitudes toward energy conservation. *Journal of Social Issues, 37,* 108-131.

Pettigrew, T. F. (1975). A sociological view of the post-Bradley era. *Wayne Law Review, 21,* 813-832.

Pettigrew, T. F. (1978). Competing evaluation models: The ESAA evaluation. *Journal of Educational Statistics, 3,* 99-106.

Pettigrew, T. F. (1979a). Race, ethics, and the social responsibility of social scientists. *Hastings Center Report, 9,* 15-18.

Pettigrew, T. F. (1979b). Tension between the law and social science: An expert witness's view. In J. Greenberg, T. F. Pettigrew, S. Greenblat, W. McCann, & D. A. Bennett (Eds.), *Schools and the courts: Volume I—Desegregation.* Eugene, OR: ERIC Clearinghouse on Educational Management, University of Oregon.

Pettigrew, T. F., & Green, R. L. (1976). School desegregation in large cities: A critique of the Coleman "white flight" thesis. *Harvard Educational Review, 46,* 1-54.

"Quake prediction rattles Peru, scientists disagree" (1981, June 29). *San Francisco Chronicle,* p. 10.

Sly, D. L., & Pol, L. G. (1978). The demographic context of school segregation and desegregation. *Social Forces, 56,* 1072-1086.

Smith, A., Traganza, E., & Harrison, G. (1969). Studies on the effectiveness of antidepressant drugs. *Psychopharmacology Bulletin,* 1-53.

Warwick, D. P., & Pettigrew, T. F. (1983). Toward ethical guidelines for social science research in public policy. *Hastings Center Report, 13,* 9-16.

Wolfgang, M. (1974). The social scientist in court. *Journal of Criminal Law and Criminology, 65,* 239-247.

PART II

Policy Areas

PART II, SECTION 1

The first three chapters in Part II focus on interventions in the economy and in the workplace. Marylee Taylor's chapter concerns social science research on affirmative action, particularly research that attempts to estimate race and sex inequities. Taylor discusses the limitations of such research, which arise largely because researchers use limited cross-sectional data sets in an attempt to estimate complex, reciprocal causal relations. Further, she points out that research on affirmative action includes choices that have hidden value implications, but are often disguised as substantive choices about research design. In doing so, Taylor emphasizes the role of political philosophy and values in decisions about both affirmative actions policy and research.

In Chapter 6, Pamela Cain discusses the role of social science research in "comparable worth"; that is, in attempts to achieve gender equity in wages by measuring the value or worth of jobs. After a brief historical review of the comparable worth issue, Cain examines how methodological limits affect comparable worth research. She also discusses the current and potential role of social scientists in the comparable worth movement and notes the extent to which values and politics necessarily mediate the role of social science research in this area.

In the final chapter on the economy and the workplace, Hank Levin examines employment policy. Levin considers the causes of and cures for unemployment from the perspective of market theory. He also briefly discusses some major limitations of research aimed at estimating the effect of a particular policy on unemployment. Levin argues that despite the limitations of research in economics, we know enough about the economy to reduce unemployment far below current levels. What is lacking, Levin contends, is (1) political consensus on higher employment as a goal and on a strategy for achieving that goal, and (2) an ongoing "experimenting society" approach to employment policy.

5

Science and Politics in Affirmative Action Research

MARYLEE C. TAYLOR

The ideal context for social policy research would be a society blessed with unified commitment to the goal of social justice, consensus on the meaning of social justice, and acceptance of collective responsibility for achieving that end. In such a tidy world, the charge to social scientists would be straightforward: Assess the discrepancy of current conditions from the desired "socially just" end state; diagnose the causes of that discrepancy and propose appropriate remedies; finally, monitor and evaluate the remedial programs. The contributions of social science would then depend on the adequacy of theory and method to the task and the professionals' ability to communicate with relevant non-scientific communities.

The reality that serves as the context for affirmative action policy research is the antithesis of the ideal described above: Given the complex and deeply rooted patterns of racial and sexual stratification in the United States, the goal of racial and sexual equity often receives more visible and potent opposition than support; definitions of equity vary over the entire range of logical possibilities; and there is no consensus regarding the apportionment of institutional responsibility to effect remedies.

Broadly defined, affirmative action consists of all efforts that go beyond "passive nondiscrimination" in attempting to eliminate racial and sexual inequities. Proponents of affirmative action base their arguments on analyses of "institutional discrimination," and court rulings as well as federal policy prescribing affirmative action incorporate the logic, if not always the language, of institutional discrimination analysis. At the heart of the institutional discrimination notion is the observation that a vast array of American institutional practices effectively build privilege on privilege, insuring that "them as has gets," a dynamic that locks victims of discrimination into their underprivileged status. (See, for example, Benokraitis & Feagin, 1978; Feagin & Feagin, 1978; Pettigrew, 1975). "Last hired, first fired" seniority practices are a prime example of institutional mechanisms that reward groups whose occupational successes came early and penalizes groups that were until recently excluded from good jobs. Here a history of discrimination in a particular institution retards the current progress of those who were earlier victimized, even though present policies of this institution may be free of overt racial or sexual bias. The matter becomes exponentially more complex when interrelationships among institutional spheres are considered. Thus, for example, insofar as occupational outcomes are conditioned on educational attainment, inequities in education are perpetuated in the occupational sphere even when occupational requirements are themselves ostensibly nondiscriminating. This interinstitutional or system dynamic was acknowledged when the U.S. Supreme Court, in its famous *Griggs* v. *Duke Power Co.* decision (401) U.S. 424, 1971), found that employment selection procedures that have an adverse impact on minority groups are potentially discriminatory and must be abandoned unless the employer demonstrates their validity as predictors of job performance.

In short, institutional discrimination analyses note that the legacy of past discrimination can be perpetuated and magnified through time and across institutional spheres, by practices that are themselves colorblind and sex-neutral. The implication is that breaking into such spirals of inequity requires active intervention, that is, special recruitment and training efforts, revision of selection criteria, and so on.

If the logic underlying affirmative action requirements and recommendations is clear, virtually all the issues raised by this analysis are unresolved, and for reasons that are not difficult to comprehend.

By definition, redistribution of privilege across gender and racial lines entails real losses for some, and dominant group willingness to relinquish its disproportionate share of resources would be an anomaly in human history. Thus it is hardly surprising that the goal of redistribution is not universally shared.

Opposition to redistribution, however, can coexist with nominal support for the goals of racial and sexual equity (indeed, propriety dictates that it usually does). Thus the battles are typically waged on more subtle grounds. Varying definitions of the equitable end state, rooted in diverse assumptions about prexisting group differences, imply widely discrepant assessments of the need for change. At one extreme, all manifest inequality is identified as inequity. From this perspective, there exist no racial or gender differences that legitimate unequal social outcomes; all inequalities derive from social injustice and all should be socially redressed. At the other extreme, the crucial inequalities are seen to derive from race or sex differences for which this society is not responsible; thus wide disparities in group outcomes are not problematic but just. For racial minorities, arguments of the latter form commonly focus on the supposed dysfunctional legacy of non-European cultural traditions, although claims of innate racial and ethnic differences have reared their head again in recent years. With sex differences, the issue is sometimes defined in terms of direct biological limitations on temperament or ability, sometimes in terms of cultural patterns presumed to stem from biologically dictated reproductive roles. If women are innately predisposed or culturally conditioned to offer indiscriminate nurturance rather than make hard-headed decisions, for example, than the absence of women from positions of authority represents neither injustice nor cause for remedial action.

Beyond these unsettled questions, there is another: On whose shoulders should the responsibility for remedy lie? Opponents of extensive redistribution predictably place minimal responsibility on any institution, whereas proponents place heavy responsibility on all, and the debates rage on. Should a given institution or organization be held responsible to redress only the direct effects of its own past discrimination, as a number of court decisions and federal agency rulings suggest? Or should a given institutional domain actively circumvent the dynamics that would perpetuate inequities rooted in other institutional spheres, as implied by proposals for on-the-job training to compensate for deficits in formal education? Or should there be even more aggressive intervention across institutional spheres, for example, following the Swedish model of giving more liberal employment leaves to new parents who share the responsibility for child care?

Social science cannot resolve any of these issues. In principle it is possible to assess the relative contributions of nature and nurture to sex differences, and of cultures of origin and cultures of victimization to race differences. But in practice such research efforts have proven futile. And the heart of the conflict surrounding affirmative action lies outside the realm of science altogether. Who should lose, and who should gain, and who should shoulder the burden of righting society's wrongs—these questions are philosophical, not scientific. Who *will* lose and who *will* gain and who *will* shoulder the burden—these outcomes must be determined not through scientific inquiry but through complex political process.

The reality, then, is that research relevant to affirmative action must operate without the idealized model's framework of givens, a fact that has telling implications for the actual and potential contributions of social science to this policy domain. Theory, method, and ability to communicate with nonscientists can be examined, and examples will be found of internal, scientific, and professional strengths and weaknesses. But account must also be taken of the societal context of dissensus on basic goals and definitions and of self-interested political struggle. This context places severe external constraints on the scientific activity of social scientists, limiting access to data and funding. Further, it virtually guarantees that individual philosophy and political inclination will mix with technical judgment to influence discretionary decisions, a phenomenon that is often unavoidable and is not necessarily problematic when underlying premises are made explicit, but that carries serious dangers when unacknowledged ideological stance masquerades as technical requirement. Finally, this context means that there are areas in which the potentially useful role for social science lies not in presenting policymakers with answers, but in presenting them with questions.

Three research tasks pertinent to affirmative action invite social science attention: (1) Estimating the extent of existing race and sex inequities; (2) identifying institutional mechanisms that perpetuate inequity and proposing remedial action; (3) monitoring the implementation of affirmative action efforts and evaluating their impact.

Each of these research areas presents a unique configuration of challenges and a unique record of successes and failures, but for all three areas the scientific problems ubiquitous to social science research are compounded by obstacles deriving from the sociopolitical conflict that surrounds affirmative action. This chapter will focus on the first of the three research domains, estimation of race and sex inequity, concluding with brief comments on the other two research domains.

ASSESSING RACE AND
SEX INEQUITY

Documentation of race and sex inequity provides the primary rationale for equal opportunity and affirmative action programs, and an extensive research literature reports assessments of inequity in employment, education, health care, and other social benefits, sometimes focusing on local conditions, sometimes on national patterns. Testimony to the contribution of this research lies in the fact that virtually every policy statement or court decision prescribing affirmative action uses social science evidence on inequity as its foundation. However, these assessments of inequity are fraught with thorny problems.

If inequality per se were the issue, the research tasks would be straightforward and the findings unambiguous. But some factors contributing to sex and race inequalities are nearly always judged to represent neither direct nor indirect discrimination, and controls are introduced to remove the effects of these "legitimate" sources of group differences before making the crucial race and sex comparisons. It is with the introduction of these controls that the problems are generated: Imprecision or inaccuracies in interpretation of complex evidential patterns are not likely to be detected by nonprofessional audiences; the needs for extensive data and sophisticated analysis give rise to other difficulties; and the most telling complexities arise with the discretionary selection of control variables, the crucial issues here being substantive rather than technical. Investigations of employment discrimination provide examples of each kind of problem.

Imprecise or inaccurate portrayal of findings The mystique surrounding statistics makes the typical reader highly vulnerable to ambiguous or misleading claims in reports of the complex analyses that control for "irrelevancies" before making race or sex comparisons. Christopher Jencks's (1983a) review article points out two such problems in Thomas Sowell's *Markets and Minorities* (1981). First, Sowell's (p. 13) discussion invites overestimation of the extent to which differing geographical distributions of racial groups account for race differences in income. Also, in the purportedly equal payoff of education for blacks and whites, Sowell (p. 23) finds evidence that black-white income differentials can be accounted for by education. A well-trained social scientist would immediately respond that income inequality not attributable to education can and does exist in the presence of equal black-white rates of income returns to education. (The absence of a race by education interaction effect on income does not imply there is no race main effect.) But the intricacy of race and sex inequity assessments leaves the nontechnical reader ill-equipped to exercise independent, critical corrective judgments, and an open door exists for intentional or unintentional miscommunication of evidence.

Data acquisition Precise partitioning of occupational achievement and income disparities into "legitimate" and "unjust" (discrimination-produced) segments depends upon control variables representing "legitimate" influences on labor market outcomes. And it is virtually never possible to obtain all the indicators needed for a thoroughly satisfactory analysis.

For example, Reynolds Farley's (1979) meticulous investigations of race and sex inequities gain considerable credibility from their dependence on U.S. Census Bureau Data, but the Census data do not include all the indicators necessary for thorough exploration of the inequity questions. Particularly troublesome is the fact that years since completion of schooling is the best available indicator for work experience, a factor that most analysts consider an essential control in sex comparisons of occupational and economic outcomes. Disproportionate discontinuities in women's labor force participation is the major issue here, and a work experience measure that does not register interruptions simply misses the point.

Another illustration is offered by the University of Michigan's Panel Study on Income Dynamics (Duncan & Morgan, 1978). The data collected for this effort are unusually sophisticated, containing, among other things, direct measures of work experience, absenteeism, and self-imposed restrictions on job location and work hours. Although these data allow for controls that put most research in the area to shame, even they are marked by deficiencies that thwart attempts to quantify the contribution of factors other than to racial and gender discrimination income gaps. The researchers explain that without information about occupational decisionmaking, there is no way to disentangle voluntarily produced discrepancies in occupational distributions that should be partialled out of inequity estimates from the involuntary discrepancies in occupational distributions that should be counted as an aspect of labor market discrimination. In the absence of such information, these analysts chose simply to omit occupation as a control in their analyses of race and sex income differentials. But the researchers are forced also to admit that without the refinements that the missing occupational decision-making data would provide, their results cannot provide an estimate of labor market discrimination.

If the most careful and intricate inequity research suffers from crucial data deficiencies, typical analyses are all the more acutely handicapped by this kind of problem. (The limitations of inadequate proxy variables and absent indicators are compounded, of course, by the ubiquitous problem of unreliability in the indicators that serve as controls.)

Data analysis Multiple methodologies have been used to estimate discrimination-produced inequity as residual inequality after controlling for the influence of "legitimate" background factors. Despite congruent intent, these strategies have idiosyncracies capable of producing substantially divergent conclusions.

U.S. Civil Rights Commission studies (1978) use a technique employed in the earlier-mentioned research of Reynolds Farley (1979): Within race by sex subgroups, income is regressed on such "legitimate" determinants as education. Then the independent variable means for the white male group are substituted into the minority group regression equation, producing an estimate of what the average white male would earn if his background characteristics paid off for him at the same rate as they pay off for minority group members. The difference between this estimate and the actual mean income for white males is taken as a measure of income discrimination.

Featherman and Hauser (1976) are among the researchers who routinely perform this operation in the other direction, estimating the income gap attributable to discrimination as the difference between the actual mean income for the minority group and the income predicted when independent variable means for the minority group are substituted into the white male regression equation.

Algebra confirms what logic suggests: These two variants of the regression technique produce estimates that predictably differ and potentially diverge dramatically. For simple bivariate regression, the magnitude of the discrepancy between estimates equals the difference between slope coefficients for the minority and white male equations multiplied by the difference between predictor variable means for the two subgroups. For multiple regression, the magnitude of the discrepancy is the sum of such products across the several predictor variables.

Applied to earnings comparisons between black and white male workers, in which slope coefficients and background characteristic means are both typically greater for whites than blacks, the Farley technique predictably yields a larger estimate of discrimination than the Featherman and Hauser method: Farley (1979, Table 3) estimated the cost of being a black rather than white male at $3630 for 1960, $3804 for 1970, and $1838 for 1977; rough calculations using the summary statistics provided by Farley suggest that the alternate Featherman and Hauser regression procedure would yield estimates of $1168 for 1960, $1749 for 1970, and $1271 for 1977. Not only do the estimates differ substantially for all dates (by more than a factor of three for 1960), but the pattern of acute decline in direct discrimination that Farley finds to have occurred between 1970 and 1977 is not revealed in the results of the alternate procedure.

How can the difference between the two techniques be understood in substantive terms? The principle becomes obvious if we focus on the salary comparison between black and white males, simplify things by assuming that education is the sole background factor used as an independent variable in the regression analysis, and visualize a graph on which both the black and white regression lines are represented. The well-documented interaction between race and education in affecting earnings, i.e., the fact that income returns to education are greater for whites than blacks implies that the regression line for whites, which lies above that for blacks, also has a steeper slope. The Featherman and Hauser technique of substituting the black mean into the white regression equation takes as its estimate of discrimination the difference between the two regression lines at the point at which education equals the average for blacks. In effect, it asks what blackness costs those whose level of education equals the average currently attained by blacks. The Farley technique of substituting the white mean into the black regression equation takes as its estimate of discrimination the difference between the two regression lines at the point at which education equals the average for whites. Thus it asks what blackness costs those whose level of education is higher, that is, equal to the average currently attained by whites. The larger estimate yielded by the Farley technique merely spells out one implication of the interaction effect revealed in the differing slope coefficients: Blackness costs the highly educated more than it costs those with lower levels of educational attainment. (By the same token, the acute 1970-1977 decline in direct discrimination revealed by the Farley technique but not the Featherman and Hauser method reiterates the oft-noted fact that recent gains have been greater for the black elite than for the black majority.)

In short, these two variants of the regression technique are by no means comparable; they provide answers to two entirely different questions. Which is the more reasonable question to ask? It seems clear that if the intent is to provide a single estimate of existing discrimination, one should ask what the average black man loses by virtue of his race, not what is lost by the atypical black man who possesses background characteristics of the average white. That is, the Featherman and Hauser technique of substituting minority means into the white regression equation is the appropriate choice. Applied to the entire population of male workers, the Farley estimate may be seen as an answer to the hypothetical question of how much his race would cost the average black man if the black male population were to attain the background characteristics currently possessed by white males (i.e., if all indirect discrimination were to cease) while direct discrimination in income was maintained at its present level. This hypothetical question is not particularly sensible to ask because most analysts assume that

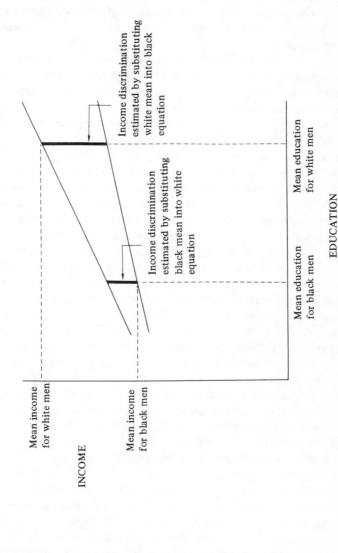

INCOME

Mean income
for white men

Mean income
for black men

Income discrimination
estimated by substituting
white mean into black
equation

Income discrimination
estimated by substituting
black mean into white
equation

Mean education
for black men

Mean education
for white men

EDUCATION

Figure 5.1   Comparison of the Two Regression Substitution Techniques

direct income discrimination will be easier to eradicate than the multiple forms of indirect discrimination that race differences in background characteristics reflect. On the other hand, the Farley estimates do focus attention on a very important subgroup: Outcomes reaped by those relatively privileged black men whose background characteristics resemble those of the average white do signal the payoff of effort and therefore have the potential to encourage or discourage other blacks from striving for similar attainment.

Thus there is value in the answers provided by each technique. The problem is that a given method is typically represented as *the* vehicle for estimating the cost of minority status, without acknowledgment of its peculiarities or explanation of its distinctiveness. Although Featherman and Hauser do offer a footnote (1976, Note 6) asserting that their method provides more conservative estimates than Farley's, they make only a start at explaining the divergence.

Still another approach to the task of estimating direct income discrimination uses regression in a different manner than has been described thus far. Instead of performing subgroup regression analyses and using the regression equation from one analysis together with independent variable means from the other, some researchers have simply computed a single regression equation for the entire population of scores, naming race and/or sex among the independent variables. The effect magnitude for race (sex) is then estimated by the respective unstandardized (partial) slope coefficient. Conventional description of the output from such analyses makes the strategy sound appropriate: "After controlling for education (and whatever else), the effect of race (sex) is___." However, the earlier discussion of regression techniques hints at some of the problems with the single regression strategy. For one thing, the single regression technique is insensitive to potentially relevant interactions between race (sex) and other independent variables; i.e., it glosses over differences in the slope coefficients of different subpopulations. For another thing, this technique is sensitive to within-subgroup background characteristic variability and to the relative sizes of the subgroups represented in the analysis, factors that in many substantive contexts should be counted as irrelevancies. For example, let us return to the simple comparison of black and white male worker incomes that takes education as the sole background control variable. Holding constant the slope coefficients and the mean levels of education and income for each subpopulation, we can alter the proportions of blacks and whites represented in the study or the variability of education within subpopulations and create acute variation in the estimates of direct race discrimination, even producing estimates that lie outside the range defined by the two subgroup regression substitution techniques. It would seem that the popular single regression technique is a trustworthy source of estimates on the cost of minority status only under certain, highly restrictive conditions.

In summary, the data analytic strategies used to produce policy-relevant estimates of existing discrimination have not been subjected to sufficient scrutiny. Many of the conclusions derived from this research are misleading. And even where appropriate analysis has been performed, the choice of analytic strategy has not been justified in terms that would guide future researchers to similarly appropriate decisions.

Selection of "control" variables The difficulties discussed above are all scientific or professional problems in one sense or another, and their solution, even if it must be envisioned rather than achieved, is defined by scientific norms. In contrast, the choice of control variables, the pivot on which the potential value of the whole research endeavor rests, raises issues that are inevitably intertwined with the unresolved political debate surrounding affirmative action and thus defy scientific solution.

Although operationalization of control variables is a common focus of discussion in published research reports, the choice of variables itself is rarely taken to require extensive justification. Reports often assure readers that prior research has been combed to aid in constructing an inclusive list; thus, convention serves as one implicit criterion for selecting controls. Methodology sections of research reports often give the impression that empirical evidence of correlation with the outcome measure has been taken as sufficient grounds for inclusion as a control. The typical operating assumption seems to be that there is some finite list of objectively appropriate control variables, and the researcher's task is simply to name them all and get them into the analysis. The most commonly expressed worry of researchers and charge by critics is that relevant variables have been omitted, predictably inflating the estimate of discrimination (which is, after all, merely a residual).

Rarely is sufficient recognition given to the fact that inclusion of a particular control variable in an analysis designed to estimate discrimination is not a technical matter: It is a policy statement about what portion of inequality in outcomes a given social institution ought *not* be held responsible to remedy. When the implicit policy statements are made explicit, it becomes evident that taken-for-granted methodological decisions have slurred over important substantive issues on which social dissensus exists.

For example, in *Affirmative Discrimination* (1975), Nathan Glazer documents his argument that labor market discrimination was rapidly disappearing even before affirmative action by citing results of a Hall and Kasten (1973) study that compared the jobs of young black and white workers after controlling for the relative "endowment" of the two. And Glazer matter-of-factly reports that father's occupation was one of the endowment measures used as a control in the earlier research. Controlling for father's occupation before making race comparisons in occupational attainment is a bit like granting the legitimacy of grandfather clauses in voting requirements: It implies that conditioning employment outcomes on father's occupation should be considered legitimate, not a problem to be remedied. Exposed to open debate, this presumption would certainly evoke objections by many, presumably by Glazer himself, given that analyst's staunch commitment to meritocratic ideals. But perfunctory mention of father's occupation as an item in a list of control variables does not invite such public debate.

If father's occupation is a control rarely included in analyses of labor market discrimination and is predictably controversial when noted, education is a standard inclusion questioned by few. However, substantive questions could be raised here as well. Recent sociological literature notes evidence that as a group American workers show educational attainment that outstrips the requirements of the jobs they actually perform (Clogg & Shockey, in press; Staines & Quinn, 1979). And in its famous *Griggs* v. *Duke Power Co.* decision, the U.S. Supreme Court decreed that employers act unconstitutionally when they use hiring and promotion criteria that have a negative impact on protected classes and are not demonstrably related to job performance. Extension of the Griggs logic suggests that education should be considered a "legitimate" determinant of labor market outcomes only to the extent that advances in education actually pay off in improved job performance. By implication, an overcorrection is performed and objectionable employment practices are systematically underestimated when education is used as a control.

Turning to another arena, a standard explanation for sex inequality in college faculty salaries is "market influences" (that is, generally higher salaries in certain disciplines, typically those with the greatest predominance of men). Many attempts to estimate sex inequity include controls for market influences, typically taken as legitimate determinants of salary. However, the clustering of women in lower-paying disciplines is no accident and can itself be considered an aspect of labor market sexism. In part this clustering may reflect the disadvantages with which women have entered the competition for the more desirable (higher paying) jobs. Beyond this, direct sex bias in wage structures, the focus of comparable worth arguments, is difficult to deny in the face of evidence such as Touhey's (1974) demonstration that manipulation of purported sex ratios affected subjects' ratings of occupational prestige. In short, the correlation between the average salary for a discipline and the sex ratio of its members can be viewed as yet another form of labor market discrimination, in which case controlling for "market influences" means underestimating salary inequity.

The examples presented above raise questions about the extent to which economic inequities faced by the previous generation, or inequities in current educational practice or traditional wage structure, should absolve employers of responsibility to redress existing economic inequalities. Additional complications arise when economic institutions are implicated in spiraling processes of reciprocal effects.

For example, Glazer (1975, p. 41) is one of the analysts who has documented a claim of minimal labor market discrimination by pointing to the near income parity of under-35 black and white husband-wife families. At first glance, it may seem reasonable to control for family structure before using a race comparison of family income to assess employment discrimination. It may make sense; that is, *until* we consider the possibility that family structure is an effect as well as a cause of family income. Lee Rainwater (1970) and others have demonstrated the profoundly disruptive effects that economic hardship has on marriage. By implication, income discrimination against blacks predictably removes its victims from the ranks of the married. Thus "controlling" for family structure by limiting samples to husband-wife families siphons off part of the income discrimination evidence that Glazer and others purport to estimate.

Christopher Jencks (1983a) has pointed to another instance in which reciprocal causal dynamics are probable. In his review of Thomas Sowell's (1981a, 1981b) recent books, Jencks suggests that real but slight attitudinally derived race differences in job performance may heighten critical appraisals by supervisors, who then overrespond and create wider attitudinal differences, and so it goes until small race differences become large ones.

Another kind of spiraling process was discussed in the Michigan Income Dynamics Study report (Duncan & Morgan, 1978), this one so diffuse that empirical dissection would be difficult even with longitudinal data. The domestic division of labor between the sexes is often used to explain differential occupational success as something other than discrimination-produced inequity. Indeed, the common decision to make the husband primary breadwinner and the wife primary homemaker does have a predictable impact on occupational outcomes. For many couples, however, this decision may be less a voluntary statement of preferences than a rational response to different job market opportunities for men and women. To the extent that traditional domestic patterns are perpetuated by labor market discrimination, biased underestimates of discrimination are produced by analyses that include indicators of domestic role as controls.

Reciprocal causal processes like those hypothesized here are virtually impossible to investigate without the kind of longitudinal data sets that are all too rarely available, and they present thorny technical challenges even when data deficiencies are not the problem. When such reciprocal causation exists, as when intergenerational transmission of disadvantage may exist or multiple institutional spheres are complicit in interlocking patterns of discrimination, we will probably never have an empirical basis on which to apportion responsibility for the creation of inequalities. However, affirmative action prescriptions are, after all, based on an acknowledgement of intricately intertwined causal processes. They represent an attempt to address race and sex inequalities even when we can't satisfactorily dissect their sources. Thorough understanding of the complicated causal mechanisms of inequality will remain a scientific goal. But the primary policy relevance of inequality research is in considerations about how much remedial effort should take place in a given institutional area. Are controls for family structure to be introduced before making race comparisons in family income? Are worker attitudes to be controlled when racial groups are compared on occupational success? Are controls for continuity of labor force experience to be used when making sex comparisons in labor market outcomes? All such decisions imply nonscientific judgments about who should be responsible for cleaning up the collaboratively produced and reciprocally spiraling mess.

Thus researchers cannot provide scientific answers to questions about the treatment of ambiguous or reciprocal causal processes in inequality research. What they can do is to explicitly raise such questions. Doing so performs two kinds of service. First, it invites critical examination of research that must, in the absence of societal consensus or well-defined policy, rest on discretionary judgments that probably reflect the researchers' ideological preferences. And more importantly, it calls attention to the need for clearer social policy decisions about the apportionment of responsibility for the remedy of race and sex inequity. The problem in existing social science research is that too often the unresolved substantive questions are buried in discussions of technical requirements, and discretionary judgments are represented as scientific imperative.

OTHER AFFIRMATIVE ACTION
RESEARCH DOMAINS

Affirmative action research of other kinds presents technical problems at least as challenging as those faced in inequity estimation research,
and the record of achievement is similarly mixed, if less extensive.
Here again, internal scientific problems are not the whole story: The
sociopolitical context provides framework and sets limits on the scientific enterprise. These other research domains will not be considered
in detail, but a few suggestive comments can be made.

*Identifying institutional discrimination mechanisms and developing
remedies* Research that focuses on the mechanisms of institutional
discrimination is crucial, carrying the potential both to demonstrate
the general need for affirmative action and to suggest specific remedies.
Among the vast array of institutional practices that may contribute
to inequities, some have been fruitfully addressed. For example, research
has amply documented the importance of informal communication
networks in employment acquisition (see Benokraitis & Feagin, 1978,
p. 77), and expanded announcement of position openings has become
one of the most widespread affirmative action practices. The concern
about bias in standardized tests used for admission to educational
institutions has provoked revision of test content and, in some quarters,
more sensitive use of test scores as admission criteria.

Employment selection practices have been the focus of an interesting
chapter in the history of social science involvement with affirmative
action policy. Relatively early, employment testing was identified by
federal agencies as a mechanism of indirect discrimination, perhaps
because these practices are circumscribed and concrete enough to be
amenable to external intervention. Federal agencies have made extensive use of social science consultants on testing throughout the last
two decades, and the standing (1978) federal guidelines on employment
selection practices depend heavily on American Psychological Association testing standards statements.

The outcome of this collaboration has not been entirely satisfactory.
After years of conflict among the several federal agencies involved,
the mere existence of the 1978 Uniform Policy (Federal Register, Vol.
43, #166, August 25, 1978) is something of a triumph. But the guidelines
that emerged are technical enough to be awesome to many of the
employers required to use them while failing to offer detailed instruction
on the test validation procedure that should be taken as crucial—
analysis of subgroup data to assess test fairness. In effect, more specific
guidelines are being hammered out in the courts. The most encouraging

result of all this is that some employers are, with the assistance of social science consultants, developing more refined and less biased employment selection strategies. But this positive sign is balanced by reports that many employers are simply being driven away from attempts at systematic, objective selection procedures, instead relying on informal decision-making practices that are at least as open to race and sex bias but are harder to monitor.

Multiple sources of these difficulties can be identified. Some are clearly scientific problems, e.g., the chronic confusion in social science discussions of validity. Incomplete communication between social scientists and policymakers appears also to have been a contributing factor. (For example, the 1978 guidelines' discussion of construct validity suggests that this framework was lifted part-and-parcel from its social science sources, without appropriate adaptation to the specific context of employment selection. Also, in their zealousness to respond to policy interest in this question, psychometricians have produced so many conflicting definitions of test fairness that the guidelines' silence on assessment procedures is reasonably interpreted as paralysis in the face of the confusion.) But these problems are compounded by others that lie outside the control of social science researchers, e.g., micropolitical squabbles among federal agencies.

With respect to other mechanisms of institutional discrimination, the record of social science involvement is briefer. Access to relevant information is a major problem. As noted by Kelman (1972) and others, the powerful are so rarely studied because they have the resources to protect themselves from scrutiny. Few institutional authorities are likely to voluntarily provide the information necessary to examine their standard operating procedures for evidence of adverse impact. And in the present political climate, government-mandated investigations will predictably become less rather than more rigorous: Recent Equal Employment Opportunity Commission budget cuts were felt most dramatically in the units assigned to consider "systemic" discrimination, the mechanisms of indirect discrimination (Bureau of National Affairs, June 3, 1982). Here, then, is another telling limit set by the sociopolitical context.

Monitoring and evaluating affirmative action programs Monitoring the details of affirmative action implementation is a research task necessarily linked to that of assessing program impact. For one thing, impact studies must incorporate some means of ascertaining that affirmative action efforts exist in practice as well as on paper; i.e., there must be manipulation checks. Beyond this, however, as is the case with school desegregation and other social intervention efforts, questions about impact must certainly be asked and answered not in the global terms favored by polemicists, but in terms of specifics. It is undoubtedly the case that when affirmative action successes exist, they are occasions in which a *particular* program has promoted *certain* outcomes for *specified* groups of people. Implementation and evaluation research must, then, be directed to distinguishing those occasions from others.

Performing this task requires difficult-to-obtain data. Certainly standard institutional reports to federal monitoring agencies are not adequate information sources on affirmative action implementation efforts. Anecdotes about academic department heads sabotaging affirmative action efforts by offering women and minorities positions with unacceptably low salaries hint at the complexity of learning the inside stories of institutional life.

Similarly, outcome statistics provided in legally mandated institutional reports are far from adequate grist for the research mill because these can so easily be tailored to suit institutional purposes (e.g., by inflating minority counts with part-time people, dual appointments, foreigners, and so on). On top of the quality control issue, there exists the need to look behind routinely available outcome measures. The perils of taking a single, obvious outcome measure as the whole answer are underlined by Lazear's (1979) finding that many employers have financed increases in entry-level wages for minority hirees by cutting back on-the-job training programs that would have promoted long-range wage equity.

In short, research on implementation and impact of affirmative action programs would, even in a more ideal situation, be faced with the complex methodological problems of dealing with aggregate, longitudinal data—problems that pervade evaluation research. But the political conflict surrounding this particular social program means that researchers must fight an uphill battle even to define their research questions in the specific terms that can actually aid policy rather than the global terms of public debate, and then they must struggle to acquire intricate data in the face of reticent institutional authorities and waning financial and staff support from the federal government.

CONCLUSIONS

In summary, the challenges facing affirmative action research are formidable. Some technical and professional difficulties have been identified—problems of data acquisition, data analysis, accurate portrayal of findings, and so on. But problems of research in this area are magnified by the political conflict that surrounds questions of major resource redistribution.

Existing scientific difficulties are amenable to amelioration through internal, professional efforts to develop data bases, refine methodologies, and clarify conceptual formulations. And, as in other areas of policy-relevant research, application of their work will become more likely as social scientists develop micropolitical skills enabling them to communicate effectively with policymakers, negotiate with competing governmental agencies, and so on. But also crucial will be social scientists' sensitivity to the ways in which macropolitical processes condition their participation in the development of affirmative action policy.

NOTE

1. The regression substitution problem described above has a parallel in the non-parametric research literature. An approach to decomposing population differences into one segment accounted for by control variables and a second, residual segment was developed by Kitagawa (1955) and has been used to estimate the cost of minority status by Seigel (1965), Johnson and Sell (1976), and Sell and Johnson (1978). Applicable to tabular data, this strategy is set apart from regression techniques by the advantage of automatically accommodating nonlinear relationships and by the disadvantage of requiring the transformation of continuous data into cruder, categorical form.

The Kitagawa decomposition technique also has two variants, quite analogous to the regression alternatives discussed above. The researcher must choose to assume that both populations have the background characteristic distributions actually manifested by one population or the other. And here too the estimates produced by the two alternate choices will differ by a known quantity. (Estimates will differ by the quantity

$$\left(\sum_i \sum_j [t_{ij} - T_{ij}] \left[\frac{n_{ij}}{n_{..}} - \frac{N_{ij}}{n_{..}} \right] \right)$$

where t_{ij} = rate for persons in the ith category of I and the jth category of J in population p; T_{ij} = rate for persons in the ith category of I and the jth category of J in population P; N_{ij} = number of persons in both the ith category of I and the jth category of J in population P; and n.. and N.. = total number of persons in populations p and P, respectively.) Again, the real problem is that the difference between the two variants has been inadequately explicated. Kitagawa understood and described the situation in technical terms. However, apparently failing to realize that a particular substantive context might provide the basis for an a priori decision between alternate analytic strategies, she advised researchers either to present both estimates as a range or to adjust calculations in a way that splits the difference. Applications of this technique to the problem of quantifying direct income discrimination faced by minorities (Siegel, 1965; Johnson & Sell, 1976; Sell & Johnson, 1978) have used the variant of the Kitagawa technique that seems most appropriate for their particular substantive purpose (the analogue of the Featherman and Hauser regression choice), but without explicit acknowledgment (and perhaps without realization) of the principle that should have guided their statistical decision. Thus these studies provide useful results, but not the guidelines that would make their results fully interpretable or encourage appropriate application of the Kitagawa technique to other substantive problems.

REFERENCES

Benokraitis, N. V., & Feagin, J. R. (1978). *Affirmative action and equal opportunity: Action, inaction, reaction.* Boulder, CO: Westview Press.

Clogg, C. C., & Shockey J. W. (in press). Mismatch between occupation and schooling: A prevalence measure, recent trends, and demographic analysis. *Demography, 21,* 235-257.

Duncan, G. J., & Morgan, J. N. (Eds.), (1978). *Five thousand American families: Patterns of economic progress* (Vol. VI). Ann Arbor, MI: Institute for Social Research.

Farley, R. (1979). *Racial progress in the last two decades: What can we determine about who benefitted and why?* Paper presented at the meetings of the American Sociological Association.

Feagin, J. R., & Feagin, C. B. (1978). *Discrimination American style: Institutional racism and sexism.* Englewood Cliffs, NJ: Prentice-Hall.

Featherman, D. L., & Hauser, R. M. (1976). Changes in the socioeconomic stratification of the races, 1962-1973. *American Journal of Sociology, 82,* 621-651.

Glazer, H. (1975). *Affirmative discrimination.* New York: Basic Books.

Hall, R. E., & Kasten, R. A. (1973). The relative occupational success of blacks and whites. *Brookings Papers on Economic Activity, 3,* 785.

Jencks, C. (1983a, March 3). Discrimination and Thomas Sowell. *The New York Review.*

Jencks, C. (1983b, March 17). Special treatment for blacks? *The New York Review.*

Johnson, M. P., & Sell, R. R. (1976). The cost of being Black: A 1970 update. *American Journal of Sociology, 82,* 183-190.

Kelman, H. C. (1972). The rights of the subject in social research: An analysis in terms of relative power and legitimacy. *American Psychologist, 27,* 989-1016.

Kitagawa, E. M. (1955). Components of a difference between two rates. *American Statistical Association Journal, 50,* 1168-1194.

Lazear, E. (1979). The narrowing of black-white wage differentials is illusory. *The American Economic Review, 69,* 553-564.

Pettigrew, T. F. (Ed.). (1975). *Racial discrimination in the United States.* New York: Harper & Row.

Rainwater, L. (1970). Poverty in the United States. In D. P. Moynihan (Ed.), *Toward a national urban policy* (pp. 195-205). New York: Basic Books.

Sell, R. R., & Johnson, M. P. (1978). Income and occupational differences between men and women in the United States. *Sociology and Social Research, 62,* 1-20.

Siegel, P. M. (1965). On the cost of being a Negro. *Sociological Inquiry, 35,* 41-57.

Sowell, T. (1981a). *Ethnic America.* New York: Basic Books.

Sowell, T. (1981b). *Markets and minorities.* New York: Basic Books.

Staines, G. L., & Quinn, R. P. (1979). American workers evaluate the quality of their jobs. *Monthly Labor Review, 10,* 3-12.

Touhey, J. C. (1974). Effects of additional women professionals on ratings of occupation prestige and desirability. *Journal of Personality and Social Psychology, 29,* 86-89.

U.S. Commission on Civil Rights (1978). *Social indicators of equality for minorities and women.* Washington, DC: Commission on Civil Rights.

6

The Role of the Social Sciences in the Comparable Worth Movement

PAMELA STONE CAIN

In 1979, Eleanor Holmes Norton, Commissioner of the Equal Employment Opportunity Commission under President Carter, predicted that comparable worth would be the equal employment issue of the 1980s (Norton, 1979). Less than halfway into the decade, her forecast is already proving correct. Comparable worth is a strategy to achieve sex equity in pay based on the value of the work performed in a job rather than on market forces. Largely unknown in the 1970s, comparable worth has gained rapid acceptance among labor unions and women's organizations. They have achieved major comparable worth victories using a variety of tactics including collective bargaining, strikes, and litigation. The social sciences have played a critical role in these efforts. Among other contributions, social scientists were instrumental in the development of a technique known as job evaluation that provides the conceptual underpinning of the theory of comparable worth as well as the methodology to implement it. Nonetheless, the role of the social sciences has often been obscured, even limited, by the highly charged, adversarial nature of the comparable worth debate.

In this chapter, I first review the history of comparable worth as a social movement, highlighting some of the major legislative and judicial actions that have shaped its progress. I then describe and critique the use of job evaluation techniques to assess the worth of jobs. Against this background, I analyze the role the social sciences have played in the comparable worth movement, their potential future contribution, and possible limits on their role. I argue that the adversarial nature of the comparable worth debate and the constituencies involved widen the gulf that typically exists between the academic social science establishment and applied practitioners. This inhibits the exchange of research and ideas that is necessary if the scientific community is to make its greatest contribution.

COMPARABLE WORTH AS A SOCIAL MOVEMENT: A BRIEF HISTORY

Sex discrimination in employment was first prohibited in 1963 with the passage of the Equal Pay Act. In 1964, Congress reiterated its commitment to sex equity in the workplace by passing Title VII of the Civil Rights Act. After two decades of enforcement under the auspices of the Equal Employment Opportunity Commission (EEOC), progress toward sex equity in employment has been limited. In 1983, women earned 62 cents for every dollar earned by men (Pear, 1983). Further, although women made well-publicized inroads into such formerly all-male professions as medicine and law, their opportunities in the labor market are circumscribed due to the existence of pervasive job segregation by sex.

Job segregation is a long-standing feature of the workplace whereby men and women select or are assigned to jobs on the basis of gender (e.g., Hartmann, 1976; Blau & Hendricks, 1979).[1] An aspect of this type of segregation is that jobs become sex-typed; i.e., closely identified with the sex of the workers performing them. Certain jobs are seen as appropriate for men, others for women. Segregation indices (denoting the proportion of workers of either sex who would have to change jobs for men and women to achieve similar occupational distributions) show only a slight decrease during the 1970s (Beller, 1982).

During this period, court cases also revealed the shortcomings of existing legislation and prevailing judicial interpretation in significantly affecting job segregation or the wage gap. The Equal Pay Act applied only to situations in which men and women performed equal or the same jobs. Title VII was interpreted similarly, although an amendment to it (known as the Bennett Amendment) was ambiguous in this regard. The existence of extensive job segregation by sex meant that for most women—working in low-paying, female-dominated jobs—there were either no male co-workers or no nearly identical, male-dominated jobs that would enable them to satisfy the equal work standard in a Title VII case.[2]

Thus, a new type of case appeared that capitalized on the ambiguity surrounding the Bennett Amendment to Title VII. This amendment, it was argued, broadened the scope of Title VII beyond that of the Equal Pay Act to cover cases in which jobs were comparable but not equal. These "comparable worth" cases also capitalized on a procedure known as job evaluation that is used by employers to establish salary structures. Job evaluation, described in greater detail in the next section, enables comparisons between otherwise dissimilar jobs and the creation of a hierarchy of jobs based on their estimated worth. Such cases advanced a theory of wage-setting based on a job's value or worth to an employer (as indicated by job evaluation) rather than on the interplay of labor supply and demand in the market, and sought to redress perceived inequities in pay between dissimilar, sex-segregated jobs. Interestingly, the comparable worth approach was first applied during World War II by the National War Labor Board in the context of settling sex discrimination cases in key wartime industries (Gitt & Gelb, 1977; Gasaway, 1981).

A common outcome of job evaluation is that jobs performed by women receive high "worth" scores, placing them relatively high in the hierarchy of jobs and, in turn, of wages. Often these plans predict higher wages for women's jobs than the wages currently being paid by the firm or by other firms in the external labor market. To avoid an increased wage bill and disruption of the existing wage structure, employers often fail to adjust the pay for women's jobs to reflect their worth as measured by the job evaluation. In failing to do so, plaintiffs held that employers merely reproduced and perpetuated the sex discrmination that occurred in the labor market at large.

Two cases that illustrate well the issues involved in comparable worth are *Lemons* v. *City and County of Denver* (620 F. 2d. 228, 10th Cir., 1980) and *Christensen* v. *State of Iowa* (563 F. 2d. 353, 8th Cir., 1977). In *Lemons,* plaintiffs were nurses who contended that they were underpaid relative to comparably evaluated male maintenance workers. *Christensen* involved a series of female-dominated clerical jobs such as library assistants and account clerks that was evaluated comparably to a male-dominated series including such titles as carpet layer and tree trimmer. Despite job evaluation evidence, both cases were rejected under Title VII; *Lemons* for failing to meet the equal work standard, and *Christensen* for failing to demonstrate a prima facie case of discrimination.

At about the time that these cases were gaining prominence, the EEOC commissioned the National Academy of Sciences (NAS) to study the potential of existing job evaluation procedures for accurate assessment of the worth of jobs. The NAS study resulted in two reports. The first (Treiman, 1979) critiqued job evaluation methodology and noted the lack of research available about these procedures. The second (Treiman & Hartman, 1981) endorsed the use of job evaluation under some circumstances to assess the comparable worth of jobs and reduce wage discrimination. In contrast, an industry-sponsored consortium of representatives of business, management consulting firms, and industrial and organizational psychologists argued against the use of job evaluation plans to assess the worth of jobs and concluded that "there is simply no known technique by which job 'worth' in any intrinsic sense can be measured" (Livernash, 1980, p. 3).

Meanwhile, progress on comparable worth in the courts continued to be blocked by a narrow interpretation of the Bennett Amendment. This obstacle was removed in June, 1981, with the Supreme Court's ruling in the *County of Washington* v. *Gunther* that the Bennett Amendment did "not restrict Title VII's prohibition of sex-based wage discrimination to claims for equal pay for 'equal work' " (U.S. Supreme Court, 1981, p. 1), thus, in effect, broadening the title's scope to cover cases of comparable but not equal jobs.

At about this same time, the American Federation of State, County, and Municipal Employees (AFSCME), which represents thousands of public-sector employees and has a large female membership, made comparable worth an organizing and bargaining theme. It won the first major comparable worth settlement by means of a strike by city employees in San Jose, California, in 1981. This action, based on the results of a half-million dollar study commissioned by the city, resulted in an upgrading of pay for various female-dominated clerical positions (Bunzel, 1982).

To date, the most sweeping comparable worth victory was won in a return to the judicial arena in a case brought by AFSCME against the State of Washington. In September, 1983, the state was found to be in violation of Title VII for continuing to pay various female-dominated jobs less than comparable jobs held predominantly by men. The comparability of these jobs had been brought to the State's attention in 1974 by a job evaluation study that it had commissioned and subsequently ignored (Willis & Associates, 1974, 1976).

The Washington State case is significant for being the first since *Gunther* to implicitly uphold the validity of a comparable worth approach. Although the court did not make its own judgment about the relative worth of the state's jobs, it acknowledged as binding the state's own valuation of them. Washington State has indicated that it will appeal the decision. This appeal will be the first direct test of the legal viability of the comparable worth theory.

Ironically, the victory in Washington State could slow the momentum the comparable worth movement has achieved. Job evaluation plans have provided the basis for legal action, new bargaining demands, and work stoppages by unions. As a result, lawyers who represent employers may well advise their clients not to institute or even to do away with such plans. A recent *New York Times* article quotes one lawyer as telling clients that they "shouldn't start a job evaluation study if they're not going to have the money to carry through on remedying any undervaluation [of women's jobs] that they find. Once you have the study, it can be used against you to make a much stronger legal case of sex discrimination" (Lewin, 1984).

JOB EVALUATION
DESCRIPTION AND CRITIQUE

Background

The strategy of comparable worth and the methodology of job evaluation are closely intertwined. Helen Remick, a sociologist who is one of the foremost proponents of comparable worth, goes so far as to define the approach in terms of one particular type of job evaluation. Comparable worth, she writes, is the "application of a single bias-free point factor evaluation system within a given establishment, across job families, both to rank-order jobs and to set salaries" (Remick, 1981, p. 377). Although there are several types of job evaluation systems, only one type—the point factor method cited by Remick—has been used in comparable worth claims. For this reason, the discussion that follows is limited to a consideration of this particular method, which is also the most widely used (Treiman & Hartmann, 1981). Different job evaluation systems share many of the same procedures and have many of the same shortcomings, albeit to different degrees. For a description of other types of job evaluation, see, for example, Livernash (1980) and Treiman (1979).

How Job Evaluation Works

Job evaluation is a "formal procedure for hierarchically ordering a set of jobs or positions with respect to their value or worth, usually for the purpose of setting pay rates" (Treiman, 1979, p. 1). Jobs, not the workers performing them, are the units of analysis. Job evaluation usually entails three steps.[3]

1. Job analysis This is a procedure used to determine the basic functions, responsibilities, and requirements of different jobs. Typically, job analysis is carried out by the human resource division of a corporation or public-sector organization, or by outside consultants. Information about jobs is solicited from interviews with, or observation of, workers, supervisors, or both. Written descriptions are usually generated using a standardized form or questionnaire specially designed for this purpose. In some applications, teams of workers and management are assembled to write or review job descriptions.

The goal of job analysis is to arrive at a description that fully and objectively conveys the job's work content, skills, and organizational importance. In most instances, this is accomplished by describing jobs in terms of the individual tasks that constitute them. Also noted in the description are the training and experience required to perform the job at an average level of competence, lines of reporting, areas of responsibility, types of equipment and materials used, and special circumstances, e.g., hazardous working conditions or licensing requirements.

In some firms or organizations, job analysis is an ongoing process, with periodic updating, the results of which are used for a variety of purposes including the development of career ladders and training programs as well as compensation. In other instances, job analysis is undertaken specifically for pay setting.

2. Job rating In order to determine the value of jobs, a set of rating factors is developed that is thought to reflect legitimate bases of compensation. In private firms, these factors embody management's priorities and correspond to the company's reward system and organizational climate. Companies may develop their own unique set of factors or, as is done more commonly, choose a commercial system whose factors are most consistent with their own priorities. Typically, the "compensable" factors represent the skill, effort, responsibility, and working conditions of jobs. For each factor a scale is devised. Each job description produced as part of the job analysis is rated on each factor by supervisors, human resource personnel, or outside consultants. Scores on the individual factor ratings are totaled to arrive at a job worth score. In some cases, factor ratings are also approved by job incumbents or by worker-management teams.

3. Pay setting These factors ratings are then used to determine wages. Wage data are taken either from the firm's existing pay scheme or from wage surveys conducted for equivalent jobs in the relevant labor market. These data are used to assign weights to each of the factors. In some applications, factor weights are assigned judgmentally to reflect the value the employer places on each of the different factors. More commonly, multiple regression is used. Once a model has been developed, either by regression or judgment, it can be used to assign wages to new jobs, to jobs not included in the original analysis, or to adjust existing job wages to conform more closely to the model. As noted earlier, the predictions of job evaluation models are not viewed as definitive, but rather serve as guides. Companies do not have to adjust their wages to those predicted by the model, although the Washington State ruling may have important implications for this practice. In instances in which the predicted wage is significantly different from the prevailing wage, the decision to conform more closely to the predicted wage will be based on a number of considerations such as the perceived importance of the job, the size of the labor pool available to fill it, the organization's competitive position in the industry, and the employer's tastes.

Although it is difficult to obtain good estimates, formal job evaluation systems are in place in most large firms and government agencies and cover millions of workers (Treiman & Hartmann, 1981). In the private sector, job evaluation systems are typically management-initiated; in the public sector, they are more likely to be implemented at the workers' behest. Job evaluation is a multimillion-dollar industry, and firms engaged in it regard their systems and the procedures for implementing them to be proprietary knowledge. Private-sector companies also regard their job evaluation systems as proprietary and confidential. As a result, details of their measurement, data collection, and implementation procedures are difficult or impossible to obtain. Dissemination is, in fact, usually prohibited. Information on job evaluation plans is more accessible in the public sector, but it is rarely written up and distributed in a systematic fashion (notable exceptions are Remick, 1980, and Witt & Naherny, 1975).

Criticisms of Job Evaluation

As the history of the comparable worth movement demonstrates, its advocates have made considerable, rapid progress using job evaluation as the basis of their actions. Job evaluation procedures, however, have been widely criticized by academicians, job evaluation practitioners, and women's groups on both sides of the issue (see, for example, Treiman, 1979; Remick, 1978; Schwab, 1980; Treiman & Hartmann, 1981; and Gottfredson, 1983). In a recent review, Schwab (1983) provides an excellent distillation of this literature.[4] Major criticisms have focused on the measurement properties of these systems, especially their reliability, possible sex bias, and choice of criterion variable.

Studies of reliability have focused on the degree to which the ratings assigned to factors are subject to random or systematic errors based on the characteristics of raters or the jobs being rated. Treiman (1979, p. 40) characterized as "not particularly encouraging" the reliability of job evaluation ratings. Total scores based on the pooled assessments of five or more raters (a situation rarely encountered in practice) appear reliable, but the ratings of individual factors often are not. Using very highly trained raters, however, acceptable reliabilities have been obtained for individual factors (see, for example, Cain & Green, 1983; Doverspike, Carlisi, Barrett, & Alexander, 1983).

With regard to systematic error, Schwab cities several studies that suggest that ratings are not affected by whether the rater is a manager, union representative, or worker. Grams and Schwab (1983) found, however, that judgments about jobs were influenced by raters' knowledge of their current salaries.

Women's groups have raised special concerns about potential sources of sex bias in job evaluation procedures. These concerns were given much attention in the NAS reports (Treiman, 1979; Treiman & Hartmann, 1981). Several sources of bias have been suggested.

The first, evaluation bias, can be manifested in many ways (Nieva & Gutek, 1980; McArthur, 1983). One that is often singled out is the choice or operationalization of factors so as to favor tasks or aptitudes associated with male-dominated jobs. For example, effort factors are commonly measured by the amount of weight lifted rather than by mental concentration or task intensity.

Sex bias has also been held to operate in the description and rating steps of job evaluation, although the few studies that have assessed this directly found little evidence of such bias. The sex of the rater does not appear to affect reliability, nor do raters evaluating the same job appear to be influenced by the sex of the worker performing it (Arvey, Passino, & Lounsbury, 1977). The pervasiveness of sex-role stereotypes and sex segregation makes it difficult, however, to interpret the results of these studies. Nieva and Gutek (1980) suggest that sex bias in evaluation may operate in subtle and complex ways, and that it is affected by: (1) The amount of information and clarity of instructions available with which to make judgments; (2) the sex-role incongruency of the situation to which ratings are to be assigned; and (3) the level of qualifications involved.

The weighting of job factors has been cited as a second potential source of sex bias. Systems that assign weights empirically using market wages as the criterion have been subjected to special criticism. These systems are the most commonly used and have been involved in several comparable worth cases. To the extent that market wages embody discriminatory elements, weights based on them will reflect this. The final NAS report (Treiman & Hartmann, 1981) concluded that discrimination did exist in the labor market. To avoid perpetuating it, the report suggested statistical techniques to adjust factor weights to purge them of discrimination. Alternatively, it recommended using another criterion variable that was itself nondiscriminatory.

In a recent article, Schwab and Wichern (1983) attempt to assess the implications for female wages of the two possible sources of bias just discussed: Evaluation and use of discriminatory wages as a criterion variable. They find that systematic evaluation bias does not necessarily disadvantage all female jobs. Use of biased market wages as the criterion variable (that which is to be predicted), however, does have the generally hypothesized negative impact on female wages.

These problems represent serious potential limits to the effective use of job evaluation to assess the comparable worth of jobs and hence, more broadly, to the ability of the social sciences to contribute to the debate surrounding pay equity. Unreliability, to the extent that it is random, will not differentially affect women's jobs, but low reliability can lead to inconsistencies that will undermine a major rationale of job evaluation, that is, to rationalize pay structures. Random unreliability can be fairly easily remedied, fortunately, by using more and/or better-trained raters.

More troublesome and potentially less easily remedied are sources of systematic error. These can result in a "built-in" disadvantage to jobs dominated by women. Even sources that are not directly sex-linked can have an adverse impact on the rating of women's jobs. For example, to the extent that raters are affected by knowledge of a job's salary, women's jobs are likely to be rated lower than men's simply because they are lower paying. Thus, sometimes insidiously, a vicious cycle is set in motion that disadvantages women. Clearly, in the context of comparable worth, systematic sources of bias and unreliability must be identified through research and then eliminated in actual implementation if job evaluation is to be used as an equitable mechanism for closing the pay gap between men's and women's jobs.

Probably the thorniest dilemma facing job evaluation practitioners is the choice of a criterion variable. The use of biased wages as a criterion has been demonstrated to adversely affect women's wages. The continued use of wages that embody discrimination undermines one of the primary goals of comparable worth: To eliminate discrimination based on sex. Efforts to adjust wages statistically to purge them of discrimination are hampered by the difficulty of directly measuring this phenomenon. Additional research on the determinants of wages is needed if this solution is to gain acceptance.

Several researchers have suggested using other criteria in place of wages. In this regard, pooled judgments about the fairness of a given wage have been advocated, most notably by Birnbaum (1983). Job evaluation models would thus seek to predict and reproduce a wage hierarchy based not directly on market wages, but on people's judgments about the relative worth of jobs and the equity of the associated hierarchy.

The idea of an alternative fairness criterion highlights the central role of values in the comparable worth debate. As the NAS report concluded (Treiman & Hartmann, 1981), in the context of pay setting, comparable worth advocates do not invoke an absolute standard of worth, but rather one based on values of fairness and sex equity. The methodology to implement a fairness criterion is still being developed, but even if technical problems were to be resolved, it is unclear that the goals of comparable worth would be achieved using this approach. The greatest potential drawback to a fairness approach is, of course, that insofar as it captures social norms or public sentiments, it may reflect discriminatory prejudices that run counter to comparable worth or any policy that seeks to promote greater equity among disparate groups. Thus, even in the hypotentical world of a perfect social science, sex equity would not be achieved unless and until equity norms prevailed in the larger society.

Conversely, in the real world, with a far from perfect social science, advocates have made some progress toward greater equity between the sexes using flawed methodology. With improved methodology, as has already been discussed, advocates can move even closer to this goal.

A recurring theme in all recent reviews of job evaluation has been the need for current applied practice to incorporate state-of-the-art developments in relevant academic disciplines. In addition to the need for research on such basic measurement issues as validity, reliability, and sex bias, other areas of concern are thus far unexplored. Implementation of job evaluation systems is usually beyond the control of social scientists. Yet anecdotal and trial evidence indicates that serious bias sometimes arises at this point. Research is needed to better elucidate the practices surrounding implementation

THE ROLE OF THE SOCIAL SCIENCES IN THE COMPARABLE WORTH MOVEMENT

As the history of the comparable worth movement illustrates, its rapid progress to date was not a function of breakthroughs in scientific knowledge or even of changes in the law. Its real turning point hinged instead on the judicial interpretation of an obscure amendment to Title VII of the Civil Rights Act. There can be little doubt, however, that the social sciences, in the hands of powerful political actors riding the crest of changing norms about women and work and showing a heightened concern for sex equity, were critical to the success the movement has thus far achieved. By documenting the persistence of inequality in the face of active interventions to overcome it, social science helped to shape public opinion and equity norms. These, in turn, prompted the application of job evaluation in an innovative way to diagnose and remedy sex discrimination using a comparable worth approach. Changing public opinion and norms very likely influenced prevailing legal interpretation too.

Because comparable worth is a politically charged issue, the most visible actors have been lawyers, judges, feminists, politicians, and union officials. In the thick of lobbying, litigation, and negotiation, social scientists have usually functioned quietly behind the scenes as technical experts. Some (e.g., Remick, 1981), however, have forsaken a detached, objective stance to act as scientist-advocates allied with activist organizations on both sides of the comparable worth issue.

Whether acting as advocates or not, social scientists served two critical functions in the comparable worth movement. First, they were instrumental in the diagnosis of the underlying problems that spawned the movement, that is, job segregation and the wage gap, as well as in the identification of specific instances of comparable worth discrimination.

Second, both advocates and foes of comparable worth used social science research to legitimate their positions. Research on the differential labor market experiences of men and women as well as job evaluation results were skillfully invoked in public education and lobbying campaigns and litigation by adherents of comparable worth. In this regard, the tentative endorsement of the approach by the prestigious National Academy of Sciences was widely cited. On the other side of the issue, opponents of comparable worth exploited the controversy surrounding job evaluation methods to discredit it.

One generally acknowledged benefit of the comparable worth movement, even among its detractors, has been the attention it focused on job evaluation. The movement has fostered a long-overdue examination of these methods. After an initial period of review and criticism, the field is attracting increased attention in the academic research community. This revitalization signals greater communication between the academic and applied worlds. It is not without tensions, however, and potential limits. As Gottfredson (1983) points out, the comparable worth movement spans several disciplines with different perspectives and languages. Moreover, business practices often conflict head-on with the professional code of ethics in science. This is most apparent with regard to freedom of information, when the scientist's need for exchange of ideas, explicitness of assumptions, and replication directly counters the business practitioner's need for secrecy and unique competitive positioning.

Historically, the lack of communication between basic and applied researchers in the job evaluation field and the insularity of practitioners in industry resulted in a situation in which job evaluation techniques fell woefully behind contemporary scientific advances. To remedy this, Gottfredson (1983) called on professionally trained psychologists to assist firms in developing improved compensation systems. He also urged that the usual closed practice surrounding these systems be discouraged as inappropriate professional behavior.

He and others have suggested that guidelines be established for the development and implementation of job evaluation systems. If this recommendation were to be adopted, social scientists would undoubtedly take the lead in their formulation, much as they did with testing guidelines (Tenopyr, 1981).

In future litigation, it appears likely that social scientists will be called on as well. The appeal of the Washington State decision will probably involve efforts to discredit job evaluation methods. The appeals process will also move beyond technical questions about job evaluation to larger issues concerning the operation of labor markets and the applicability of a comparable worth approach therein. In answering these questions, social scientists will play a key role. If the comparable worth approach is upheld under appeal, social scientists will continue in their current capacity. Both the Supreme Court in the *Gunther* case and the recent ruling in Washington State indicate that the courts do not want to get directly involved in evaluating jobs and are happy to leave the task to outside experts.

The ability of social scientists to play a fully effective role in these different scenarios will depend on whether or not the cross-fertilization between job evaluation research and practice that is now being established can be maintained. As the comparable worth movement achieves more victories, there will undoubtedly be increased pressures against open communication. If so, social scientists will be called on for more than technical expertise. It will fall on them to develop a set of professional and ethical standards that can meet the demands of real-life application in the highly adversarial context of comparable worth, while at the same time maintaining scientific integrity and credibility. This task, obviously, is not an easy one. The broader ethical and scientific issues that are raised in applied work are still being grappled with. New standards, informed by practice, are still evolving and are not without controversy (see, for example, Cronbach & Associates, 1980).

CONCLUSION

The larger social issues surrounding comparable worth—literally timeless battles between the sexes and between management and labor—mean that the social sciences qua science must ultimately take a back seat to normative and political struggles. Whether or not comparable worth will be endorsed as a policy by the public and private sectors is not a scientific question, but a political one. Comparable worth will not depend on social science for a judgment that it is desirable and fair, but on the collective judgments of workers, employers, the legal establishment, and legislators. Informed social science can inform these judgments, however. Social scientists will be more or less effective in facilitating the comparable worth debate depending on the rigor and quality of their research and their ability to surmount the fray in communicating their knowledge and expertise to relevant decision makers.

NOTES

1. Within firms, Bielby and Baron (1982) document the existence of virtually complete sex segregation of jobs for a sample of California establishments during the 1960s and 1970s.

2. Title VII is broader in scope than the Equal Pay Act and is usually preferred by plaintiffs in a sex discrimination case.

3. The following discussion draws on Treiman and Hartmann (1981).

4. Hereafter, references to Schwab pertain to Schwab (1983) unless otherwise indicated.

REFERENCES

Arvey, R. D., Passino, E. M., & Lounsbury, J. W. (1977). Job analysis results as influenced by sex of incumbent and sex of analyst. *Journal of Applied Psychology, 62,* 411-416.

Beller, A. (1982). Occupational segregation by sex: Determinants and changes. *Journal of Human Resources, 17,* 371-382.

Bielby, W., & Baron, J. (1982, May 24-25). *A woman's place is with other women: Sex segregation in the workplace.* Paper presented at the Workshop on Job Segregation by Sex, National Academy of Sciences, Washington, DC.

Birnbaum, M. H. (1983). Perceived equity of salary policies. *Journal of Applied Psychology, 68,* 49-59.

Blau, F. D., & Hendricks, W. E. (1979). Occupational segregation by sex: Trends and prospects. *Journal of Human Resources, 14,* 197-210.

Bunzel, J. (1982). To each according to her worth? *The Public Interest, 72,* 77-93.

Cain, P. S., & Green, B. F. (1983). Reliabilities of selected ratings available from the Dictionary of Occupational Titles. *Journal of Applied Psychology, 68,* 155-165.

Christensen v. Iowa (1977). 563 F. 2d 353, U.S. Court of Appeals for the Eighth Circuit.

Cronbach, L. J., & Associates (1980). *Toward reform of program evaluation.* San Francisco: Jossey-Bass.

Doverspike, D., Carlisi, A. M., Barrett, G. V., & Alexander, R. A. (1983). Generalizability analysis of a point-method job evaluation instrument. *Journal of Applied Psychology, 68,* 476-483.

Gasaway, L. M. (1981). Comparable worth: A post-*Gunther* overview. *The Georgetown Law Journal, 69,* 1123-1169.

Gitt, C., & Gelb, M. (1977). Beyond the equal pay act: Expanding wage differential protections under Title VII. *Loyola University of Chicago Law Journal, 8,* 723-767.

Gottfredson, G. G. (1983). *On the equivalent value of different kinds of work.* Paper presented at the annual meeting of the Eastern Sociological Society, Baltimore, MD.

Grams, R., & Schwab, D. P., (1983). Impacts of sex composition and salary level on judgments of content in job evaluation. *Proceedings of the Midwest Academy of Management, 26,* 285-293.

Hartmann, H. I. (1976). Capitalism, patriarchy, and job segregation by sex. *Signs, 1*(2), 137-169.

Lemons, M., et al. v. City and County of Denver. (1978). Cases 906, 907 (The United States District Court for the District of Colorado); Civil Action No. 78-1499, U.S. Court of Appeals for the Tenth Circuit.

Lewin, T. A. (1984, January 1). A new push to raise women's pay. *New York Times.*

Livernash, E. R. (Ed.). (1980). *Comparable worth: Issues and alternatives.* Washington, DC: Equal Employment Advisory Council.

McArthur, L. Z. (1983, October 7-8). *Social judgment biases in comparable worth analysis.* Paper presented at the Seminar on Comparable Worth Research, National Academy of Sciences, Hilton Head, South Carolina.

Nieva, V. F., & Gutek, B. A. (1980). Sex effects on evaluation. *Academy of Management Review, 5,* 267-276.

Norton, E. H. (1979, October 30). Speech to conference on pay equity. *Daily Labor Reporter.*

Pear, R. (1983, October 3). Earnings gap is narrowing slightly for women. *New York Times.*

Remick, H. (1978). Strategies for creating sound, bias free job evaluation plans. In *Job evaluation and EEO: The emerging issues* (pp. 85-112). New York: Industrial Relations Counselors, Inc.

Remick, H. (1980). Beyond equal pay for equal work: Comparable worth in the State of Washington. In R. S. Ratner (Ed.), *Equal employment policy for women: Strategies for implementation in the United States, Canada, and Western Europe,* (pp. 405-448). Philadelphia: Temple University Press.

Remick, H. (1981). The comparable worth controversy. *Public Personnel Management Journal 10,* 371-383.

Schwab, D. P. (1980). Job evaluation and pay setting: Concepts and practices. In E. R. Livernash (Ed.), *Comparable worth: Issues and alternatives.* Washington, DC: Equal Employment Advisory Council.

Schwab, D. P. (1983, October 7-8). *Job evaluation research and research needs.* Paper presented at the Seminar on Comparable Worth Research, National Academy of Sciences, Hilton Head, South Carolina.

Schwab, D. P., & Wichern, D. W. (1983). Systematic bias and market wages: Implications for the comparable worth debate. *Journal of Applied Psychology, 68,* 60-69.

Tenopyr, M. L. (1981). The realities of employment testing. *American Psychologist, 36,* 1120-1127.

Treiman, D. J. (1979). *Job evaluation: An analytic review* (Interim report to the Equal Employment Opportunity Commission). Washington, DC: National Academy of Sciences.

Treiman, D. J., & Hartmann, H. I. (Eds.). (1981). *Women, work, and wages: Equal pay for jobs of equal value.* Washington, DC: National Academy Press.

U.S. Supreme Court, (1981). County of Washington, Oregon v. Gunther, No. 80-429.

Willis, N. D., & Associates (1974). *State of Washington comparable worth study.* Seattle, WA: Norman D. Willis and Associates.

Willis, N. D., & Associates (1976). *State of Washington comparable worth study, Phase II.* Seattle, WA: Norman D. Willis and Associates.

Witt, M., & Naherny, P. K. (1975). *Women's work—up from 878: Report on the DOT research project.* Madison, WI: University of Wisconsin Extension.

7

Can the Social Sciences Solve the Problem of Unemployment?

HENRY M. LEVIN

Perhaps one of the most distressing of all human experiences is that of not being able to find employment. Not only is one's social stature and sense of self-worth deeply affected by occupational and employment status, but the vast majority of the population must depend upon the earnings from their labor as the principal or only source of income. Thus, the inability to find employment can represent a serious blow to an individual's health, ego, and standard of living. At the extreme, both psychological and physical survival may hang crucially on the ability to obtain a job (Ferman & Gordus, 1979).

Although productive employment has primacy as a human need, it does not merit the same priority as a social right. At the peak of the recession of 1982, some 12 million Americans were unemployed, accounting for almost 11 percent of the labor force (Economic Report of the President, 1983, pp. 198-199). Even with the strong recovery and falling unemployment rates in 1983 and 1984, the hope was that the rate might decline to 7 percent. Few expected unemployment rates to fall below that mark before rising once again.

Unemployment has traditionally been worse for nonwhites and youth than for whites and adult workers. The nonwhite unemployment rate at the end of 1982 was almost 19 percent, and the rate for all 16- to 19-year-olds was almost 25 percent (Economic Report of the President, 1983, pp. 199, 201). For minority teenagers the unemployment rate approached 50 percent (Economic Report of the President, 1983, p. 201). Of course, the unemployment situation affected not only these men and women, but their families as well, for many were the sole or principle sources of income for children and other dependents.

Even these numbers understate the true extent of unemployment by virtue of the fact that employment statistics include only those persons who are looking for work at the time of the survey. Persons who have given up looking because of the bleakness of the job situation— the so-called discouraged workers—are not included in the labor force, so they are not counted as unemployed. Likewise, persons who are underemployed in the sense of working at part-time jobs, even though they desire full-time work, or working in low-level jobs that do not draw upon their skills and training are counted among the employed with no qualitative distinctions regarding their status. Any unemployment measure that takes account of discouraged and underemployed workers would provide an even more distressing picture than the present statistics reflect (Sorkin, 1974, Chap. 1).

Given the seriousness of the unemployment situation, it is no surprise that many social scientists—especially economists—have devoted considerable attention to the study of labor markets and employment (Levitan, Mangum, & Marshall, 1972). Despite the considerable research output on this subject, unemployment is more serious and threatening today than it has been since the great depression. Table 7.1 shows the highest and lowest average annual rates of unemployment by recent decade and illustrates the rising trend since 1950.

SOCIAL SCIENCE AND POLICY

Any attempt to construct a course of action to reduce unemployment must be premised on the answers to two questions: (1) What are the levels and causes of unemployment? and (2) How much unemployment ought the society to permit, and how should the goal be attained? The first addresses a description of positive reality or "What is." The second addresses the question of normative reality or "What is desirable." It is the difference between the answers to these two questions that determines not only whether there is a tension, but what type of social and political response is appropriate.

The social sciences in the United States are dedicated primarily to answering the first question. Virtually all of the social sciences and their constituent epistemologies are dedicated to explaining positive reality or how the world works by measuring phenomena and using

TABLE 7.1
Highest and Lowest Annual Unemployment Rates by Decade

Decade	Highest	Lowest
1950-59	6.8%	2.9%
1960-69	6.7	3.5
1970-79	8.5	4.9
1980-83	9.7	7.1

Source: Bureau of Labor Statistics.

theoretical constructs to formulate and test causal relations. Typically these exercises take the form of description, definition, measurement, analysis, and prediction as well as attempts to improve the underlying theory and empirical methods. The goal is to develop an understanding of social, economic, cultural, and political behavior of individuals and social groups that is sufficiently generalizable and powerful to predict outcomes under a wide variety of conditions.

In the present context, an understanding of what factors contribute to unemployment can only be one part of the policy process. Equally important are the answers to questions of normative reality. That is, even if the social sciences share a consensus on the causes of unemployment, action is not possible without a consensus on normative reality or goals regarding unemployment. This is hardly as straightforward as it may appear. Although everyone may be in favor of reducing unemployment, it is likely that this can only be done in reality by making other changes in society. For example, reducing unemployment may require raising taxes, tolerating inflation, imposing mandatory reductions in retirement age, and a number of other social burdens or "trade-offs."

This is the basic dilemma of the social sciences as they address policy. Although they can contribute to an understanding of positive reality, they are quite marginal to the political process that determines normative reality and political strategy. It is unfortunate that this aspect of policy has been largely misunderstood by social scientists. Indeed, English is unique among modern languages in having separate words for policy and politics. In other languages, a single word such as *politique, politik,* or *politica* refers to a single realm of action, encompassing our version of both policy and politics. For at bottom, policy *is* politics. The fact that we have a distinct word for each gives the unfortunate and misleading impression that policy is a technocratic act based upon expertise that is largely removed from politics.

The center of policy is the political process. The social sciences can contribute information to the political arena, information that may have a powerful impact because of the special prestige conferred upon "science" in modern societies. However, this should not obscure the fact that the findings and view of social scientists are only one set of influences on the political process. They rarely dominate it. For this reason, there can be an enormous gap between what is known about the world and what is actually done to address important social issues. Even when the findings of social science are unanimous on a particular issue, they may be given little weight in the political arena if they suggest strategies that violate important political constraints on action.

In summary, when issues can be decided based on information alone, the social sciences can be a powerful ally to policy. Knowledge will be power. However, when a situation cannot be resolved because of deep ideological differences and inherent political conflict in taking action, the social sciences will be unable to provide a solution. A great deal is known about how to solve the unemployment problem, but these solutions cannot easily be applied in the existing political setting in the United States.

SOCIAL SCIENCES AND UNEMPLOYMENT

The social sciences can provide an understanding of the causes of unemployment in two ways. First, they can develop an analytic or theoretical scheme for understanding unemployment. Second, they can evaluate unemployment within that framework in order to establish the empirical magnitudes of the various causes of unemployment and the probable consequences of policy changes. In essence, these are exercises in positive reality (Friedman, 1953). That is, the social science approach to unemployment is an attempt to understand the nature and determinants of unemployment and how unemployment would be affected if that world were to be manipulated in different ways. Such research may be premised upon a specific view of normative reality, that unemployment should be alleviated. However, given that all alternatives for reducing unemployment will have costly consequences for some groups, research cannot provide particular solutions that will necessarily survive the political process. And there is no assurance that there are technical solutions if the stalemate on a subject is essentially political, not technical.

In the case of employment and unemployment, social science analysis is drawn primarily from economics. Within economics there are two broad frameworks for explaining unemployment: Market theories and

Marxian ones. According to the Marxian explanation, unemployment is an important dimension of capitalism (Edwards, Reich, & Weisskopf, 1972). The existence of substantial unemployment tends to discipline the workforce so that more work can be derived from employees who fear losing their jobs under such conditions. Further, the Marxian explanation argues that over the long run there will be a tendency for the "reserve army of labor" to expand as increasingly productive capital displaces labor. Thus, it is argued that unemployment is functional to capitalist development and will increase over time until workers take over the means of production to meet the needs of the working class (Gordon, 1972, Chap. 5).

Economic policy in the United States does not consider the Marxian perspective for both ideological and pragmatic reasons. Even if Marxian analysis is applicable, the policy consequences are generally beyond the scope of any action that could be taken by policymakers. That is, Marxian analysis generally rejects "reforms" of the capitalist system as an alternative to revolution. In fact, often such reforms are seen as obstacles to revolutionary change (Gorz, 1968). Nevertheless, some scholars who share the Marxian perspective have proposed a policy agenda to increase employment within the capitalist system by democratizing investment decisions and economic ownership of productive enterprises (Carnoy & Shearer, 1980; Bowles, Gordon, & Weisskopf, 1983). Because these types of decisions are consistent with a modified capitalist economy, they do not really derive directly from a Marxian explanation for unemployment. Rather, they can be evaluated within a market analytic framework.

Market Theory

Market theories refer to those in which the free workings of competitive economic markets allocate resources (Dorfman, 1967). Goods and services are produced by large numbers of firms, each one producing such a small portion of total market output that it cannot affect market price. Each firm accepts the market price for the good or service that it is producing and hires productive inputs of capital and labor at their competitive prices, producing that amount of output that will maximize profits. In order to maximize profits it is assumed that each firm will hire each input, including labor, up to the point at which the additional cost of another unit of input is just equal to the value of additional output produced by that unit of input. Thus, the demand for workers is determined by the wage that the employer must pay, worker productivity, and the costs and productivities of other inputs that can substitute for workers in production. Other things being held constant, the higher the wage, the less the labor that will be demanded by employers as they substitute other relatively cheaper inputs for some of the labor input.

The supply of labor is determined primarily by prevailing wage rates, the size of the productive population, and tastes for income versus leisure. Each individual and household attempts to maximize its welfare by obtaining an optimal combination of income and leisure. Because most households have little or no income-producing property, the typical household must provide labor services to obtain the income that will enable it to purchase goods and services in the market place. Work is assumed to have disutility in that individuals would rather have leisure than productive work, but it is a source of earnings that can be used for goods and services that do have value. Each individual is assumed to determine the number of hours that he or she will work according to the wage that is offered. The higher the wage, the greater the cost of leisure in terms of the value of market goods and services that the individual must sacrifice by not working. Accordingly, workers will generally wish to offer more hours of work at higher wages, and it is assumed that the supply of labor is positively related to wages.

It is assumed that firms are maximizing profits, households are maximizing the utility derived from their consumption of market goods and leisure; there are very large numbers of firms competing both in product markets and in labor and other input markets; there is perfect information on market prices, wages, technology, and the productivity of different workers and other inputs on the part of firms; and there is perfect information on employment alternatives and wages. On the basis of these assumptions the market establishes a competitive equilibrium for the production of all goods and services, and the hiring of inputs into production including labor. That competitive equilibrium reflects a set of prices and wages at which all resources will be employed in their most productive uses so that there will be no unemployment of workers or other productive resources.

This can be observed in Figure 7.1 that shows supply and demand relations in a competitive labor market. Supply is an increasing function of the wage level, and demand is a decreasing function as explained above. Only at the point of intersection of the two relations does the amount of labor supplied equal that which is demanded. At that point there is full employment of M workers at a wage of N. The question may arise as to why the wage would not be higher than N at Q. The answer is that at Q there is an excess of supply relative

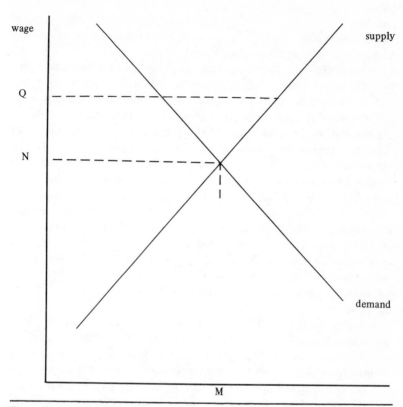

Figure 7.1   A Competitive Labor Market

to demand that results in unemployment. Workers would have an incentive to compete with each other for existing jobs by accepting a lower wage until the equilibrium wage, N, was reached. For a similar reason, the wage could not remain for long below N. Firms would have an inadequate number of workers and would respond by bidding up the wage until N was reached. On the basis of this logic, full employment is assured in the long run, and unemployment can only be created by tampering with the perfectly competitive market. It is important to note that this is not the only version of how labor markets function (Okun, 1981, Chap. 2), but it is the dominant one. A more complete development of the economics of labor markets can be found in Hamermesh and Rees (1984).

Defining Full Employment

Before considering the causes of unemployment, it is important to consider what is meant by full employment (Sorkin, 1974, Chap. 1). Economists have found it useful to differentiate conceptually between three components of unemployment: Frictional unemployment, cyclical unemployment, and secular or structural unemployment.

Even when there are adequate jobs for all at market wages, some persons will be between jobs. That is, at all times, some employers will be searching for prospective employees and job seekers will be searching for employment prospects. Job openings are not filled instantly, for job seekers must obtain information and go through the various steps of application, interview, and selection before a hire is made. The fact that some persons will always be between jobs—even in a full employment economy—is recognized under the category of frictional unemployment. Although such persons will be counted as unemployed, there is rarely deep concern about them. At the most, policy interventions should be limited to providing information about job opportunities and available workers in order to more quickly fill positions.

It is also recognized that unemployment will vary considerably over the business cycle. Capitalist economies have been characterized historically by wide swings in economic activity from prosperity to recession. Although unemployment rises with recession, such swings are not considered to represent long-run changes because the unemployment rate will decline as economic activity rises. Thus, some portion of unemployment will be attributible to the particular stage of the business cycle, and economists and policymakers have generally viewed this type of unemployment differently than secular unemployment. Cyclical unemployment is generally treated through government fiscal and monetary policies based on increased government spending, reduced taxation, and monetary measures that will reduce interest rates. As the economy approaches what is defined as full employment, such policies are modified to adjust to existing economic conditions (Campagna, 1974, Chaps. 13-15),

Secular unemployment refers to unemployment that is neither frictional nor cyclical. This type of unemployment occurs even in times of prosperity. Some of it is considered to be "structural" in the sense that the unemployed are located in different geographical areas than the jobs available or lack the skills required for available jobs. This may be due to industrial and occupational shifts as some industries and occupations decline while others expand. But another portion may be due to the fact that the economy is just unable to generate enough jobs, even in good times, for those who wish to work. Recent empirical estimates suggest that this situation is worsening as the ratio of unemployed persons to available job openings seems to be increasing substantially (Abraham, 1983).

Historically, in the United States, an unemployment rate of 2 percent was accepted as being "frictional," although in countries like Sweden and Japan there is deep concern when unemployment rises to this level (Ginsburg, 1983; Taira, 1983). In recent years there has been a tendency to define full employment at some higher rate of unemployment such as the 4 percent reflected in the Humphrey-Hawkins Bill that was considered by Congress in the mid-1970s. The premise behind the rise in tolerable unemployment rates is the view that frictional unemployment is rising as individuals extend the length of their search for a good job at a time when unemployment insurance, higher family incomes, and two-income families enable individual job seekers to be more selective. Some economists have even viewed full employment as taking place when unemployment is as high as 6 percent on these grounds, and others have dismissed unemployment as being no more serious than the idle time spent in waiting for a plane (Hall, 1983), even though for many of the unemployed there will not be enough flights to accommodate them. Others argue that there is a "natural rate of unemployment" in that only one rate of unemployment is consistent with a constant change in price levels (Friedman, 1968), although this notion has been heavily criticized (Cherry, 1981).

In terms of diagnosing unemployment, frictional, cyclical, and secular components are considered to have different causes and potential consequences. In general, frictional unemployment is largely ignored except to the degree that better information and lower unemployment benefits will reduce the time of workers between jobs. Cyclical unemployment is considered to require only temporary alleviants because it is inherently temporary in nature. And secular unemployment is considered to be the subject of the most serious concern for policy because it is neither as inevitable as frictional unemployment nor as temporary as cyclical unemployment.

Causes of Unemployment

Because the perfectly competitive market is supposed to provide full employment, nonfrictional unemployment must be due to the fact that markets are not functioning as advertised. The culprits that are usually blamed are wage rigidities; monopoly concentration of industry; international barriers to trade; imperfect information; restrictive monetary policy; and inadequate effective demand.

Wage rigidities refer to the fact that wages might not adjust downward as in the move from Q to N in Figure 7.1 because of minimum wage legislation or trade union power. Minimum wages are designed to make certain that a full-time worker will earn at least enough to provide a minimal standard of living. Market economics does not promise such an outcome, so government has stepped in to assure it. But, in doing so, it has been argued that jobs that would have been forthcoming at a lower wage will not be provided by firms, contributing to unemployment (Brown, Gilroy, & Cohen, 1982). Trade unions, too, wish to improve the earnings of their members. Although in recent years both unionized automobile and steel workers have taken some pay cuts to save jobs, trade unions usually are vigorously opposed to cuts in wages. Further, government jobs are usually characterized by salary schedules that are rarely, if ever, revised downward. Thus, it is argued that wages may rise above the equilibrium level that would guarantee full employment.

Monopoly concentration of industry refers to the fact that many industries do not have a large number of firms competing in the marketplace. In such industries a few firms tend to dominate output, and they have incentives to restrict output to a lower level than would be produced under competitive conditions. Lower levels of output for an industry will also reduce employment below what it would have been under competitive circumstances.

International barriers to trade include trade restrictions practiced by the United States and other countries such as tariffs, quotas, subsidies, and the maintenance of international exchange rates for currencies that do not reflect accurately their values in international trade. These barriers are mainly created by government intervention that can distort foreign exchange rates and trade patterns, creating greater employment in some sectors and lower employment in others.

Further, market economies do not adjust instantaneously to changes in technologies and market conditions. Rather, it is assumed that over the long run there are appropriate responses. At any one time, imperfect information on alternatives and changing conditions will create a lag between the stimulus and response. During the interim there is a period of adjustment characterized by resource unemployment as resources shift from declining industries and markets to emerging ones.

Restrictive monetary policy refers to government expansion of the money supply that is inadequate to sustain expansion of the economy at a full-employment level (Duesenberry, 1967). The Federal Reserve

Bank has a number of tools for altering the money supply of which the most prominent are its power in setting reserve ratios of member banks for loans; buying and selling securities through open market operations; and altering the level of the discount rate for purchasing debts from member banks. If the money supply grows too slowly, interest rates rise and borrowing for business investments is reduced, resulting in a rise in unemployment. If the money supply increases too rapidly, interest rates decline and investment expands, raising both employment and inflation. Thus, the Federal Reserve Bank must chart a narrow course between the Scylla of unemployment and the Charybdis of inflation. When it errs on the side of a rate of monetary growth that is too sluggish, unemployment will increase.

A final reason that is given for unemployment is that there is a tendency for mature capitalist economies to fail to sustain the level of market demand that will employ all resources. This was essentially the criticism of Keynes to neoclassical economics. He argued that there will be some circumstances in which investors will be so pessimistic about the future that inadequate investment will be forthcoming to promote and sustain expansion. In that case, unemployment will be too high and incomes will be too low to create a high enough effective demand for goods and services. Under such circumstances, he maintained that government must make the investment to raise effective demand to a level that would assure full employment (Musgrave & Musgrave, 1976, Chap. 24). Although this would entail budgetary deficits in times of poor economic conditions, those deficits would be repaid through budgetary surpluses in prosperous times. However, if there is a long-term trend toward underconsumption, then the problem of stimualting demand becomes a secular one.

Cures for Unemployment

The cures for unemployment can be analyzed as they affect the market for labor and aggregate economic conditions. In general they divide into those for improving the functioning of labor markets; those for reducing or altering the supply of workers; and those for increasing the demand for workers.

Improvements in general market functioning refer to ways of attaining a free market equilibrium that approximates the perfectly competitive market. The most important of these include:

(1) reducing wage rigidities
(2) reducing monopoly concentration

(3) reducing international barriers to trade
(4) improving information

The reduction of wage rigidities refers primarily to the elimination of the minimum wage and other impediments to the free adjustment of wages so that they can fall as well as rise. Presumably it also means reducing the power of trade unions to bargain over the wages of their members.

Reducing monopoly concentration refers to the need to create greater competition in markets for goods and services so that output and employment expand in those industries. Reducing international barriers to trade refers to the dismantling of tariffs, duties, and quotas on imports and subsidies on exports as well as the promotion of freely floating international exchange rates without governmental intervention. Obviously, such measures would have to be undertaken by major groups of trading nations simultaneously because there are disincentives to any single nation taking unilateral steps in these directions.

Finally, the provision of better information on the availability of jobs and their requirements as well as the availability of labor and its characteristics would serve to reduce the time required to fill positions. All of these would presumably improve the functioning of labor markets, reducing unemployment over the long run.

But, as Keynes suggested: "We are all dead in the long run." Accordingly, economists have devoted themselves to suggesting specific interventions in labor markets to reduce unemployment by altering the supply of, or demand for, labor. Supply-side interventions include reducing the labor supply or altering its skills to make it more employable. They include:

(1) education and training policies
(2) reducing population growth
(3) reducing immigration
(4) increasing compulsory schooling
(5) increasing armed forces
(6) increasing taxes on labor earnings
(7) lowering retirement age
(8) raising entry age for child labor

Education and training policies refer to ways of improving the qualifications of labor for existing jobs, a strategy that was central to the War on Poverty (Levin, 1977) and the Comprehensive Employment Training Act (CETA) programs. Reducing family size refers to discouraging larger families to slow future labor force growth. This can be done by reducing the tax deductions for dependents and the subsidies for children's services as well as through the proliferation and subsidization of campaigns on family planning and birth control.

Reducing immigration, increasing the amount of compulsory schooling (e.g., from age 16 to 18), increasing the size of the armed forces, and lowering the retirement age will all reduce the size of the civilian labor force. The retirement age can be lowered by law for public employees, and the receipt of public pensions can be tied to withdrawal from the labor market. Increasing taxes on labor earnings will encourage some persons to withdraw from the labor market or to reduce their hours of work. Finally, raising the entry age for child labor to 18 years will reduce the number of the young in labor markets.

It is clear that there are a large number of policy interventions for restricting the labor supply and reducing unemployment. Likewise, there are also a substantial number of potential interventions for increasing the demand for workers:

(1) an expansionary monetary policy
(2) an expansionary fiscal policy
(3) wage subsidies
(4) industry subsidies
(5) mandated staffing ratios
(6) expansion of government employment
(7) promotion of labor intensive enterprises
(8) reduction of plant closings

An expansionary monetary policy is designed to encourage rising business activity and employment through reducing interest rates, thus encouraging business borrowing and investment. This is achieved primarily through a purposive expansion of the money supply by the Federal Reserve Board. An expansionary fiscal policy entails some combination of tax reduction and increased government spending to stimulate the economy through increasing effective demand for goods and services.

Wage subsidies are designed to reduce the cost of employing particular kinds of workers. For example, subsidies have been used to provide incentives to hire youth and the disadvantaged (Hammermesh, 1978). Subsidies can also be used to protect particular industries with heavy employment bases or particular firms. The recent federally guaranteed loans to Lockheed and Chrysler were certainly defended on the grounds of preventing catastrophic unemployment consequences. Subsidies can also be used to assist industries in holding their market positions in international trade (e.g., low-cost loans to foreigners from the U.S. Import-Export Bank for purchasing American goods), a policy that is clearly at odds with reducing international trade barriers.

Mandated staffing ratios can increase employment in the private sector. For example, federally regulated industries can require specific staffing patterns such as those stipulated for cockpit crews in airliners. It is possible to extend this logic to other types of employment endeavors on health and safety grounds or on military self-sufficiency grounds such as the maritime subsidies provided to the U.S. Merchant Marine Fleet and to shipbuilders.

Obviously, expansion of government employment is the most direct way of reducing unemployment (Palmer, 1978). Increasing jobs in the government sector through the expansion of existing programs or the creation of new ones such as the Public Works Administration (PWA) and the Civilian Conservation Corps (CCC) during the 1930s enabled important social tasks to be accomplished with a larger public workforce (Kesselman, 1978). In some countries, important industries have been nationalized to attempt to retain their employment base.

The promotion of labor intensive enterprises can be accomplished in a number of ways (Levin, 1983b). Government purchases can be made from small businesses rather than large ones whenever possible because the former tend to have far higher ratios of labor to output and have had a greater contribution to employment in recent years (U.S. Small Business Administration, 1979; World Bank, 1978, Chap. 2). Likewise, the substitution of tax incentives for hiring labor rather than investing in capital would alter the present bias in favor of capital over labor. Present tax policies provide accelerated depreciation and tax credits for capital investment without a compensating benefit for expanding employment. The government can also promote the establishment of worker cooperatives that tend to be very labor intensive. Large industrial worker cooperatives have been found to be more productive than comparable traditional firms while providing considerably more employment at the same output levels (Levin, 1983a).

Finally, the government could cushion impending business closures by requiring advance notice and making plans to assist workers in obtaining new employment. Attention could also be addressed to reducing tax and other incentives that make it more profitable under some circumstances to shut down profitable businesses than to continue operations (Bluestone & Harrison, 1982).

Estimating the Magnitude of Effects on Unemployment

Although the theoretical analysis of supply and demand provides an overall framework for formulating policies, economists are also concerned with estimating the magnitudes of unemployment reduction associated with a particular policy. The basic approach is to formulate a pertinent model of the specific labor markets to be addressed; to specify a system of structural equations that would incorporate the policy variable within the labor market framework; to obtain appropriate data and estimations of the equations; and to interpret the findings within a policy framework. These procedures can be found in basic texts on labor economics (Hamermesh & Rees, 1984) and in standard econometric texts (Johnston, 1963; Theil, 1971). They are also reflected in specific studies of labor markets such as those in the *Journal of Labor Economics* or in the *Brookings Papers on Economic Activities,* and they are found in surveys of unemployment research such as those on labor market dynamics and unemployment (Clark & Summers, 1979), and the minimum wage and unemployment (Brown, Gilroy, & Cohen, 1982).

These econometric studies are helpful in understanding the potential effects of different policies, but they have a number of deficiencies with respect to their prescriptive abilities. First, they are generally based upon either historical time series on labor market behavior or cross-sectional analysis among individuals or states as units of analysis. Thus, the empirical results may not be especially applicable to changing economic conditions or labor markets. This problem even holds for experimental manipulation of policy variables such as those of the Negative Income Tax Experiment (Rossi & Lyall, 1978). Such experiments are limited to specific populations and to a particular time period characterized by certain labor market conditions. Generalization requires viewing the prospective effects for broader audiences and a more general time frame.

Moreover, labor market dynamics vary considerably over the business cycle so that empirical estimates may vary according to which part of the cycle the data are taken from. This factor inhibits the use of empirical results for long-term policy interventions. For example, the demand of employers for labor in response to a change in wages will vary considerably within the relatively short period covered by a typical economic cycle (Hamermesh, 1978, pp. 99-101).

A second deficiency is that the research variables may be considerably different than the policy ones. For example, the effects of wage subsidies on employer hiring and reduction in unemployment are typically assessed by estimating the demand elasticity for labor. The latter is based upon the hiring response of employers to different wage levels in the natural environment—with statistical controls for other obvious influences—rather than a direct evaluation of wage subsidies. The expectation is that a wage subsidy can be viewed as a reduction in the wage that ëmployers pay so that the employer response can be determined from the more general estimates of demand elasticity for labor. Even when experimental interventions are attempted in these areas (Ball et al., 1981), they are still subject to the limits of time and sample specificity rather than being useful for general policies.

Finally, the implementation of any policy to reduce unemployment will also have potential effects on inflation and other areas of social concern. Although the area of unemployment and inflation has been heavily addressed, the findings are hardly conclusive (Baily, 1982; Ginsburg, 1983, pp. 22-29). The unemployment-inflation trade-off does not seem to be stable, inevitable, or fully understandable in the policy context, even though recent national policies are predicated on the assumption that the relations are understood (Economic Report of the President, 1983, pp. 37-38).

In summary, there are a large number of options available to reduce unemployment in the United States. Much of the empirical work in labor economics represents an attempt to understand the magnitude of employment that could be created by particular strategies such as monetary and fiscal policy or reduction of the minimum wage, government employment programs, and retraining approaches. However, the research is of such a nature that it can only be used to set broad guidelines on effects of different policy interventions. It cannot be used to provide precise estimates in a complex and dynamic labor market situation, but it can support the formulation of broad dimensions of policy. The "fine-tuning" must be carried out at the implementation stage. My contention is that research has shown productive policy directions for reducing unemployment considerably below current levels. In order to understand why that body of knowledge is not used more fully, one must return to the politics of unemployment.

THE POLITICS OF
UNEMPLOYMENT POLICY

If we have the knowledge and tools to reduce unemployment, and there is a general consensus that unemployment ought to be reduced, why is there an obvious failure to make significant inroads into the unemployment problem? For some reason, existing knowledge has not been translated into political action or outcomes that are sufficient to address the issue.

The simple answer to this paradox is that virtually none of the policies that follow from this analysis are costless. All require some

TABLE 7.2
Consequences of Different Unemployment Strategies

Consequences	Strategies
Tax increase or inflation	Education and training
	Increased compulsory schooling
	Increased armed forces
	Increased taxes on labor earning
	Wage subsidies
	Industry subsidies
	Expansion of government employment
Inflation	Expansionary monetary policy
	Expansionary fiscal policy
Reduced freedom of action	Reduced union power
	Reduced minimum wage
	Reduced monopoly concentration
	Reduced compulsory schooling
	Increased armed forces
	Lowered retirement age
	Higher entry age for child labor
	Mandated staffing ratios
	Reduced plant closings
Government competition with private sector	Expanded government employment
Favoring some industries over others	Education and training policies
	Reduced immigration
	Wage subsidies
	Industry subsidies
	Promote labor intensive enterprises

type of sacrifice of other valued goals in order to implement them. And often the sacrifices that are required must come from the most powerful constituencies. We are referring not only to economic sacrifices or trade-offs, but also to the loss of freedom required by some of the policies.

Table 7.2 represents an attempt to list the consequences of different strategies for reducing unemployment. Each type of consequence is listed along with the policies that are likely to create it. Virtually all strategies that are designed to increase government spending are likely to entail a tax increase or create inflationary pressures from that portion of additional spending that is funded through government borrowing or expansion of the money supply (Baily & Tobin, 1978). Expansionary monetary and fiscal policies also can have profound inflationary consequences. Many of the strategies are associated with reduced freedom of action for firms and individuals. Some entail a potential increase in competition between the public and private sector as the government creates additional employment. Finally, many of the strategies would tend to favor some industries and firms over others, as the policies would impact quite differently on different economic sectors.

One could add to this list the issue of who is responsible for assuring a minimum standard of living when minimum wages are cut. Or one could address the implications for job displacement of such high technologies as microprocessors, robotics, and biotechnologies in which some groups will gain in income and employment, others will lose, and net job losses may result (Levin & Rumberger, 1983).

The reduction of unemployment is not costless. The question is: Who will bear these costs? Although there is strong support among many elements in American society to reduce unemployment, there is no strong consensus on how it should be done. There is simply no strategy or set of strategies that seems to be capable of winning political consensus, a fact that tells more about the politics of American society than about its social science. In contrast, a country like Sweden has ordained the right to a job as a basic social right. In recognition of this commitment, Sweden has adopted an active labor market policy of integrating monetary and fiscal policy; engaging in vigorous retraining programs for workers in declining skill areas and industries; providing incentives and subsidies for retraining of workers; and providing subsidies to firms in order to retain or expand employment in crucial geographic areas and industries (Ginsburg, 1983, pp. 109-211; Rehn, 1980; Rehn & Lundberg, 1963).

These efforts have resulted in unemployment levels that have rarely exceeded 2 percent, as reflected in Table 7.3. This table shows unemployment rates from 1960-1979 for both Sweden and the United States, adjusted to the U.S. concepts of unemployment. The U.S. rate of unemployment averaged about three times that of Sweden despite the fact that a higher proportion of the Swedish population was in the labor force. Although inflation was higher in Sweden than in the United States over this period (an annual average price rise in Sweden of about 8.9 percent between 1971-1978 compared with 6.7 percent in the U.S.), this was viewed by Swedish polity as a reasonable price to pay for high employment levels (Ginsburg, 1983, pp. 123-124).

In contrast, the political process in the United States seems to use the unemployment issue as a political excuse to pursue policies that are responsive to constituencies other than the unemployed while defending the policies as ones designed to reduce unemployment. Thus, it is no surprise to find some conservatives arguing for tax reductions that favor the rich, the reduction of union power, and the reduction

TABLE 7.3
Unemployment in Sweden and the United States, 1960-1979,
Adjusted to U.S. Concepts
(percentages)

	Unemployment Rate			Unemployment Rate	
Year	United States	Sweden	Year	United States	Sweden
1960	5.5%	NA	1970	4.9%	1.5%
1961	6.7	1.4%	1971	5.9	2.5
1962	5.5	1.5	1972	5.6	2.7
1963	5.7	1.7	1973	4.9	2.5
1964	5.2	1.5	1974	5.6	2.0
1965	4.5	1.2	1975	8.5	1.6
1966	3.8	1.6	1976	7.7	1.6
1967	3.8	2.1	1977	7.0	1.8
1968	3.6	2.2	1978	6.0	2.2
1969	3.5	1.9	1979	5.8	2.1
Average 1960-1969	4.8	1.7	1970-1979	6.2	2.1

Source: Ginsburg, H., 1983, p. 121, *Full employment and public policy: The United States and Sweden.* Reprinted by permission of Lexington Books, D. C. Heath and Company, Lexington, MA.

or elimination of minimum wages and health and safety regulations in the workplace on the basis that these changes will make it possible for the economy to create new investments and hire more workers. Although these proposals have been argued on the basis of reducing unemployment through either direct or "trickle-down" effects, there is little evidence that they will have a major effect on unemployment even though they will surely be favored by conservative constituencies. Indeed, studies of the effects of minimum wages on employment show only the most trivial effects. For example, a reduction in the minimum wage from $3.35 an hour to $2.00 an hour would appear to reduce the rate of teenage unemployment by about three percentage points (Brown, Gilroy, & Cohen, 1982). Such a change would hardly make a dent in teenage unemployment.

In like manner, some liberals have used the unemployment issue to push for expansion of programs that support such traditional liberal constituencies as government workers and those in the social services. The levels of funding that are within the realm of political possibility tend to create few additional jobs for the unemployed relative to their number but relatively large numbers of jobs for middle-class government workers and professionals.

And this is the dilemma that must be faced. Addressing unemployment in the long run will require a large number of measures, not just a single one that will provide the "quick fix" (Levin, 1983b).

The basic directions for policy are clear, and, like the Swedes, the United States must adopt similar active labor market policies if it is serious about reducing unemployment. This can be done within the spirit of social reforms-as-experiments advocated by Don Campbell (1975), in which an experimenting society would use the policy levers identified by social scientists to address unemployment and other concerns. However, such an endeavor assumes the same powerful commitment as the Swedes to the right to productive work. This is a serious political challenge. The social sciences can only attempt to answer questions about the causes of unemployment and what alternative cures are available. They cannot legislate and implement the policies.

REFERENCES

Abraham, K. G. (1983). Structural/frictional vs. deficient demand unemployment: Some new evidence. *American Economic Review, 83,* 708-724.

Baily, M. N. (1982). *Workers, jobs and inflation.* Washington, DC: The Brookings Institution.

Baily, M. N., & Tobin, J. (1978). Inflation-unemployment consequences of job creation policies. In J. Palmer (Ed.), *Creating jobs* (pp. 43-73). Washington, DC: The Brookings Institution.

Ball, J., et al. (1981). *The participation of private businesses as work sponsors in the youth entitlement demonstration.* New York: Manpower Demonstration Research Corporation.

Bluestone, B., & Harrison, B. (1982). *The deindustrialization of America.* New York: Basic Books.

Bowles, S., Gordon, D. M., & Weisskopf, T. E. (1983). *Beyond the wasteland: A democratic alternative to economic decline.* New York: Anchor Press/Doubleday.

Brown, C., Gilroy, C., & Cohen, A. K. (1982). The effect of the minimum wage on employment and unemployment. *The Journal of Economic Literature, 20,* 487-528.

Campagna, A. S. (1974). *Macroeconomics theory and policy.* Boston: Houghton Mifflin.

Campbell, D. T. (1975). Reforms as experiments. In E. Struening & M. Guttentag (Eds.), *Handbook of evaluation research* (Vol. 2) (pp. 71-100). Beverly Hills, CA: Sage.

Carnoy, M., & Shearer, D. (1980). *Economic democracy: The challenge of the 1980s.* White Plains, NY: M. E. Sharpe.

Cherry, R. (1981). What is so natural about the natural rate of unemployment? *Journal of Economic Issues, 15,* 729-743.

Clark, K. B., & Summers, L. H. (1979). Labor market dynamics and unemployment: A reconsideration. *Brookings Papers on Economic Activity, 5,* 13-60.

Dorfman, R. (1967). *Prices and markets.* Englewood Cliffs, NJ: Prentice-Hall.

Duesenberry, J. S. (1967). *Money and credit: Impact and control,* 2nd ed. Englewood Cliffs, NJ: Prentice-Hall.

Economic Report of the President (1983, February). Transmitted to the Congress, Washhington, DC.

Edwards, R., Reich, M., & Weisskopf, T. (1972). *The capitalist system.* Englewood Cliffs, NJ: Prentice-Hall.

Ferman, L. A., & Gordus, J. P. (Eds.). (1979). *Mental health and the economy.* Kalamazoo, MI: W. E. Upjohn Institute for Employment Research.

Friedman, M. (1953). The methodology of positive economics. In M. Friedman (Ed.), *Essays in positive economics* (pp. 1-43). Chicago, IL: University of Chicago Press.

Friedman, M. (1968). The role of monetary policy. *American Economic Review, 58,* 1-17.

Ginsburg, H. (1983). *Full employment and public policy: The United States and Sweden.* Lexington, MA: Lexington Books.

Gordon, D. M. (1972). *Theories of poverty and underemployment.* Lexington, MA: D.C. Heath.

Gorz, A. (1968). *Strategy for labor.* Boston: Beacon Press.

Hall, R. (1983). Is unemployment a macroeconomic problem? *American Economic Review: Papers and Proceedings, 73,* 219-222.

Hamermesh, D. S. (1978). Subsidies for jobs in the private sector. In J. Palmer (Ed.), *Creating jobs* (pp. 87-114). Washington, DC: The Brookings Institution.

Hamermesh, D. S., & Rees, A. (1984). *The economics of work and pay* (3rd ed.) New York: Harper & Row.

Johnston, J. (1963). *Econometric methods.* New York: McGraw-Hill.

Kesselman, J. (1978). Work relief programs in the great depression. In J. Palmer (Ed.), *Creating jobs* (pp. 153-229). Washington, DC: The Brookings Institution.

Levin, H. M. (1977). A decade of policy developments in improving education and training for low-income populations. In R. Haveman (Ed.), *A decade of federal antipoverty programs.* New York: Academic Press.

Levin, H. M. (1983a). Raising employment and productivity with producer cooperatives. In P. Streeten & H. Maier (Eds.), *Human resources employment and development, Vol. 2: Concepts, measurement and long-run perspective* (pp. 310-328). Proceedings of the Sixth World Congress of the International Economic Association held in Mexico City, 1980. London: Macmillan.

Levin, H. M. (1983b). The workplace: Employment and business interventions. In E. Seidman (Ed.), *Handbook of social intervention* (pp. 499-521). Beverly Hills, CA: Sage.

Levin, H. M., & Rumberger, R. W. (1983, August/September). The low-skill future of high technology. *Technology Review,* (pp. 18-21).

Levitan, S. A., Mangum, G. L., & Marshall, R. (1972). *Human resources and labor markets.* New York: Harper & Row.

Musgrave, R. A., & Musgrave, P. B. (1976). *Public finance in theory and practice* (2nd ed.). New York: McGraw-Hill.

Okun, A. M. (1981). *Prices and quantities.* Washington, DC: The Brookings Institution.

Palmer, J. L. (1978). *Creating jobs.* Washington, DC: The Brookings Institution.

Rehn, G. (1980, July). Expansion against stagflation—some unorthodox reflections based on the Swedish experience. *Working Life in Sweden,* No. 18. Available from the Swedish Information Service, Swedish Consulate General.

Rehn, G., & Lundberg, E. (1963, February). Employment and welfare: Some Swedish issues. *Industrial Relations, 2,* 1-4.

Rossi, P. H., & Lyall, K. C. (1978). An overview evaluation of the NIT experiment. In T. D. Cook (Ed.), *Evaluation studies review annual* (Vol. 3). (pp. 412-428). Beverly Hills, CA: Sage.

Sorkin, A. L. (1974). *Education, unemployment, and economic growth.* Lexington, MA: Lexington Books.

Taira, K. (1983). Japan's unemployment: Economic miracle or statistical artifact? *Monthly Labor Review, 106,* 3-10.

Theil, H. (1971). *Principles of econometrics*. New York: John Wiley.

U.S. Department of Labor (1983). *Monthly Labor Review, 106,* 59.

U.S. Small Business Administration (1979). *1978 annual report*. Washington, DC: U.S. Government Printing Office.

The World Bank (1978). *Employment and development of small enterprises*. Sector Policy Paper. Washington, DC: The World Bank.

PART II, SECTION 2

The next three chapters center on educational policy and child care. In the first chapter of this section, Bob St. Pierre discusses social science research on compensatory education. He begins by differentiating between two criteria for evaluating research: "Useful," which refers to the study's quality in answering some question of interest, and "Use," which refers to whether the study affects some user's actions or decisions. St. Pierre then describes and constrasts two large-scale compensatory education studies in which he has participated. Based upon this comparison, he discusses several obstacles to the successful application of the social sciences and offers recommendations for making research both more useful and more likely to be used.

In Chapter 9, Bob Crain and Karen Carsrud discuss the roles of the social sciences in school desegregation policy. They debunk the myth of the social scientist as "Philosopher-King" in the area of desegregation. Crain and Carsrud also criticize the traditional research focus on the global causal question, "does desegregation work?" and on questions that are of primary interest to the academic community, but not to administrators and judges who must construct desegregation plans. Crain and Carsrud contend that research on desegregation should instead focus on "nuts and bolts" issues in search of more effective ways to implement desegregation.

Jay Belsky, in the final chapter of this section, examines the science and politics of day care. Belsky briefly reviews the methodological shortcomings of day-care research. He concludes that despite its limitations, this research provides useful policy guidelines for day-care centers. These research-based guidelines have not translated into policy, however. Belsky considers why in a review of the political deliberations about day-care policy.

8

Are the Social Sciences Able to Answer Questions about Compensatory Education Programs?

ROBERT G. ST. PIERRE

The task given to writers in this section of the book is to offer evidence bearing on the ability of the social sciences to answer questions about selected social policy areas and to consider the impact of several potential obstacles to the successful application of the social sciences. To address these issues, I begin by first dealing with what it means to "answer a question" about social programs and what it means to "successfully apply" the social sciences. Next, I review selected compensatory education evaluations and draw conclusions about the questions they answered and the degree to which they are successful applications of the social sciences. Then comes a discussion of the obstacles faced in applying the social sciences to provide knowledge about compensatory education programs. The final section offers general conclusions about the application of social science research.

The chapter's main conclusion is that the social sciences have proven themselves capable of answering questions about compensatory education programs, but that they have not done so consistently. This conclusion was not drawn by performing a meta-analysis or meta-evaluation of compensatory education studies, but rather by integrating the author's own impressions gathered from doing and reading about compensatory education studies, and by reviewing studies for this chapter. Instead of providing an overall assessment of the efficacy of the social sciences in

AUTHOR'S NOTE: The author wishes to thank Bob Dentler, Lance Shotland, and Mel Mark for their comments on earlier drafts of this chapter.

obtaining information on compensatory education, this chapter offers examples that illustrate substantial variability in the success of the social sciences. Therefore, this chapter focuses on two compensatory education studies: The National Follow Through Evaluation conducted between 1967 and 1977 for the U.S. Office of Education, and the Compensatory Education Study, conducted between 1974 and 1978 for the National Institute of Education. These two evaluations illustrate diversity in terms of methodology, research questions, and the degree to which they answer questions. Further, the author played parts in both studies, and so the reviews and conclusions presented here are based on these firsthand experiences.

ANSWERING QUESTIONS AND APPLYING THE SOCIAL SCIENCES

To address the question posed in the title, it is necessary to specify what is meant by "answering questions" about a social program and about "successfully applying" the social sciences. Two criteria will be used in determining whether a question has been answered and whether the social sciences have been successfully applied. The first criterion pertains to the conduct of a well-designed and well-implemented study that yields believable results; by definition, such a high-quality study is a "useful" evaluation. This assertion is based on the notions that evaluations exist independent of their actual use and usefulness is a characteristic of the evaluation, not of what is done with the evaluation. The second criterion is the degree to which the evaluation results are actually "used" by some audience. Most of the literature on evaluation use fails to distinguish between "useful" and "used" (although this distinction has been made in other fields, e.g., Helmreich, 1975, distinguishes between "applicability" and "utilization" in the applied social psychology literature). It is often stated that an evaluation was not useful because it was not used. However, in the framework presented here, to be used is not a precondition to being useful, and although the sets of "used" and "useful" evaluations overlap, each contains a relatively large, unique number of studies.

Given the simplifying assumption of two levels (high and low) for each of the two criteria, Table 8.1 shows what can be concluded about answering questions concerning social programs and successfully applying the social sciences when different assumptions are made about evaluation use and evaluation usefulness (quality). To *answer a question*

TABLE 8.1
Conclusions to be Drawn Based on Different Assumptions
about Evaluation Quality (Usefulness) and Actual Use

		Actual Use	
		Low	High
QUALITY (Usefulness)	Low	(1) Cannot answer questions, waste of money (not useful and not used)	(2) Cannot answer questions, but may influence evaluation users (not useful but used)
	High	(3) Answers questions, but not a successful applicaton (useful but not used)	(4) Answers questions, successful application (useful and used)

about social programs, it is necessary to satisfy only the criterion of usefulness; i.e., to conduct a high-quality study (as in cell 3 or 4). It is not necessary for the study actually to be used for decision making or in any other sense. The provision of high-quality information is enough—the question gets answered regardless of the degree to which the answers are or are not used. On the other hand, a *successful application* of the social sciences requires that both criteria be met. The study must both answer questions (be useful, be of high quality) and be used (cell 4). In this framework, low-quality studies by definition are not capable of answering questions, and even if such studies are used, they do not qualify for a successful application of the social sciences. The low-quality, low-use study is simply a waste of money (cell 1). The low-quality, high-use study (cell 2) does not provide answers any more than the low-quality, low-use study, but for some reason it manages to influence evaluation audiences.

Having made the simple two-level distinctions between evaluations that do and do not answer questions, and between evaluations that are and are not successful applications of the social sciences, it is important to raise two complicating factors. First, some persons would argue that answering questions requires aggregating the results of several studies. Witness the recent increase in the use of meta-analysis as a technique for generating new knowledge. For the sake of simplicity we have limited our discussion of answering questions and successfully applying the social sciences to the case of a single study; however, the logic can be extended to cases in which multiple studies are of interest. Second, in practice, evaluations rarely fall neatly into one of the four cells defined in Table 8.1. It is often the case that an evaluation provides answers to some questions but not others; that the design is strong in one or two areas but weaker in others; or that the findings are only partly used, are neglected by the primary audience but used by a secondary audience, or are used for purposes not originally envisioned. As will be seen throughout the chapter, my preference is to be generous, to declare an evaluation partly useful if it is able to answer at least a subset of the questions that it set out to answer and to declare it a partly succesful application of the social sciences even if the users and uses differ from those originally intended.

THE FOLLOW THROUGH EVALUATION

An early Head Start evaluation (Wolff & Stein, 1966) stated that Head Start increased children's school readiness, with a later dropoff in public school. Based in part on this study, the Johnson administration proposed a Follow Through program to continue similar services to disadvantaged children through grade three. Because full funding for the program was not available, Follow Through's emphasis was changed from a full-scale service program to a demonstration program in which several educational specialists (called model sponsors), with widely divergent views of how early childhood education should be conducted, each implemented an educational model in several school districts. The Follow Through models included: Highly structured models emphasizing academic skills in reading and arithmetic; models stressing cognitive thinking through asking and answering questions, problem solving and creative writing; models emphasizing social-emotional development and encouraging exploration and discovery in academic areas; and models focusing on preparing parents to improve the education and development of their children (U.S. General Accounting Office, 1975, pp. 3-4). The model sponsors were responsible for designing an educational program (model) consistent with the learning theory in which they believed, implementing that model in multiple school districts, and monitoring the status of the model and improving it over time.

Evaluation Design

The National Follow Through Evaluation was quasi-experimental in nature. Expectations for success ran high at the beginning of the study in the late 1960s, and design considerations were not given high priority. It was assumed that program effects would be so large that they would be apparent regardless of the design. According to Egbert (1973):

> Its design stemmed from the conviction that sufficient improvement could be effected in the institutions serving children that children's development would be so markedly superior as to be readily demonstrated. . . .Follow Through's design was born also from the conviction that unless such substantial differences were manifest, the really massive increases in spending that would be required could not be justified. (p. 25)

In 1969 the U.S. Office of Education (USOE) contracted with SRI International to conduct the National Follow Through Evaluation. In 1972, when Abt Associates, Inc., became involved in Follow Through, USOE had focused the evaluation on a comparision of the effectiveness of different educational models, specified evaluation questions comprising only a subset of the broad goals of Follow Through, and limited the outcome measures to a few that could be used to compare sponsors (Haney, 1977). Thus, the primary question addressed by the national evaluation was whether the various educational models being tested in Follow Through had differing impacts on the academic and affective levels of pupils they served: To find out which model "works best."

Findings

The findings of the national evaluation are presented by Stebbins, St. Pierre, Proper, Anderson, & Cerva (1977), Anderson (1977), and Kennedy (1978). The purpose of presenting findings at this point is to set the stage for a discussion of the debate about the evaluation and the degree to which the evaluation was able to "answer questions" about Follow Through. Thus, only certain evaluation findings are reviewed: The most important ones and those that motivated much of the controversy.

The primary conclusion of the study was that "the effectiveness of each Follow Through model varied substantially from site group to site group; overall model averages varied little in comparison" (Stebbins et al., 1977, p. 135). The strength of this finding is better understood when one realizes that 11 of the 13 models with three or more school districts in the evaluation had at least one district with a positive average effect on basic skills (covariance-adjusted comparisons showed that Follow Through children performed better than comparison children), and that all 13 models had at least one district with a negative average effect (covariance-adjusted comparisons showed that comparison children performed better than Follow Through children). Another way to view the finding of district-to-district variability is to note that in each model with more than three districts, the range of average district effects was greater than the range of average model effects.

Models were grouped according to their domain of primary emphasis (behavioristic, cognitive, developmental, psychodynamic), and the ranks of the models in each group were averaged to allow statements about "types" of models rather than individual models. Based on this grouping, a secondary finding, not to be taken out of the context of the primary conclusion, was that "models that emphasize basic skills succeeded better than other models in helping children gain these skills. . . . Models that emphasize basic skills produced better results on tests of self-concept than did other models" (Stebbins et al., 1977, pp. 143, 147).

Conclusions were also drawn about the effectiveness of individual models, the differences in the effectiveness of models that implemented their programs in large cities as opposed to other locales; differences between Head Start as opposed to non-Head Start children; differences between children from high-income as opposed to low-income families; differences between kindergarten and first grade as opposed to second and third grades; and differences between later as opposed to earlier cohorts. The interested reader is referred to Stebbins et al. (1977) for specific conclusions in these areas.

Answering Questions and Applying the Social Sciences to Follow Through

What conclusions can be drawn about the degree to which the social sciences have answered questions about Follow Through and the degree to which the Follow Through evaluation was a successful application of the social sciences? In answering we must realize that different observers, faced with the same evidence, have come to very different conclusions about whether the Follow Through evaluation provided answers about Follow Through or whether the evaluation was a successful application of the social sciences.

Evidence that this is the case comes from the debate that took place upon release of the Follow Through evaluation. The debate occurred not so much because the evaluation was perceived as having immediate policy consequences for the Follow Through program, but more because of the size and scope of the evaluation and because it entailed a test of the effects of several different methods of educating children and was of potential interest to a wide public audience. Therefore, it had potential consequences for education in general. The debate over the evaluation is particularly relevant to the present discussion because it focused precisely on the issue being addressed here: Whether the evaluation was of sufficiently high quality to be useful.

Some of the controversy over the Follow Through evaluation was fanned by the popular press's interpretation of the findings. A front-page article in the *Washington Post* proclaimed in its header, "Basic Teaching Methods More Effective" (Feinberg, 1977, P.1). A similar message was delivered by LaTour (1977) in the *National Observer*. This article claimed "Basic Skills Found Lagging in 'Open' Classrooms" (p. 6). An article in *Newsweek* (Basic is better, 1977) cited the evaluation as finding that "children from low-income families fare far better in programs that emphasize structure and basic skills" (p. 76). Finally, Kilpatrick (1977), in a *Boston Globe* editorial, stated that the Follow Through study "confirmed the obvious: in education, basics are better" (p. 19). Although all of these examples took the secondary "basics are better" finding out of context, it is clear that much of the public accepted the evaluation as useful and providing legitimate answers about important educational questions.

On the other hand, evaluation findings were criticized by parties within the research community. For example, the evaluation was condemned for not making stronger statements about model effectiveness by the sponsor with the best evaluation results. In the *Education Daily* (1977), Wes Becker, sponsor of the District Instruction model, claimed that Abt Associates "tried to make the Oregon Direct Instruction model look bad by distorting the data to make it look as if things weren't as successful (p. 4). Becker complained about the finding of district-to-district variability, claiming that the finding was included to "justify continuing Follow Through's planned variation approach" (p. 4).

The evaluation was also criticized by the sponsors who didn't do as well in the evaluation. Hal Freeman, sponsor of Fordham University's Interdependent Learning model, stated in the same issue of *Education Daily* that "this longitudinal evaluation reduced this vastly complicated human enterprise into a few numbers. It's not just and it's not real" (p. 5). Freeman further asserted that Becker's Direct Instruction model looks good because "the kinds of instruments selected were in agreement with the practices in some models and not with others" (p. 5).

The major attack on the Follow Through evaluation came from a Ford Foundation-funded panel led by Ernest House. In the *HEW Monitor* (1977), House stated that the evaluation had "gross problems from the start" and "is widely regarded as a bad evaluation" (p. 338). Further, the panel's published critique (House, Glass, McLean, & Walker, 1978), although agreeing with the major finding of the study (that there is great site-to-site variation in the effectiveness of each model), was markedly critical of almost all aspects of the evaluation, contending that:

> The Follow Through evaluation was defective in a number of ways. The classification of models and outcome measures is misleading and perhaps untenable. The outcome measures assess very few of the model's goals and strongly favor models that concentrate on teaching mechanical skills. The definition of model effectiveness and the statistical procedure, analysis of covariance, employed to assess effectiveness are questionable. And the unit of analysis, the individual pupil, apparently favors the basic-skills models. (p. 156)

So, House et al. attacked the evaluation's findings on the basis that the evaluation was of low quality, was not useful, and that it therefore did not provide answers to questions.

The charges by House et al. were rebutted by Anderson, St. Pierre, Proper, & Stebbins (1978) and Wisler, Burns, & Iwamoto (1978). Support for the evaluation came from academicians such as Richard Elmore, who was involved with Follow Through for several years. In a letter to Richard Anderson, the Abt Associates Follow Through Project Director, Elmore (1978) stated, "House et al. have made a disastrously inaccurate reading of the Abt report on Follow Through . . . your report very skillfully addressed the most difficult issues that have arisen in the evaluation."

My own assessment of the usefulness of the Follow Through evaluation rests on the belief that evaluation is an imperfect tool and that evaluations can always be criticized on methodological grounds. Field-based evaluations are simply too difficult to conduct flawlessly; and although evaluation theorists can design top-notch studies, evaluation implementers understand that magnificent plans can easily be ruined by any of a wide range of circumstances. Because evaluations of any importance will engender debate, it is not surprising that critics typically attack a study's methodology. For example, the criticisms leveled by House et al. can be separated from the Follow Through evaluation and applied to many evaluations of field-based education programs; e.g., problems with treatment/comparison group mismatch, the use of covariance analysis to adjust for pretreatment differences between nonrandomly formed treatment and comparison groups, and the dispute over the appropriate unit of analysis. These represent a standard list of methodological problems, widely recognized in the field and discussed in the Follow Through evaluation report. This does not relieve Follow Through of the burden of these problems, but rather points out that the Follow Through evaluation shares a well-occupied spot with many other evaluations that have been accused of having faulty methodologies.

To show that those who critique evaluations do not have easy answers to the problems they raise, it can be noted that House et al.'s critique of Follow Through contained a reinterpretation of the results in which the authors argued that no model did especially better or worse than any other. However, in making this argument, House et al. relied on exactly the analytic outcomes that they had criticized earlier for being derived using faulty analytic techniques and poor measurement. Thus, it appears that for one purpose (trying to show that the evaluation was invalid) House et al. give no credit at all to the measures and analyses used in the evaluation, whereas for another purpose (trying to show that the models oriented to teaching basic skills did not work better than other models) they are willing to accept part of the analytic results. A detailed discussion of the major methodological points in the debate over the Follow Through evaluation is given by St. Pierre (1979).

A more refined assessment of the usefulness of the Follow Through evaluation may be reached by expanding the two levels of quality (high versus low) shown in Table 8.1 into a continuum so that evaluations do not have to be classified as only "good" or "bad." The Follow Through evaluation was neither exemplary, nor was it a disaster. Although it certainly had its drawbacks, it had its share of high spots. So, did it give us answers about Follow Through? Yes and no. The Follow Through evaluation provided convincing answers to some questions, especially those dealing with the performance of children in different educational programs on standardized achievement tests (the outcome measures in these areas were more reliable than the measures in other areas). It did a poorer job of answering other questions; e.g., measuring the implementation of each sponsor's model or assessing model effectiveness in noncognitive areas. Thus, the Follow Through evaluation was useful with respect to answering some questions and not useful with respect to others. However, even studies of partial utility, ones that are not able to answer all questions posed by evaluation users, still qualify for examination as potentially successful applications of the social sciences.

Did the Follow Through evaluation entail a successful application of the social sciences? The criteria for this are that the study be both useful (high quality) and used, and, again, the answer is partly yes and partly no. The extent to which the Follow Through evaluation met the criterion of usefulness has already been discussed. With respect to the criterion of actual use, the evaluation ran for so long (1967-1977) that many of the original intended users had left government service by the time it was completed. So, who used the evaluation? When the evaluation was completed it was assumed that the findings would be of potential use to several parties including Congress, Follow Through program administrators, USOE policymakers, Follow Through sponsors, and the educational community.

However, information from the evaluation was not used immediately by Congress or federal budget analysts for increasing or decreasing program funding. It was not used by model sponsors to improve their programs. It was not used by Follow Through program administrators for any particular purposes.

How was the evaluation used? Two main uses have been documented by Boruch and Cordray (1980) and St. Pierre (1979). The first and most immediate use of the evaluation was as ammunition for proponents of the "back to basics" movement. As noted earlier, popular press accounts of the evaluation picked up on the finding that models emphasizing the basic skills resulted in better pupil test scores on those skills. Thus, the general educational community was the first user of the evaluation.

The second use of the evaluation was not so immediate but was closer to what most evaluators think of as "legitimate" evaluation use. The evaluation was completed in April, 1977, and during the period between 1977 and 1980 many Follow Through sites applied to the Joint Dissemination Review Panel (JDRP) for status as validated, "exemplary" educational programs. The JDRP is a panel of persons from the U.S. Department of Education that meets periodically to review the evidence of effectiveness submitted for a wide variety of educational products and programs. Projects that meet JDRP standards may be endorsed by the Department of Education as exemplary and may be disseminated using Department of Education funds.

Follow Through sites applying for JDRP approval used data from the national evaluation as part of the evidence for their effectiveness. Though JDRP approval was seen initially as a means of acquiring additional funds for use in disseminating educational interventions, the impact on Follow Through sites and sponsors of having JDRP approval changed drastically when funds for the Follow Through program—for reasons extraneous to the program's merit—were cut under the Carter and Reagan administrations. Funding has decreased each year since 1980, and although some of the cuts have been absorbed across the board by all sponsors, the majority of cuts were made by eliminating entire sponsors and their sites. And, the order in which sponsors and sites were defunded was based in large part on whether they had received JDRP approval. This provides evidence for the assertion that the Follow Through evaluation was, in part, a succssful application of the social sciences, and it is a rather striking example of how evaluation use can occur some years after completion of a study.

THE COMPENSATORY EDUCATION STUDY

Providing a contrast with Follow Through, which involved a single large-scale, quasi-experimental evaluation, is the largely descriptive Compensatory Education Study that was funded by the National Institute of Education (NIE). Mandated by Congress in the 1974 Education Amendments, the Compensatory Education Study was to include an examination of the fundamental purposes and effectiveness of compensatory education programs; an analysis of ways to identify children in greatest need of compensatory education; an exploration of alternative ways of meeting those children's needs; and an examination of the feasibility, costs, and consequences of alternative ways of distributing federal compensatory education funds. To address these objectives, NIE built an in-house evaluation team that funded and monitored over 30 contractors who conducted work in four main areas: (1) The way in which compensatory education funds were currently being distributed and the effects of changing the formula for allocating funds; (2) the types of services provided to children who received compensatory education; (3) the effects of those services on students; and (4) the ways in which compensatory education programs were administered. Findings from the study covered all of the above areas and are illustrated by the following examples (NIE, 1978, pp. 3-8). Note how different they are from the types of findings presented in the Follow Through evaluation.

- The Title I formula (for allocating funds) accomplishes the purposes intended by the framers of the statute.

- The largest proportion of Title I money is directed to the two areas with the most formula-eligible children: Large central cities and rural sections outside metropolitan areas.

- Compensatory instructional services clearly emphasize the basic skills of reading and mathematics.

- Services are generally targeted for public elementary school students.

- States are unclear about their administrative responsibilites, and, as a result, have adopted widely different policies.

Did this evaluation answer questions about compensatory education? Most assuredly it did. The House Committee on Education and Labor stated that "the Committee has found the quality of the research by NIE to be excellent and has consequently relied upon these reports in formulating amendments to Title I" (U.S. House of Representatives, 1978, p. 5). Similarly, the Senate Committee on Human Resources noted that "The Committee wishes to commend the National Institute of Education for the uniformly high quality of its study, as well as its timeliness, as it proved invaluable to the Committee in the formulation of the Education Amendments of 1978" (U.S. Senate, 1978, p. 7). According to Cross (1979), the "study has been the single most productive piece of evaluation work ever undertaken on a federal education program" (p. 25). In a similar comment, House (no date) stated that "the federal government. . .conducted an evaluation that was helpful to Congress, that was valid, that was worthy of the name" (p. 2). These, as well as other reviews, demonstrate reasonable agreement in the research community about the high quality of the Compensatory Education Study. In general, researchers believe the evaluation answered most of the questions it set out to address, though House comments that the studies of student development were "less satisfactory than the rest of the NIE study" (p. 32). So, even though there is general agreement that the Compensatory Education Study provides an example of an outstanding evaluation, not all questions were answered. The study was useful in most but not all respects.

Given that the study did answer questions, was it a successful application of the social sciences? Yes. Boruch and Cordray (1980), as well as the other sources cited above, credit the study with contributing substantially to the deliberations of Congress when enacting the 1978 Education Amendments. In this respect the study is especially commendable for it was, in fact, used primarily for the purposes for which it was intended and by the audience as originally envisioned.

OBSTACLES TO THE SUCCESSFUL APPLICATION OF THE SOCIAL SCIENCES

Keeping in mind the earlier-stated definitions of answering questions and successfully applying the social sciences, and considering the two evaluations that have been reviewed, the question now becomes, "What can be said about obstacles faced in applying the social sciences to compensatory education programs?"

Problem Definition

Many, if not most, compensatory education studies have been plagued by inadequate problem definition. Follow Through is an exemplar in this respect. The program had multiple contradictory purposes, and no predominant group of evaluation users was ever able to shape the evaluation to its needs. In fact, the evaluation became focused only when a federal evaluation manager exercised his authority and pared down a wide range of evaluation questions to a manageable set. Though this act enabled us to learn something from Follow Through, it alienated many potential users by reducing the evaluation's relevance for them.

Quite the opposite from Follow Through, the Compensatory Education Study is noted for its solid foundation in terms of problem definition. In his review of the process used by NIE in conducting the Compensatory Education Study, Hill (1980) discussed how NIE moved from the broad research areas identified by Congress to specific research questions. In doing this, NIE spent a great deal of time across a two-year period building a research strategy. This included reaching agreement with Congress on a proper response to the mandate, asking Congress to identify topics that the mandate omitted, and reviewing additional areas of research with Congress. In sum, NIE spent a great deal of effort in specifying the questions of greatest concern and most use to Congress, and a large part of the study's success is attributable to this up-front work.

Therefore, one approach that evaluators can take in attempting to gain a clear definition of problems to be addressed is to point out to evaluation users the importance of being clear about what is wanted from an evaluation and to work with them to ensure that their information needs are being met. In their study of educational program evaluations, Boruch and Cordray (1980) address the complaints that evaluators do not deal with the issues faced by Congress and that information is not targeted to congressional needs and recommend that "evaluation statutes identify the specific questions which need to be addressed and specific audiences for results" (Executive Summary). In a companion study, Raizen and Rossi (1981) also call for greater specificity in congressional requests for information and note that "a call for evaluation that does not specify what questions are being asked can lead to the mismatching of expectations and performance by Congress and the evaluators" (p. 55). A similar message is relayed by Levine (1981) who holds that "the 'ideal legislation' will specify the scope of the evaluation activity, the questions to be addressed, and the procedure for reporting these results to Congress, and to the responsible program and oversight groups" (p. 19). Thus, evaluators are responding to the issue of problem definition in part by asking evaluation users for more direction, by saying that more targeted information will result from more targeted questions.

However, it is not reasonable to place all or even most of the burden in this area on evaluation users. Evaluators must assume the responsibility for working with users to clarify vague mandates, to illustrate the types of information that can be supplied in a given area, and to help generate additional questions. Evaluators understand what types of information can and cannot be provided much better than evaluation users, and perhaps the most important and most neglected part of our job is helping evaluation users frame clear questions and then giving them a notion of what information we can provide for them.

Some Questions Are Easier to Answer than Others

A second major obstacle to the successful application of the social sciences in compensatory education stems from the fact that some research questions are easier to answer than others. Put another way, social science methodology can do a better job at obtaining some types of information than others, and therefore some evaluations, or parts of evaluations, are much easier to conduct successfully than others. For example, information on who is being served and on services received is much easier to obtain than information on the effects of those services. Further, the majority of large-scale compensatory education evaluations conducted over the past 10 to 15 years has attempted to address difficult rather than easy questions. The two studies cited in this chapter provide examples of very different evaluations, answering different questions with different degrees of success. The Compensatory Education Study was concerned primarily with a very large, ongoing program (Title I of the Elementary and Secondary Education Act). The evaluation questions focused more on an assessment of what services were being provided, how, and to whom than on program outcomes. Thus, the questions were able to be addressed primarily by descriptive, cross-sectional methods. Because the study was aimed at discovering how an ongoing program operates, there was no assignment to treatment or control groups, and many of the rigidities of social experimentation were not required.

On the other hand, Follow Through involved an evaluation of a large-scale demonstration program. Although the "simple" collection of data required for the Compensatory Education Study was indeed obtrusive for the participating schools, the problems posed by a descriptive study of an operating program are nowhere near as difficult as those that occur in the implementation of a social experiment or demonstration program such as Follow Through. In this case the evaluator is typically dealing with fewer organizational units (schools, school districts), but the relationship is intensive and demanding. Pressures are put on program administrators to comply with the rigors of experimental or quasi-experimental designs, and the evaluators experience counterpressures to relax technical standards. The longitudinal nature of such studies dictates a host of problems that simply do not occur when using cross-sectional methods.

The problems involved in conducting randomized, controlled experiments have been chronicled at length by others (e.g., Cronbach, 1982). And though I am an advocate of the appropriate use of those methods, during the 1960s and 1970s many evaluation users asked premature questions about program impact. That is, evidence about impact was of primary interest, even when it was not at all obvious that programs were providing the intended services serving the intended populations, and so on. In such cases, it can be argued that descriptive information is an important precondition to conducting an impact evaluation. Further, evaluators did little to move evaluation users away from asking impact questions because impact studies are what "classical" evaluation research is all about. Thus, many evaluations conducted during the past 10 to 15 years adopted the experimental model when descriptive information on program operations, costs, targeting, and implementation (which can be gathered more easily, more quickly, and less expensively than information on impacts) would have been more useful to evaluation users. For example, when discussing the Compensatory Education Study, Cross (1979) noted that in 1974, after a decade of federal evaluations of compensatory education program, "almost no data existed on how much money from the Title I allocation was then being spent on basic skills" (p. 16). House's (no date) view in this area is that "federal officials in the Office of Education have attempted to evaluate these programs by an inappropriate approach to evaluation" (p. 2), and he commended NIE's Compensatory Education Study team for not relying on the experimental model.

How is this problem to be solved? The responsibility must be shouldered jointly by evaluators and evaluation users. For their part, evaluators must help evaluation users understand the value of information in nonimpact areas. They must also be willing to conduct "simple descriptive" studies, ones that are not as glamorous as large-scale, controversial impact evaluations. Next, evaluation users must be willing to do without information on program impacts if that information is premature or, at least, to add descriptive components to impact studies. Further, as noted earlier, evaluation users must be willing to participate more actively in the process of formulating research objectives and questions.

In closing this section, it is important to reiterate that randomized, controlled studies do indeed have a place in compensatory education evaluation. I have done such studies myself, and they have been worthwhile. However, the point is that increasing the ratio of descriptive studies to impact studies will lead to an overall improvement in the utility of the social sciences in compensatory education.

Some Outcomes Are More Easily Measured Than Others

This obstacle stems from the nature of the outcomes that an evaluation assesses and the degree to which those outcomes can be reasonably attained by the program. Consider Figure 8.1 that roughly orders several hypothesized outcomes of the Follow Through program on the dimension of "proximity," meaning the degree to which outcomes are temporally and conceptually proximate to or distal from the treatment. Outcomes such as the development of curriculum packages and the receipt of classroom instruction are proximate to the treatment, whereas an outcome such as "improved life chances" is distal, it is separated in both time and theory from the treatment (Schwartz, 1980).

The relationships between proximity of an outcome and three other outcome characteristics are of particular interest. First, proximate outcomes tend to have low social desirability and policy relevance whereas distal outcomes are high on this dimension. Improvements in the life chances of a child or overall school success are more socially desirable outcomes and policy relevant than, for example, training teachers to implement a given curriculum. Second, it is generally the case that social and educational programs can have a larger effect on proximal outcomes than distal outcomes. It is easier to provide mathematics instruction to children than to change their self-esteem. Third, if a relationship is found between participation in a program and an outcome, it is easier to argue that the relationship is causal when the outcome is proximal rather than distal. For example, the causal link between implementation of a curriculum and gains on a standardized achievement test is easier to demonstrate than the link between implementation of the curriculum and improved life chances.

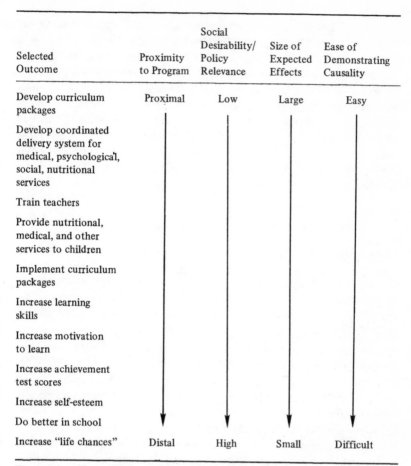

Selected Outcome	Proximity to Program	Social Desirability/ Policy Relevance	Size of Expected Effects	Ease of Demonstrating Causality
Develop curriculum packages	Proximal	Low	Large	Easy
Develop coordinated delivery system for medical, psychological, social, nutritional services				
Train teachers				
Provide nutritional, medical, and other services to children				
Implement curriculum packages				
Increase learning skills				
Increase motivation to learn				
Increase achievement test scores				
Increase self-esteem				
Do better in school				
Increase "life chances"	Distal	High	Small	Difficult

Figure 8.1   Characteristics of Selected Follow Through Outcomes

Many compensatory education evaluations have failed to find program effects, not because the program was ineffective in a proximal sense, but because the only measured outcomes were distal ones. The difficulty in detecting impacts on distal measures is not a function of faulty research design. It doesn't have to do with whether a randomized, controlled study is implemented. Rather, it stems from the fact that program impacts on distal outcomes are mediated by many factors outside the control of any single program. For example, if only "life chances," measured as, say, percentage of children graduating from high school, were assessed in the Follow Through evaluation, no educational model may have been found to be effective. Would this mean that all the educational models tested were of no value? Not necessarily. The program might have been very effective at changing the more proximal variables of reading or math skills, but in this scenario they were not measured. Alternatively, life chances are affected by so many factors besides the Follow Through program that it may be impossible to detect any impact on this variable, regardless of "true" program impact. Whether or not attempting to measure changes in more distal outcomes is worth the effort is a value question for the policymaker, not one for the evaluator. However, the implication is that measurement of proximal outcomes is crucial to a thorough examination of the program's efforts.

Administrators Are Tied to Their Programs

Another obstacle that complicates the job of a social scientist involved in answering questions about compensatory education programs stems from the close tie of most program developers and administrators to their programs. Although this holds in all fields, the ties may be closer in compensatory education, which has had a longer history than many other areas. Taking Follow Through as an example, the evaluation was set up to compare explicitly the effectiveness of different educational programs, many of which were the products of several years of work for the program developers. When faced with such an evaluation, it makes sense for program developers who fare poorly to complain about the methodology, the fairness of the evaluation, or anything else. It is much harder to conduct such an evaluation than, for example, it was to conduct the Compensatory Education Study, which was largely descriptive and did not make judgmental comparisons among the effects of programs that were each defended by enthusiastic stakeholders. These circumstances made the Compensatory Education study more politically acceptable to all parties than the Follow Through evaluation.

Disagreement on Judging Evaluation
Quality and Evaluation Use

The final obstacle to consider is one of definition: There is limited agreement on what constitutes a successful application of the social sciences. Researchers may disagree about the success of the social sciences because they hold different perspectives on what is and is not important in assessing the quality of an evaluation, they are more conservative in what they regard as believable evidence, or they simply interpret the results of studies differently. At this point it would be possible to launch into extended definitions of how to judge the quality (usefulness) of an evaluation and how to assess the degree to which evaluations are actually used. However, this chapter will only note that high-quality evaluations are measured against three criteria: Whether they are conducted in accordance with generally accepted technical standards, whether they are completed on time, and whether they are completed within budget. Each of these criteria have been given operational definitions elsewhere. For example, the Joint Committee on Standards for Educational Evaluation (1981), the ERS Standards Committee (1982), and the U.S. General Accounting Office (1978) have all issued "standards" for conducting evaluations, and Chelimsky (1983) discusses the criteria of timeliness and cost.

Boruch and Cordray (1980) analyzed six such sets of standards and found a high degree of overlap among them, leading to the conclusion that indeed there are generally accepted standards among evaluators for assessing an evaluation's quality. However, the application of such standards calls for personal judgment, and debates over the quality of specific evaluation studies are common. Such debates can occur with respect to any evaluation, simply because no evaluation is perfect and a determined critic will always be able to find flaws, even in the best studies. The crucial point is whether one considers an evaluation's flaws so severe as to undermine the validity of the study, or whether one takes the position that in spite of its flaws, an evaluation still yields believable conclusions. The determined critic will use any flaw to condemn an entire study. A more reasonable approach is the one used by House (no date) in his critique of the Compensatory Education Study in which he offered an overall opinion of the study, but also examined the study on a research question-by-question basis, thus affording a much more fine-grained assessment of evaluation quality.

The same kind of analysis pertains to assessing the degree to which an evaluation has been used. The past few years have seen several writings on the issue of defining evaluation use (e.g., Leviton & Hughes, 1981). And, as is the case with assessing evaluation quality, it is easier to gain a smattering of agreement among evaluators with respect to defining evaluation use than it is to gain consensus about the degree to which a particular evaluation has or has not been used. Boruch and Cordray (1980) have documented that a similar problem occurs with evaluation users who often do not recognize when they are using evaluation information: "We encountered a Congressional staffer who announced flatly at the beginning of an interview that evaluations were useless to his Committee. Five minutes later, he said that his

Committee used evaluations regularly in guiding the questioning of witnesses" (p. 6-1).

So, the final obstacle is related to the way in which we define and apply measures of evaluation quality and evaluation use. Though there is some agreement about definitions, putting those definitions into practice illuminates differences among researchers.

CONCLUSION

Program evaluations are just plain difficult to do. Just as there are few "slam-bang" social programs—programs that demonstrate large and impressive effects (Gilbert, Light, & Mosteller, 1975)—there are few slam-bang evaluations—ones that are well-designed, implemented without problems, and used for policy purposes. The problem is not that evaluation theorists do not know how to design studies, or that evaluation practitioners can never implement a study as designed, or that the intended evaluation users always neglect the evaluation findings. The problem is that few evaluations manage to accomplish all of these things. In this respect social scientists are as guilty of overselling themselves as program administrators: Both groups expect their work to make a big difference when, in fact, most programs do not make big differences, and most evaluations of those programs do not have great impacts. Just as a social program is only one input in the lives of program participants, evaluations of those programs are only one input into any given decision-making process. Overly high expectations for use thus make some evaluators feel that the social sciences are less successful than they actually are. Others never develop inflated expectations.

As should be clear by now, my approach is to give an evaluation the benefit of the doubt by looking for areas in which it is strong and can provide convincing answers, rather than by throwing out the entire evaluation if it is weak in one area. Rather than having to label an entire evaluation as useful versus useless, or as successful versus unsuccessful, it is preferable to make these judgments with respect to specific evaluation questions or objectives. An evaluation can be useful for answering questions a. b. and c, but not for questions d, e, and f. Of questions a, b, and c, we may find that only the information relative to question b was never used in any way. Such an evaluation can be labeled as one that did, in fact, answer questions about a social program and involve a partly successful application of the social sciences. Thus, the Follow Through evaluation answered *some* questions about compensatory education and was a *partly* successful application of the social sciences. The Compensatory Education Study answered *almost all* of its questions and was a *mostly successful* application of the social sciences.

To sum up, it is clear that the social sciences are able to answer questions about compensatory education programs, but that they have not done so consistently. The inconsistencies will not go away, however, their number can be reduced, and the chances of successfully applying the social sciences in compensatory education can be enhanced under the following conditions:

(1) When evaluation users have specific information needs and communicate those needs to evaluators;
(2) when evaluators work with evaluation users to clarify vague information needs;
(3) when evaluators are receptive to the expressed needs of evaluation users, tailoring research methods to questions rather than questions to methods;
(4) when the ratio of descriptive studies to impact studies is increased;
(5) when descriptive substudies and proximal outcomes are included in impact evaluations; and
(6) when social scientists realize that decisions about programs get made with or without information, and that in most cases, imperfect information is far better than no information at all.

NOTE

1. Clearly there are problems with this approach. For example, there may be disagreement about whether policy should be based on the answers to some questions in the absence of answers to others. If one believes that the Follow Through evaluation did provide convincing answers to questions about effects on standardized achievement tests, is it appropriate to make decisions on these answers when questions about the effects of Follow Through models in the affective domain are lacking?

REFERENCES

Anderson, R. B. (1977). The effectiveness of Follow Through: Evidence from the national analysis. *Curriculum Inquiry, 7*(3), 209-226.
Anderson, R. B., St. Pierre, R. G., Proper, E. C., & Stebbins, L. B. (1978). Pardon us, but what was the question again? A response to the critique of the Follow Through evaluation. *Harvard Educational Review, 48*(2), 161-170.

Basic is better. (1977, July 4). *Newsweek,* p. 76.

Boruch, R. F., & Cordray, D. B. (1980). *An appraisal of educational program evaluations: Federal, state and local agencies.* Evanston, IL: Northwestern University.

Chelimsky, E. (1983). The definition and measurement of evaluation quality as a management tool. In R. G. St. Pierre (Ed.), *New directions for program evaluation: Management and organization of program evaluation* (pp. 113-126). San Francisco: Jossey-Bass.

Conflicting follow-ups on Follow Through. (1977, July 11). *HEW Monitor,* p. 338.

Cronbach, L. J. (1982). *Designing evaluations of educational and social programs.* San Francisco: Jossey-Bass.

Cross, C. T. (1979). Title I evaluation—a case history in Congressional frustration. *Education Evaluation and Policy Analysis 1*(2), 15-21.

Egbert, R. L. (1973, April). *Planned variation in Follow Through.* Paper presented at the Brookings Institution Panel on Social Experimentation, Washington, DC.

Elmore, R. F. (1978, January 18). Personal communication to Richard Anderson.

Evaluation Research Society Standards Committee (1982). Evaluation Research Society standards for program evaluation. In P. H. Rossi (Ed.), *New directions for program evaluation: Standards for program evaluation: Standards for evaluation practice* (pp. 7-19). San Francisco: Jossey-Bass.

Feinberg, L. L. (1977, June 20). "Basic" teaching methods more effective, study says. *Washington Post,* p. 1.

Follow Through is questioned by winners, losers. (1977, June 14). *Education Daily,* pp. 4-6.

Gilbert, J. P., Light, R. J., & Mosteller, F. F. (1975). Assessing social interventions: An empirical base for policy. In C. A. Bennett & A. A. Lumsdaine (Eds.), *Evaluation and experiment.* New York: Academic Press.

Haney, W. (1977). *A technical history of the national Follow Through evaluation.* (Report to the U.S. Office of Education pursuant to Contract No. OEC-0-74-0394). Cambridge, MA: Huron Institute.

Helmreich, R. (1975). Appl;ied social psychology: The unfilled promise. *Personality and Social Psychology Bulletin, 1*(4).

Hill, P. T. (1980). Evaluating education programs for federal policymakers: Lessons from the NIE Compensatory Education Study. In J. Pincus (Ed.), *Educational evaluation in the public policy setting* (pp. 48-76). Santa Monica, CA: The Rand Corporation.

House, P. T. (no date). *A review of the National Institute of Education Compensatory Education Study: Collected reports.* Report commissioned by the National Academy of Education.

House, E. R., Glass, G. V., McLean, L. D., & Walker, D. F. (1978). No simple answer: Critique of the Follow Through evaluation. *Harvard Educational Review, 48*(2), 128-160.

Joint Committee on Standards for Educational Evaluation (1981). *Standards for evaluations of educational programs, projects, and materials.* New York: McGraw-Hill.

Kennedy, M. M. (1978). Findings from the Follow Through planned variation study. *Educational Researcher, 7*(6), 3-11.

Kilpatrick, J. J. (1977, July 1). Basics better in education, Cambridge group finds. *Boston Evening Globe,* p. 19.

LaTour, K. (1977, July 4). More high marks for the three r's: Basic skills found lagging in "open" classrooms. *National Observer,* p. 6.

Levine, R. A. (1981). Program evaluation and policy analyis in western nations: An overview. In R. A. Levine, M. A. Solomon, G. M. Hellstern, & H. Wollmann (Eds.), *Evaluation research and practice: Comparative and international perspectives* (pp. 27-60). Beverly Hills, CA: Sage.

Leviton, L. C., & Hughes, E.F.X. (1981, August). Research on the utilization of evaluations: A review and synthesis. *Evaluation Review, 5*(4), pp. 525-548.

National Institute of Education (1978, September). *Compensatory education study: Final report to Congress.* Washington: DC: National Institute of Education.

Raizen, S. A., & Rossi, P. H. (Eds.). (1981). *Program evaluation in education: When, how, to what ends?* Washington, DC: National Academy Press.

Schwartz, P. A. (1980). Program devaluation: Can the experiment reform? In E. H. Loveland (Ed.), *New directions for program evaluation* (Number 6). San Francisco, CA: Jossey-Bass.

Stebbins, L. B., St. Pierre, R. G., Proper, E. C., Anderson, R. B., & Cerva, T. R. (1977). *Education as experimentation: A planned variation model. Volume 4-A: An evaluation of Follow Through* (Report to the U.S. Office of Education pursuant to Contract No. 300-75-0134). Cambridge, MA: ABt Associates, Inc.

St. Pierre, R. G. (1979). The Follow Through debate. *Curriculum Inquiry, 9*(2), 149-161.

U.S. General Accounting Office (1975). *Follow Through: Lessons learned from its evaluation and need to improve its administration* (Report to Congress, MWD-75-34). Washington, DC: U.S. General Accounting Office.

U.S. General Accounting Office (1978). *Assessing social program impact evaluations: A checklist approach.* Washington, DC: U.S. General Accounting Office.

U.S. House of Representatives, Committee on Education and Labor (1978, May 11). *Report: The education amendments of 1978, H. R. 15.* 95th Congress, Second Session, Report No. 95-1137. Washington, DC: U.S. Government Printing Office.

U.S. Senate, Committee on Human Resources (1978, May 15). *Report: The education amendments of 1978, S. 1753.* 95th Congress, Second Session, Report No. 95-856. Washington, DC: U.S. Government Printing Office.

Wisler, C. E., Burns, G. P., & Iwamoto, D. (1978). Follow Through redux: A response to the critique by House, Glass, McLean, and Walker. *Harvard Educational Review, 48*(2), 171-185.

Wolff, M., & Stein, A. (1966). *Six months later, Head Start evaluation project.* New York: Yeshiva University, Ferkauf Graduate School of Education.

9

The Role of the Social Sciences in School Desegregation Policy

ROBERT L. CRAIN
KAREN BANKS CARSRUD

School desegregation is often cited as the best example of social scientists trying to redesign society to further social goals. However, there is surprisingly little evidence that social science actually affected the course of school desegregation. There is a myth of omnipotent social science as "philosopher-king," decreeing that schools should be desegregated, but this is myth. There was, and is, a real opportunity for social science to help school desegregation by what we will call social engineering—designing better desegregation plans or helping teachers in biracial classrooms—but most social scientists have expressed little interest in doing this. In short, social science refused to do what it could, while pretending to have done what it did not do.

THE MYTH: SOCIAL SCIENCE AS PHILSOPHER-KING

The vision of social science as philosopher-king, of a world where key decisions are made by applying the principles of social science, is an almost irresistable vision. For the Orwells of the radical right, school desegregtion is *1984* at its most horrible. Much as we might dislike doing so, we can reassure those who are frightened by this vision. Granted, many social scientists wrote on school desegregation and no doubt thought they were serving their social conscience. The

New York Times and *Saturday Review* quoted them. But we cannot see that this accomplished very much. Desegregation would probably have occurred in basically the same way if the social scientists had paid no attention.

It is easy to understand why the courts were accused of playing with social science. Chief Justice Warren's opinion in *Brown* v. *Topeka Board of Education* contains a paragraph famous among social scientists:

> The policy of separating the races is usually interpreted as denoting the inferiority of the Negro group. A sense of inferiority affects the motivation of a child to learn. Segregation with the sanction of law therefore has the tendency to retard the educational and mental development of Negro children and to deprive them of the benefits they would receive in a racially integrated school system.
>
> Whatever may have been the extent of psychological knowledge at the time of Plessy v. Ferguson, this finding is amply supported by modern authority. (Kluger, 1977, pp. 705-706)

What followed was the famous social science footnote that cited Clark (1950), Deutscher and Chein (1948), Frazier (1949), and others, and ended with the phrase "see generally Myrdal, *An American Dilemma*" (1944).

This footnote reflects a concerted effort by social scientists to aid the lawyers of the National Association for the Advancement of Colored People in the Brown suit. (Legal scholars have argued for years whether social science had any actual influence on the court.) In the passage quoted above, Warren was actually quoting a lower court ruling, and the passage was based heavily upon the testimony of a psychologist who was an expert witness, Louisa Holt (Kluger, 1977, pp. 419-422). What she told the Kansas court was very much the conventional wisdom of academic psychology in 1950—that isolating minority students gives them a warped perception of the world they lived in and hence a warped perception of their own worth. Her views were widely held. Deutscher and Chein (1948) had published a poll of American social scientists showing overwhelming agreement with the view that racial segregation in schools was harmful to black students.

Perhaps social science would have attracted a lot less attention had it not been for the dolls. When Kenneth Clark arrived in a South Carolina court room testifying for the NAACP about experiments in which black children reacted to black and white dolls presented to them in an experimental design, it was suddenly guaranteed that the Brown case would be viewed as a social science decision. Clark's black children preferred the white dolls (Clark & Clark, 1947), and according to psychological inference, thereby expressed a self-hatred presumably attributable to the discrimination black Americans had experienced. American social scientists and other intellectuals had been prepared for Clark's statements by the publication of *An American Dilemma* (Myrdal, 1944). *An American Dilemma* was in many ways a harbinger of the social science reports to be written later during the years of the Great Society, even by a research leadership team balanced by race, gender, and nationality. It was good social science, impressive and provocative; and it came along when the society was ready for it, at the end of World War II.

Even before the Supreme Court ruled on *Brown*, sociologists were also writing about what we would now call the "implementation" problem of school desegregation. At the request of the NAACP, a number of prominent social scientists issued a statement drawing on research about attitudes and behavior that argued that the best way to win support for school desegregation was to move quickly, quietly, and decisively to desegregate schools, with the expectation that public opinion would change to become consonant with mandated public behavior (Kluger, 1977, pp. 718-720). Once whites were confronted with the reality of desegregated schools, they would presumably accept them more readily.

Social science was also ready to start evaluating the policy it was supporting. Scientists predicted that black achievement test scores would go up as a result of desegregation, and the comparison of test scores before and after desegregation soon became a favorite dissertation topic. Today it is widely believed that desegregation does in fact enhance the learning of minority students (Crain & Mahard, 1983), and there is evidence that it improves their opportunity for success in adult life, in college, and at work (Braddock & McPartland, 1983).

This seems to be almost a model of social science as the philosopher-king, as the inventor of a grand strategy for human benefit that has improved its world. Perhaps so, but we have oversimplified the story a good bit. First, it is not obvious that social science was the cause of the social policy. Gunnar Myrdal may have brilliantly predicted that a revolution in American race relations would come after World War II, but predicting the future is not the same thing as causing it to happen. It seems unlikely tha the Supreme Court ruled the way it did primarily (or even secondarily) because of Kenneth Clark and Louisa Holt; surely the court knew it was making a moral, not a scientific, decision.

The second problem with this model of social science creating a better world is that science got off the bandwagon that it had supposedly started before the parade had much more than begun. The federal government ignored the social scientist's plea for quick implementation, instead allowing nearly 15 years of "massive resistance," "token integration," and local officials "standing in the schoolhouse door." Desegregation did not begin in earnest until the late 1960s. By then there should have been ample evidence of the educational worth of desegregation; in fact there was not much research, and the results were inconclusive. Many social scientists had discovered black self-determination as a socially superior goal to integration, and by the middle 1970s other scientists had become neoconservatives. Nowadays, social science is given credit for discovering that desegregation can cause white flight (Coleman, Kelly, & Moore, 1975) and that private schools are supposedly better than public ones (Coleman, Hoffer, & Kilgore, 1982). When the newspaper quotes someone as saying that desegregation has failed or that someone is as likely to be a professor as a southern senator, this is not because science discovered new evidence; there was little empirical research supporting community control in the 1960s (Hixson, 1974) and little evidence today for the claimed failure of desegregation. It is not that the data taught us that we were wrong in our earlier judgment. Perhaps newspapers sought out the more conservative voices or some social scientists changed their politics. If so, it is too bad because philosopher-kings are not supposed to be easily enamoured of the latest fad.

But even with all these caveats, we cannot resist giving social science an acceptable grade for creative social policy. If Frank Read, Dean of the University of Florida Law School, was correct when he stated that "the desegregation of southern schools is the greatest revolution in social mores to have occurred without bloodshed in the written history of man (1973)," even a tiny share of credit is worth a better than passing grade.

THE SOCIAL SCIENTIST AS SOCIAL ENGINEER

There is a second way to evaluate the social scientist: as the social engineer whose task is not to proclaim great social reforms or change social values but to assist the leaders of a democratic society in implementing policy. One could imagine that, in a perfect world, social science would by now have provided us with a vast number of books and articles telling the policymakers such things as:

- how to design the best desegregation plan for cities of various sizes and racial mixes,

- how to develop plans that would maximize the opportunity for housing to become integrated and lead to the elimination of the need for busing,

- how to decide what school racial mix will maximize achievement and minimize racial tension,

- how to devise the curriculum and teaching strategies needed for integrated classes, and

- how to develop a school discipline policy for newly desegregated schools that would reduce vandalism and racial violence and protect minority students from discriminatory discipline practices

One could expect that in the 30 years since *Brown* social science could have produced advice on all these issues. We think a fair evaluation would conclude that social scientists did rather badly in living up to this expectation:

(1) Have we determined the best desegregation plan for cities of various sizes and racial mixes? No, we do not have the ideal desegregation plan, one that addresses the legal issues of equal educational opportunity and simultaneously deals with issues such as white flight, practical problems in transportation students, or the financial costs of busing plans. Many of the refinements in desegregation, such as the creation of magnet schools, occurred with almost no help from social scientists.

(2) As for the desegregation plans that enhance desegregated housing, we can give social scientists credit for having belatedly demonstrated that a good school desegregation plan can increase the amount of housing desegregation (Pearce, 1980) but there is no "how to do it" manual on using schools to desegregate housing, and we are not aware of any school desegregation plan being drawn with a more than token concern for housing issues.

(3) In planning for desegregated schools, what racial mix will maximize achievement and minimize racial tension? We still do not know for certain. Until recently, there was almost no research about the optimal racial mix for a desegregated school. Earlier work in the area was opinion-based, and those opinions were clearly more heavily influenced by individual value preferences of scientists than by research data.

(4) We can give science credit for developing new curricula and teaching strategies for integrated schools. Individualized instruction, mastery learning, and cooperative learning strategies all evolved from the need to deal with the heterogeneity of classrooms (Brown, Davidson, Hoffman, & Patchen, 1977; Proshansky, 1966; Slavin, 1980, 1983). We should also give science a sizable part of the credit for the considerable improvement in the basic skills performance of minorities in the past two decades because science developed the tests that are universally used. Without those tests it is unlikely that basic skills and the achievement gap between blacks and whites could have become national issues;

without the public clamor, the movement to improve basic skills probably
would not have appeared.
(5) Do we know how to improve school discipline, reduce violence, or
reduce discriminatory discipline practices? No, there does not seem
to be much credit to distribute to social scientists in the area of school
discipline. Minority students are still suspended disproportionately in
most schools. Parents are still concerned about the lack of discipline
they perceive in desegregated schools. There is very little known about
how to prevent violence or improve race relations in desegregated secondary schools. No doubt there are many school principals who have
done good work, but we do not think they would give much of the
credit for their success to social science.

Looking at this very mixed bag of results, it is hard to give social
science more than a barely passing grade. Social science frequently
missed the opportunity to make specific recommendations to make
desegregation work better. Consider the following few examples. Some
research suggests that students who live very close to their elementary
schools make greater achievement gains than do students who are
bused into the school, perhaps because the school can more easily
involve parents (Howell, 1983). One can imagine that research on
this important topic could have been done; we could have arrived
at a reasonably clear conclusion and developed implications for public
policy; for example, worked on new kinds of desegregation plans that
used less busing or made busing equal for both racial groups. Or
consider a second example. There is a small amount of research that
suggests that racial violence in schools could be considerably reduced
if ninth-grade students were educated in high schools rather than in
junior highs (National Institute of Education, 1978). One can again
imagine that considerable research could have been done, a reasonably
clear conclusion drawn, and a policy recommendation in favor of
four-year high schools widely disseminated. There is, in fact, a national
trend toward moving the ninth grade into high school, but there is
no indication that this is because of scientific advice. We have seen
some scientific data (unpublished) suggesting that sixth graders can
be best educated in self-contained classrooms; if this is true, than
the widespread movement of sixth graders out of elementary schools
into middle schools could be disastrous and another indication of
the failure of social science to influence social policy. Because nearly
every city desegregates its schools by rearranging the distribution of
grades among school buildings, the failure of social science to have
anything to say about the educational effectiveness of different grade

configurations is a nontrivial omission (see testimony by Walberg in *Hoots,* 1982, pp. 213-214).

To give another example, a mass of educational research has concluded that ability-grouping or tracking of students can be educationally harmful to low-achieving students and can lead to resegregation within the classroom (Everston, Sanford, & Emmer, 1981; Findley & Bryan, 1971; Green & Griffore, 1978; NWREL, 1981; Simmons & Brady, 1981). Despite the literally scores of papers on this subject, the practice continues. In this case we cannot say that social science has failed because it has not done the research or not synthesized the research that has been done. Rather, social science has been insensitive to contextual factors. Teachers find heterogeneous classes difficult to teach (Goldberg, Passow, & Justman, 1966; Wilson & Schmidt, 1978), and social science has not produced an alternative teaching technology that makes heterogeneous classes as easy for a teacher to handle as homogeneous classes are.

Finally, consider a very small issue that has no major political or practical issues to deal with. Janet Scholfield has suggested, based on her research in a magnet middle school, that the standard student desks be replaced with tables that several students can share (Schofield, 1982). The use of tables furthers interracial relationships. One can imagine that this result could be replicated in other schools, a modest amount of evidence accumulated, and a recommendation made to school architects across the nation. This has not happened. Perhaps this is a failure of dissemination rather than a failure to do the research, but it is a failure nevertheless.

In summary, we are convinced that social science could have done a good deal more to make desegregation work. Social science, busy playing at being philosopher-king, has mostly missed the opportunity to play a critically needed role as social engineer.

Why Social Science Has Not Done More

In considering why social science has had so little impact on school desegregation practice, we have become convinced that the serious problems are not problems of method. Although there are methodological problems, they are no worse than those problems confronted in other types of social research.

We think the real answer lies in the peculiar relationship between academic social science and the public schools. Academic research has its own value system and its own reward structure; it does not value applied educational research and, hence, does not reward it.

Shotland and Mark, in their introduction to this volume, present a paradigm listing some possible obstacles limiting the role of social science in policymaking. In our view, the most important obstacle in that list is confusion over problem definition.

It is often the case in academic evaluations that a policymaker has one set of questions about a policy and the evaluator answers a different set. This is clearly what has happened in desegregation research. Social scientists became excited at the opportunity to struggle with grand questions about whether schools should or should not desegregate that were likely to attact the attention of the *New York Times* and our colleagues. The important academic rewards are controlled by the University; we succeed in our careers by collecting accolades from colleagues, in scholarly reviews from those in our field at other schools and in informal interdisciplinary recognition from the faculty on our campus. Most academic research has focused on arguing about whether desegregation raises the test scores of minority students. The question is of great interest, but the constitutional requirement of schools to desegregate would not be changed if minority test scores did not go up in integrated schools. Although we scientists debate grand questions about the overall impact of desegregation, the school administrators and judges, who do not have the luxury of reopening the *Brown* case, would much rather we had something to say about the nuts and bolts issues of how to draw a desegregation plan.

It is also not clear that anyone is interested in paying social scientists to do applied research on desegregation. An individual school district, confronted with its own desegregation problems, cannot reasonably be expected to fund research that is applicable to any of ten thousand other school districts. (And they probably also realize they may not want or be able to implement the research recommendations.) For this reason, the federal government has stepped in to finance most educational research. The problem is that the federal government has at various times made it clear that it also is not interested in supporting research on some important issues on school desegregation. For example, at the same time that the federal government has appropriated considerable funds for technical assistance in desegregation, it has prohibited these funds from being used for the actual drafting of desegregation plans. But the issues of whether the ninth grade should be put in junior high or senior high school is not the sort of exciting intellectual problem that would prompt most social scientists to work nights and weekends without a government grant. We think most of the social engineering associated with school desegregation fits perfectly under what we will call Crain and Carsrud's law: "If research is useful to the society, but is not suitable for faculty cocktail conversation and cannot be construed as elegant basic science, than the research will not be done unless there is a federal contract issued."

Even if there is a federal contract, it is not easy to persuade academics to accept the money or to deliver a useful product in return. In one Rand study of desegregation technical assistance, it was found that the more distinguished the university that received a federal contract to provide technical assistance, the worse the quality of assistance provided (Crocker et al., 1976, pp. 124-125). What are the implications of this bias of academics toward basic reseach and away from specific applied problems? The most important is that social science, by trying to evaluate school desegregation with the only measurement readily available, the standardized test score, attempted to refine desegregation from a moral issue in which social science had no special competence into an educational intervention, presumably to be cancelled like the open classroom fad if test scores did not improve to our liking. It is sobering to realize that if black student test scores had not gone up markedly in the last two decades, social scientists might have created a situation wherein Congress would have been under even greater pressure to act to limit judicial authority over school desegregation. A good case can be made that improvement in academic test performance was at best a secondary goal in the minds of the lawyers who brought the Brown suit to court. For them, the schools were the keystone of an edifice of segregated institutions. The fall of school segregation was supposed to lead to a collapse of segregation and discrimination in public accommodations, voting, housing, and employment. It did that and more, for it led to a call for "equality of educational opportunity" and to massive federal funding to help low achieving students. But most academics paid little attention to this and defined the significance of school desegregation quite narrowly as an effort to erase the "gap" between black and white IQ and achievement test scores.

The social scientists, in inventing the concept of IQ, provided scientific evidence for the inferiority of blacks; and by correlating desegregation with achievement test growth, they created scientific evidence for and against the merits of school desegregation. It is not clear that either of these acts was particularly helpful to schools or the black students facing desegregation.

To make matters worse, the social scientists debated the effect of desegregation on achievement inconclusively for many years. (The issue may be settled now, but it is too early to be sure; see Crain & Mahard,

1983, for a review of this large literature). The problem is that the research studies were primarily small and badly funded, and we do not have a very satisfactory method for synthesizing educational research results such as those produced by such studies in order to decide whether we've learned something or not. Meta-analysis, the statistical pooling of results from many studies, is a step in the right direction but is not an answer in itself, in part because we do not have in social science a sensible and meaningful way to interpret the importance of the effect of a policy on a social outcome. Thus one group of reviewers of the relationship between desegregation and minority achievement scores seemed to be in close agreement about the numerical magnitude of desegregation's effect on achievement but in almost no agreement as to whether that number should be considered large or small (Cooper, 1983). If this problem in interpreting research findings cannot be solved, the social sciences are going to have a great difficulty drawing policy-relevant conclusions from its research.

Perhaps one reason why academics focused so heavily on IQ and achievement scores is that academics themselves performed very well on such tests. It is always tempting to believe that the areas in which one does especially well are the most important, so it is difficult for academics not to elevate intelligence and all things intellectual into positions of sacred honor.

Many social scientists resist working with schools to improve school desegregation because they are enmeshed to some degree in writing—an almost simpleminded ethnic one-upmanship. It sometimes appears as if the function of social science has become reduced to the elementary process of deciding which racial group is morally upset. Scientists appear to fall into opposing camps: Those whose research searches for relationships between the social deprivation of minorities and low ability, family disorganization, or criminal behavior, and an opposing group whose research always finds the problem to be the racism of white individuals and white institutions. Scientists in the first group are not interested in improving methods of desegregation, whereas those in the second group probably have little desire to have a school district as a client.

There is another reason why social scientists resist working for school districts: They share with other intellectuals a bias against government. There is a surprising tendency for academics to believe that anyone who would consent to teach public school is at least feebleminded. Thus all government agencies are bad, but schools are worse. It is difficult to pursue applied work in education if one is constrained by assuming that schools are incompetent and teachers are fools.

This is only part of the adversarial relationship that exists between the academics and the school practitioners. Not only do the academics look down their noses at the school practitioners, but some practitioners consider academics to be time wasters at best and dangerous at worst. One can hardly blame the practitioner for wanting to ignore academic research when so much of it seems to be of so little value. But when research is policy-relevant many school officials are uninterested because they reject the basic tenant of science, that of generalizability. For many school administrators, nothing is true unless there is evidence in their own district—evidence from a statistical study done in the rest of the United States is meaningless.

The final major obstacle to the implementation of social science research is politics. The impressive way in which social science has learned about white flight from desegregation might lead us to expect this research to have had an impact on the way desegregation plans are drawn, but on the whole it has not. Decisions about desegregation plans are very much political decisions in which school board members must balance legal constraints and public sentiment—often leaving little room for consideration of complex research issues. Social scientists are not political actors; they hold no elected positions, and this means that when they work with policymakers they must be value-subservient. The policymaker has the responsibility for taking value positions and certainly cannot surrender that to the scientist. Social scientists interested in influencing social policy must compromise their own values. Scientists may resent having to do so, but the alternative is to retreat into a position of morally superior impotence.

The Social Scientist as Broker

Where does that leave social scientists? It seems to us that it leaves most social scientists in ineffective roles. By choosing to be philosopher-kings and arbiters of major moral issues, they have chosen not to provide the sort of scholarly work on desegregation that could be of value to policymakers. But social science need not be ineffective. Some university professors have chosen to step out of the traditional researcher's role to become directly involved with practitioners. In doing so they become "brokers" at the boundary between science and policymaking, synthesizing their own research with the work of others, creating policy-relevant conclusions, and then working with policymakers to implement the research results.

When we look at examples of social scientists serving in this role, we see cases in which science has had considerable impact. Most of the desegregation plans in the United States show the influence of a small group of social scientists who have served as consultants to civil rights groups, courts, and school districts. It would be difficult to exaggerate the impact that Gordon Foster of the University of Miami and other desegregation planners have had. Their notebooks and desk calculators have given us the basic framework for nearly every desegregation plan in the United States—the idea of creating pairs or clusters of white and black schools, assigning all the students in the pair or cluster to a formerly black school in certain grades and to the formerly white schools for other grades. This simple idea has been worked out in detail and used in thousands of school districts.

But courts are reluctant to use it in the large central cities with declining white populations, cities like Philadelphia, Los Angeles, and Atlanta, where desegregation would produce schools with heavy black majorities. Civil rights lawyers have attempted to persuade the courts to force the merger of these central city districts with the surrounding suburbs. However, the courts have only done so in two cases: Louisville and Wilmington. In this rather pessimistic environment a new plan— also developed by a professor—brings a new ray of hope. Gary Orfield, of the University of Chicago, serving as a consultant to the court, encouraged local planners to develop a voluntary cross-district solution for St. Louis. In this plan, existing school districts are not abolished, but minority students in the central city are permitted to volunteer to attend suburban schools while suburban whites are permitted to come into the city. This voluntary program represents an ideological compromise that has been embraced and denounced by both conservatives and liberals. It will be another decade before we know how important the St. Louis model is for other school districts, but as of now it is the most promising strategy we have for solving metropolitan segregation.

If we look at the professor-brokers like Foster and Orfield who stand between social science and the practitioner, we see some important differences in the methodology of their scientific work compared to the methods of more academic researchers. One is their different orientation to problem definition. Their involvement in the real world sensitizes them to everyday practical problems. But the most important difference is that they are more aware of political issues, are more able to establish a relationship of trust with practitioners, and are willing to devote the time and energy required to turn a scientific idea into a working policy.

An example of policy-relevant research methodology is the work of a third academic-broker, Robert Slavin of Johns Hopkins. He has worked on developing cooperative group learning systems that work in all types of classrooms, but are especially well-suited to integrated schools. Other academics (Aronson, 1978; Cook, 1978; Johnson & Johnson, 1981) have written on this and have carried out experiments showing the value of cooperative techniques; but Slavin has gone further, developing and manufacturing the curriculum materials and distributing them to thousands of classrooms. Most academic social scientists would consider such behavior inexplicably self-sacrificing.

Federal funding has been small in educational research but has nevertheless played an important role in encouraging the scientist-brokers. The government has recognized that applied work will not be done unless a counterpressure to the university's value system is created. Several government agencies have given preference in their funding to proposals intended to solve real world problems. More importantly, some agencies have established policy research centers to provide permanent funding to individuals who want the opportunity to work in a broker role.

Non-Academic Broker Roles:
School District Research and Evaluation

There is another approach to solving the academic-practitioner gap; instead of asking the university professor to become more practitioner-oriented, we can ask school districts to become more research-oriented. To date, only a few districts have strong independent research departments, but we expect more districts to strengthen their research capability in the future. In this chapter, we will single out the work in one school district as an example of the way technical assistance can be provided in large school districts by social scientists working in research and evaluation departments. It is to be understood that this school district, the Austin (Texas) Independent School District, may be atypical. It has repeatedly won prizes for the superiority of its evaluation reports. Its professional evaluation staff is relatively large and well trained; most are not ex-teachers, but instead have Ph.D's in Psychology, Educational Psychology, Communications, etc. Following are five brief examples of work done by this department.

One of the important ways Austin uses research is to clarify and rationalize the political process. For example, the Austin evaluation groups' evidence that white achievement test scores have been rising after desegregation has defused at least some of the opposition to busing there. Our other four examples are of technical assistance provided by the evaluation group resulting in changes in educational practice, in some cases through original research.

An interview with white parents who withdrew their children from public school in the year following a court order to desegregate was an important bit of market research. The report documenting parent concerns about discipline and disruption helped remind the school district to continue efforts to revise its school discipline practices, continue funding of monitors on school buses, and emphasize discipline in its public relations.

A survey of parents who did not withdraw their children from the public schools was fruitful. In addition to the collection of quite specific suggestions for ways the district might improve, it also became clear that many parents felt the extracurricular activities offered by the public schools were superior to those in private schools. A student involved in varsity athletics, band, orchestra, or drill team would lose those opportunities in most private schools. The data were useful in many ways. Although severe cuts in federal funding for desegregation programs have occurred, the district has continued the use of extra late-afternoon buses for any secondary students wishing to participate in after-school activities. Also, when district staff, board members, or other supporters met with parents, information about the activities and programs can be mentioned as part of the ongoing public relations function. Perhaps these actions would have been taken without the data, but perhaps not. The information at least had an obvious potential for usefulness and presumably played at least some part in the policymaking process.

A study was also undertaken to identify which schools had principals who dealt particularly well with court-ordered desegregation. Strategies used by those principals to facilitate the process were then identified, synthesized, and disseminated (Carsrud & Welsh, 1982).

Less political but equally important to issues of racial equity, the staff drew on both internal research and evidence from other researchers to argue against compensatory education programs that pull students out of the class for special tutoring—the research indicating that the disruption of the student's schedule and the resegregation and homogeneous ability groups that result are so harmful as to nearly wipe out the benefits of the additional resources provided. One result was a transfer of compensatory education funds from so-called "pullout" programs to an overall reduction in class size in certain low-income schools. This program has been quite effective (Carsrud & Doss, 1983).

If we compare the research and dissemination in Austin to the scholarly literature we immediately see the difference. Austin is concerned with the nuts and bolts of programs, conceptualized in a virtually atheoretical frame.

CONCLUSIONS

The American university is having difficulties dealing with its role as a disseminator of scientific research. The scientists who aspire to do policy-relevant work in social science must either do academically respectable work in addition or else content themselves with appointments at less prestigious universities. The elite universities are apparently the ones least able to provide competent assistance to policymakers in the case of school desegregation. The conflict between applied and basic research would be less serious if most academic researchers concerned with school desegregation were based in schools of education in which applied work is more respectable. Unfortunately many of them have appointments in academic departments such as psychology or sociology, in which the system of rewards discourages practical research. The federal government has been sensitive to this problem for some time and has attempted to compensate for it by putting more of its research funds into contracts that specify the research area rather than leaving it up to the scientist's discretion to select a topic. The federal government has also required researchers to include plans for dissemination of findings to practitioners in their proposals and has provided long-term funding for technical assistance centers and research and development centers dealing with various social policy topics, including school desegregation. Unfortunately, the federal government has repeatedly cut its budget for educational research and has been particularly cautious about spending money on politically sensitive research on desegregation. It remains an empirical question whether or not federal money can outperform the academic prestige hierarchy as an incentive for choosing one type of research over another.

In conclusion, we give social science bad grades. We social scientists have contributed to school desegregation policy, but far less than what we could have done. And we don't think it is because we lack the sophisticated statistical methods. The explanation is simpler: It is because we have worked on questions that will get us tenure, not questions that help kids; and it is because Congress and the Education Department have been reluctant to spend money on the research that needed to be done. When social science has worked, it is because some scientists have been willing to step out of their traditional role and the government or a local school district has been willing to support them while they have gotten their hands dirty.

Those who have stayed behind, keeping their hands clean inside the ivory tower, may feel that they have made great contributions to public policy, but we disagree. Many academic intellectuals were surprised that the Reagan budget cuts in research created no public outcry. We might like to believe that the school superintendents and the minority leaders did not protect because they are prejudiced against research. But it may also be because they think they do not need more research to study such things as the correlation of the religious background of school board members with their attitudes toward busing (Crain, Inger, McWorter & Vanecko, 1972).

NOTE

1. One area in which a synthesis seems to have developed is in the analysis of white flight. We seem to know a great deal about how much white flight occurs in desegregation, how long it persists, and what factors in desegregation plans can minimize the loss of white students. Perhaps the reasons why we know so much in this area is that one researcher, Christine Rossell, has devoted most of her professional career to this single question (Rossell, 1978; Rossell & Hawley, 1981, 1982).

REFERENCES

Aronson, E. (1978). *The jigsaw classroom.* Beverly Hills, CA: Sage.

Braddock, J. M., & McPartland, J. M. (1983). *More evidence on social-psychological processes that perpetuate minority segregation: The relationship between school desegregation and employment.* (Report No. 338.). Johns Hopkins University: Center for Social Organization of Schools.

Brown, W., Davison, J., Hoffman, G., & Patchen, M. (1977). Determinants of students' interracial behavior and opinion change. *Sociology of Education, 50,* 55-75.

Carsrud, K. B., & Doss, D. A. (1983). *Title I schoolwide projects: An alternative to pull out?* Paper presented at the annual meeting of the American Education Research Association, Montreal, Canada.

Carsrud, K. B., & Welsh, D. J. (1982). *On implementing court-ordered desegregation: What successful principals do.* Paper presented at the annual meeting of the American Educational Research Association, New York City. (ERIC Document No. 215 027).

Clark, K. G. (1950). *Effect of prejudice and discrimination on personality development.* Midcentury White House Conference on Children and Youth.

Clark, K. B., & Clark, M. (1947). Racial identification and preference in Negro children. In T. M. Newcomb & E. L. (Eds.), *Readings in social psychology* (pp. 551-560). New York: Holt, Reinhart & Winston.

Coleman, J. S., Kelly, S. D., & Moore, J. (1975). *Trends in school segregation, 1968-1973.* The Urban Institute.

Coleman, J. S., Hoffer, T., & Kilgore, S. (1982). *High school achievement.* New York: Basic Books.

Cook, S. W. (1978). Interpersonal and attitudinal outcomes for cooperating interracial groups, *Journal of Research and Development in Education, 12,* 97-113.

Copper, H. (1983). *Six reviews of research on desegregation and black achievement: What they tell us about knowledge synthesis.* Paper presented at 1983 meetings of the American Educational Research Association, Montreal, Canada.

Crain, R. L., Inger, M., McWorter, G. C., & Vanecko, J. S. (1972). *The politics of school desegregation.* Chicago: Aldine.

Crain, R. L., & Mahard, R. E. (1983). The effect of research methodology on desegregation-achievement studies: A meta-analysis. *American Journal of Sociology, 88,* 839-854.

Crocker, S., Crain, R. L., Graubard, M. H., Kimbrough, J. M., King, N. J. Thomas, M. A., Wirt, F. M. (1976). *Title IV of the Civil Rights Acts of 1964: A review of program operations.* Santa Monica, CA: The Rand Corporation.

Deutscher, M., & Chein, I. (1948). The psychological effects of enforced segregation: A survey of social sciences opinion. *Journal of Psychology, 26,* 259-287.

Everston, C. M., Sanford, J., & Emmer, E. T. (1981). Effects of class heterogeneity in junior school. *American Educational Research Journal, 18,* 219-232.

Findley, W. G., & Bryan, M. M. (1971). *Ability grouping, 1970: Status, impact, and alternatives.* Athens, GA: University of Georgia Center for Educational Improvement.

Frazier, E. F. (1949). *The Negro in the United States.* New York: Macmillan.

Goldberg, M., Passow, A., & Justman, J. (1966). *The effects of ability grouping.* New York: Teachers College Press, Columbia University.

Green, R. L., & Griffore, R. (1978). School desegregation, testing, and the urgent need for equity in education. *Education, 99,* 16-19.

Hixson, J. (1974). Community control: The values behind a call for change. In *Cultural pluralism.* Berkeley, CA: McCutchan Publishing Company.

Hoots v. Commonwealth of Pennsylvania (1982, April 24). 71 U.S. 538, testimony of Herbert Walberg, p. 165-221.

Howell, J. F. (1983). Walking or riding: Does it make a difference in black student achievement? *Journal of Educational Equity and Leadership, 3,* 127-133.

Johnson, D. W., & Johnson, R. T. (1981). Effects of cooperative and individualistic learning experiences on interethnic interaction. *Journal of Educational Psychology, 73,* 444-449.

Kluger, R. (1977). *Simple justice.* New York: Random House.

Myrdal, G. (1944). *An American dilemma: The Negro problem and modern democracy.* New York: Harper & Row.

National Institute of Education (1978). *Violent schools—safe schools: The Safe School Study Report to Congress.* Washington, DC: Government Printing Office.

Northwest Regional Educational Laboratory (1981). Topic summary reports on instructional grouping: Ability grouping (Research on school effectiveness project). Portland, OR: NWREL.

Pearce, D. (1980). *Breaking down barriers: New Evidence on the Impact of Metropolitan School Desegregation on Housing Patterns,* Washington: Center for National Police Review, School of Law, Catholic University.

Proshansky, H. M. (1966). The development of intergroup attitudes. In *Review of child development research* (Vol. 2). New York: Russell Sage.

Read, F. T., (1973). The Bloodless revolution: The judicial integration of the deep South. Brigham Young University, Welch lecture.

Rossell, C. H. (1978). *Assessing the unintended impacts of public policy: School desegregation and resegregation.* Washington, DC: National Institute of Education.

Rossell, C. H., & Hawley, W. D. (1981). Understanding white flight and doing something about it. In W. D. Hawley (Ed.), *Effective school desegregation equity, quality and feasibility.* Beverly Hills, CA: Sage.

Rossell, C. H., & Hawley, W. D. (1982). Policy alternatives for minimizing white flight. *Educational Evaluation and Policy Analysis, 4,* 205-222.

Schofield, J. W. (1982). *Black and White in school: Trust, tension, or tolerance?* New York: Praeger.

Simmons, C. A., & Brady, N. M. (1981). The impact of ability group placement decisions on the equality of educational opportunity in desegregated elementary schools. *The Urban Review, 13,*(2), 129-131.

Slavin, R. E. (1980). Cooperative learning. *Review of Educational Research, 50,* 315-342.

Slavin, R. E. (1983). *Cooperative learning.* New York: Longman.

Wilson, G. J., & Schmidt, D. W. (1978, April). What's new in ability grouping. *Phi Delta Kappan,* pp. 535-536.

10

The Science and Politics of Day Care

JAY BELSKY

The rising rate of women in the labor force represents one of the most pronounced changes in the American family since the turn of the century, with the most marked increase occurring since World War II. This dramatic change in American economic and family life has been most pronounced for women with children, with the number of working mothers increasing eight-fold between 1940 and 1975 (Hill, 1977, 1978). Projections reveal that this rate of growth will continue to produce an expected six million working mothers with children under six by 1985—a 32% increase over a brief 10-year period (Hill, 1978). Indeed, it is estimated that by 1990 three of every four mothers will work (Urban Institute, 1980).

Because increasing numbers of women with children are entering the labor force, either for reasons of personal fulfillment or economic need, increasing numbers of their offspring are being cared for by persons other than parents. Until recently, such nonparental care was viewed as a necessary evil, to be employed by the working poor or to be called upon in times of national emergency (e.g., World War II industrial mobilization). But, as the women's movement has gained increased acceptance, and as economic pressures, including inflation, unemployment, and high interest rates, have made middle-class lifestyles all the more difficult to achieve and maintain, the utilization and acceptance of day care has grown.

According to the most recent but already outdated data gathered by the United States Department of Health, Education, and Welfare, as of June 1978 about 2.6 million families used in-home care for more than 10 hours per week; 3.4 million relied on family day care; and

1.3 million relied on center care. What we see here, then, is that the type of care that is most publicly visible (day-care centers) is the least used. And, as we will see when we consider the effects of day care, we know most about this kind of care that we have the least of and far less about the kinds of care that are most widely employed.

Which families use day care? As a group, they can be distinguished from the general population on several dimensions. Although most children enrolled in day-care centers are white, minorities (especially blacks) are disproportionately represented among users of center care. Many of the families using day care, and virtually all who receive public subsidies, are either low-income single parents struggling to stay off welfare and to remain self-sufficient or dual-worker households in which a second parent's income keeps the family above the poverty line. Thus, millions of American parents have essentially no choice but to share the rearing of their children with others for extended periods of time each week (Ruopp & Travers, 1982).

Recent census bureau projections that estimate an average of 2.1 children per family suggest that the demographic pressures that affect the demand for supplementary child care will increase greatly in the 1980s (Hofferth, 1979). There should be little doubt, then, despite its ever-present critics (e.g., Fraiberg, 1977), that supplementary, non-maternal child care, commonly known as day-care, is here to stay. In view of this reality and the demographic character of contemporary American society that determines it, there should be little argument that day care is, and ought to be, an issue of public policy. And there are many groups sharing interest in day care that are concerned about public policy. Some of these, such as children and parents, are beneficiaries of day care, whereas others may be regarded as "gatekeepers," such as the researchers and policymakers who control public information and decision making. Because these interest groups hold distinct (though by no means mutually exclusive) concerns, those issues that public policy does or could address and that day-care research does address are not equally valued by all constituencies (Travers, Beck, & Bissell, 1982).

It is beyond the scope of this chapter, as well as my own expertise in and concern for child development, to address all policy-related issues. Thus, my intention is to restrict this analysis of day care and public policy to questions of specific interest to those concerned with the effects of this experience on children's development. In view of this restricted focus, two particular issues that have been of concern to child developmentalists will be the focus of my analysis of social science research, social policy, and day care. The first has to do with the effects of supplementary child care on children's cognitive, emotional, and social development. Some developmental theory and past research on the psychological impairment of institutionalized children (especially infants) suggested that day care would prove harmful to children (e.g., Spitz, 1945). Thus, the basic question for policymakers, and indeed the principal question that guided initial child development research on day care, was, "Is day care bad for young children? That is, does rearing outside the confines of the family in a group program adversely affect intellectual, social, and emotional development?" It should be clear that this specific interest in the developmental consequences of day care, and particularly a concern for negative effects, derived from policymakers' and scientists' obligation to protect the public from harm. If day care proved detrimental to development, it would be hard to make the case that day care was in the public's best interest; consequently, it would be difficult to endorse policies to promote, or even support, the group-rearing of young children beyond the confines of the family.

If, on the other hand, group-rearing did not prove harmful to children, a second issue would be raised: "Under what conditions would children fare the best in day care? That is, what types of rearing environments prove most supportive of children's development?" Because the day-care research I will review does not indicate that day care is necessarily harmful to children, this second issue has become the principal concern in recent years of policy-minded child developmentalists studying day care. Presumably, if conditions of care that promote optimal development can be identified, then a policy imperative would exist to encourage such conditions. At the very least, there would exist an obligation to assure that inadequate conditions of care not be tolerated, especially if purchased with tax revenues.

In the course of this chapter I will review social science research evidence that does, in fact, address and even answer both sets of questions raised above—one conerned with the effects of day care, the other with the conditions that define quality or growth-facilitating care. Before presenting this review, that itself draws heavily upon analyses offered elsewhere (Belsky & Steinberg 1978; Belsky, Steinberg, & Walker, 1982), I consider issues of measurement and evaluation that serve to qualify some of the conclusions that can be drawn from available day-care research. After reviewing limits of day-care research and what is known about the effects of day care and the nature of quality care, I will turn attention to the policymaking process, drawing heavily upon an insightful analysis of its recent history presented by Nelson (1982). My point here will be to demonstrate that although all the day-care research to be reviewed provides policy-relevant information, day-care policy seems to develop out of a political process that has little if anything to do with scientific inquiry.

SOCIAL SCIENCE RESEARCH AND DAY CARE

Scientific Limitations

It is a scientific truism that the validity of conclusions that can be drawn from research is a function of the adequacy of a research design. In the area of day-care research there exists a variety of measurement and design problems that undermine the confidence that can be placed in the results of many studies. In part this is a function of the fact that day-care research is, by its very nature, field research. Indeed, in those instances in which research on day care is most carefully controlled to conform to the requirements of experimental design, the circumstances of the research are often so unusual as to make the generalizability of the findings to the population at large highly questionable. There seems to be a trade-off, then, between methodological elegance (i.e., internal validity) and substantive significance (i.e., external validity) in this field of inquiry. All this is not to say that poor research is to be accepted or that good day-care research cannot and has not been carried out. In point of fact, the research, although by no means being elegant or without its methodological limitations, provides valid and useful information for scientists and policymakers alike.

Sample Limitations

Initial research on day care was restricted to university-connected centers providing especially high-quality care. Staff-child ratios were especially good (few children per caregiver); the training of staff both in child development and child care was often extensive; and the day-to-day experiences made available to children were frequently based upon formal curriculums specifically intended to foster cognitive, social, and emotional development (e.g., Ricciuti, 1974; Ramey & Campbell, 1979; Kagan, Kearsley, & Zelazo, 1978). Obviously, such care is not representative of that experienced by most children in this country. Although such sampling restrictions in day-care research may limit the degree to which results can be generalized, this does not necessarily mean they are without value. When the evidence indicates that high-quality care is not detrimental to development, there is good scientific reason to refute the claim that daily separation of young children from their mothers *necessarily* impairs the child's psychological functioning. It should be noted, moreover, that in recent years this tendency to study only optimal caregiving environments is changing. More than ever, social scientists are moving beyond highly controlled settings to investigate the nature and effects of community-sponsored day care (e.g., Blanchard & Main, 1979; Clarke-Stewart, 1980; Cummings, 1980; Golden, Rosenbluth, Grossi, Policave, Freeman, & Brownless, 1978; Rubenstein & Howes, 1979).

Design Limitations

There exist two principal limitations of day-care research with respect to design. The first has to do with the immediacy of the effects of day care that are evaluated, the second with the comparability of home-care samples that are often compared in order to discern day-care effects.

With the exception of three investigations (Moore, 1975; Robertson, 1982; Barton & Schwarz, 1981), there are no follow-up studies of children exposed to home care versus day care beyond the preschool years. And two of these studies are retrospective in nature, such that only Moore's (1975) research in England involves a prospective, longitudinal design. It is entirely possible, therefore, that any effects of day care that have been discerned may disappear, or conversely that effects not observed initially might appear with time. Because we know little if anything about the long-range impact of day-care experience, there is reason to be cautious in drawing any conclusions, positive or negative, about the effects of day care.

Even more serious a concern from the standpoint of design are the potential preexisting differences that characterize children reared in day-care centers and at home. In most investigations of the effects of day care, two samples are compared, one using day care, the other being reared at home. Such comparative designs are founded upon the assumption that when developmental differences exist they can be attributed to variation in child care experience. But a major problem, perhaps *the* major problem of such designs, and indeed the "Achilles' heel" of day-care research, is that important differences are likely to characterize home-reared and day care-reared comparison groups *before* variation in child care is experienced (Roopnarine & Lamb, 1978). Under such circumstances the attribution of subsequent developmental differences to day care, and thus the very notion of day-care effects, may be inappropriate.

There have been two generally sound methodological approaches to dealing with this problem—each of which has serious limits. The first is to include in study designs matched samples that vary only in the rearing environment to which they are principally exposed (home or day care). A variation on this theme is to statistically control for preexisting group differences in any evaluation of day-care effects. The major problem with these approaches is the assumption that the important domains of potential differences are known and well measured. Not surprisingly, studies have implemented controlled designs that equate groups (through matching or statistical analyses) on routine demographic factors such as parental education, income, and birth order of child. Yet it is likely that significant variations remain uncontrolled in such studies. Indeed, it has been shown that families that place their children in day care differ in important respects from those that do not (Hock, 1976, 1980; Sibbison, 1973). Hock (1976) found, for example, that mothers who rely upon day-care services for their infants possess different attitudes toward the maternal role than those who do not. Families that use day care are likely, then, to differ from those that do not—a serious problem for virtually all studies of the effects of day care. In some respects, studies of the effect of day care may involve the comparison of apples and oranges.

The traditional solution to such methodological difficulties is to adopt a truly experimental, as opposed to quasi-experimental, design by randomly assigning subjects to treatment conditions. In the real world this is quite difficult. Indeed, I am aware of only a single investigation that has pursued this strategy (Ramey & Campbell, 1979). And because such control can only be implemented when one has control of the day-care facility, this project, not surprisingly, involved one of those nonrepresentative, high-quality, university-based, research-oriented day-care centers mentioned earlier. An understandable, yet no less noticeable, trade-off was made in this investigation, then, between experimental control and generalizability of results.

Two investigators have implemented creative strategies to try to overcome the inherent limits of such trade-offs by using families waiting to be enrolled in oversubscribed day-care centers as comparisons for families with children already in day care (Cochran, 1977; Peters, 1973). But even this design that controls for the important variable of *motivation to use supplementary care* has its problems. If families desire entry into a day-care center and are not enrolled either for reasons of experimental design or because an insufficient number of spaces are available to accommodate them, it remains quite possible, perhaps probable, that they will seek to have their child care needs met elsewhere— either by finding another center, a family day-care home, or relying on a babysitter. To the extent that such alternative child-care arrangements are made, the very purpose and function of experimental control are subverted by the exigencies of the real world.

Experimentally controlled designs that permit comparison of home-reared and day care-reared children may simply not be possible in day-care research because their successful implementation would require denying some families access to all types of day care. What this suggests is that quasi-experimental designs may be the best we can hope for, and we have already documented the limits of research that has adopted, or is likely to adopt, such an approach.

Measurement

The measurement problems that characterize research on day care are no different from those that characterize developmental psychology and the social sciences more generally. When it comes to assessing children's intellectual, social, and emotional development in order to chronicle day-care effects, the scientist is faced with very real limits in available technology. Once again a trade-off characterizes the scientific process. The assessment of intellectual development represents a case in point. One can opt, as many have, for standardized developmental assessments that, although being highly reliable and well standardized, may not be representative of many cognitive skills, such as everyday problem solving, in which scientists, policymakers, and the public are most interested.

The study of social development has somewhat greater problems. The reasons for this are varied. First, there is little agreement about what ought to be measured if one wants to assess social competence, for example. Second, and probably as a consequence, there are few well-standardized instruments to select from. Thus, most day-care researchers rely upon observed behavior to gather data on cooperation, aggression, and the like. But although such strategies possess a fair degree of face validity, their psychometric properties and predictive utility are far from established.

Conclusion

This analysis of limits in day-care research could easily and understandably lead the rigorous scientist to conclude that research on the

effects of day care cannot be done well, or at least not well enough
so that it is useful to policymakers. There are two reasons why I would
not draw this conclusion. The first is that if the principal question
is whether day care is bad for children, then even nonperfectly controlled designs can answer this question. Unless we presume that families
that place their children in day care do a better job of caring for
their offspring before and during their placement (and no such evidence
has even been gathered), then comparisons that consistently reveal few
differences between day-care and home-reared children should allay
most fears that policymakers are likely to have. Thus, although the
feasible research designs may not be ideal for documenting the effects
of day care per se, they appear good enough to chronicle deficits
that would be associated with (as opposed to caused by) day-care rearing.

My second cause for confidence in available day-care research derives
from the data themselves. Despite limits in design and especially
measurement, findings across studies are surprisingly consistent, even
if not perfectly uniform. And, as I hope to show, when inconsistency
is apparent, this too appears both explainable and meaningful.

THE DEVELOPMENTAL EFFECTS
OF DAY CARE

Having arrived at this conclusion, I will proceed to summarize the
effects of day care upon the intellectual, emotional, and social development of young children.

Intellectual Development

The overwhelming majority (over 80 percent) of studies of the effects
of day care on subsequent intellectual development reveal few differences between day care-reared childen and matched home-reared
controls (Belsky, Steinberg, & Walker, 1982). Although a number of
investigators discerned initial gains in one or many test subscales, all
significant differences between day-care children and matched controls
disappeared during the program or soon after its termination. In the
only long-term follow-up study in this area, 102 or 120 Swedish children
initially investigated by Cochran (1977) during infancy were found
at 5½ years of age to be equal in intelligence regardless of whether
they had been continuously reared in a day-care center, family day-care
home, or in their own homes by their parents (Gunnarson, 1978).
For children from relatively advantaged families, then, exposure to

day care, even to high-quality, cognitively enriched programs, does not appear to result in any long-term gains in IQ test performance. Neither, though, does it seem that any losses in intellectual performance result from enrollment in day care.

In contrast to this conclusion regarding children from advantaged families, it is of significance that positive effects of the day-care experience on performance on standardized tests of intellectual development have been reported by a handful of investigators for those children who have been categorized as higher risk for developmental delay than the average middle-class child. By positive effects I am referring not to improvement in intelligence test scores but to the prevention of the all too often discerned decline over time in IQ scores of children growing up in poverty. In this regard, Ramey, Dorval, and Baker-Ward (1981) found that for children reared continuously in center care since early infancy, only 11 percent of the day care-reared children scored in the range of cognitive-educational handicap (IQ $\leq$ 85) at age five, whereas a full 35 percent of equally impoverished home-reared controls scored below this level of functioning. It must be noted, however, in this and most other experimental studies of the effects of day care on children from low-income families, that the children were enrolled in centers specifically designed to provide cognitive enrichment, with programs varying widely in the kind of special enrichment offered.

The overall picture of evidence, duly qualified, suggests that the day-care experience has neither beneficial nor adverse effects on the intellectual development (as measured by standardized tests) of most children. For economically disadvantaged children, however, day care may have an enduring positive effect; that is, it appears that day-care experience may reduce the drop-off in test scores that typically occurs in high-risk populations after 18 months of age (Belsky & Steinberg, 1978; Belsky, Steinberg, & Walker, 1982).

Emotional Development

Historically, the mother-child bond has been of prime concern to those interested in the influence of early experience upon emotional development. Psychoanalytic theory and early research on institutionalized children (e.g., Bowlby, 1951; Spitz, 1945) suggested that any arrangement that deprived the child of continuous access to the mother would impair the development of a strong maternal attachment and thereby adversely affect the child's emotional security. Because day care, by its very nature, entails the daily separation of mother from child, a good deal of attention has been devoted to discovering whether child care outside the home does indeed disrupt the child's emotional tie to his mother. The major strategy for making such an appraisal has been to observe young children's responses to separation from and reunion with their mothers (usually in an unfamiliar laboratory playroom) and to see whether children prefer to interact with their mothers, their caregivers, or a stranger in free play situations.

In a very early, and therefore noteworthy, study, Blehar (1974) observed children aged 30 and 40 months of age who were enrolled in day care for five months. She observed disturbances in the attachment relationships that these children had developed with their mothers. In each age group, the home-reared comparison subjects were more likely to greet their mothers positively following the stressful separation experience, a behavioral style that is considered to index a secure emotional attachment (Sroufe, 1979). Much criticism has been wielded against this study (Belsky & Steinberg, 1978), and an attempt to replicate Blehar's 40-month results, using many more methodological controls, failed to find the home-care/day-care differences she discerned (Moskowitz, Schwarz, & Corsini, 1977). Although a few investigations do indicate that day-care children are more likely to become distressed following separation from caregiver (Cochran, 1977; Ricciuti, 1974), evidence of similar patterns of emotional development in day care- and home-reared children comes from a series of studies of 10- to 12-month-old, (Brookhart & Hock, 1976), 5- to 30-month old (Doyle, 1975), 36-month-old (Roopnarine & Lamb, 1978), and 41- to 45-month-old children (Portnoy & Simmons, 1978). In each investigation, response to separation from and reunion with mother were generally equivalent between groups that varied in early rearing experience. Why then do Blehar's (1974) previous results differ so markedly from the major trend in the literature? Two explanations come to mind—one historical, the other developmental.

Blehar's children were enrolled in day care in the early 1970s, a time when day care, especially for very young children, was still looked upon negatively by many. Possibly, then, the guilt that parents experienced in violating cultural standards, or even the quality of care that was offered when day care was such a relatively new phenomenon, could have adversely influenced the Blehar subjects. Thus, a cohort effect, emphasizing the historical timing of day-care enrollment, might be responsible for her divergent results.

Additionally, it needs to be noted that Blehar's children were only in day care for five months when evaluated. And recent evidence indicates that a "transient distress reaction" may be associated with initial adaptation to daily separation from parents and thus may account for Blehar's data. This explanation was first proposed by Portnoy and Simmons (1978), who were unable to replicate Blehar's results, but studied children who averaged 9½ months of day care experience prior to assessment. And, in an entirely independent study, Blanchard and Main (1979) found that avoidance of mother (both during daily pickup from day care and in a structured laboratory situation), decreased the longer the child had been in day care. These findings suggest, then, that young children may go through a period of stressful adaptation to supplementary child care. But once they come to understand that regular separation from parent need not imply loss of the attachment figure, adaptation is achieved and problematic behavior is reduced.

Beyond the just discussed transient-distress reaction, negative effects of day care may be absent primarily when supplementary child care arrangements are reasonably stable and care is of a reasonable quality. In fact, a recent study of infants enrolled prior to their first birthday in unstable (i.e., frequently changing) day-care arrangements reveals that children in such poor quality care arrangements are at risk for developing anxious-avoidant attachment relations with their mothers (Vaughn, Gove, & Egeland, 1980). Such attachment relations, it is important to note, have been found to predict problems in adjusting to peers during the preschool years (Arend, Gove, & Sroufe, 1979).

A follow-up study of these same children led its authors to conclude, however, that even these effects may not be long lasting: "At two years of age the effects of out of home care were no longer striking. . . . For this sample, then, it appears that the cumulative adverse effects of out-of-home care were minimal" (Farber & Egeland, 1982, p. 120). Despite these conclusions, it should be noted several trends were apparent in Farber and Egeland's data on children's behavior during a problem-solving episode that could lead a more cautious reader to a different conclusion. Specifically, toddlers whose mothers began working prior to their infants' first birthday displayed significantly less enthusiasm in confronting a challenging task than children who had no day care experience. Furthermore, they tended to be less compliant in following their mothers' instructions and were less persistent in dealing with a difficult problem than children who had never been in day care or who began day care after their first birthday. Finally, they, like the late-entry day-care children, tended to display more negative affect.

These mostly near significant ($p < .10$) trends that qualify the Farber and Egeland (1982) conclusions are important in view of two additional and recent studies that also raise questions about early entry into day care. In one that was conducted in Bermuda that will be discussed in more detail when we consider the conditions of quality care, McCartney and her colleagues (1982, p. 148) found that "children who began group care in infancy were rated as more maladjusted (when studied between three and five years of age) than those who were cared for by sitters or in family day care homes for the early years and who began group care at later ages." In a retrospective investigation of 8- to 10-year-olds who had varied in their preschool experiences. Barton and Schwarz (1981) found day-care entry prior to 12 months to be associated with higher levels of misbehavior and greater social withdrawal, even after controlling for the education of both parents.

These new data lead me to modify conclusions that have been arrived at in past reviews in order to underscore the potentially problematical nature of early entry into community-based, as opposed to university-based, day care (Belsky & Steinberg, 1978; Belsky, Steinberg, & Walker, 1982). Supplementary child care exerts little influence on the child's emotional ties to his or her mother (other than transient distress) except under certain conditions, as when children are enrolled in unstable or poor quality day-care arrangements prior to their first birthday. Under such conditions, infants may be more likely to develop a particular kind of disturbance in their relations with their primary attachment figure: They will be likely to avoid her. Further, they may be more likely to display emotional and social problems in subsequent years. Important to note, though, is the fact that such deleterious consequences may not be long lasting or inevitable. Recall that Farber and Egeland themselves felt that little effect of early entry was evident at two years of age. Further, studies of high-quality care have failed to discern negative consequences of early entry (Ricciuti, 1974; Kagan, Kearsley, & Zelazo, 1978; Ramey, Dorval, & Baker-Ward, 1981).

Social Development

Earlier it was noted that both economics and ideology play a major role in the utilization of day care in the United States, as increasing numbers of mothers with young children are working outside the home— either for reasons of financial necessity or personal fulfillment. To fully understand such early reliance on group-rearing, one also needs to recognize the value that American culture places on independence. In marked contrast to the Japanese, for example, who view their newborns as independent and thus in great need of developing dependency relations with parents, family, and community, Americans view newborns as exceedingly dependent, needing to be weaned from their excessive reliance on others if they are to suceed in a society as competitive and individualistic as the United States (Caudill & Weinstein, 1969; Kagan, Kearsley, & Zelazo, 1978). Thus, it should be of little surprise that one important reason why American families place their children in group-rearing situations is to give them an opportunity to be independent of their families and to learn how to get along with others, most especially their peers. When it comes to assessing the effects of day care on social development, then, primary attention has been directed toward children's behavior toward their agemates.

With respect to peer relations, available evidence indicates that day care has both positive and negative effects. On the positive side, Ricciuti (1974) and Kagan et al. (1978) have shown that one- to two-year olds with group experience during infancy are more willing to approach a strange peer or continue their play in the presence of an unfamiliar agemate, and Clarke-Stewart (1979) has reported that two- and three-year olds cared for in day-care centers, nursery schools, or family day-care homes display more cooperation while playing with a strange peer and are better able to appraise the perspective of another than are agemates reared by their mother or a babysitter at home. More recently, Vliestra (1981) has reported, on the basis of obsrvations of 2½- to 4½-year-olds, that those experiencing full-time day care in contrast to those experiencing half-time day care (for at least six months) engaged in significantly more positive interactions with peers and displayed more of what she regarded as prosocial aggression (tattling, defending property against counterattack, command, enforcing rules), but not more hostile aggression (physical or verbal attack on others). Studies such as these and others (Gunnarson, 1978) clearly suggest that day care may enhance certain social competencies, probably by providing children with early and increased opportunities to relate to peers. That these effects may be enduring is suggested by Moore's (1975) study of adolescents: Boys who had experienced group-rearing prior to the age of five reported higher concern for social activities and were also observed to be more sociable with peers and found to be chosen more regularly by peers as likable than were boys who were home-reared during their preschool years.

On the negative side, Moore (1964) observed that when these children were preschoolers, those in supplementary child-care arrangements (which were often unstable) were more prone to toilet lapses and were more self-assertive. Schwarz, Strickland, and Krolick (1974) found in one of the first studies to raise concerns about the effect of day care that preschoolers with day-care experience in infancy were more aggressive (both physically and verbally) toward peers than a group of home-reared children who were enrolled in day care for the first time when three- to four-years-old. And more recently, Barton and Schwarz (1981) found that eight- to ten-year-olds who had been in day care on a full-time basis during their preschool years were rated by peers as more aggressive and prone to misbehavior. Although all the evidence is by no means totally consistent (see Vliestra, 1981; Barton & Schwarz, 1981), it does repeatedly suggest that in some respects day-care children engage in more negative interactions with peers. My own reading of these data is that with greater peer exposure comes greater peer interaction, which is more likely to be both positive and negative in quality.

Conclusion

Some of the effects of day care do appear problematical. Early entry during the first year may adversely influence the child's emotional functioning. Further, the increased peer contact intrinsic to day care, when coupled with often lax controls, promotes more negative interactions between peers. Such behavior could well be a function of greater peer contact and could well be eliminated with a greater degree of authoritative control. After all, it is not observed in Israeli and Soviet group-rearing situations. The fact, however, that even such apparently negative effects as these are not discerned in many studies clearly suggests that although such disturbing consequences can be produced by day-care rearing, they need not be.

This point is extremely important from the standpoint of policy. In response to the policy-oriented question, "Is day care bad for children?", it seems appropriate to conclude that it usually is not and certainly does not have to be, but that it can be. In view of this conclusion, the policy orientation is forced to shift from one of day-care effects to the conditions of care that produce different consequences. This would seem to be especially so because parents who work need child care of some sort. If some arrangement must be made it would seem to be incumbent upon a society to know what are the best conditions for such care or, at the very least, what are the conditions to be avoided. Fortunately, day-care research by child developmentalists has responded to this shift in focus; indeed, it may have even preceded it.

CONDITIONS OF QUALITY

Research designed to evaluate the effects of day care routinely involves the comparison of children whose experiences vary markedly.

Some have been reared in day care, others by their own parents. Such between-group designs afford scientists and policymakers little insight into those contextual conditions that are most supportive of development. Indeed, such inference is possible only indirectly by comparing the results of investigations that sampled children from different day care-rearing milieus. Such between-study comparisons are inherently problematical because of the large number of factors across which investigations vary in addition to the quality of programs from which they have sampled children.

Recognition of this limit has led policy-minded students of child development to examine variation within day care milieus in recent years. In part this work has been motivated by the recognized limits of home-care versus day-care comparisons. It is also motivated, however, by the realization that day care is here to stay, and thus that policymakers need to know about the conditions of day care, especially those that can be regulated, and how they affect the child's development. Toward this end, three approaches to specifying quality have been undertaken.

One set of studies documents relationships between variation in the social structure of day care and child development. Such studies that focus upon dimensions of care like group size, caregiver-child ratio, and staff training permit several conclusions. Most significant in this regard are the findings of the National Day Care study that involved 67 day care centers and approximately 1,000 children. Both small group size and caregiver training in child development-related areas were found to be positively related to children's intellectual development (Ruopp & Travers, 1982). Indeed, except in the case of infant care, group size rather than the ratio of caregivers to children was the most important contextual determinant of how children developed. Similarly, Schwartz and his colleagues (1981) found large group size to undermine social functioning in their study of 64 two-year-olds in Bermuda. Group size emerges, then, as a significant (and regulatable) social structural parameter of day-care centers with respect to both social and intellectual development.

From a scientific standpoint, investigations that link social structural dimensions of day care directly to child development outcomes are limited because they cannot specify why or how such social structural parameters influence the child. In recognition of this weakness, a second set of studies attempts to link social structure with experience because social structure is presumed to directly influence the types of experiences children actually have on a day-to-day basis in day care. But why is this important? Because it is assumed that it is experience that influences development. In other words, this second set of investigations represents an effort to identify the experiential consequences of social structure.

Center and group size as well as child-caregiver ratio are the social structural characteristics of centers that have received the most empirical attention in efforts to understand how variation in program structure affects children's experiences, which we will eventually see are related to children's development. More rules, regulations, and controls are observed in large groups (Prescott, Jones, & Kritchersky, 1967), and in smaller groups teachers display more sensitivity to the individual needs of children (Heinicke, Friedman, Prescott, Pancel & Sab, 1973) and engage in more embellished caregiving (e.g., questioning, responding, praising, comforting), less straight monitoring of children, and less interaction with other results (Travers & Ruopp, 1978). Probably as a consequence, preschoolers in smaller groups are more actively involved in classroom activities (Travers & Ruopp, 1978), and such activities likely mediate the relationship between size and developmental outcomes.

In the case of infants, the National Day Care study found that better ratios (fewer children per caregiver) were associated with less crying by children and more informal teaching (Connell, Layzer, & Goodson, 1979; Travers & Ruopp, 1978; see also Biemiller, Avis, & Lindsay, 1976). Similar observations were made by Howes (in press) in her work in day-care homes. She also found more experience as a child care worker and more formal training in child care to be positively related to the provision of "high quality" care (i.e., provision of social stimulation, expression of positive affection).

On the basis of such work, we see that those aspects of the social structure of day care that have been related to the developmental consequences of day care tend also to covary in a meaningful manner with variation in day-to-day experiences in day care. Such a pattern of covariation provides support for the assumption that size, ratio, and training influence child development by shaping experience. In order to make the strongest case possible for this inference, we turn next to investigations linking variation in day-to-day experience to variation in the effects of day care.

Studies that speak to this issue involve the assessment of a variety of outcomes that can be broadly distinguished in terms of those that evaluate socioemotional development and those that focus upon cognitive-linguistic development. Interestingly, there exists striking similarity across studies in the dimensions of experience that have been sampled, even though measurement procedures vary from caregiver or maternal reports to systematic behavioral observation. The fact, too, that results are strikingly consistent makes these studies relatively easy to summarize. In general, children who experience higher levels of cognitive and social stimulation from their caregivers while in day care look more competent than those who experience care that is more custodial in nature (Golden, Rosenbluth, Grossi, Policave, Freeman, & Brownless, 1978; Kermoian, 1980; Anderson, Nagel, Roberts, & Smith, 1981; Rubenstein, Howes, & Boyle, 1979).

The developmental significance of the quantity and quality of caregiver involvement is most apparent in a comprehensive investigation of 156 families with preschoolers in day-care centers on the island of Bermuda (McCartney, Scarr, Phillips, Grajek, & Schwarz, 1982). The subjects of this study, it is of interest to note, ranged in age from 36 to 60 months and represented virtually the entire population of preschoolers in day care on the island. Observations of children and interviews with directors were used to gather information on the activities children were exposed to and the stimulation they encountered. Results revealed, even after controlling for family background characteristics, that variation in quality significantly predicted linguistic and social competence. Specifically, a measure of adaptive language and two ratings of intelligence and task orientation were strongly related to variation in quality among centers. In fact, in the case of language, nearly 20 percent of the variance was accounted for by differences in quality. With respect to social development, nearly half the variance in sociability (i.e., extroversion) from a standardized measure of classroom behavior (filled out by parents and teachers) was accounted for by total quality; similarly a measure of consideration for others was also predicted by positive aspects of the day-care milieu. In contrast, children rated as dependent tended to come from centers with low overall quality. Furthermore, poor emotional adjustment (i.e., anxious, hyperactive, aggressive), as rated by caregivers, tended to occur in centers with low levels of adult verbal interaction with children.

On the basis of the preceding analysis, it should be clear that not all day care is the same. There exists great variation in social structure, experience, and the outcomes associated with day-care exposure. Further, on the basis of the data reviewed, a case can be made for the claim that social structure influences experience that, in turn, affects child development. As we have seen, in centers and family day-care homes in which group size is modest, ratios are low (for infants), and staff training is high, caregivers tend to be more stimulating, responsive, and positively affectionate, as well as less restrictive. Moreover, children who experience such care tend to be more cooperative, more intellectually capable, and more emotionally secure.

THE POLITICS OF
DAY CARE

There should be little doubt, despite its limitations, that social science research on day care is policy-relevant. The evidence reviewed demonstrates not only that day care need not undermine human development, but that certain contextual conditions, many of which are amendable to legislative regulation, foster optimal development. This value of social science research for the policymaking process should not be confused, however, with the utilization of such research in making day-care policy. Indeed, Nelson's (1982) analysis of the politics of federal day-care regulation convincingly demonstrates what most students of any legislature know so well: Policy is principally a function of politics. Let us see the extent to which this is true of contemporary day-care legislation.

Day care has been conceptualized at the federal level with one of two purposes in mind (Nelson, 1982). The developmental approach conceives of supplementary child care as a strategy for enhancing the psychological well-being of children from economically distressed households. The welfare approach, in contrast, conceives of day care principally as a strategy of reducing welfare expenditures by enabling mothers to seek employment. By no means, of course, are these perspectives mutually exclusive. After all, both have the common purpose of reducing poverty and welfare dependency.

Nevertheless, each perspective, with its somewhat different emphasis, results in different policy options. Welfare day care, essentially targeted at adults, seeks to minimize costs of care and thereby make parental employment possible. Comprehensive developmental day care, in contrast, seeks to break the poverty cycle by targeting children. Consequently, it calls for high staff-child ratios, well-trained staff, and good facilities; from this perspective, cost is not a concern.

In view of these competing perspectives, it should not be surprising that the regulation of day-care programs receiving federal dollars has been an issue around which there has been great debate. The bottom line, in this debate, always comes down to cost, even if dictated by more philosophical considerations.

In 1967, the labor committee of the United States Senate "sought to bring some order to the plethora of social welfare initiation by mandating a set of interagency regulations to govern numerous federal day care programs" (Nelson, 1982, p. 273). The actual writing of legislation began in 1968 when HEW Secretary Wilbur Cohen created the Federal Panel on Early Childhood. Given the nature of democratic representation, the panel was evenly divided between those favoring comprehensive developmental services and those advocating minimum costs to facilitate the employment of welfare mothers. As a result of the make up of the panel, a compromise solution was arrived at that made the Federal Interagency Day Care Regulations (FIDCR) very general, nonspecific and, consequentially, unenforceable (Nelson, 1982).

Following Nixon's election in 1968 and his sweeping proposal for welfare reform, Edward Zigler, as Director of the Office of Child Development, sought to establish a set of day-care requirements that could be enforced and would provide a minimal level of care consistent with the child's health and development. By 1972 the task was complete, and on every aspect of a center's operation requirements were specific. Moreover, these regulations expanded the scope of federal oversight to home care. But problems arose almost immediately. The Office of Management and Budget opposed the regulations, and Elliot Richardson, then the HEW Secretary, refused to proceed without their support. Also important in the eventual failure of these requirements was the protest by child-care advocates in favor of comprehensive day care. Those supportive of proprietary day care also had difficulties with the regulations. They would raise costs to the point at which many providers would no longer find the provision of day-care services profitable. Zigler's revisions, then, were soundly condemned by all sides. The art of compromise failed (Nelson, 1982).

In the context of more general Title XX legislation, the issue of day-care regulation arose several years later. The issue this time focused upon categorical approaches detailing specific programs and expenditures versus block grant approaches that would leave decision making in the hands of local communities. In this context, FIDCR was raised again and some modification of the still standing 1968 guidelines were made on the basis of several of Zigler's earlier proposals to enhance quality (e.g., provision of ratios for the zero to three-year-old age groups) and to reduce costs (e.g., waiving the requirement for provision of educational experience in group care). By the time these changes passed both houses of Congress and were signed into law by President Ford, delays in the legislative process had pushed FIDCR enforcement into the new Carter administration. Debate in FIDCR continued along the lines of past argument—proprietary versus developmental.

In view of this long-standing disagreement, an appropriateness study was undertaken that further delayed implementation. In February, 1978, an ambiguous report was presented. But fortunately at this time, a four-year study by Abt Associates, the National Day Care Study, was just being completed. This timely, but unplanned occurrence provided data to make the basis for any conclusion appear scientifically sound. Because the Abt study found size rather than ratio to be significant, harmony was possible between the two day-care lobbies. Those who could not meet stringent ratio requirements were saved and those concerned with the maintenance of quality were provided evidence that size was critical. Thus the grounds for rapproachement existed, or at least so it seemed. Although social science research was responsible for fostering a climate in which consensus was possible, it cannot be emphasized enough that the influence of the Abt data on regulation was more coincidental than intentional. Thus, policy and science were almost accidentally wed in this situation, which from the outside looks so premeditated as to make one mistakenly respect the wisdom of policymakers for pursuing scientific answers to policy-relevant questions in the first place.

Even though consensus seemed to be emerging, problems arose because actual ratio requirements had to be specified, even though they were no longer regarded as central to the quality care debate. Several alternatives, along with cost analyses, were prepared by Abt, but this process regenerated the conflict that for a moment seemed might subside. The proprietary lobby was in favor of the least stringent requirements, whereas several children's interest groups, like the Children's Defense Fund, were in favor of the strictest staff-child ratios. As Nelson (1982) chronicles the history, HEW Secretary Patricia Harris was leaning toward the less expensive requirements when a confidential memo on this topic was leaked into the hands of ACYF, which then appealed to White House Domestic Affairs advisor, Stuart Eizenstadt. Most significant here with respect to the policymaking process is the fact that contact with Eizenstadt was made through a personal relationship between one of the strict ratio proponents and Eizenstadt's wife! Eizenstadt then sent a memo, actually drafted by the Children's Defense Fund, to Secretary Harris, expressing strong White House support for stricter ratios. This input prevailed and requirements were issued in March, 1980. In view of this process, a reasonable question to ask is, "Is this any way to make policy?"

Despite the promulgation of the new requirements, reality prevailed. By the time of their issuance, inflation was at 20 percent and elections were around the corner. Budget cutting and deregulation were the order of the day. Congress once again suspended the regulations for more cost studies and, then—enter the Reagan Administration. All the hard work of FIDCR went down the tubes. The regulations were not reinstated—at least not yet. Indeed, the issue of federal regulations became moot. Federal funds for the support of day care were channeled by Reagan to states in the form of block grants, thereby foreclosing the federal role in standard setting (Maccoby, Kahn, & Everett, 1983). As a result, some states like Mississippi have no statutory requirements regulating infant day care. Others, like Arizona, have extremely loose requirements, allowing one adult to care for as many as 10 children under two years of age even in federally funded centers (Zigler & Muenchow, 1983).

CONCLUSION

What conclusions can be drawn from all this? On the one hand it can be confidently stated that day-care research is relevant to and should be helpful in the promulgation of public policy. On the other hand it can be stated that the policymaking process is political, and susceptible to the influence of personal friendships to say nothing of the changing winds that whip through Washington with each change in administration; as a result, day-care research, although theoretically useful, is of little consequence, at least insofar as issues such as the effects of day care and the conditions of quality care are concerned.

Consider for a moment the first substantive scientific issue addressed in this chapter. One may argue that because day care has not been found to be bad for children, that such information has served an important function in policymaking. Other results, so this argument may go, would have led policymakers to discourage the use of day care. A historical analyses of day care that extends beyond that reviewed here provides a strong basis for disputing this claim (Belsky, Steinberg, & Walker, 1982). The government has sponsored day care when it has been in its best interest, irrespective of results from day-care research. During World War II, for example, the mobilization of women for factory work resulted in the establishment of programs that served more than 105,000 children (under the Lanham Act). Furthermore, given the desire to take welfare mothers off the welfare roles, many job programs have included funds for day care (e.g., Title XX of Social Security Act, Title II of Manpower Training Act). Day-care research in these instances had had absolutely nothing whatsoever to do with day-care policy. Indeed, I suspect it was never even considered as relevant to the issues under consideration because the principal concern was employment not child care.

It is also worth considering the contemporary scene. Day care is here to stay not because research indicates it need not be harmful to children, but because women are in the work place, either for reasons of economic necessity or personal fulfillment. How many of these women would not be working, and would not use day care in one form or another, it research indicated that day care was not in children's best interest? I suspect that in those cases in which families did not need the income mothers earn or in which working was not essential to a women's sense of self that research might influence day-care usage and, therefore, social policy. But in view of the fact that of all the women working relatively few probably fall into this category, there is additional support for the contention that research, although relevant, is not really all that influential in policymaking.

This point seems to be underscored even more strongly by the policymaking process pertinent to the second research issue that was considered: the conditions of quality care. By no means is it clear that the results reviewed seriously influence policymaking. Long before these results emerged positions were taken that had to do with cost versus developmental effects, with the proprietary centers and even the women's movement lining up on one side and the children's lobbies on the other.

In this context, it is worth wondering it, had the results of the National Day Care Study been different, the Children's Defense Fund, for example, would have altered its position with respect to what is necessary to provide quality care. Had the data indicated that neither group size, caregiver ratio, nor staff training were related to day-to-day experiences and developmental outcomes, attitudes probably would not have changed. Flaws can always be found in research, and in the case of the National Day Care Study they would have been searched for. Inappropriate instrumentation, measurement, or design would have been singled out to demonstrate the limits of the research and thus the value of the position held before, during, and after the research was conducted. The data would have been dismissed out of hand. Because this was not found, however, the data were instead embraced.

Scientific findings, it would seem, are of consequence when a prevailing ideology needs fuel for its arguments. Indeed, Maccoby, Kahn, and Everett (1983, p. 81) have observed that "whether a particular piece of research is drawn upon. . . depends greatly upon its timing in relations to various aspects of the sociopolitical climate. . . although available knowledge is frequently not utilized because the political climate is not receptive to it, the reverse situation may also occur." Science, it would seem, is more likely to serve as political ammunition than as a tool for policy illumination.

In view of this reality, scientists ought to be concerned. Ideally, we generate data presumably for purposes of understanding. We are, presumably, open to the rejection of our hypotheses and thus are willing to let the data speak for themselves. Although this is by no means always the case, it does not seem as if policymakers approach scientific information in the way scientists believe it ought to be approached. In some respects our research is used to market a position. Data are sorted through to find those that conform to prevailing notions; such evidence is then presented as scientific. The purpose of the political process does not seem to find answers but to make opinions prevail. Given this situation, one may contend that scientists become the prostitutes of politicians. We are called upon when desired, ignored when not.

REFERENCES

Anderson, C. W., Nagle, R. J., Roberts, W. A., & Smith, J. W. (1981). Attachment to substitute caregivers as a function of center quality and caregiver involvement. *Child Development, 52,* 53-61.

Arend, R., Gove, F., & Sroufe, L. (1979). Continuity in early adaptation from attachment in infancy to ego-resiliency and curiosity at age 5. *Child Development, 90,* 950-959.

Barton, M., & Schwarz, C. (1981, August). *Day care in the middle class: Effects in elementary school.* Paper presented at the American Psychological Association Annual Convention, Los Angeles, CA.

Belsky, J., & Steinberg, L. (1970). The effects of day care: A critical review. *Child Development, 49,* 929-949.

Belsky, J., Steinberg, L., & Walker, A. (1982). The ecology of day care. In M. E. Lamb (Ed.), *Nontraditional families: Parenting and child development.* Hillsdale, NJ: Erlbaum.

Blehar, M. (1974). Anxious attachment and defensive reactions associated with day care. *Child Development, 45,* 683-692.

Bowlby, J. (1951). *Maternal care and mental health.* Geneva, Switzerland: World Health Organization.

Biemiller, A., Avis, C., & Lindsay. A. (1976, June). *Competence supporting aspects of day care environments—a preliminary study.* Paper presented at the Canadian Psychological Association Convention, Toronto, Canada.

Blanchard, M., & Main, M. (1979). Avoidance of the attachment figure and social-emotional adjustment in day-care infant. *Developmental Psychology, 15,* 445-446.

Brookhart, J., & Hock, E. (1976). The effects of experimental context and experimental background on infants' behavior toward their mothers and a stranger. *Child Development, 47,* 333-340.

Caudill, W., & Weinstein, H. (1969). Maternal care and infant behavior in Japan and America. *Psychiatry, 12,* 32-43.

Clarke-Stewart, K. A. (1980). Observation and experiment: Complement any strategies for studying day care and social development. In S. Kilmer (Ed), *Advances in early education and day care.* Greenwich, CT: JAI Press.

Cochran, M. (1977). A comparison of group day and family child-rearing patterns in Sweden. *Child Development, 48,* 702-707.

Connell, D. B., Layzer, J. I., & Goodson, D. (1979). *National study of day care centers for infants: Findings and implications.* Unpublished manuscript, ABT Associates Inc., Cambridge, MA.

Cummings, E. M. (1980). Caregiver stability and day care. *Developmental Psychology, 16,* 31-37.

Doyle, A. (1975). Infant development in day care. *Developmental Psychology, 11,* 655-656.

Doyle, A., & Somers, K. (1978). The effects of group and family day care on infant attachment behaviors. *Canadian Journal of Behavioral Science, 10,* 38-45.

Farber, E. A. & Egeland, B. (1982). Developmental consequences of out-of-home care for infants in a low-income population. In E. Zigler & E. W. Gordon (Ed.), *Day care: Scientific and social policy issues.* Boston: Auburn.

Fraiberg, S. (1977). *Every child's birthright: In defense of mothering.* New York: Basic Books.

Golden, M., Rosenbluth, L., Grossi, M. T., Policave, H. J., Freeman, H., Jr., & Brownless, M. (1978). *The New York City Infant Day Care Study: A comparative study of licensed group and family day care programs and the effects of these programs on children and their families.* New York: Medical and Health Research Association of New York City, Inc.

Gunnarson, L. (1978). *Children in day care and family care in Sweden: A follow-up.* Bulletin No. 21, Department of Educational Research, University of Gothenburg.

Heinicke, C., Friedman, D., Prescott, E., Puncel, C., & Sale, J. (1973). The organization of day care: Considerations relating to the mental health of child and family. *American Journal of Orthopsychiatry, 43,* 8-22.

Hill, C. R. (1977). The child care market: A review of evidence and implications for federal policy. In *Policy issues in day care: Summaries of 21 papers.* Washington, DC: Department of Health, Education, and Welfare.

Hill, C. R. (1978). Private demand for child care: Implications for public policy. *Evaluation Quarterly, 2,* 523-545.

Hock, E. (1976). *Alternative approaches to child rearing and their effects on the mother-infant relationship. Final report.* Washington, DC: Department of HEW, Office of Child Development, Grant No. OCD-490.

Hock, E. (1980). Working and nonworking mothers and their infants: A comparative study of maternal caregiving characteristics and infant social behavior. *Merrill-Palmer Quarterly of Behavior and Development, 26,* 79-101.

Hofferth, S. (1979). Day care in the next decade: 1980-1990. *Journal of Marriage and the Family,* 644-658.

Howes, C. (in press). Caregiver behavior and conditions of caregiving. *Journal of Applied Developmental Psychology.*

Howes, C., & Rubenstein, J. L. (1981). *Determinants of toddler experience in daycare: Social-affective style age of entry and quality of setting.* Unpublished manuscript, University of California, Los Angeles.

Kagan, J., Kearsley, R., & Zelazo, P., (1978). *Infancy: Its place in human development.* Cambridge, MA: Harvard University Press.

Kermoian, R. (1980, May). *Type and quality of care: Mediating factors in the effects of day care on infant responses to brief separation.* Paper presented at the International Conference on Infant Studies, New Haven, CT.

Lally, R. (1973). *The family development research program: Progress report.* Unpublished paper, Syracuse University.

Maccoby, E., Kahn, A., & Everett, B. (1983). The role of psychological research in the formation of policies affecting children. *American Psychologist, 38,* 80-84.

McCartney, K., Scarr, S., Phillips, D., Grajek, S., & Schwartz, J. C. (1982). Environmental differences among day care centers and their effects on children's development. In E. Zigler & E. Gardon (Eds.), *Day Care: Scientific and social policy issues.* Boston: Auburn House.

Moore, T. (1964). Children of full-time and part-time mothers. *International Journal of Social Psychiatry, 2,* 1-10.

Moore, T. (1975). Exclusive mothering and its alternative: The outcomes to adolescence. *Scandinavian Journal of Psychology, 16,* 255-272.

Moskowitz, D., Schwarz, J., & Corsini, D. (1977). Initiating day care at three years of age: Effects on attachment. *Child Development, 48,* 1271-1276.

Nelson, J. R., Jr. (1982). The politics of federal day care regulation. In E. Zigler & E. Gordon (Eds.), *Day care: Scientific and social policy issues.* Boston: Auburn House.

Office of Assistant for Planning and Evaluation. (1978, June). *The appropriateness of the Federal Interagency Day Care Requirements (FIDCR): Reports on findings and recommendations.* Washington, DC: United States Department of Health, Education, and Welfare.

Peters, D. (1973). *A summary of the Pennsylvania Day Care Study.* University Park: Pennsylvania State University.

Portnoy, F., & Simmons, C. (1978). Day care and attachment. *Child Development, 49,* 239-242.

Prescott, E., Jones, E., & Kritchevsky, S. (1967). *Group day care as a child rearing environment.* Final report to Children's Bureau. Pasadena, CA: Pacific Oaks College.

Ramey, C. T., & Campbell, F. A. (1979). Compensatory education for disadvantaged children. *School Review, 87,* 171-189.

Ramey, C., Dorval, B., & Baker-Ward, L. (1981). Group day care and socially disadvantaged families: Effects on the child and the family. In S. Kilmer (Ed.), *Advances in early education and day care.* Greenwich, CT: JAI Press.

Ricciuti, H. (1974). Fear and development of social attachments in the first year of life. In M. Lewis & L. A. Rosenblum (Eds.), *The origins of human behavior: Fear.* New York: John Wiley.

Robertson, A. (1982). Day care and children's responsiveness to adults. In E. Zigler & E. Gordon (Eds.), *Day care: Scientific and social policy issues.* Boston: Auburn House.

Roopnarine, J., & Lamb, M. (1978). The effects of day care on attachment and exploratory behavior in a strange situation. *Merrill-Palmer Quarterly, 24,* 85-95.

Rubenstein, J. L., & Howes, C. (1979). Caregiving and infant behavior in day care and in homes. *Developmental Psychology, 15,* 1-24.

Rubenstein, J. L., Howes, C., & Boyle, P. (1979, March). *A two year follow-up of infants in community based infant day care.* Paper presented at the biennial meeting of the Society for Research in Child Development, San Francisco, CA.

Ruopp, R., & Travers, J. (1982). Janus faces day care: Perspectives on quality and cost. In E. Zigler & E. W. Gordon (Eds.), *Day care: Scientific and social policy issues.* Boston: Auburn House.

Schwarz, J. C., Scarr, S. W., Caparulo, B., Furrow, D., McCartney, K., Billington, R., Phillips, D., Hindy, C. (1981, August). *Center, sitter, and home day care before age two: A report on the first Bermuda infant care study.* Paper presented at the American Psychological Association Annual Convention, Los Angeles, CA.

Schwarz, J., Strickland, R., & Krolick, G. (1974). Infant day care: Behavioral effects at preschool age. *Developmental Psychology, 10,* 502-506.

Sibbison, V. (1973). The influence of maternal role perceptions on attitudes toward and utilization of early child care services. In D. Peters (Ed.), *A summary of the Pennsylvania Day Care Study.* University Park: Pennsylvania State University.

Spitz, R. A. (1945). Hospitalism: An inquiry into the genesis of psychiatric conditions in early childhood. *Psychoanalytic Study of the Child, 1,* 53-74.

Sroufe, L. (1979). The coherence of individual development. *American Psychologist, 34,* 834-841.

Travers, J., Beck, R., & Bissell, J. (1982). Measuring the outcomes of day care. In J. Travers & R. White (Eds.), *Learning from experience: Evaluation early childhood education program.* Washington, DC: National Academy of Sciences.

Travers, J., & Ruopp, R. (1978). *National Day Care Study: Preliminary findings and their implications: 31 January, 1978.* Cambridge, MA: Abt Associates.

Urban Institute. (1980). *The subtle revolution: Women at work.* Washington, DC: The Urban Institute.

Vaughn, B., Gove, F., & Egeland, B. (1980). The relationship between out-of-home care and the quality of infant-mother attachment in an economically disadvantaged population. *Child Development, 51,* 1203-1214.

Vliestra, A. G. (1981). Full versus half-day preschool attendance: Effects in young children as assessed by teacher ratings and behavioral observations. *Child Development, 52,* 603-610.

Zigler, F., & Muenchow, S. (1983). Infant day care and infant-care leaves: A policy vacuum. *American Psychologist, 38,* 91-94.

PART II, SECTION 3

The final set of chapters in Part II deals with social science and the criminal justice system. Charles Tittle begins with a critical review of the methodologies that can be applied to the study of deterrence. Tittle reaches a pessimistic conclusion about our current ability to reach confident conclusions about deterrence; this parallels Greenwood's (1984, p. 6) recent conclusion that "the magnitudes or even existence of any deterrent effects cannot be estimated, due to a variety of methodological problems." Tittle further argues that without confident, specific conclusions about deterrence, social scientists should not offer specific policy recommendations on this subject.

Chapter 12, by Jeanne Marsh, is based on a recent study of a change in Michigan's rape legislation. Much of Marsh's discussion focuses on the implementation process and its role in assessing the impact of legal change. Marsh points out that a good theory of the implementation of legal change can lead to more effective law reforms and, based on the Michigan reform, offers some suggestions about what factors may facilitate successful implementation of a legal reform. In addition, Marsh reviews some of the methodological limitations that beset studies of law reform. Marsh concludes her chapter with a more general discussion of policymaking processes and the potential role of the social sciences in them.

Peter Rossi and Jim Wright's chapter on gun control concludes the section on criminal justice issues. Rossi and Wright review various approaches to the study of gun control, including both studies of public opinion toward gun control and studies designed to assess the effectiveness of gun control legislation. They note the difficulties that arise because of specification errors, both in survey research and in impact assessments. In so dong, Rossi and Wright point out the potential for both use and misuse of social science data in policymaking processes. They also point out the value of studies of the implementation of gun control laws. Rossi and Wright conclude with a discussion of the way in which social science research might best fit into political deliberations on gun control.

REFERENCE

Greenwood, P. W. (1984). Selective incapacitation: A method of using our prisons more effectively. *NIJ Reports, SNI, 183*(3), 6-7.

11

Can Social Science Answer Questions about Deterrence for Policy Use?

CHARLES R. TITTLE

In this chapter I suggest that (1) sensible research-based policy must rest on scientifically sound principles: (2) such principles do not now exist and are unlikely to be developed in deterrence; and (3) even if scientific principles of deterrence were finally established, their implementation would probably be impractical.

Deterrence occurs when potential criminal acts are suppressed because people fear penalties. Scholars recognize many forms of deterrence, the most important distinction being between general and specific (Gibbs, 1975). Specific deterrence refers to fearful inhibition of subsequent crime among recipients of punishment whereas general deterrence denotes curtailment of crime among a population of potential offenders who may not have been punished individually. Scholars must explain and specify the conditions, if any, under which various deterrent effects are produced. In this chapter I try to show that real progress in accomplishing this task is unlikely and that this situation makes policy applications impractical.

The discussion is organized into five general sections. The first identifies the requirements for sensible policy. The other four sections outline the reasons those requirements are not met in the deterrence area. Among these reasons are methodological problems, which are discussed in the second section. The methodologies of both general deterrence and specific deterrence are considered in turn. Critique of the general deterrence methodology differentiates defects of ecological-type research, self-report surveys, natural intervention studies, and experiments. Discussion of specific deterrence methodology details difficulties in follow-ups, comparison groups, and other issues. The third section highlights theoretical problems, describing deficiencies in deterrence theory and their consequences. The fourth part outlines practical problems of cost and ethics. Finally, lay and scientific biases retarding research success are identified.

WHAT IS NEEDED

Scientific knowledge useful for policy must be based on theory that answers the question why, that allows derivation of the contingencies under which causal effects are or are not expected, and that has been empirically verified through tests replicated frequently enough so that a broad consensus within the scholarly community endorses its validity. This does not mean that science produces perfect knowledge or that complete and total understanding is essential for policy relevance. It does mean that we ought to be right considerably more often than we are wrong. Knowledge in the deterrence area simply does not qualify on these grounds.

My thesis imposes unusually stringent criteria for policy-relevant research. Suppose, for instance, that social researchers found that increases in statutory penalty for a particular offense were usually followed within two years by reductions in the rate of that offense. Some people believe this would be enough for policy. It would not matter to them that greater (or lesser) changes in penalty may produce different results, that the connection between the statutory change and recorded rates of offense may be due to something besides deterrence, that the association may be limited to this specific offense in this kind of context, or even that covariation between the two might be incidental, due entirely to some prior conditions (such as, perhaps, the public debate that preceded the statutory change, as described in Ross, 1982). What would matter is that the specific statutory changes apparently "work" and therefore may be used in other circumstances.

In my opinion, however, policy recommendations based on "raw," ad hoc empirical conclusions like this are unwise, even if they could be reliably established. There are two important reasons for this view. First, the likelihood that the same exact conditions that produced the result would prevail in other circumstances in which the policy might be applied is quite low. Any application stands a good chance of failure without more complete knowledge concerning such things as the range of penalties that would produce various changes in offense rate; whether the empirical relationship is causative; whether the actual intervening mechanism was deterrence, increased social cohesion, or some other mechanism; and whether the relationship is generalizable to other offenses, kinds of sanctions, and situations. Each failure of a social science based policy undermines public confidence in our ability and precludes a meaningful role in instances in which actual scientific knowledge may be brought to bear. One need only observe later public reaction to permissive education, juvenile justice diversion programs, prison rehabilitation schemes, and numerous economic policies to recognize the low state of public esteem to which our craft can fall.

A second reason is that the information missing from "practical" research is often necessary for prudent policy. The famous Minneapolis experiment concerning the effect of various police strategies for handling domestic assault (Sherman & Berk, 1984) illustrates the danger. The authors interpret their results as showing that arresting assaulters will deter them from repeating their behavior, and on the basis of this interpretation unabashedly recommend arrest policies for police in dealing with domestic violence; however, their design, in fact, does not rule out several rival interpretations of the outcome. For instance, one plausible alternative is that fewer repeat instances were found among the arrestee group because victims in those cases were more likely to have been intimidated into silence after the offenders were released from custody. Perhaps the victims were afraid to activate the police again or to report victimizations to the follow-up interviewers who could easily have been perceived by victims and offenders as police associates. Thus, policy based on this experiment might "work" to make domestic violence less of a problem for police, but the wisdom of such policy would be debatable if the victims, rather than the offenders, were deterred. Moreover, even if this experiment were unambiguously interpretable, it may not be generalizable to other crimes, cities, police, or offenders. Implementation elsewhere may mean failure at the expense of alternative strategies.

Therefore, until social science can collectively speak with reasonable confidence, it runs an awful risk in recommending policy. Unfortunately, even if social science ultimately establishes confident generalizations about deterrence, realities will probably still preclude meaningful application. Public policy in a democratic society always represents reconciliation of diverse interests through compromise. Hence, implemented programs rarely preserve the highly specific and contingent features of complex cause and effect schemes produced by science. If recent research trends are indicative, deterrence researchers may find that any reasonably sound conclusions they finally reach will indicate that deterrence by legal threat can occur only under narrow conditions and that it may hinge on largely "irrational" perceptual and cognitive processes. Policy recommendations, therefore, may eventually take the form of statements such as the following: Deterrence may be expected only for potential first commissions of particular crimes among specific age/gender/class categories in certain kinds of neighborhoods when controllers threaten specific kinds of sanctions with particular degrees of credibility communicated interpersonally, and then only if all of these conditions are simultaneously present. Implementation plans simply could not maintain such precise parameters (and would, in any case, violate the requirement of equal protection under the law although that is not my primary point here). Thus if scientific principles of deterrence ever do emerge they are likely to mandate delicate surgery when only meat-axe approaches can be employed.

Not only would deviations from a precise plan likely fail, but any success might produce costly side effects of unknown magnitude. For instance, suppose the above recommendation ended up in a policy of increasing penalties of many kinds to be imposed on all age/gender/class categories in many neighborhoods on the logic that at least some will be affected, and that those in circumstances fitting the precise description did show a decline in crime, but those in circumstances not fitting the precise description ended up despising the law, fearing their government, and perhaps even increasing their criminal behavior because of their decreased respect for the laws. Whether the gain would have justified the cost would be debatable—in the same way that the desirability of risking heart damage in treating rheumatism is debatable when the degree of potential heart damage and the probable success of implementation are unknown. Intelligent discussion of the merits of either action would depend upon the advance ability to identify and estimate the likelihood and magnitude of various outcomes. That ability does not now exist with respect to deterrence; in fact, we cannot now adequately measure the deterrent or side effects even after the fact.

The prospect of reasonable scientific recommendations for policy, whether they be highly contingent or otherwise, lies far in the future if it can be expected at all. For now, we know very little, and the climate for learning more is not favorable. Let's consider why this is so.

METHODOLOGICAL BARRIERS

The following discussion of methodological problems in assessing the effect of sanctions is divided into two main parts to correspond with the major distinction between general and specific deterrence. In each case, potential alternative strategies are critiqued.

General Deterrence

Ecological analysis Most research concerning general deterrence, especially that influencing the priorities of funding agencies and being brought into public debates, has been, and continues to be, of an ecological type (e.g., Ehrlich, 1975, 1977). Indicators of sanction characteristics, crime, and population variables for political units (such as states, cities, or countries) are extracted from government documents (such as police, prison, or census publications) and statistically analyzed to determine if sanction variables predict crime rates when other factors are controlled. Although ecological studies have sometimes been simplistic, involving no more than a comparison of similar population units, recent ones have used statistical techniques designed for studying causal sequences and reciprocal relationships (e.g., Greenberg & Kessler, 1982; Loftin & McDowall, 1982; and many of the studies listed in Palmer, 1977). Consequently, debate over technical issues and reanalyses reflecting minute statistical modification and critique of previous work now dominate the literature (e.g., Bowers & Pierce, 1980; Jacob & Rich, 1980; McQuire & Sheehan, 1983; Passell & Taylor, 1977) so that practically every study is controversial. Critics have found many reasons to question the findings from ecological research.

First, statistical problems preclude confident conclusions (Blumstein, Cohen, & Nagin, 1978; Brier & Feinberg, 1980; Cousineau, 1973; Logan, 1982; Yunker, 1982). Variables thought to be important in the deterrence process and that can be measured using official data are so interrelated that their effects on each other cannot be reliably disentangled, especially when the models incorporate possible reciprocal causation. In the terminology of causal modeling, if a model is complex enough to reflect the deterrence process, at least some of the equations in the model often cannot be "identified." In other words, any proposed causal system is so complex and the data so limited that an infinite number of structures might be consistent with the results, making it impossible for analysis to reveal which causal system is actually operating (see Nagin, 1978; Hanushek & Jackson, 1977; Namboodiri, Carter, & Blalock, 1975; Yunker, 1982).

A possible solution to the identification problem is to locate (and measure) additional variables that play the role of "instruments" in the causal system. For instance, if a researcher wishes to estimate the effect of one endogeneous variable, Y_1, on another, Y_2, it is usually helpful to introduce into the model a variable that is related to Y_1

(often because it has a direct effect on Y_1), but that is not related to the error term of Y_2. When such variables can be found and brought into a model, the identification problem can sometimes be solved and estimates made of the effects of some Y's on other Y's. But if, as is often the case, appropriate instrumental variables cannot be found, estimating the most interesting causal effects will be impossible (see especially Nagin, 1978; Yunker, 1982). Further, even when a unique set of estimates is obtained, many of the coefficients may be statistically unstable because the instrumental variables are weak (for a discussion of this general problem and related problems in causal modeling, see Cramer, 1980).

Unfortunately this problem appears to be endemic; it does not seem to be solvable simply with better measurement or statistics. In studying sanctions, even conceiving of possible instruments is difficult, not to mention finding suitable indicators of them. Imagining something that affects the crime rate but does not also affect law enforcement challenges the best minds. Thus, scholars can never be sure if results represent statistical artifacts or real evidence.

Second, were these statistical problems corrected, causal models using ecological-level data would still be misleading because many potentially important variables cannot be measured for aggregate populations with official or documentary data (cf. Greenberg, 1977). This problem, which in causal modeling language is called misspecification, poses the classical third variable causation problem and also limits the study of process or interactions among variables. Many variables, such as social cohesion, the general degree of criminal motivation, or the aggregate amount of moral condemnation of specific criminal acts within the different ecological units, may represent contingencies on which a deterrent effect depends or that render an apparent effect spurious. For instance, Erickson, Gibbs, & Jensen (1977) argue that if crime is regarded as highly repugnant in an area, then severe sanctions are likely, citizens will more readily aid in law enforcement, and fewer people will be motivated to commit crimes. Therefore, if moral condemnation cannot be measured and brought into a model, a potentially spurious association between sanction severity or certainty and the crime rate may be erroneously taken as evidence of deterrence. Conversely, threats may be more effectively communicated to potential criminals within morally conscious contexts (Geerken & Gove, 1975). If so, an association between sanction characteristics and crime rate would exist only in specific places where moral consciousness about crime is high. In such a case, research may discount deterrence when, in fact, it is conditional.

And so it is with numerous theoretical variables. Many aggregate-level factors cannot be measured using official statistics, even when researchers recognize their importance. Substituting data such as proportion of blacks or poverty level to represent level of moral condemnation of criminal acts or general criminal motivation, as is typical, simply will not do, particularly in light of contemporary controversy about socioeconomic distribution of criminal behavior (see Braithwaite, 1981; Kleck, 1982; Thornberry & Farnworth, 1982; Tittle, 1983; Tittle, Villemez, & Smith, 1978, 1982). Futhermore, even though one can imagine using individual survey data aggregated for large numbers of separate ecological units to measure collective characteristics such as moral condemnation, it is not likely to be done, for reasons to be detailed later.

Third, the ecological approach involves a crucial but dubious assumption about *process* that is untestable using ecological data themselves. When a researcher establishes that some sanction measured for political units as wholes causes or predicts lower crime rates, this is taken as evidence for deterrence; that is, the researcher assumes that the intervening link between the cause and effect is a psychological process occurring in the minds of some or all of the individual members of the political units (see in particular Cloninger & Sartorius, 1979). This process presumably involves accurate perceptions by potential law breakers of official sanction characteristics and, then, suppression of criminal impulses because of fear of those sanctions (Erickson & Gibbs, 1976, 1978; Henshel & Carey, 1975; Parker & Grasmick, 1979). But as Gibbs (1975) so cogently argues, an ecological relationship between sanctions and crime rates may rest on any number of intervening factors including restrictions on opportunities for crime brought about by sanctions, moral and normative reinforcements, incapacitation of potential offenders, and others (Bankston & Cramer, 1974; Greenberg, 1977).

For example, punishing or threatening to punish offenders may heighten awareness within a population of the danger of crime, thereby inducing citizens to take greater precautions to avoid being victimized. Or, as Durkheim (1933) long ago noted, it may unify the population into a more cohesive and tightly knit group (Scott, 1976). The result could be better security on property, altered lifestyles to minimize the chances of being assaulted, raped, or robbed, as well as greater preventative surveillance. Thus sanctions or sanction threats may reduce crime by eliminating some of the opportunities for victimization rather than by scaring potential offenders (cf. Cohen & Felson, 1979). Similarly, threatening or actually invoking punishment may generate or reinforce moral feelings about the law by reminding individuals that the behavior in question is wrong (Andenaes, 1974). Sanctions may diminish the crime rate by lowering motivation to offend or by activating morally rooted self-control. And if it is true that most crime is committed by a few career criminals (an assumption yet to be established), punishment might control crime by incapacitating potential offenders rather than by deterring them (Cohen, 1978; Greenberg, 1975; Shinnar & Shinnar, 1975; Wilson, 1983).

The only direct way to learn if deterrence constitutes the causal link between rates of sanctioning and crime is to find out how sanction threats in various ecological units are perceived by individuals in those units. But this is a task ecological studies cannot perform, and until it is performed, accumulated research will remain uninterpretable. Some evidence already suggests the absence of a perceptual link betwen official sanctioning and individual behavior. Not only do individual citizens seem to know little about actual laws or probabilities of sanctions (Assembly Committee, 1975; Richards & Tittle, 1982; Williams & Gibbs, 1981), but a growing body of social psychological literature suggests that even with such information, individuals might rarely use it in evaluating their own risk (e.g., Bar-Hillel, 1980; Bar-Hillel & Fischoff, 1981; Nisbett & Ross, 1980; Tyler, 1980). As this literature indicates, there appears to be a widespread tendency to ignore actuarial data in favor of idiosyncratic, individualizing information in judging personal risk ("the base rate fallacy"). Hence, the major source of supposed information about deterrence for now and apparently for some time in the future—ecological analysis—seems seriously flawed.

Of course, some may say this is all true and relevant for social science but is of little consequence for policy. As noted earlier, some think that an established association between punishment and crime rates would be useful for policy because it suggests that reducing crime by increasing the severity or certainty of penalties is possible, no matter what the causal mechanism. But imagine that an ecological association between penalties and crime were established (which it hasn't been), but that the intervening process was not, in fact, deterrence, but, rather, heightened awareness; that is, because of sanctions most citizens become more conscious of the chances of being victimized and take precautions to protect themselves, thereby lowering the crime rate. This would mean that a policy increasing the chances of apprehension, conviction, and execution for homicide might "work," but it would do so inefficiently and at a great and unnecessary cost. The price would include the loss of freedom for every citizen, needless loss of life of those executed, and probably massive expense for additional police and equipment, even though the goal may as easily be achieved through advertising.

Hence, it may make a great deal of difference, even for policy, that ecological-type research continues to depend upon an untestable and dubious assumption about how sanctions are linked to rates of crime in political units.

Consequences of the inability to link individual perceptions with ecological-level variables is further illustrated by "aggregation bias" (Grasmick, 1982; Greenberg, Kessler, & Logan, 1981; Greenberg & Kessler, 1982). Ecological researchers use as units of analysis entities for which data are routinely collected and reported. These units were designed for political, not research purposes. As a result, they often do not represent truly viable social units to which individual residents may look for behavioral guidance, nor are statistics representing their characteristics necessarily meaningful reflectors of social realities. For instance, numerous less populated areas of a state may have high crime rates and relatively low punishment probabilities whereas a few highly populated areas may have high crimes rates and relatively high punishment probabilities. Aggregating these data for the state as a whole exaggerates the influence of the higher population areas so that the total political entity will seem like a high crime, high punishment area, and it will be assumed that all residents of the state perceive and act (or fail to act) on the "high punishment" message. In an ecological study using the 50 states, this particular state will influence the overall results toward a nondeterrent conclusion when, in fact, most subunits within it showed characteristics consistent with a deterrent interpretation. On the other hand, treating less populous and more populous states equally in an analysis of 50 states distorts results by weighting the influence of the smaller states disproportionately. Thus aggregation biases run in both directions and may be compounded. Nobody knows what official sanctions are taken into account by people (or even if they are taken into account at all). It is hard to believe that citizens actually perceive and act on arrest or imprisonment rates prevailing in an entire state, and some even question whether potential offenders take into account arrest or punishment probabilities in cities. Grasmick (1982) maintains that the most likely level of sanctioning for individuals to comprehend and act upon is the neighborhood. But "neighborhood" is not a political unit for which sanction and population data are reported (not to mention the other necessary variables), nor is it one that is easily defined if one were trying to reaggregate raw census or police data. Furthermore, it appears that statistical biases inherent in inappropriate levels of aggregation are monstrous (Greenberg & Kessler, 1982). Yet, ecological research is tied to these unrealistic territorial aggregates.

Fourth, another aggregation problem bears on the time lag between threats expressed through the ongoing sanctioning process (such as arrest rates) in political units and inhibitions of criminal impulse that presumably result. Official statistics confine a researcher to assumptions that match bureaucratic patterns of record keeping and reporting. As Grasmick points out, it makes little sense to imagine that a convenient one-year interval is the appropriate one for sanction threats (changes in rates of apprehension or punishment) to influence criminal impulses. Moreover, using official statistics typically involves aggregating presumed causal intervals of as little as one day (December 31 of one year to January 1 of the next) to as long as several years (when researchers merge data into two-, three-, or even five-year bunches) into one average category. Surely this involves much distortion even if the real causal interval happened to be about one year. But the error may be even greater if the deterrent process is more or less instantaneous. Are a person's actions logically influenced by his or her fear of sanctions last year or now? Will a person's actions a year from now logically be influenced by current fear or that which he or she will experience next year? Unless individual perceptions about sanctions and the presumed resulting fear are stable over time (an assumption contrary to current evidence, see Minor & Harry, 1982; Paternoster, Saltzman, Waldo, & Chiricos, 1983), conclusions from ecological-type research may be completely meaningless.

Fifth, data in the official reports on which ecological studies are based are biased (McCleary, Nienstedt, & Erven, 1982; Sherman & Glick, 1982; Skogan, 1974) because only a fraction of committed crimes is actually recorded by the police—a fraction that is not constant from political unit to political unit. Moreover, indicators of sanctioning such as arrest, clearance, or imprisonment rates are biased becaue of varied practices of recording or defining "arrest" or "clearance" in different jurisdictions (DeFleur, 1975) and the hiatus between crimes committed and those for which people are eventually convicted and/or incarcerated.

Finally, if deterrence is contingent, as many suspect, ecological analysis will never discover it. There are theoretical reasons to believe that some demographic categories, kinds of populations, and types of sanctions may reveal deterrent influence whereas other categories, populations, or types of sanctions will not (Zimring & Hawkins, 1968, 1973). But because ecological data represent political units, they cannot be reaggregated to study which gender, race, SES category, or age group is more or less likely to be deterred. In addition, researchers are limited to whatever natural variations happen to be there. Perhaps deterrence can only occur above various thresholds of certainty or severity (Tittle & Rowe, 1974)—levels that may not actually be reached in any of the political units under study. If such were true, ecological analysis would produce erroneous conclusions, but scholars would not know they were wrong, especially if, ironically, such research actually were implemented so that the higher levels of variation in sanctioning were precluded. It could also be that deterrence requires some interactive combination of certainty and severity—a combination that may not be typically found in existing natural variation. In this particular instance, data limitations may render conclusions using ecological analysis practically useless.

In summary, all ecological analyses suffer from severe statistically based limitations because of the nature of the research problem and the types of data employed. Moreover, they cannot fully model the presumed deterrent process because they cannot get at individual cognitive processes, focus on specific categories or individuals, or take into account some contextual variables that have theoretically important consequences. For these reasons the ecological strategy seems to have exhausted its potential without much payoff.

Self-Report surveys There are, of course, alternative ways to address general deterrence: The most popular one currently is the self-report survey. The basic strategy is to sample some population, query respondents about their perceptions of various aspects of sanctions such as the likelihood of apprehension or punishment for themselves or others in case of law violation, and then obtain reports of their delicts in the recent past and/or their willingness to violate in the future, as well as to measure demographic, attitudinal, and other traits of the individual (e.g., Grasmick & Bryjak, 1980; Jensen, Erickson, & Gibbs, 1978; Silberman, 1976). These individual data are then statistically analyzed to see how well cognitions about sanctions predict the person's behavior when crucial variables like personal moral commitment are held constant. Potential advantages of the survey approach include testing the deterrence process directly; measuring the important variables that remain untapped by ecological analysis (such as perceptions about sanctions and their source, or moral commitments); and examining variations in deterrence among demographic categories, contextual situations, and for various kinds of sanctions. Unfortunately, these advantages are not easily realized because of unique difficulties in survey methodology.

First, self-report data may contain systematic errors. Memory failure, distortion, and deliberate nondisclosure are all especially troubling because they may be directly related to the variables of interest when studying sanctions. Although various tests do suggest reasonable accuracy, and ingenious methods for enhancing or estimating truthfulness have been developed (Akers, Massey, Clarke, & Lauer, 1983; Bradburn & Sudman, 1979; Clark & Tifft, 1966; Tittle, 1980; Tracy & Fox, 1981), scholars will probably never fully trust self-reported data, especially those concerning criminal behavior. Even cooperative respondents may inadvertently mislead researchers. Psychological processes are always at work, tending to lead respondents toward consistency in answers and toward selective perception of events and phenomena (Abelson, Aronson, McGuire, Newcomb, Rosenberg, & Tannebaum, 1968). For example, individuals tend to regard information with which they agree to be even closer to their own positions than it really is (assimilate) and to push that which they think is contrary to their own positions even farther away (contrast; see Sherif & Hovland, 1961). If a respondent thinks crime is bad he or she may well "assimilate" information about chances of punishment; that is, respondents may think their perceptions are closer to their ideal behavior than they really are or were over the time period in question. Similarly, survey respondents may reduce the "dissonance" inherent in simultaneous cognitions that they have committed a criminal act and that they are basically law-abiding citizens by distorting their opinions about the moral status of particular acts (Festinger, 1957). And image management to elicit favorable positive feedback (even from interviewers or unknown readers of anonymous questionnaires) is commonly postulated (Goffman, 1959).

Furthermore, even the most truthful respondents have difficulty assessing and communicating some important things about themselves. For instance, the deterrent doctrine assumes that people are deterred when their perceived costs (usually expressed in terms of chances of apprehension and perceived severity of punishment) exceed the rewards to be gained from a criminal act. Analysis of cost and behavior alone, as is almost always done, deceives because those individuals for whom a particular criminal act has low utility may be deterred even by a small perceived chance of punishment (cost still exceeds benefit) whereas people for whom that act has extremely high utility may be undeterred even though they perceive very high chances of punishment (benefit still exceeds cost). Unless utility is measured and taken into account, it will appear that neither is influenced by sanctions; the first because they have little fear of them, and the second because they commit the crime despite great fear. But utility has not been measured because researchers cannot figure out how respondents can express the personal value or benefit of potential criminal acts, especially because utility may fluctuate from time to time and from situation to situation. The benefit from stealing $5 is much greater when one is stranded than at home. The value of stealing $5 may continually be greater for some than for others. Clearly, utility is relative; without a standard of comparison across repondents, it is impossible for any given person to meaningfully convey it, and it is even difficult to express an "average" utility across various personal situations.

Surveys may also mislead because sampled individuals who cannot be located or who refuse to participate may be crucial. And because the kinds of people most likely to break laws (see Zimring & Hawkins, 1968) are not actually known, it is impossible to estimate systematic error. The assumption that some social classes, races, or nationality groups have greater criminality is currently in doubt, so oversampling selective categories of the presumed "criminally prone" to adjust is unjustified. It is not even practical to "correct" a sample by including known offenders. Although offenders were obviously undeterred from committing the act for which they were apprehended, this does not mean that they were more or less undeterred overall than others or that they were, or are, more criminally motivated. A convicted person could have contemplated hundreds of criminal acts only to have been deterred from committing all but the one for which convicted, whereas another individual may have contemplated hundreds of illegal acts, committed some, and escaped apprehension altogether. Moreover, "rehabilitation" may reduce previous criminal motivation. Inescapably, if deterrence is conceivable only among a subpopulation—the criminally motivated—it may be missed in a survey.

Sample defects cloud the picture in another way. Because some offenses, especially serious ones, are relatively rare, there will be few instances of actual or contemplated acts of these types, even in a completely representative sample. Insufficient natural variation in some variables may preclude meaningful conclusions. For example, some evidence (which incidentally may be questioned in the same way that other deterrence-relevant evidence has been questioned in this chapter) suggests that perceived certainty and severity of sanction must reach particular thresholds before a deterrent effect is likely (Tittle, 1980; pp. 223-242). But for some crimes almost everybody sampled might anticipate severe sanctions. Therefore, it would be difficult to determine if perceived sanction severity affects actions because there would be few instances of perceived low severity, even with a complete census.

The survey approach, at least as it is likely to be practiced in the foreseeable future, suffers, as does ecological analysis, from an inability to measure social characteristics of the group or environment of which the sampled respondent is a part. Surveyors can obtain individual perceptions about contextual characteristics, but they cannot obtain data about actual contextual traits to determine if such variables influence the individual sanction-behavior relationship. A national sample may include only 40 or 50 people from each state, perhaps only a few from some cities or counties within each state, and only one or so from a select few of all possible neighborhoods. Respondents can report things about themselves, such as moral feelings concerning a type of crime, and these reports can be aggregated to estimate characteristics of total populations; however, because samples are usually chosen to represent large total populations, the collectivity closest to the individual respondents will be poorly described by aggregation. The alternative of selecting separate samples for many neighborhoods, cities, counties, and states so that aggregation could be accurate to all relevant contexts requires an enormous N, the cost of which would be prohibitive even if meaningful "neighborhoods" could be identified. Hence, self-report studies may never incorporate the necessary variables for correct inferences about deterrence.

In addition, self-report researchers face the same previously described statistical problems that plague ecological studies. Multicollinearity, misspecification, inappropriate causal lags, identification problems, and reciprocal causation are prevalent. This has not been widely recognized because survey researchers have generally used more simplistic approaches, rarely modeling relationships among a large number of relevant self-report variables and attempting to estimate parameters with more advanced techniques (see Grasmick, 1981; Greenberg, 1981). When this is widely attempted, it may become clear that disentangling interrelations among perceptual variables is as different as disentangling ecological variables.

Natural intervention studies Effects of naturally occurring changes in sanctioning can also be studied to learn about deterrence. A legislature may authorize more severe penalties for a specific violation or a police agency may step up surveillance. In such cases a scholar can sometimes estimate whether the rate of violation decreases in response to the alterations in sanctioning. But meaningful research like this can seldom be conducted.

First, implementation may be defective. Simple legislative authorization does not guarantee change in some deterrent-relevant variable. Attempts to implement changes in drunk-driving laws or their enforcement dramatically illustrate this (see Ross, 1982). Police or court officials often subvert the law (Shover, Bankston, & Gurley, 1977), and sometimes potential violators misperceive or remain totally unaware of the legal or enforcement changes. In addition, indicators of violation independent of enforcement activity itself can seldom be found. Crackdowns to nab speeders may reveal previously unrecorded violations. Similarly, intensified patrolling of neighborhoods increases the probability of finding already existing crime (see Chambliss, 1975). To register a deterrent effect, an outcome must, therefore, be great enough to overcome this initial apparent growth in offense rate because in most cases there are no unbiased proxies like those used in drunk-driving studies (such as nighttime fatalities or single-car crashes). Third, if implementation is successful and good measures of offense change can be found, researchers must be able to ascertain how much change is due to the presumed causative variable rather than to seasonal fluctuations or to some extraneous factor such as unusual political change, a unique weather occurrence, or some national or world event (Cook & Campbell, 1979). Ruling out seasonal fluctuations is conceivable although it requires reliable, long-term, periodic data that are sometimes missing (Campbell & Ross, 1968; Glass, 1968; McCain & McCleary, 1979; McCleary & Hay, 1980; Ross, 1982). But discounting external factors necessitates comparing several similar cases—something usually quite difficult to do.

Finally, provided all this can be successfully accomplished, it may be impossible to isolate changes due to deterrence from those attributable to incapacitation, victim preventive maneuvers, or other factors that may accompany modification of the sanctioning process. Moreover, were all this possible, the conclusion would still apply only to the type of sanction, the specific offense, the particular kind of political unit and population, and the actual range of variation present in the instant case. "Ideal" natural intervention cases that could yield confident causal inferences about deterrence do not exist. Even imperfect ones permitting "reasonable" conclusions are rare. No doubt natural intervention studies will accumulate over time and may prove to be useful adjuncts in the quest for knowledge, but as likely as not they will point toward incorrect or problematic conclusions.

Experiments The experimental method probably contains the fewest *inherent* defects, and in form and structure it holds the greatest promise of providing reliable information about the effects of sanctions. Methodological and practical considerations limit their value, however. An "ideal" deterrence experiment may involve random assignment of political entities, such as cities within a particular size range, to several groups to be subjected to various degrees and types of sanction effort ranging from none to very intense. After an appropriate causal interval, the groups of cities could be compared in number of criminal victimizations. If there were a deterrent effect, presumably all the groups of cities "treated" with increased sanction effort would show less crime than the control or the group in which sanction effort was diminished, and "no sanction effort" cities should show a much greater volume of crime than the control group. Moreover, by comparing the several "increased sanction effort" groups among themselves one should be in a position to decide which element of the deterrent formula is more important.

But difficulties intrude. First, managing the political and organizational problems to manipulate sanctioning in even one city, much less a lot of them, boggles the mind. Few citizens or community leaders would appreciate the value of experimental work enough to endorse it, and functionaries would not be likely to alter their normal patterns of behavior in response to research demands (see Fishman, 1977; Sherman & Berk, 1984). Even when legislatures make severe sanctions mandatory, they often find sabotage by judges who resent loss of discretion (Ross, 1973; Shover, Bankston, & Gurley, 1977). One can easily imagine some vested interests (possibly including the police) resisting reductions in enforcement required in one group of these cities, whereas others would try to prevent the huge costs of surveillance and victim surveys necessary to establish outcomes. In short, experimental treatments cannot often be imposed, and even if imposed they frequently don't "take."

Second, it would be impossible to guarantee that all conditions among the groups of cities except the experimental treatments would remain the same. Among the many contaminating influences might be differential migration. Some residents of the "no sanction effort" cities might flee to the enforcement cities out of fear whereas some people might move to the "open" cities looking for opportunities to commit crimes or to escape police intrusion in their lives. These movements would not be random and therefore would taint the results.

Third, even if the hypothesized outcomes were observed it might not be possible to infer that they were due to deterrence. For one thing, the effects of incapacitation could not be separated from, say, the effects of sentence severity. Alternatively, results may be due to self-protective responses by citizens to reduce criminal opportunities. Moreover, all the experimental groups could show relatively equal reductions in crime due to a "Hawthorne effect." If citizens became aware that their city was part of an experiment (which they almost certainly would), they might draw together in a self-conscious solidarity that could reduce crime, even in the "no sanction effort" cities.

Finally, measuring criminal behavior in a reasonably accurate way independent of law enforcement may limit such experiments to victim-producing crime and would introduce the kind of error always present in survey research. Furthermore, if survey measurements of crime (victimization) were repeated intervally, they could themselves influence outcomes by heightening citizen awareness of the crime problem even if independent samples were employed in each wave. Repeatedly reminding citizens of possible victimization may have wide ripple effects.

The best that can be hoped for is to use experimental methods in limited situations or in the laboratory. Although it is comparatively easy to invent laboratory experiments testing the effect of sanction threat or implementation on various forms of noncriminal deviance, the laboratory has obvious external validity limitations (Cook & Campbell, 1979).

Multiple methods Although each of the particular methodological approaches social science might use in trying to answer questions about general deterrence is flawed, the possibility remains of employing several of these methods simultaneously to compensate for the weaknesses of each. Survey methods could conceivably be combined with ecological analysis to learn whether legal threats are perceived and acted on by individuals. Or survey methods could be incorporated into experiments or natural intervention situations to produce better measurement of subsequent crime. Although desirable and promising for improvement of research, eclectic approaches nevertheless fail to solve the problems of multiple defects that characterize each separate method. There are just too many ways our methods are seriously marred. For instance, statistical problems that follow from the entanglement of variables cannot be corrected by merging methods. Further, merger could add problems such as those of sample and response bias when surveys are combined with other methods. In fact, multiple methods may actually compound rather than balance some problematic elements.

Indirect tests also appear promising. For instance, experiments along the line of the "base rate fallacy" research could presumably establish the conditions, if any, under which individuals use actuarial data such as apprehension and punishment rates to judge their own risk, thus indirectly addressing the major assumption of ecological research. Randomly assigned treatment groups could be exposed to actual sanctioning rates and then be asked to judge personal risk, whereas the control group judges personal risk without benefit of such exposure. But again, such strategies may reveal more problematic elements than they resolve. If such research showed little account being taken of actuarial facts about sanctioning, questions about representativeness of subjects and artificiality of experimental situations would blunt the impact. Also, such findings would not preclude the possibility that actuarial facts somewhere along the line were relevant in forging perceptual habits that continue to affect how one behaves. In the deterrence area, there always seems to be room for reasonable doubt, even with multiple methods, because each method adds its own problems without clearly compensating the weaknesses of it complement.

Finally, it cannot be assumed that the collective product is believable because defects of various research approaches or of particular studies will automatically "cancel each other" or have random consequences. It would be reassuring to find a variety of types of studies pointing in the same direction, but it might mean only that they are all wrong in complementary ways. Without reliable information about the exact ways the various methodological problems discussed in this chapter affect outcomes, concluding that the total body of evidence is somehow more correct than its separate defective parts is wishful thinking.

Specific Deterrence

The question here is whether punishments cause the particular individuals punished to avoid future offense. To answer it, the number of violations occurring after punishment must be compared with the number of offenses in equivalent groups of unpunished offenders (or possibly among those punished to a lesser degree). But methodological problems in trying to do this are legion.

Official data Official records cannot reliably reveal recidivism. Although FBI records can show rearrest they are poor indicators of criminal behavior (and, in addition, are not readily available to scholars). Obviously, offenders may commit other crimes without being arrested, convicted, or incarcerated. And they can be rearrested or reincarcerated without having committeed a new crime (Glasser, 1964) despite the habit of the FBI and others of equating arrest with guilt. In addition, record follow-ups cannot distinguish deterrent consequences from maturation, death, or rehabilitative outcomes (Tittle, 1974). One releasee may conform due to successful treatment for a psychological disorder that caused the original offense. Failure to appear in arrest files within a follow-up period would suggest deterrence. But this hypothetical subject did not stop offending because of punishment fear; instead, the motivation to offend was extinguished. Another releasee may recidivate despite having come to loath prison because stigma denies him or her opportunities for employment, thereby increasing previous criminal motivation to a level exceeding the intensified fear of prison.

Even if offense patterns could be reliably traced through official records, there is no way to assure that those experiencing various degrees of punishment are alike in other ways that could affect recidivism. In addition, it would be important to include unpunished offenders to learn if punishment per se serves as a deterrent. But using police data restricts samples to those at least experiencing police contact—itself a degree of punishment. Furthermore, official data permit study only of the possible deterrent effects of punishment severity, although deterrence might depend not on severity of punishment but on the perceived certainty that punishment will occur, and certainty can be investigated only if one could determine the number of actual offenses preceding the punishment (not just those leading to arrest). The possibility of erroneously ruling out deterrence is, therefore, great.

Limitations of official data also preclude effective field experiments. Offenders could conceivably be assigned randomly to experimental groups varying in degree of punishment to be administered. But measuring subsequent offense would involve police data with all their attendant problems (there are a few exceptions in which victim response could be monitored, see Lempert, 1981; Sherman & Berk, 1984). Results would be unreliable, and, in addition, interpretation uncertain. If no effects were found, the possibility would still remain that deterrence could arise from certainty of punishment, which is unmanipulable because it cannot be known from police data whether this is the first, third, or later actual offense. And if the study did show progressive effects for severity, they might not be due to deterrence, but rather to some other factor.

Nevertheless, the idea of randomly assigning offenders to punishment severity groups and then measuring recidivism, however it might be done, appeals to many because it ostensibly seems to be the kind of study in which limited practical aims of a deterrent nature can feasibly be evaluated with scientific methods (cf. Sherman & Berk, 1984). From a policy standpoint it might appear that it doesn't matter that such an experiment could consider only criminal acts that result in arrest, would be unable to deal with the effects of certainty of punishment (except to hold them constant through randomization), or could not isolate the causal mechanism. Reliable experimental demonstration that severity of punishment "works" to reduce future recorded contact with police may seem to have direct practical application (of course, by the same token, failure to find such an effect may seem less useful because the possible deterrent effect of punishment certainty would remain).

But such a hypothetical case constitutes yet another instance in which the concerns of genuine science, although appearing too demanding for the world of policy, may nevertheless be the sounder guidelines. Here I have in mind not the unmeasurable side effects discussed before, but rather the consequences of being unable to certify the unidentified causal process as one of specific deterrence. Suppose, for instance, that the unattended causal mechanism in the example was actually something like disablement (the human spirit of the offenders was broken by extended incarceration so that they became incapable of any autonomous action, including crime), rather than deterrence (inhibition of criminal behavior because of fear of further sanction). This would mean that policymakers, using research as a guide, might unwittingly create a cadre of dependent automotons rather than deter future law violation. To be sure, such a policy might diminish the crime problem (in the same way that capital punishment undeniably has a specific preventive effect), but it might not be regarded by most citizens as a wise policy if they knew why and how it worked. That is one reason why I believe deterrence scholars would do well to satisfy the main requirements of science before setting forth their product for public action, even when it appears that practical applications are "obvious."

Other kinds of data Successful investigation of specific deterrence may hinge upon the ability to use respondent reports or laboratory observations. Populations can be sampled and queried about past patterns of offense, punishment, and subsequent offense, or individuals can be interviewed periodically. Subsequent offenses of those reporting having offended but escaping punishment could be compared with those admitting offending and being punished while other differentiating variables are statistically controlled (cf. Gold, 1970). Offenders randomly assigned to groups for receiving varied degrees of punishment could also be surveyed to identify subsequent crime through self-report or by reports from family and associates. And perhaps individuals experiencing various degrees of punishment could be traced after release for self-reports of subsequent offense as well as other characteristics that could be controlled statistically to rule out differences among the punishment groups. But all these raise again issues about survey and self-report methodology discussed before, especially truthfulness in disclosure of criminal behavior or discrediting punishment, and sample bias.

Similarly, laboratory experiments could be devised to measure the effect of certain kinds of punishments on subsequent behavior. But the limitations of the laboratory often noted—artificiality, limited time periods and causal intervals, and selected samples—once again frustrate the plan. In short, methodological problems blocking knowledge of specific deterrence are as severe as those involved in studying general deterrence, and they appear equally difficult to solve.

THEORETICAL BARRIERS

Methodological barriers inhibit scientific and policy-useful knowledge about deterrence; yet, of equal or greater import is the inadequacy of theory. If solutions to methodological problems were found, questions about deterrence would still be unanswerable. Indeed, without more adequate theory, scholars cannot pose the right questions or know when some have been answered.

The consequences of theoretical inadequacy usually noticed by researchers include inability to specify causal intervals between sanction threats and hypothesized response, absence of guidelines concerning the political level at which formal sanctioning might influence individual perceptions and behavior, and the uncertainty of identifying crucial antecedent, intervening, or conditional variables. But this is only the tip of the iceberg. "Theory" about deterrence basically consists of: (1) One general principle or axiom (Gibbs, 1975, calls it a doctrine) stating that certain and severe punishment will curtail crime; (2) some unconnected ideas about why deterrence might operate under some conditions but not others (Andenaes, 1974; Chambliss, 1967; Tittle, 1980; Zimring & Hawkins, 1973); and (3) identification of some conditional or control variables that perhaps ought to be taken into account (Geerken & Gove, 1975; Tittle & Logan, 1973).

In fact, deterrence "theory" is not much better than "rainmaker theory" (Etzioni, 1983). "Rainmaker theory" asserts that a dance will produce rain. When rain follows the dance (no matter how long afterward or how much it rains—and, of course, it will eventually rain), this can be interpreted as evidence for the accuracy of the theory. On the other hand, critics will always claim that it didn't rain enough (how much is enough?), soon enough (what is the causal interval?), often enough (how strong must the association be?), or in the right places (what are the conditional expectations?) to credit the theory. Or perhaps critics will acknowledge the association but point out that it could be spuriously due to other variables not measured and taken into account (what are those variables and why must they be taken into account?). Similarly, absence of rain within a reasonable time after the dance (what is reasoanble?) can be interpreted as negative evidence for the theory, although proponents will maintain that failure could be due to improper performance of the dance (what is proper performance?). Still other proponents will reason that the dance obviously works sometimes because they have personally witnessed its effects in certain instances, whereas others will argue that because the dance was shortly followed by rain sometimes, the task is simply to isolate the conditions under which it works.

These contradictory interpretations are all possible because the "theory" is not really a theory. It doesn't say how much rain is supposed to be produced by the dance or how long it will take. It does not say exactly how the dance must be performed, where it must performed, or for how long, nor does it explain how the dance and the outcomes are supposedly connected. Moreover, it does not say what other conditions must be present or absent for the results to be forthcoming. Thus, little can be learned about rainmaking because the basis for posing answerable questions is absent.

So it is with deterrence; so little can be specified theoretically that almost any outcome of a test can be interpreted in numerous ways. When a given study shows the crime rate, or the criminal behavior of some individuals, to vary negatively with sanctions, proponents rejoice, claiming more vindication for deterrence. But critics scoff, viewing the effects as too small, too late, not generally distributed enough, or spuriously attributable to other variables not measured or taken into account. On the other hand, when a study reveals sanctioning to be unrelated or positively related to crime, critics rejoice in rejection of the deterrence argument while proponents maintain that failure in this instance was due to the improper imposition of sanctions (such as not certain or severe enough), the unusual nature of the offense or offenders, or absence of some favorite condition the particular advocate thinks is necessary for the operation of deterrence. Finally, some fans (or foes) regard all the systematic evidence as irrelevant because they "know from common experience" that sanctions do (or do not) deter. In short, because sanctioning theory is so weak, scholars cannot agree whether, in any test, the conditions for deterrence have been fulfilled; therefore, meaningful inferences cannot be drawn. Under such conditions research can never provide conclusive answers to questions about deterrence.

Theoretical deficiency is especially curious because there are numerous theories in sociology and social psychology relevant to the question of how and why individuals become motivated to commit crimes, and there are also theories about how and why individuals form perceptions about, and come to fear, various things. True enough, most of these theories are themselves imprecise and often lack coherence. But little effort is being devoted to integrating existing theories into a scheme that explains how and why crime might be deterred under what conditions and from which systematic predictions about deterrence could be formulated and tested empirically. Until that is done, there is little hope.

PRACTICAL BARRIERS

Cost

The best hope for progress seems to be in marrying survey with ecological approaches and experimentation on a larger scale. The first involves extensive surveys within numerous ecological units. Aggregating respondent data by ecological unit would permit: (1) Measurement of variables now untapped; (2) study of the supposed linkage between official sanctioning in ecological/political units and perceptions about sanctions among residents of those units; and (3) exploration of the various levels (neighborhood, city, state) at which official action might influence behavior and/or perceptions of sanctions. Periodic surveys within the same ecological units, particularly if respondents were panelled, would make study of alternate causal intervals possible and help solve the causal order problem. But this strategy would be incredibly costly. To be representative of a variety of different kinds of ecological units, large and small, would require an enormous number of cases, and exceptionally careful data collection and verification would be needed to permit inferences about ecological units from respondent data. In addition, great expense in managing, analyzing, and interpreting the data would be encountered. Such costs could easily be out of the range of normal social science funding.

Similarly, setting up and executing numerous experiments using a wide range of subjects and relatively minute variations in conditions would be prohibitively expensive. The cost of even one major experiment using batches of randomly assigned cities might be shocking; the price of a whole series of needed experiments or simulations could stun the imagination. Although such expenditures may be minute compared to those involved with other policy-relevant research (such as developing a single major military weapon), it still seems unlikely that our society will make such a commitment to deterrence research, particularly because inherent methodological problems would still render the results problematic.

Ethics and legality Some policy-relevant knowledge could conceivably be gained if scholars were able and willing to manipulate research subjects strictly for scientific purposes. But the vast majority of researchers are not "mad scientists," and the world is not at their command. Consequently, some important things can never be known. For example, to increase confidence in deterrence research three improvements in method seem particularly important. One is to determine the truthfulness of individual survey responses; the second is to ascertain the number of crimes those released from custody actually commit; and the third is to establish the extent to which experimental subjects commit crimes of interest to experimenters. But despite fantasies by some social scientists of subjecting survey respondents to polygraph exams or truth serum (cf. Clark & Tifft, 1966), surreptitiously wiring releasees for electronic monitoring (cf Ingraham & Smith, 1978), or tempting experimental subjects to commit serous crimes while under surveillance, few responsible scholars would actually do such things, even if they were allowed; and, of course, political, professional, and constitutional constraints prohibit them. Hence incomplete and flawed data will always prohibit confidence in research results. And so it is with many issues relevant to the deterrence question. The need to know the effects of sanctions will probably never outweigh the need to protect citizens from arbitrary harm or intrusion.

CONTEXTUAL BARRIERS

The Lay Context of Research

Another factor standing in the way of policy-relevant research is an antiscientific bias among lay persons. It is questionable whether bureaucrats, politicians, government officials, judges, lawyers, police, or citizens who may be involved in the funding, participation in, or implementation of research really want to know the answers to questions about deterrence. To many, no doubt, such knowledge would be of little importance. Some believe policy ought to be based on moral, political, or commonsensical considerations, or that punishment is self-justifying as vengeance or retribution. Others think they already know the answers, and many of those who doubt their judgments distrust social science's ability to contribute to knowledge. In addition, some have vested interests in the sanctioning system. The possibility that prisons might be shown to be superfluous, for instance, or that legal threats might be proven to be useless or highly limited is economically or ideologically threatening to some. Indeed, even hypothesizing about the inefficacy of sanction often leads to lay outrage or ridicule. Thus it is unrealistic to expect the kind of mandate from citizens and authorities that would permit deterrence questions to be thoroughly addressed.

The Social Scientific Context of Research

Equally limiting are defensive maneuvers by social scientists themselves. Despite claims of self-corrective peer review, conscious efforts to keep open minds, and presumed rigorous scientific training, the social science disciplines that deal with deterrence are riddled with inadvertent antiscientific elements. Some scholars appear to be committed to the theoretical (perhaps "ideological") notion that deterrence *must* work, and they seem bent on proving it, whereas others appear equally committed to the idea that deterrence cannot work and to disproving the doctrine. Some even equate the truth of the deterrence doctrine with the validity of particular academic disciplines (see Beyleveld, 1982). Personal status and prestige are staked on the "right" outcome of research. Is it any surprise, then, that some researchers always seem to find supportive evidence whereas others always find negating evidence? And in view of this, isn't intolerance of criticism or innovative methodologies, willingness to accept outrageous assumptions in conducting and interpreting research, and avoidance of creative theory understandable?

Other scholars are crippled by methodological commitments. "Ecological" researchers have little understanding or sympathy for survey methods or experimental work; surveyors distrust experiments and official data; and "natural interventionists" scoff at the rest. Alone this would not be so bad, but practitioners of particular methods dominate and control review panels of the main granting agencies. Any research "establishment," especially the current one, encourages scholars to repeat the same kind of work using the same kind of data, making only minor specification adjustments, and ignoring the same errors. Innovation requires potential jeopardy of continued support as well as personal prestige and power. Because these problems represent natural products of academic organizations or particular social processes rather than deliberate or conscious biases, they are unlikely to abate.

CONCLUSION

It appears that methodological, theoretical, practical, and contextual hurdles may forever prevent social science from answering questions about deterrence in a confident way. Certainly methodological and theoretical problems have so far precluded a sound body of knowledge. Every issue bearing on deterrence is currently controversial, and every empirical finding is contradicted. Anything social science says about deterrence, other than that we don't know, stands a good chance of being wrong. There is now no compelling reason to believe that social science-based policies concerning sanctions would be any more efficient, useful, or morally justifiable than those that emerge from ordinary public debate.

In view of this, good sense would seem to demand extreme caution. Even when ad hoc, "raw," empirical findings about the effects of sanctions in specific situations appear to be policy-relevant, their use may be dangerous because the "missing scientific links" may be of critical relevance in judging the wisdom of various policies.

Perhaps a useful but honest policy role for deterrence scholars would be as "nervous Nellie's," helping to shape the form of public debate by reminding others that things are not as simple as they seem, by confessing our ignorance, and by making plain that unknowns can be ignored only at potentially great peril. Anything beyond that is pretentious.

REFERENCES

Abelson, R. P., Aronson, E., McGuire, W. J., Newcomb, T. M., Rosenberg, M. J., & Tannebaum, P. H. (Eds.). (1969). *Theories of cognitive consistency: A sourcebook.* Chicago: Rand McNally.

Akers, R. L., Massey, J., Clarke, W., & Lauer, R. M. (1983). Are self-reports of adolescent deviance valid? Biochemical measures, randomized response and the bogus pipeline in smoking behavior. *Social Forces, 62,* 234-251.

Andenaes, J. (1974). *Punishment and deterrence.* Ann Arbor: University of Michigan Press.

Assembly Committee on Criminal Procedure (California). (1975). Public knowledge of criminal procedure. In R. L. Henshel & R. A. Silverman (Eds.), *Perception in criminology* (pp. 74-90). New York: Columbia University Press.

Bankston, W. B., & Cramer, J. A. (1974). Toward a macro-sociological interpretation of general deterrence. *Criminology, 12,* 251-280.

Bar-Hillel, M. (1980). The base rate fallacy in probability judgments. *Acta Psychologica, 44,* 211-233.

Bar-Hillel, M., & Fischoff, B. (1981). When do base rates affect predictions. *Journal of Personality and Social Psychology, 41,* 671-680.

Beyleveld, D. (1982). Ehrlich's analysis of deterrence. *British Journal of Criminology, 22,* 101-123.

Blumstein, A., Cohen, J., & Nagin, D. (Eds.). (1978). *Deterrence and incapacitation: Estimating the effects of criminal sanctions on crime rates.* Washington, DC: National Academy of Sciences.

Bowers, W., & Pierce, G. (1980). Deterrence or brutalization: What is the effect of executions? *Crime and Delinquency, 26,* 453-484.

Bradburn, N. M., & Sudman, S. (1979). *Improving interview method and questionnaire design.* San Francisco, CA: Jossey-Bass.

Braithwaite, J. (1981). The myth of social class and criminality reconsidered. *American Sociological Review, 46,* 36-47.

Brier, S., & Feinberg, S. (1980). Recent econometric modeling of crime and punishment: Support for the deterrence hypothesis? *Evaluation Review, 4,* 147-191.

Campbell, D. T., & Ross, H. L. (1968). The Connecticut crackdown on speeding: Time series data in quasi-experimental analysis. *Law and Society Review, 3,* 33-53.

Chambliss, W. J. (1967, Summer). Types of deviance and the effectiveness of legal sanctions. *Wisconsin Law Review,* 703-719.

Chambliss, W. J. (1975). *Criminal law in action.* Santa Barbara, CA: Hamilton.

Clark, J. P., & Tifft, L. L. (1966). Polygraph and interview validation of self-reported deviant behavior. *American Sociological Review, 31,* 516-523.

Cloninger, D., & Sartorius, L. C. (1979). Crime rates, clearance rates and enforcement effort. *American Journal of Economics and Sociology, 38,* 389-402.

Cohen, J. (1978). The incapacitative effect of imprisonment: A critical review of the literature. In A. Blumstein, J. Cohen, & D. Nagin (Eds.), *Deterrence and incapacitation: Estimating the effects of criminal sanctions on crime rates* (pp. 187-243). Washington, DC: National Academy of Sciences.

Cohen, L. E., & Felson, M. (1979). Social change and crime rate trends: A routine activities approach. *American Sociological Review, 44,* 588-608.

Cook, T. D., & Campbell, D. T. (1979). *Quasi-experimentation: Design and analysis issues for field settings.* Chicago: Rand McNally.

Cousineau, D. F. (1973). A critique of the ecological approach to the study of deterrence. *Social Science Quarterly, 54,* 152-158.

Cramer, J. C. (1980). Fertility and female employment. *American Sociological Review, 45,* 167-190.

DeFleur, L. B. (1975). Biasing influences on drug arrest records: Implications for deviance research. *American Sociological Review, 40,* 88-103.

Durkheim, E. (1933). *The division of labor in society.* New York: The Free Press.

Ehrlich, I. (1975). The deterrent effect of capital punishment: A question of life and death. *American Economic Review, 65,* 397-417.

Ehrlich, I. (1977). The deterrent effect of capital punishment: Some further thoughts and additional evidence. *Journal of Political Economy, 85,* 741-788.

Erickson, M., & Gibbs, J. P. (1976). Further findings on the deterrence question and strategies for further research. *Journal of Criminal Justice, 4,* 175-189.

Erickson, M., & Gibbs, J. P. (1978). Objective and perceptual properties of legal punishment and the deterrence doctrine. *Social Problems, 25,* 253-264.

Erickson, M., Gibbs, J. P., & Jensen, G. F. (1977). The deterrence doctine and the perceived certainty of legal punishments. *American Sociological Review, 42,* 305-317.

Etzioni, A. (1983, March 16). Rainmakers in the university: Economists keep their variables vague. *Chronicle of Higher Education, 27,* 72.

Festinger, L. (1957). *A theory of cognitive dissonance.* Evanston, IL: Row, Peterson.

Fishman, R. (1977). *Criminal recidivism in New York City: An evaluation of the impact of rehabilitation and diversion services.* New York: Praeger.

Geerken, M. R. & Gove, W. R. (1975). Deterrence: Some theoretical considerations. *Law and Society Review, 9,* 498-513.

Gibbs, J. P. (1975). *Crime, punishment, and deterrence.* New York: Elsevier.

Glaser, D. (1964). *The effectiveness of a prison and parole system.* Indianapolis, IN: Bobbs-Merrill.

Glass, G. V. (1968). Analysis of data on the Connecticut speeding crackdown as a time-series quasi-experiment. *Law and Society Review, 3,* 55-76.

Goffman, E. (1959). *The presentation of self in everyday life.* New York: Anchor.

Gold, M. (1970). *Delinquency in an American city,.* Belmont, CA: Wadsworth.

Grasmick, H. (1981). The strategy of deterrence research: A reply to Greenberg. *Journal of Criminal Law and Criminology, 72,* 1102-1108.

Grasmick, H. (1982). *Linkages between ecological and perceptual data: Methodological issues in deterrence research.* Paper presented at annual meeting of American Society of Criminology, Toronto, Canada.

Grasmick, H., & Bryjak, G. (1980). The deterrence effect of perceived severity of punishment. *Social Forces, 59,* 471-491.

Greenberg, D. F. (1975). The incapacitative effect of imprisonment: Some estimates. *Law and Society Review, 9,* 541-580.

Greenberg, D. F. (1977). Deterrence research and social policy. In S. Nagel (Ed.), *Modeling the criminal justice system* (pp. 281-295). Beverly Hills, CA: Sage.

Greenberg, D. F. (1981). Methodological issues in survey research on the inhibition of crime. *Journal of Criminal Law and Criminology, 72,* 1094-1101.

Greenberg, D. F., & Kessler, R. C. (1982). The effect of arrests on crime: A multivariate panel analysis. *Social Forces, 60,* 771-790.

Greenberg, D. F., Kessler, R. C., & Logan, C. H. (1981). Aggregation bias in deterrence research: An empirical analysis. *Journal of Research in Crime and Delinquency, 18,* 128-137.

Hanushek, E. A., & Jackson, J. E. (1977). *Statistical methods of social scientists.* New York: Academic Press.

Henshel, R. L., & Carey, S. H. (1975). Deviance, deterrence, and knowledge of sanctions. In R. L. Henshel & R. A. Silverman (Eds.), *Perception in criminology* (pp. 54-73). New York: Columbia University Press.

Ingraham, B. I., & Smith, G. W. (1978). Electronic surveillance and control of behavior. In N. Johnston & L. D. Savitz (Eds.), *Justice and corrections* (pp. 966-977). New York: John Wiley.

Jacob, J., & Rich, M. (1980). The effects of the police on crime: A second look. *Law and Society Review, 15,* 109-122.

Jensen, G. F., Erickson, M. L., & Gibbs, J. P. (1978). Perceived risk of punishment and self-reported delinquency. *Social Forces, 57,* 57-78.

Kleck, G. (1982). On the use of self-report data to determine the class distribution of criminal and delinquent behavior. *American Sociological Review, 47,* 427-433.

Lempert, R. (1981). Organizing for deterrence: Lessons from a study of child support. *Law and Society Review, 16,* 513-568.

Loftin, C., & McDowell, D. (1982). The police, crime and economic theory: An assessment. *American Sociological Review, 47,* 393-410.

Logan, C. H. (1982). Problems in ratio correlation: The case of deterrence research. *Social Forces, 60,* 791-810.

McCain, L. J., & McCleary, R. (1979). The statistical analysis of the simple interrupted time-series quasi-experiment. In T. D. Cook & D. T. Campbell (Eds.), *Qusai-experimentation: Design and analysis issues for field settings* (pp. 233-293). Chicago: Rand McNally.

McCleary, R., & Hay, R. A., Jr. (1980). *Applied time series analysis for the social sciences.* Beverly Hills, CA: Sage.

McCleary, R., Nienstedt, B. C., & Erven, J. M. (1982). Uniform crime reports as organizational outcomes: Three time-series experiments. *Social Problems, 29,* 361-372.

McQuire, W. J., & Sheehan, R. G. (1983). Relationships between crime rates and incarceration rates: Further analysis. *Journal of Research in Crime and Delinquency, 20,* 73-85.

Minor, W. W., & Harry, J. (1982). Deterrent and experiential effects in perceptual deterrence research: A replication and extension. *Journal of Research in Crime and Delinquency, 19,* 190-203.

Nagin, D. (1978). General deterrence: A review of the empirical evidence. In A. Blumstein, J. Cohen, & D. Nagin (Eds.), *Deterrence and incapacitation: Estimating the effects of criminal sanctions on crime rates* (pp. 95-139). Washington, DC: National Academy of Sciences.

Namboodiri, N. K., Carter, L. F., & Blalock, H. M., Jr. (1975). *Applied multivariate analysis and experimental designs.* New York: McGraw-Hill.

Nisbett, R. E., & Ross, L. (1980). *Human inference: Strategies and shortcomings of social judgment.* Englewood Cliffs, NJ: Prentice-Hall.

Palmer, J. (1977). Economic analyses of the deterrent effect of punishment: A review. *Journal of Research in Crime and Delinquency, 14,* 4-21.

Parker, J., & Grasmick, H. G. (1979). Linking actual and perceived certainty of punishment: An exploratory study of an untested proposition in deterrence theory. *Criminology, 17,* 366-379.

Passell, P., & Taylor, J. (1977). The deterrent effect of capital punishment: Another view. *American Economic Review, 67,* 445-451.

Paternoster, R., Saltzman, L. E., Waldo, G. P., & Chiricos, T. G. (1983). Estimating perceptual statibility and deterrent effects: The role of perceived legal punishment in the inhibition of criminal involvement. *Journal of Criminal Law and Criminology, 74,* 270-297.

Richards, P., & Tittle, C. R. (1982). Socioeconomic status and perceptions of personal arrest probabilities. *Criminology, 20,* 329-346.

Ross, H. L. (1973). Law, science and accidents: The British road safety act of 1967. *Journal of Legal Studies: 2,* 1-78.

Ross, H. L. (1982). *Deterring the drinking driver: Legal policy and social control.* Lexington, MA: D. C. Heath.

Scott, R. A. (1976). Deviance, sanctions, and social integration in small-scale societies. *Social Forces, 54,* 604-620.

Sherif, M., & Hovland, C. I. (1961). *Social judgment: Assimilation and contrast effects in communication and attitude change.* New Haven, CT: Yale University Press.

Sherman, L. W., & Berk, R. A. (1984). The specific deterrent effects of arrest for domestic assault. *American Sociological Review, 49,* 261-272.

Sherman, L. W., & Glick, B. G. (1982). *The regulation of arrest rates.* Paper presented to the American Sociological Association Annual Convention, San Francisco, CA.

Shinnar, R., & Shinnar, S. (1975). The effects of the criminal justice system on the control of crime: A quantitative approach. *Law and Society Review, 9,* 581-611.

Shover, N., Bankston, W. B., & Gurley, J. W. (1977). Responses of the criminal justice system to legislation providing more severe threatened sanctions. *Criminology, 14,* 483-499.

Silberman, M. (1976). Toward a theory of criminal deterrence. *American Sociological Review, 41,* 442-461.

Skogan, W. (1974). The validity of official crime statistics: an empirical investigation. *Social Science Quarterly, 55,* 25-38.

Thornberry, T. P., & Farnworth, M. (1982). Social correlates of criminal involvement. *American Sociological Review, 47,* 505-518.

Tittle, C. R. (1974). Prisons and rehabilitation: The inevitability of disfavor. *Social Problems, 21,* 385-395.

Tittle, C. R. (1980). *Sanctions and social deviance: The question of deterrence.* New York: Praeger.

Tittle, C. R. (1983). Social class and criminal behavior: A critique of the theoretical foundation. *Social Forces, 62,* 334-358.

Tittle, C. R., & Logan, C. H. (1973). Sanctions and deviance: Evidence and remaining questions. *Law and Society Review, 7,* 371-392.

Tittle, C. R., & Rowe, A. R. (1974). Certainty of arrest and crime rates: A further test of the deterrence hypothesis. *Social Forces, 52,* 455-462.

Tittle, C. R., Villemez, W. J., & Smith, D. A. (1978). The myth of social class and criminality: An empirical assessment of the empirical evidence. *American Sociological Review, 43,* 643-656.

Tittle, C. R., Villemez, W. J., & Smith, D. A. (1982). One step forward, two steps back: More on the class/criminality controversy. *American Sociological Review, 47,* 435-438.

Tracy, P. E., & Fox, J. A. (1981). The validity of randomized response for sensitive measurements. *American Sociological Review, 46,* 187-200.

Tyler, T. R. (1980). Impact of directly and indirectly experienced events: The origin of crime related judgments and behaviors. *Journal of Personality and Social Psychology, 39,* 13-28.

Williams, K., & Gibbs, J. P. (1981). Deterrence and knowledge of statutory penalties. *Sociological Quarterly, 22,* 591-606.

Wilson, J. Q. (1983). *Thinking about crime.* New York: Basic Books.

Yunker, J. A. (1982). The relevance of the identification problem to statistical research on capital punishment: A comment on McGahey. *Crime and Delinquency, 28,* 96-124.

Zimring, F., & Hawkins, G. (1968). Deterrence and marginal groups. *Journal of Research on Crime and Delinquency, 5,* 100-114.

Zimring, F. E., & Hawkins, G. J. (1973). *Deterrence: The legal threat in crime control.* Chicago: The University of Chicago Press.

12

Obstacles and Opportunities in the Use of Research on Rape Legislation

JEANNE C. MARSH

In recent years, all 50 states have made some modifications in their rape and sexual assault statutes (Benien, 1980). These changes reflect (1) the increasing use of law as a mechanism of social change, and (2) the increasing political sophistication of women as an interest group concerned about issues of sexual assault.

Reflecting the need to understand and document the efficacy of sexual assault law reform as a social policy instrument, the number of "legal impact" studies of these reforms has increased along with the number of law reform efforts (Deming, 1982; Loh, 1981). In this chapter, an evaluation of the earliest and most comprehensive reform, Michigan's criminal sexual conduct law, will be examined (Marsh, Geist, & Caplan, 1982). Evidence from this evaluation will be the basis for (1) identifying appropriate ways to analyze legislative reform as a social change mechanism, and (2) specifying realistic expectations regarding the use of such knowledge for the development of social policy.

THE LIMITATIONS OF LEGAL IMPACT STUDIES

Studies concerned with the impact of sexual assault legislation are plagued by problems that characterize legal impact studies more generally:

(1) failure to examine the implementation of the reform
(2) limited scope of outcome measures
(3) failure to apply or develop an underlying conceptual framework

In this section, these three problems will be discussed briefly. Methods employed in a study evaluating Michigan's criminal sexual conduct law (Marsh, Geist, & Caplan, 1982) will be used to illustrate strategies for addressing these problems.

1. Implementation analysis Recent legal impact studies include classic quasi-experimental studies such as the evaluation of the British breath-analyzer laws (Ross, 1973), the Connecticut speeding crackdown (Glass, 1968), and the 1968 Federal Firearms statute (Zimring, 1975). Many of these studies have combined archival data such as crime statistics with quasi-experimental interrupted time-series designs to evaluate the impact of laws. Such studies have strengthened causal inference about the capacity of laws to bring about changes. They have provided, for example, clear evidence that gun control laws have been unsuccessful whereas speeding "crackdowns" have evidenced discernible effects. Whether or not they have incorporated the interrupted time-series design, legal impact studies have been concerned almost exclusively with documenting the effectiveness of specific reforms and have ignored the general process of reform (Feely, 1976; Nimmer, 1978). These studies fail to investigate the extent and nature of a statute's implementation and factors that influence both implementation and impact.

There are several reasons for the focus of these studies on causal analysis. Assessing the impact of legal change is important to the policymaker deciding whether to push for a similar reform elsewhere. The desire to answer, in the most valid manner, the question, "Does the law work?" has no doubt contributed to a preoccupation with designs and measures required for establishing causal relations. Thus, there is a pragmatic explanation for the underemphasis of implementation in legal impact studies: The information derived from such studies has little immediate utility for the policymaker.

There are substantive and methodological explanations as well. Conceptual models that seek to identify factors that are important to the successful implementation of a law are scarce. As a result, little theoretical guidance exists for designing studies of implementation. From a methodological perspective, strategies appropriate for implementation analyses are not as well-documented as those for impact analyses and, according to Williams and Elmore (1976, p. xiii), are "likely to require time-consuming and tedious activities unlikely to bring about striking breakthroughs in terms of understanding."

Despite the factors that have discouraged implementation analyses, such analyses are important for two reasons. First, in order to interpret findings from analyses of impact, it is necessary to document the nature of and extent to which revised laws are, in fact, administered by criminal justice officials. If laws are not carried out, or only partially carried out, then little measured effect can be expected. Second, it is important to describe the way in which laws are implemented as a first step in increasing knowledge of successful implementation strategies. In this way, the factors influencing implementation can be identified. For example, an implementation analysis may seek to identify characteristics of the law, the criminal justice system, or the political context necessary for successful implementation. Or implementation studies could examine the way in which characteristics of cases influence how the law is administered. For example, most sexual assault legal revisions are germane primarily in cases in which the defense is consent (as opposed, for instance, to defenses of false identification or diminished responsibility). An impact study that fails to consider the nature of cases tried could result in misleading conclusions about the law's effect. This point is illustrated by a case-by-case analysis of sexual assault cases coming through an Indiana court. Reskin and LaFree (1980) found that a reformed law had little impact because most of the cases did not center on a defense of consent.

As mentioned previously, strategies for conducting implementation analysis are not well-developed. In the evaluation of the Michigan law, the in-depth survey was the means for exploring the implementation of the law. To measure the nature and extent of adherence to the law, judges, prosecutors, defense attorneys, and rape crisis counselors were interviewed about how frequently specific provisions of the law were applied. They were also interviewed about the situations requiring the actual application of specific provisions. Observation obviously represents a powerful tool in implementation analyses. Although this was not an explicit strategy employed in the Michigan study, substantial incidental contextual information was acquired through observation as a result of researchers' direct involvement in conducting interviews. More extensive discussions of appropriate approaches to implementation analyses can be found elsewhere (Rossi & Freeman, 1982; Williams & Elmore, 1976).

2. Measurement Two types of measurement problems plague legal impact studies. First, outcome measures often are restricted in scope. Many studies identify the law as the independent variable and use only one or two measures of outcome as dependent variables. The use of quasi-experimental interrupted time-series designs limits outcome measures to those indices available over time such as crime statistics. Given the broad purposes served by legal reform, the examination of only one or two measures provides a relatively narrow view of the impact of the law. Second, measures used frequently have serious biases that may distort estimates of impact. All measures are in some way fallible. For example, biases in crime statistics that result from their vulnerability to political influences and from data collection methods varying over time and place are well-documented (Wolfgang, 1963).

The evaluation of the Michigan law provides an example of how these problems can be addressed. Outcome measures were derived from the analysis of crime statistics as well as from survey items. The approach allowed for multiple measures of outcome, combining objective crime statistics with the subjective perceptions of impact held by criminal justice officials and rape crisis counselors.

The multimethod approach provided a remedy for the method bias of each approach. Additionally, care was taken to reduce bias in each approach separately. For example, the survey was administered to individuals playing a variety of roles inside and outside the criminal justice system; police officers, prosecutors, defense attorneys, judges, and rape crisis counselors. Perspectives represented by any one role were balanced by others. The problems inherent in crime statistics were addressed in several ways. The crime statistics used were those collected by the Michigan State Police for the Uniform Crime Reporting (UCR) system. Individuals responsible for these statistic were interviewed to document the way in which statistics were collected, to assess the completeness of the data, and to determine any changes in the data collection strategies during the period of interest. These interviews provided no indication that the implementation of the law with the revised definitions of the crime altered data collection strategies. In Michigan, crimes labled forcible rape under the old law and CSCI under the new law were reported consistently as forcible rape in the UCR statistics. Once the comparability of the data before and after the law was determined, this statistic was the basis for the interrupted time-series analysis.

In general, evaluation studies, like all studies, must attend to data quality issues. The use of archival data such as crime statistics provides particular challenges due to the difficulties of evaluating the comparability of data collection procedures over time and place. Interviewing responsible individuals can often reveal the character of data collection procedures. Additionally, anomalous trends in the data, such as sharp, unexplained increases or decreases, can suggest possible changes in data collection procedures that can be investigated.

3. Adequacy of underlying conceptual framework The quality of any evaluation is improved by the explication of an underlying conceptual framework. Chen and Rossi (1983) discuss the importance of using existing theory and knowledge to construct a reasonable model of how a program can be expected to work before evaluating it. As in many areas in which evaluations are conducted, theory and knowledge relevant to the reform process are scarce. Factors that determine the success or failure of legislative reform have not been clearly identified. However, Freeman (1973) has identified three factors that are important in successful reform efforts. First, she suggests a law with supportive judicial interpretation must be in place that states public support for the change and that specifies explicitly the means for the change. Second, the law must be implemented and enforced by an administrative structure sympathetic to the intent of the law. And finally, the beneficiaries of the change must be organized to take full advantage of the change and to exert pressure on the administrative structure to improve implementation efforts. Robertson and Teitlebaum (1973) and Handler (1978) support the importance of taking account of the organization responsible for administering the reform and the groups responsible for promoting the reform in addition to the specific characteristics of the legislation (Robertson & Teitlebaum, 1973; Handler, 1978).

The analysis and interpretation of the findings of the Michigan study were guided by a conceptual framework that included these factors.

MICHIGAN'S CRIMINAL SEXUAL CONDUCT LAW

The reform in Michigan was intended to effect changes that were both symbolic and instrumental. The symbolic goals of the reform were to raise the issue before public consciousness and to counteract the traditional biases against the rape victim. Reformers viewed the reform as a "visible place to start the process of change" (BenDor, 1976). They noted the following:

> Despite the fact that rape reform legislation does not provide a total solution to the problem, it should be enacted since it will, at the very least, establish a strong policy in support of the rape victim. Such a policy should counteract the historical bias against rape victims by giving notice that the rights of the rape victim will no longer be subordinated to those of the accused. (Sasko & Sesek, 1975, pp. 502-503)

The instrumental goals of the law were: (1) To redefine and recriminalize rape and other forms of sexual assault extending equal protection to excluded groups; (2) to normalize requirements for evidence, bringing the legal standards for rape cases in line with those used in other violent crimes; and (3) to exercise control over decisions made in the criminal justice system (BenDor, 1976). These goals were addressed through the following legal changes:

(1) Restriction on the use of sexual history evidence. Perhaps the most important innovation of this law was the prohibition on the use of evidence of the victim's prior sexual conduct with persons other than the accused. This prohibition was based on the irrelevance of such evidence and its highly prejudicial and inflammatory nature.

(2) An elimination of the resistance and consent standards. Under the new law, resistance by the victim is no longer an element of the prosecutor's evidence. This makes the prosecution of rape cases comparable to other crimes by eliminating the requirement that victims risk death in order to have a case against their assailant.

(3) A degree structure. The degree structure in Michigan's law is an explicit description of criminally assaultive sexual acts articulated in four degrees. These are assessed by the seriousness of the offense, the amount of coercion used, the inflation of personal injuries, and the age and incapacitation of the victim. The codification of offenses and the clarification of language are crucial aspects of the degree structure because they reduce the amount of discretion that law enforcement officials exercise. Under the new law, police and prosecutors may investigate and pursue cases they would not have taken previously; those "marginal" cases in which the victim was not injured, did not strenuously resist, knew the offender, or was a prostitute.

(4) An extension of protection to previously unprotected groups. The law explicitly extended protection to males and to legally separated spouses.

Findings from the Study of Michigan's Criminal Sexual Conduct Law

The effectiveness of Michigan's criminal sexual conduct law can be documented directly in terms of the tangible goals that were achieved. Convictions for criminal sexual conduct in the first degree (formerly "forcible rape") have increased substantially as a function of the reformed law. Consistent with this finding, prosecutors report that their chances of achieving convictions have improved. They additionally report that they are able to win more types of cases than they were in the past, suggesting that the law's protection extends to more groups of people. The findings further reveal that the law in Michigan has been implemented in such a way that the procedures used in sexual assault cases are now in many ways similar to those used for other crimes. (For further detail on these and other findings, see Marsh et al., 1982.)

The causal link between the changes and the law gains support from the fact that criminal justice officials cite specific provisions of the law as responsible for the positive changes documented. The law shifts the burden of proof by prohibiting the use of sexual history evidence and eliminating the need to prove resistance and nonconsent. Prosecutor's improved chances to win convictions seem to derive from this shift. The law also improves chances of convictions by structuring the offense into degrees, with punishment commensurate with the seriousness of the crime. This feature of the law provides police and prosecutors with specific guidelines for investigating and charging decisions. Further, it allows prosecutors to plea bargain down to a sex offense that reflects the nature of the crime. Police, prosecutors, defense attorneys, and judges believe that the gender neutral language of the law and its increased capacity to protect those with potentially prejudicial sexual histories also increases the types of cases that have a chance for conviction. They further feel that the victim's experience in the criminal justice system, although still difficult, is less onerous than it was in the past. The law's limitation of sexual history evidence was overwhelmingly credited with this improvement.

The evidence is more equivocal with regard to the law's capacity to change officials' perceptions of the boundaries of sanctioned sexual behavior toward women. The data reveal that criminal justice officials have not yet assimilated the explicit redefinition of rape contained in the law's new structure. Both crime statistics and interview data reveal that officials continue to adhere to a simple dichotomy between "real rape" and other sex crimes. According to this perspective, "real rape" is committed by sexual psychopaths who prey on strangers. There is no argument about the relevance of the law in these brutal cases. But the application of the law to other areas of sexual conduct is considered, according to one judge, to be "messing with the folkways."

In sum, criminal justice officials report carrying out specific procedural changes related to the implementation of the law. Implementation of the law may be responsible for discernible impact in the form of increased convictions. Nevertheless, criminal justice officials reveal few nontraditional attitudes toward the crime and its appropriate handling in the criminal justice system.

Having documented the specific impact of the reform, interest remains in understanding factors that influenced the results. In other words, not only the question, "Does the law work?", but also the question, "How does the law work?", is relevant. The model of law reform developed in the study indicates that success is determined by the characteristics of the law itself, the system implementing it, and the forces outside the system that pursued the change (Freeman, 1973; Handler, 1978; Robertson & Teitelbaum, 1973). To better understand the reform, these three clusters of variables were analyzed.

The nature and provisions of the law What is known about the capacity of laws to influence behavior? Existing evidence suggests the potential for impact is increased when laws specify the formal procedures through which cases must be processed (Nummer, 1978) as the sexual assault law does. For example, law-mandated preliminary hearings and grand jury or other routine court appearances are more likely to be complied with than other types of laws (Nimmer, 1978). The greater likelihood of compliance with laws that change procedures no doubt results from the fact that they are techically simple and easily monitored; these characteristics increase the implementability of any law reform (Handler, 1978). Laws perhaps have their most powerful influence on the way in which jury trials, as compared to other aspects of the legal process, are conducted. This is in part due to the careful recording of the trial process and to the monitoring function of a potential appeal. In addition, the formal and adversarial nature of trials may contribute to the implementation of legal change.

In part, the success of Michigan's criminal sexual conduct law occurred because the procedures outlined in the rape law were technically simple, easily monitored, and focused primarily on trial proceedings. In addition, the degree structure clarified the evidence needed to convict for each charge of criminal sexual conduct, and other provisions specifically prohibited evidence related to the victim's sexual past.

Rape law reforms have been faulted for focusing on procedural changes related to the conduct of trials because more than three-quarters of these cases never reach trial. This is a legitimate concern, but the criticism ignores the evidence that laws can have only a minimal impact outside the courtroom; most research suggests that laws have little or no influence on the routine day-to-day practices of the criminal justice system. For example, in addition to documenting that the law had its greatest impact on trial proceedings, the findings suggest that warrant issuing and polygraph use are unaffected by the law.

Nature of the criminal justice bureaucracy The repeated failure of reforms in the criminal justice system is well documented. Nimmer (1978) specifically attributes this failure to inattention to existing knowledge of the organizational characteristics of the system. Evidence provided by Nimmer (1978) suggests that the decentralized, highly complex, and informal structure of the criminal justice system is not conducive to implementing change. However, its functional characteristics can be exploited to counteract bureaucratic inertia. The capacity for change derives from the ability of the law, the law reformers, or both to appeal to the primary interests of the participants in the criminal justice system, that is, to minimize time and resources and to maximize individual power and prestige. Implementation of the criminal sexual conduct statute was enhanced because the law and its advocates reduced costs and increased benefits to important parties in the criminal justice system.

There were several ways in which the law addressed criminal justice participants' need to cope with overwhelming case loads. The study results show that once officials in the criminal justice system became familiar with the law, their jobs became easier and they were able to perform them more efficiently: For police officers, the law specified evidence required for each sexual assault and contributed to a more straightforward investigation procedure; for prosecutors, the law gave specific guidelines for charging decisions and increased the likelihood of achieving convictions through plea bargaining or through trial.

In addition, implementation of the new legislation was facilitated by its capacity to increase officials' power and prestige. When the law was enacted, several prosecutors responded to the increased legitimacy the law brought to the crime of rape by setting up special prosecutorial units to speed up and consolidate sexual assault case processing. In some jurisdictions, the unit was collapsed with existing select units designed to handle the most serious cases, such as those committed by repeat offenders. In other jurisdictions, the special unit retained its own social worker or crisis counselor to aid the victim and, in turn, the prosecutor. Respondents in every county said that these special units attracted the most able and ambitious prosecutors and could be used to demonstrate the concern and sensitivity of the chief prosecutor with respect to this crime. Because the law additionally made it easier for prosecutors to achieve convictions, and because convictions are a central criterion for career advancement among prosecutors, in many counties the law served as a mechanism for expanding prosecutorial power and influence. Thus, despite the fact that the organizational structure of the criminal justice system generally goes not facilitate change, the Michigan law reform appeared to accomplish some important procedural reforms through its compatibility with the functional characteristics of this organization; i.e., the law facilitated more efficient case processing and expanded influence among criminal justice personnel.

Influence of the law reformers Models of interest group politics shed some light on the influence of the activists responsible for the passage and implementation of the law. The initiation or adoption of change depends on the degree to which an organization is accountable to outside groups, whether for funds, political support, or clients.

For many criminal justice officials, accountability takes the form of responsibility to those who elect them. Ideally, if constituencies are to succeed, they must design reforms whose costs to the organization do not outweigh benefits; they must establish and maintain legitimacy; and finally, because the enactment of the law and its implementation are two different matters, they must remain organized and committed long enough to monitor and augment the system's compliance with the reform.

The implementation of the criminal sexual conduct law sets up a situation in which costs of implementation and change are concentrated in the criminal justice system while the benefits are dispersed to the population of potential victims. Wilson (1974) and Handler (1978) argue that in such situations opposition to change tends to be intense, and, because there are no tangible benefits to those pushing for change, it is often difficult for those groups to organize and remain organized. The Michigan law reformers were able to overcome these problems for two reasons.

First, because the law is compatible with the interests of criminal justice officials, the difficulties it initially seemed to present were neutralized or converted to assets. A new constituency to promote implementation has emerged within the system precisely because the early effects of the law benefitted many officials. Maintaining the status quo now means preserving the salutory effect of the law both structurally, through continuation of highly professionalized sexual assault units, and functionally, by preserving the efficiency the law lends to case processing. Furthermore, a growing number of criminal justice officials, from elected chief prosecutors to police detectives, have established reputations for themselves or their units by promoting the law.

Second, the nature of the coalition formed to revise Michigan's rape law has contributed both to its legitimacy and its capacity to sustain activity. Members of the Michigan Task Force on Rape achieved crucial support for the law by aligning themselves with conservative legislators and other law-and-order advocates. It is partly because this coalition was possible that rape law reform became a target of the movement. Of greatest importance is the advocates' monitoring of the statute's implementation. Crisis center counselors are often present in court as victim advocates. They not only offer support to victims but can observe the extent of compliance or noncompliance with the law. These activities have kept the issue before the public and exerted pressure on the criminal justice system. It remains unclear how long and how intense this monitoring must be to overcome the natural resistance of criminal justice organizations to changes required by law.

The tendency for social reform groups, if not to lose interest in particular issues, to at least turn their attention to other related concerns is problematic. Sustained pressure from these groups is such a crucial ingredient in the implementation of the reform.

In sum, the study drew upon relevant legal, organizational, and political science knowledge to develop and explore a model of legislative reform. This developing model suggests that laws that focus on procedural reform, that appeal to the requirements of criminal justice officials to minimize time and resources and maximize prestige, and that are carefully monitored by activists are the most likely to succeed.

APPLICATION OF RESEARCH ON RAPE LEGISLATION

Much of the growth in the social sciences is based on the hope that they can improve the human condition. There is, however, uncertainty about (1) the validity of social science knowledge relevant to the formulation of social policy and (2) the ways in which social science is useful is resolving social policy issues.

A significant portion of the literature concerning the use of social science in social policymaking and, indeed a significant portion of this chapter has been devoted to descriptions of strategies for improving the validity of social science research. However, a look at the policy process and the role of research or any other kind of information in the process reveals validity is not a primary determinant of research utilization. It is not the inadequacy of theory or methods (although they are far from perfect), the unavailability of relevant data (although this remains a problem), or the inappropriateness of problem definition (although intellectual hazards remain in this area as well) that hinder the direct application of social sciences to policy decisions. It is the character of the policymaking process itself that limits the rational application of social science knowledge to policy problems. Research on knowledge utilization has in many ways idealized the policymaking process, positing a logical, rational process. As a result, this research, which has focused primarily on factors affecting utilization or hindrances to utilization, has had limited payoff.

The Social Policy Process

The development of social policy is indeed a process rather than a single decision (Lynn, 1977). It begins with the recognition and legitimation of a social problem and includes the development of programs or policies to deal with the problem, the passage of legislation, the allocation of funds, and the monitoring and evaluation of the programs. In a pluralistic society, these decisions are influenced primarily by interest groups and critical events. Decisions are only minimally influenced by relevant knowledge. Because many policy choices require value choices, even if information were perfect and complete, it would not provide an adequate basis for policy decisions (MacRae, 1976). Furthermore, social problems are seldom solved with a single program or policy. Instead, changes are accomplished incrementally through successive program and policy modifications. Often in the process, societal perceptions of a problem change the direction of policy initiatives. Thus, the policy process is value-laden, incremental, and adaptive.

Social Science and the Social Policy Process

The policy process is such that there are at least two major ways social science can inform the development of social policy. The first is the capacity of the social sciences to use scientific discipline to collect accurate and reliable facts about the nature of social problems and the consequences of altering factors that influence these problems. The capacity for the social sciences to establish causal relations among social phenomena is perhaps the unique contribution they make to understanding the social conditions of humankind (Cronbach, 1975). The purpose of this activity is to improve the ability to predict and control situations in the short run. Accurately documenting the effect of an income maintenance program or a compensatory education program permits better prediction of the effects of these programs in different settings or the comparison of various programs on policy-relevant criteria. This application of the scientific method to the study of social phenomena has been refined in the United States to the point that some view the development of the social sciences as an valuable national resource.

Social scientists contribute as well to the development of social policy through their efforts to build models to understand and explain social phenomena. Although social scientists may not be able to achieve theories capable of the precise predictions possible in the natural sciences, they are capable of collecting empirical observations and structuring them into general laws (Cronbach, 1975). The focus of this activity is the development of explanatory concepts—concepts that may ultimately alter our view of social phenomena; i.e., how we think about social problems.

The first of these activities has, perhaps, the most immediate instrumental value for the policymaker. However, the research utilization literature indicates that social science research primarily influences policy through the second activity (Caplan, Morrison, & Stambaugh, 1975; Weiss, 1977). Research that shapes the rhetoric for a problem or transforms ideas about the source or expression of a problem is referred to more often in the policy process.

Characteristics of the policy process have several additional implications for the application of social scientific knowledge. They suggest that the development of policy-relevant social science need not operate on the short time frames of legislative and budgetary cycles. As new policy initiatives are developed to address enduring social problems, the findings of social science research has ongoing applicability. Additionally, the model-building explanatory aspects of research are as important to the policymaking process as the carefully controlled assessments of policy impact. Knowledge of fundamental social processes related to the social problems and interventions will have ongoing significance.

Recent studies of the impact of technological research and development on industrial innovation point to fruitful directions for future work (Mosteller, 1981; Nelson & Langlois, 1983). These studies suggest that innovations result from several sources, rather than a single breakthrough or piece of research evidence. And research influencing a given innovation may have occurred as much as twenty years prior to the breakthrough. Further, the most successful innovators are those sensitive to user needs.

Such evidence indicates the need for continued insistence on the development and use of research techniques that allow a historical, longitudinal approach to the study of social issues. Such techniques include social indicator measures, time-series designs, and other longitudinal data analytic techniques. Despite a recognition of the importance of such products and techniques, there are few studies that take a historical, longitudinal approach to the study of social issues.

Although too great a policy impact has been expected from results of a single study, a variety of methods for systematically accumulating knowledge from research on a given problem has been developed. Secondary analysis, meta-analysis, and data synthesis represent approaches for aggregating and summarizing results that are increasing in adequacy and sophistication. This is an important direction for continued work.

Finally, the characteristics of users of social science research and the nature of their information needs must be more clearly identified. In part because the prevailing view of the policymaking process has been so simplistic, the diversity of users of policy-relevant social science and the diversity of their needs are not understood. This question was addressed as part of the study of Michigan's criminal sexual conduct law (Marsh, 1981). Through a brief telephone interview of self-identified users, five distinct groups of users and several types of use were identified. Many users reported requesting the findings for conceptual use; i.e., to develop a counseling or victim assistance program or to develop a strategy for reforming laws in their state (36 percent). A substantial number also reported use of the results to legitimize or promote a particular political position (29 percent). None of these respondents identified plans for using the findings in ways consistent with the prevailing definition of instrumental use (Leviton & Hughes, 1981). These data are interesting primarily as indicators of how much more there is to learn about user information needs.

To summarize, social scientists influence both overtly and covertly the nature and direction of social policies that promote social justice in society. Although the results of a single investigation compete with the results of other studies as well as with a myraid of other influences in the policymaking process, evidence of the impact of social science on social thought and social policy cannot be ignored. Two ways in which social science influences social policy are (1) by providing reliable facts about the short-term impact of policy and program change and (2) by providing some understanding of the reason why change does and does not occur. A review of an analysis of the impact of a reformed criminal sexual conduct law illustrates these two types of contributions. Despite the evidence that social science can produce policy-relevant information, we remain relatively ignorant as to the process by which this information can be used to promote social justice through the policy process. However, there is some evidence that (1) a longer time frame, (2) a view toward the systematic accumulation of knowledge, and (3) a greater sensitivity to the needs of users of our product all hold promise for improving the utilization of results from social science research.

This understanding suggests that ongoing social science research relevant to sexual assault policy development will consist of targeted evaluation research examining the impact and implementation of specific policies. In addition, more general social science research relevant to the reform process—e.g., research in the areas of discretionary decision making, organizational development, and social movements—will contribute to sexual assault policy formulation through the development of explanatory models. The importance of a consistent, ongoing program of research is clear from the consideration that an accumulation of knowledge is more likely to influence policy than a single breakthrough study. Finally, there is much that remains to be learned about the information needs of decision makers dealing with the problem of sexual assault, from rape crisis counselors to state legislators. Increased sensitivity to the needs of these research consumers will provide guidance and direction for improving the relevance of social research to social policy in the area of sexual assault.

REFERENCES

Benien, L. (1980). Rape III—National developments in rape reform legislation. *Women's Rights Law Reporter, 6,* 170-213.

BenDor, J. (1976). Justice after rape: Legal reform in Michigan. In M. Walker & S. Brodsky (Eds.), *Sexual assault: The victim and the rapist.* Lexington, MA: Lexington Books.

Caplan, N., Morris, A., & Stambaugh, R. (1975). *The use of social science knowledge in policy decisions at the national level.* Ann Arbor, MI: ISR.

Chen. H., & Rossi, P. (1983). Evaluating with sense: The theory-driven approach. *Evaluation Review, 7,* 283-302.

Cronbach, L. J. (1975). Beyond the two disciplines of scientific psychology. *American Psychologist, 30,* 116-127.

Deming, M. (1982). Personal communication. Social Science Research Institute, University of Southern California, Los Angeles, CA.

Feely, M. M. (1976). The concept of laws in social science: A critique and notes on an expanded view. *Law and Society Review, 10,* 497-523.

Freeman, J. (1973). *The politics of the women's liberation movement.* New York: David McKay.

Glass, G. V. (1968). Analysis of data on the Connecticut speeding crackdown as a time-series quasi-experiment. *Law and Society Review, 3,* 55-76.

Handler, J. F. (1978). *Social Movements and the legal system: A theory of law reform and social change.* New York: Academic Press.

Leviton, L. C., & Hughes, E.F.X. (1981). Research on the utilization of evaluations: A review and synthesis. *Evaluation Review, 5,* 525-548.

Loh, W. (1981). What has reform of rape legislation wrought? *Journal of Social Issues, 37,* 28-52.

Lynn, L. (1977). Policy relevant social research: What does it look like? In M. Guttentag (Ed.), *Evaluation studies review annual* (Vol. 2, pp. 63-76). Beverly Hills, CA: Sage.

MacRae, D., Jr. (1976). *The social function of social science.* New Haven, CT: Yale University Press.

Marsh, J. (1981). *Evaluation consumers report.* Paper presented at the Evaluation Research Society meetings, Austin. TX.

Marsh, J., Geist, A., & Caplan, N. (1982). *Rape and the limits of law reform.* Boston, MA: Auburn House.

Mosteller, F. (1981). Innovation and evaluation. *Science, 211,* 881-886.

Nelson, R. R., & Langlois, R. N. (1983). Industrial and innovation policy: Lessons from American history. *Science, 219,* 814-818.

Nimmer, R. T. (1978). *The nature of system change: Reform impact in the criminal courts.* Chicago: American Bar Foundation.

Reskin, B., & LaFree, G. (1980). *Studying jury verdicts in sexual assault cases: Some preliminary conclusions.* Paper presented at the American Society of Criminology, San Francisco, CA.

Robert, J., & Teitelbaum, P. (1973). Optimizing legal impact; A case study in search of a theory. *Wisconsin Law Review,* 665-726.

Ross, H. L. (1973). Law, science and accidents: The British road safety act of 1967. *The Journal of Legal Studies, 2,* 1-78.

Rossi, P., & Freeman, H. E. (1982). *Evaluation: A systematic approach.* Beverly Hills, CA: Sage.

Sasko, H., & Sesek, D. (1975). Rape reform legislation: Is it the solution? *Cleveland State Law Review, 24,* 422-463.

Weiss, C. H. (1977). *Using social research in public policy making.* Lexington, MA: D. C. Heath.

Williams, W., & Elmore, R. E. (1976). *Social program implementation.* New York: Academic Press.

Wilson, J. Q. (1974). The politics of regulation. In J. W. McKie (Ed.), *Social responsibility and the business predicament* (pp. 135-168). Washington, DC: Brookings Institution.

Wolfgang, M. E. (1963). Uniform crime reports: A critical appraisal. *University of Pennsylvania Law Review, 11,* 708-738.

Zimring, F. E. (1975). Firearms and federal law: The gun control act of 1968. *The Journal of Legal Studies, 4,* 133-198.

13

Social Science Research and the Politics of Gun Control

PETER H. ROSSI
JAMES D. WRIGHT

This chapter is concerned generally with the relationship between social science research and public policy formation. Many interesting, and at times rather disconcerting, aspects of this relationship are illustrated in the uses made of social science research by partisans on both sides of "The Great American Gun War" (Bruce-Biggs, 1976)—the perennial debate in American political life over what to do about crime and the firearms with which crimes are committed.

It perhaps goes without saying that the gun control issue is an inordinately complex and hotly debated one, and, thus, one that has been argued in any number of manifestations. Some aspects of the larger political debate have progressed more or less independently of anything the social sciences have had to say. To illustrate, much of the disputation, at least in some quarters, revolves around one's interpretation of the intent of the Second Amendment, and here, social sciences clearly has had little to contribute.

There are, however, many aspects of the gun control debate in which social science has become at least peripherally involved, and at least

AUTHORS' NOTE: Preparation of this chapter was supported by Grant 78-NI-AX-0120 from the National Institute of Justice. We draw heavily here on research reported in J. D. Wright, P. H. Rossi, and K. Daly, Under the Gun: Weapons, Crime and Violence in America *(Hawthorne, NY: Aldine Publishing Co., 1983). The acknowledgement of support from the National Institute of Justice does not imply endorsement of the views expressed in this chapter, for which we bear sole responsibility.*

two areas in which the available social science research has played
a distinctive, indeed, critical role. The first concerns the extent to which
public opinion favors or opposes new and more stringent gun regulations. And the second concerns the question of whether gun control
laws "work" in reducing the rates of violent crime. These two specific
issues therefore constitute the substance of this chapter.

PUBLIC OPINION ON
GUN CONTROL ISSUES

Partisans in virtually every public policy debate find it convenient,
whenever possible, to claim that public opinion is favorable to their
point of view, and the gun control debate is certainly no exception.
To illustrate, we can quote briefly from the Executive Summaries of
two recent studies of this topic:

> Majorities of American voters believe that we do not need more laws
> governing the possession and use of firearms and that more firearms
> laws would *not* result in a decrease in the crime rate.

> It is clear that the vast majority of the public (both those who live
> with handguns and those who do not) want handgun licensing and
> registration. . . . [T]he American public wants some form of handgun
> control legislation.

Only the extremely naive would misidentify the sources of these
two quotations. The first is from a report entitled, "Attitudes of the
Electorate Toward Gun Control 1978," prepared by Decision-Making
Information, Inc., of Santa Ana, California, for the National Rifle
Association (NRA). The second quotation is from a report entitled,
"An Analysis of Public Attitudes Toward Handgun Control," prepared
by Cambridge Reports, Inc., for the Center for the Study and Prevention
of Handgun Violence. Both studies are opinion surveys based on national probability samples, were done in the same few months (April
through June of 1978), and deal ostensibly with the same subject
matter. And yet the "policy conclusions" appear, at least initially,
to be polar opposites.

These two surveys, of course, are not the first soundings of public
opinion on gun control issues. Indeed, the first "gun control" poll
was conducted by Gallup in the 1930s, and literally hundreds of polls
on the topic have been conducted since (Erskine, 1972; Wright, Rossi,
& Daly, 1983, Ch. 11). The two 1978 surveys differ from previous
polls in devoting their entire questionnaires to gun control issues; in-

deed, taken as a set, these two polls are nearly encyclopedic in their coverage. But even here, each survey focuses on different aspects of the larger issue and poses those issues to respondents in very different ways. Indeed, a quick scanning of the two interview schedules brings to light two salient features of these surveys. First, the Caddell survey emphasizes in each item that the question refers to handguns and "handgun violence," whereas the DMI survey focuses on firearms generally and on "crime control." Second, although the two surveys are ostensibly on the same issue, there are very questions that deal with the same specific topic.

The differing emphases of the two surveys are themselves instructive. Many people who favor stricter controls over the ownership and use of handguns nonetheless oppose further controls over the ownership and use of shoulder weapons by the civilian population. Symbolically, handguns are nasty little things that evoke potent and emotional responses in many people; rifles and shotguns usually do not evoke the same kinds of responses. Interestingly, although perhaps not surprisingly, the Caddell poll emphasizes handguns in nearly every question, whereas in the DMI poll, specific references to handguns (as distinct from guns in general) tend to be avoided.

In the same vein, Caddell's questions emphasize "handgun violence, " whereas the DMI questions focused on crime and its control. "Handgun violence," symbolically, seems to be the sort of thing that sensible firearms policies might fruitfully address; "crime," again symbolically, is clearly a more obdurate problem, and one may appropriately wonder whether "gun control" per se would contribute anything to its solution. Thus, through phrasing and emphasis, both survey organizations provide contextual cues that, in comparison, clearly seem intended to elicit the "right" answers from their respondents.

The contrasts between the contents of the two surveys also indicate that public opinion on gun control is sufficiently complex and multifaceted that two entire surveys can be devoted to the topic and still touch upon relatively little common ground. This also means that considerable latitude is given to the researchers in defining the issue operationally, a condition that invites partisan selectivity.

The Caddell survey has a lengthy sequence of questions on specific handgun control measures, prefaced, as we have just indicated, by a lead-in statement that the measures in question are to be considered as devices to "control handgun violence." The DMI survey has relatively few questions on handgun control.

As in most prior polls on the topic, Caddell finds large majorities favoring most, but not all, of the handgun controls mentioned. Some of the larger majorities are registered for relatively innocuous items that are easy to agree with because they call only for an endorsement of the status quo. For example, we should not be surprised to learn that some 85 percent would favor a crackdown on illegal gun sales because "cracking down" on anything illegal is simply an endorsement of existing laws. Several of Caddell's larger majorities are obtained from items of this general sort.

Several items dealing with the registration of handguns and the issuing of permits for handgun ownership or possession all elicit sizable majorities in favor of them. One should again be wary, however, of reading more into these results than is warranted. Many states and local communities already have laws of these kinds on the books. For example, Cook and Blose (1981) report that about two-thirds of the American population reside in jurisdictions that require handgun purchasers to be screened by the police. Hence, many who favor this provision, or other similar provisions, may again simply be endorsing the status quo within their jurisidictions.

Measures more extreme than those currently in use in many jurisidictions do not enjoy much public support. Substantial majorities, for example, oppose a "buy back" law, such as was once tried in Baltimore and a few other places. The idea of an outright ban on the manufacture, sale, or ownership of handguns is also rejected by sizable majorities, with the exception of the fairly strong endorsement (70 percent in favor) of a ban on the manufacture of "cheap, low-quality handguns."

There is very little in the DMI survey to which the Caddell findings just summarized can be directly compared. One item shows that 13 percent believe that there are already too many laws governing the possession and use of firearms, a proportion roughly on the same magnitude as the proportions who oppose each of the Caddell items concerning registration and permits. Some 41 percent say that "the present laws are about right," and 44 percent—the plurality— believe that we need even more laws along these lines. We can only speculate about the additional laws that this 44 percent say they want, suspecting that many of them may already be on the statute and or- dinance books in their home towns and states. Correspondingly, the fact that the majority does not want more laws is also ambiguous. Indeed, these findings are by no means inconsistent with the large majorities who favor many of the measures that were included in the Caddell survey; as we have already stressed, many of these measures are already on the books in many jurisdictions.

The finding that the "majority" of the population does not want more gun laws is, of course, heavily stressed in the DMI report and was, indeed, the finding that was summarized in the quotation from their report cited earlier. It will be quickly seen, given the actual empirical results, that the DMI summary is a masterfully rhetorical formulation. As we have just seen, the actual result is as follows: 13 percent believe there are too many gun laws already, 41 percent believe that the present laws are about right, and 44 percent believe we need more laws. Given these results, it is worth emphasizing that all three of the following are true (and equally misleading) statements: (1) The majority does *not* believe there are too many laws; (2) the majority does *not* believe present laws are about right; (3) the majority does *not* believe that we need more laws.

A final set of items that touch upon the same subject matter in both surveys—although in different ways—concerns endorsement of gun registration programs. The DMI item finds that 61 percent of the electorate opposes "the Federal government's spending four billion dollars to enact a gun registration program." On the surface, this finding appears to contradict the Caddell finding of large majorities favoring gun registration. But, there is obviously no inconsistency between wanting gun registration and also wanting it to cost less than four billion dollars.

Both surveys have comparable questions about proposals for an outright ban on handguns. The Caddell survey finds that 31 percent of the population would favor such a ban, 18 percent are neutral, and 51 percent are opposed. The comparable DMI item is somewhat different, especially in not allowing respondents to select a neutral position and in being phrased in an "agree-disagree" framework. DMI finds that more than 80 percent disagree with the statement that "no private individual should be allowed to own a handgun." It is thus plain in both studies that the majority of the U.S. population oppose outright bans on private ownership and use of handguns.

Both surveys also find very large majorities (80 to 90 percent) supporting the concept of severe mandatory prison sentences for persons who use a gun to commit a crime. Caddell finds that 55 percent would favor mandatory prison sentences for persons carrying unlicensed handguns, whereas DMI does not have a comparable item. Both surveys find large majorities (again, in the range of 80 to 90 percent) agreeing that criminals will always be able to arm themselves no matter what laws are passed.

On the expected effects of gun control, DMI asks whether respondents anticipate that crime rates would decrease or increase if more firearm laws were enacted. The plurality (43 percent) expect a decline in the crime rate, most by only a small amount; a large minority, 41 percent believe crime rates would be unaffected; and a smaller minority, 16 percent, believe that crime rates would actually increase. Caddell's version is an agree-disagree question with no middle or neutral category: He finds 49 percent who agree that licensing all handgun owners would reduce crime, 42 percent who disagree, and 10 percent holding no opinion. Despite the differences in the wording of the two items, the two surveys achieve close to identical results; roughly 40 percent to 50 percent of the population believe that crime would go down with stricter gun controls, with the remainder thinking that crime rates would either remain the same or increase. Our review of these two opinion polls, although brief, provides the basis for at least a few generalizations.

First, these two polls amply demonstrate (as if further demonstration were necessary!) the important point that "gun control" is an inherently ambiguous term, one that has been used to refer to a wide range of possible interventions spanning the entire policy space from simple registration and licensing requirements to mandatory sentences for using a gun in commiting a crime and, at the outer edge, outright bans on the manufacture, sale, and possession of certain types of guns. The polls also demonstrate that large majorities of the public do indeed favor *some kinds* of gun controls, and that equally large majorities oppose *other kinds* of gun controls. To say that the public somehow "favors" or "opposes" gun control *in general* is obviously to speak in meaningless ambiguities and thus to confuse rather than clarify the issue.

Second, when the two surveys are comparable in detail, results are similar at least in magnitude. Slightly different questions do not change the distributions (at least for this topic) by more than a few percentage points in either direction.

Third, the surveys differ primarily in the ways in which the many facets of the larger issue are covered or not covered in the respective questionnaires and ensuing reports—what specific topics are chosen for coverage, how questions are phrased, and, in particular, which findings are most heavily emphasized in the analysis. Thus, Caddell sticks to handguns and handgun violence throughout his survey and DMI phrases questions in terms of firearms and crime control. Caddell's survey contains many questions about specific handgun control measures whereas DMI asks rather vaguely about "more" or "less" firearms legislation.

The rough comparability of the actual empirical findings from these two surveys leads to an interesting thought experiment to wit: Could Caddell sit down with the DMI results in hand and write a report that would satisfy the Center for the Study and Prevention of Handgun

Violence? Could the DMI staff use Caddell's results to prepare a report that would satisfy the National Rifle Association? The answer to both questions is almost certainly yes. The studies differ primarily *not* in what they actually find, but in the emphasis and significance attached to the various findings. The *accuracy* of a finding is a matter about which all technically trained people would normally be able to agree; the *significance* of a finding derives mainly from one's prior values.

It does not take a very fertile or subtle imagination to see how these two questionnaires were constructed to fulfill the needs of the respective sponsoring organizations—in a word, to find "strong popular support" for the client's point of view. Given the five-decade history of public opinion polling on gun control issues, each of the client organizations (and both survey organizations) must have had considerable prior knowledge about the kinds of specific proposals and questions that would produce findings supporting or opposing "gun control." (DMI, in fact, had done an earlier 1975 poll on the topic, also in behalf of the NRA.) The end result, as we have seen, is a pair of surveys, each with remarkably convenient findings for its sponsor.

Social scientists, of course, are accustomed to the perils of specification errors, especially in the construction of explanatory models of social phenomena. The presence and consequence of specification errors in descriptive studies are not ordinarily pointed out in social science work, perhaps because we value descriptive studies so little. (To be sure, similar concerns are sometimes raised in terms of "construct validity.") In any event, the major faults in the two surveys reflect specification errors: Each survey incompletely, and therefore incorrectly, maps out the domain of gun control policy, gerrymandering more or less at will to exclude areas in which their clients could be expected to fare poorly and to include areas in which popular support would no doubt prove to be strong.

And yet, there are limits even here. Certain aspects of the gun control issue are so obviously central to the relevant policy domain that one omits them only at the risk of losing all credibility. Thus, Caddell had to include questions about an outright ban on handguns in his survey, knowing full well (or so one presumes) that those questions would elicit little popular support; and, likewise, the DMI survey had to include items on gun registration and licensing, again knowing in advance that majorities would be in favor of such measures. (In the latter case, of course, DMI managed to cope effectively with the problem with some highly "creative" versions of the relevant questions.)

Despite the limits we have just discussed, there remain obvious gaps in the topical coverage of each survey. Indeed, one will find entire sections in one of the questionnaires that have no counterpart in the other. Perhaps, the principle used is simply that if one does not ask the question, then one does not have to cope with the answer. This, clearly, is an extremely useful principle when the survey is meant to serve mainly polemical purposes. If the intent, however, is to inform the client (or legislators or the public) as fully and accurately as the state of public opinion measurement allows, then specification errors of the sort we have discussed are seriously misleading.

On the other hand, neither Caddell nor DMI is in the business of "informing" anyone "as fully and as accurately as possible." Both organizations sell services to clients, and like all other organizations, they have some obligation to be sensitive to the client's needs. If either of these surveys had been done as an academic poll of public opinion (for example, with funds from the National Science Foundation), one would immediately (and rightly) question the competence and integrity of the principal investigator. In the present case, it is clear that both clients pretty much got what they paid for: A technically competent poll that shows the client's viewpoint in the most favorable possible light.

Interestingly enough, however, in providing these services for their clients, the two organizations have also (inadvertently, no doubt) done the science of public opinion research a service as well. We know quite a bit more about the complexities of public thinking on the gun control issue than we knew before these two polls were conducted. In comparing the two polls, it becomes obvious not only what each of them managed to leave out, but what all the other, more academic polls on the topic have also left out. By raising some issues more pointedly than the more neutral polling firms would ever dare to, by considering in detail aspects of the issue that neutral pollsters would never touch, these two polls, unquestionably, have enlarged our understanding of public opinion and gun control, even though in isolation each poll is as much a political document as it is social science research.

ASSESSING THE EFFECTIVENESS OF GUN CONTROL LEGISLATION

A second major area in which social science research has figured prominently in the gun control debate concerns the evaluation of firearms laws and their effects on the crime rates. Partisans on both sides of the issue have for many years argued vehemently over the question of whether gun control, in fact, reduces crime. Social science interest in the topic corresponds to the emergence over the past two decades of a strong interest in applied work in the various social science disciplines (Rossi & Wright, in press).

If we have learned anything from the spate of applied social research of the recent past, it is that the expected value of the effectiveness of any social program or policy intervention hovers close to zero. We have also learned something about why policies and programs tend to be ineffective or only marginally effective. First, policymakers and their staffs often do not have the basic social science knowledge that would enable them to design programs in consonance with existing knowledge. Second, the required basic knowledge is often missing altogether and/or incomplete or otherwise defective. Finally, our knowledge about how human organizations work in the implementation of policy is extremely fragmentary, and it is often a mystery why some policies seem to be implemented in ways that preserve the integrity of the social programs involved and why others are implemented so badly that serious distortions occur.

This litany of why programs fail generally is particularly appropriate to a discussion of the assessment of the impact of gun control policies. In a word, there have been failures all along the line: In basic social science knowledge, in the art of implementing policies, and in the expertise of policymakers and their advisers in designing policy interventions.

The debate over proper civilian firearms policy remains among the more hotly contested political issues in present-day America. Much of the heat (certainly not all!) is generated in disputes about whether "gun controls" are effective in reducing crime, and in such issues, social science becomes inevitably and inextricably involved. Crime, after all, is a *social* problem of the purest sort; it is hard to imagine a technological intervention that would somehow solve the crime problem. Policymakers who deal with crime therefore turn, inevitably, to the social sciences for guidance on intervention strategies.

It is possible to deal with the issue of effectiveness to some degree because our political jurisdictions have experimented with a wide variety of gun control measures. Indeed, it appears that there are at this moment some 20,000 federal, state, and local laws regulating firearms ownership or use in one way or another (Wright et al., 1983, Ch. 12). Thus, almost every proposal that has ever been put forward by the proponents of stricter firearms controls is likely already to be in effect in some jurisdiction somewhere in the United States.

Cross-Sectional Comparisons

The diversity of "gun control" measures presently in force in the United States suggests that there are opportunities to test the relative effectiveness of different approaches to gun control. In principle, all that appears to be necessary is to contrast crime rates in jurisdictions with certain kinds of regulatory strategies to the rates prevailing in otherwise "comparable" jurisdictions that employ different strategies. On the face of it, it seems that we should be able to learn quite a bit from these "natural experiments." As we have learned, however, the results of natural experiments are as difficult to interpret in this field as in any other area of social policy.

Ordinarily, the person who asks whether gun control "works" wants to know whether there is any evidence that gun control measures reduce crime levels. A candid and considered, if rather depressing, response to such a question is that *nothing* seems to work very well in reducing crime. As we all know, crime rates in the United States have shown a very distressing upward trend since World War II that only in the last few years appears to be levelling off, and then only slightly. Nothing that has been attempted in the way of policies and programs designed to reduce crime has influenced the post-World War II crime rate trends very much.

Despite the obvious problems in so doing, social scientists have tried in various ways to answer the question of whether gun control policies of one sort or another lower crime rates. One approach has attempted to estimate effects by contrasting political jurisdictions that have relatively strict gun control laws with jurisdictions that have less strict laws, thus capitalizing on the "natural experiment" opportunities discussed above.

In their crudest form, these attempts show up in the polemical literature as simple zero-order comparisons between nations. For example, as is well-known, Great Britain has much stricter gun control laws and much less crime than the United States. From this it has been concluded that strict gun laws reduce crime! The Swiss require every able-bodied male to be a member of the national militia and thus to keep a military weapon and ammunition ready in their homes. The result is that the proportional density of firearms possession is clearly higher in Switzerland than in the United States. And yet, the Swiss have much less crime. And from this it has been concluded that crime and gun ownership are not related!

No technically competent social scientist would mistake either of the above comparisons for real evidence on whether guns or gun laws are or are not related to crime. The methodological problem encountered here, however, is formally identical to the problem that arises in other apparently more sophisticated and persuasive studies; namely, deciding what to hold constant in the comparisons.

In general, any two political jurisdictions—be they nations, states, or local communities—will differ in many ways, any one or combination of which may constitute the explanation for the observed differences in crime rates. If we had a credible, empirically persuasive macrotheory of crime, we would know just what to hold constant in making jurisdictional comparisons of this sort. Because we possess no such theory, these studies have typically held constant whatever happened to be available in the data sets used in the hopes that these variables would serve as suitable proxies for a good theoretical model. The results of such shotgun approaches should come as no surprise: different studies, holding different jurisdictional characteristics constant, produce remarkably different results. Consider the following two quotations:

> The data indicate that gun control legislation is related to fewer deaths by homicide, suicide and accidents by firearms. (Geisel, Roll, & Wettick, 1969, p. 666)

> On the basis of these data, the conclusion is, inevitably, that gun control laws have no individual or collective effect in reducing rates of violent crime. (Murray, 1975, p. 88)

In both of the studies cited, the data consist of state-level crime rates (the dependent variable), coded variables indicating the stringency of each state's gun laws (as shown in a compendium of state gun control laws), and an ad hoc selection of state-level demographic and economic data to be used as statistical controls. However, each investigator used a slightly different ad hoc selection of control variables. Depending on what was held constant, the stringency of gun control laws was either related or not related to the state-level crime rates. Neither study, incidentally, provides a plausible theoretical rationale for the set of control variables employed; as such, it is impossible to decide which is the more correct specification and therefore equally impossible to decide which conclusion is more credible.

Implementation Studies

A second category of research on the impact of gun laws has generally been more informative, mainly because it is more descriptive and hence is less dependent on the existence of sensible theory. These are "process" or "implementation"studies, centered on describing the actual "delivery" of gun control policies using data gathered in field research.

The importance of implementation research has only recently been recognized in the applied social sciences, a recognition that resulted more or less directly from the persistent string of "no effects" findings in the major evaluation studies (Rossi & Wright, in press). In speculating on the reasons *why* most social policies appeared not to produce their intended effects, it became apparent that part of the explanation was that programs were often implemented in ways that subverted the original intent (or, in some cases, were simply not implemented at all). These days, as a result, implementation research is considered to be an integral part of a comprehensive evaluation and a necessary precursor of informative impact assessment studies: It is, after all, rather foolish to assess the impact of a policy until one is clear just what policy is actually being delivered in the field.

Leading examples of implementation research in the gun control area include Zimring's definitive (1975) study of the Gun Control Act of 1968 and Beha's (1977) analysis of the implementation of the Barley-Fox gun law in Massachusetts, a law that was intended to impose mandatory one-year sentence enhancements for the unlicensed carrying of firearms. Both studies demonstrate that legislative intent can be, and often is, modified in actual enforcement to conform to the organizational imperatives of the criminal justice system.

To illustrate, the Gun Control Act (GCA) of 1968 required Federal licenses for all over-the-counter retail firearms dealers. However, the legislation did not enact any sensible procedures by which these licensed dealers would be supervised; indeed, Congress appropriated no funds for the purpose. Congress also failed to anticipate that the nominal fee required for licensure would result in several hundreds of thousands of licenses being issued. The number of licensees vastly exceeded the supervisory capacity of the relevant Federal agency (the Bureau of Alcohol, Tobacco, and Firearms). What appeared on paper as a new method of regulating retail gun dealers proved, in fact, to amount to no regulation of them at all.

Other provisions of the GCA of 1968 forbid firearms sales to convicted felons, the mentally disturbed, and out-of-state residents, but again, no procedures were specified for ascertaining whether these disqualifications were obtained or not. The result was an overload of applicants, far too few resources to police the actions of licensees, and, thus, widespread and rather simple circumvention of the intent of the legislation.

The general point to be gleaned from these studies is that unenforced and unenforceable laws and regulations cannot possibly achieve their intended goals. Such laws tend to satisfy symbolic needs, to create the impression that something is being done about the problem, but usually little more.

Time-Series Analyses

Most recently, various analysts have used more or less sophisticated time-series research designs to investigate the crime reductive effects of gun control legislation. These studies take advantage of the fact that states or other political jurisdictions often enact new gun control laws. If the appropriate time series of data exist, one can compare the behavior of the time series before and after enactment of new legislation and learn at least something of value about the net impacts.

The studies in question range in sophistication from simple pre- and posttest studies without control groups to quite complex inter-rupted time-series designs. No matter how sophisticated, however, such studies are not exempt from criticism or rancorous dispute. The essence of an interrupted time-series analysis is deceptively simple. One first models the time series prior to enactment of new legislation. On this basis, one then projects what the likely postenactment trends would have been had no new legislation been introduced. Comparisons between these projections and the observed behavior of the time series postenactment therefore provide the measure of net impact.

Clearly, the critical step in the above process is the projection of what "might have been" absent the intervention, a projection that can only be as valid as the analyst's prior understanding of why the time series behaves as it does. Sensible projections therefore require, once again, a credible, empirically based theory of how crime rates are produced. Lacking such a theory, all time-series analysts must make more or less plausible assumptions about the processes that underlie the behavior of the time series, and on the basis of those assumptions, choose the seemingly most appropriate statistical models for the data analysis. Unsurprisingly, different analysts then get different results, depending on the analytical models chosen.

Thus, the time-series analysis by Deutsch and Alt (1977) of the effects of the Bartley-Fox law in Massachusetts was challenged by Hay and McCleary (1979) on the grounds that the original analysis employed inappropriate time-series models. A reanalysis of the data, using different models, produced different findings: The original analysis suggested a small reduction in armed robbery and gun assaults as a result of Bartley-Fox, whereas the reanalysis concluded that these effects were not statistically significant. Which of these is the correct conclusion depends entirely on what kinds of assumptions one is willing to make, absent an appropriate theory, about how crime in Massachusetts is generated.

The best available time-series analysis of Bartley-Fox was conducted in a multimethod fashion by Pierce and Bowers (1979). These investigators enlarged the time frame for the study, compared the observed trends in Massachusetts and in Boston with trends in other states and communities, and, unlike previous studies, considered trends outside of Boston as well as in Boston itself. All told, the Pierce-Bowers study is more detailed and comprehensive than any of the previous Bartley-Fox analyses and does report some modest effects that consist of statistically significant but substantively small reductions in some but not all categories of gun-related crimes.

Most recent time-series studies, however, have found no discernible effects at all, for example, Loftin and McDowell's (1981) study of Detriot's recently enacted add-on sentence enhancement law, or Jones's (1981) study of the seemingly drastic Washington, D.C., gun control law.

No study has shown (or even claimed to show) *dramatic* effects of gun control legislation on gun-related crimes or crime rates generally. None of the studies claiming modest effects has yet had a long enough run to determine whether the effects persist beyond the first 12 to 18 months. The principal generalization to be made from these studies is thus that gun laws have (at best) modest and (at worst) nonexistent crime reduction effects.

Is it legitimate, then, to conclude that social science has proved that "gun control doesn't work?" Not quite! First, we must remember that "gun control" refers to an exceedingly wide range of policy interventions; the studies reviewed above deal with a fairly narrow spectrum of the broader policy space—mainly, that part of the range that involves mandatory sentence enhancement strategies. Other strategies, once enacted and evaluated, may prove somewhat more efficacious toward their intended goals.

Even restricting ourselves to the kinds of strategies that have been evaluated, however, the most we can conclude is that if these kinds of gun control laws do reduce crime, they do not work strongly enough to overpower specification errors or any of the other infirmities in the current state of the social research art. Or, to state the same point somewhat differently, if there are crime reduction effects to be obtained from these kinds of gun control laws, they lie just at or somewhere beyond the threshold of detectability through present-day social research methods.

Why don't gun control laws of the sort that have been evaluated work better than we have been able so far to detect? Why does the criminal abuse of firearms seem to persist more or less unabated in the face of whatever gun control measures we have enacted? In speculating about the possible answers to this question, we can illustrate in some fairly concrete ways how social science research and data can contribute to the design of sensible civilian firearms policies.

Jurisdictionally Specific Laws

Many diverse answers have been given to the question of why gun laws do not seem to work very well. For example, persons who favor gun control as a crime reduction measure often argue that gun control laws in the United States have never worked very well because every jurisdiction has enacted different laws. The result is that jurisdictions with very strict gun control laws often border on jurisdictions that have very lax laws. Beyond all question, there is some merit in this position: No law can be very effective if it can be circumvented by driving to the next political jurisdiction. Studies of the flow of illegal firearms into Eastern cities with very restrictive firearms laws (e.g., Brill, 1977) amply document just how futile these jurisdictionally specific laws can be.

The American "Gun Culture"

Another serious obstacle is that gun ownership is so widespread among the civilian population. Regulating the ownership and use of firearms therefore presents a considerable problem of scale. For a variety of reasons discussed in Wright et al. (1983, Chs. 2 to 5), it is difficult to know with much precision just how many guns are "out there" in private hands; a reasonable guess, however, is that there are at the present time approximately 120–130 million firearms in the United States, with one or more firearms being held by half the households in the country. Furthermore, unlike other possessions that are licensed (e.g., automobiles), gun ownership as a household characteristic is not obvious in casual observation.

Although there are many firearms held by civilians, few of them are ever involved in the roughly 1,000,000 "unfortunate gun incidents" that occur annually (events ranging from minor accidents to homicides, which are calculated quite loosely; see Wright et al., 1983, Ch. 8, for details). Serious firearm abuses that define chargeable offenses in criminal law are much fewer—approximately 300,000 annually. Social research on private weapons ownership and on the incidences of firearms crimes has thus made it clear that persons who use their firearms legally and carefully outnumber the firearms abusers by about three orders of magnitude, even if we assume that each abuse involves a separate offender, a dubious assumption. This, of course, implies that if we want to control *criminal* firearms abuse by somehow keeping tabs on all civilian ownership and use of firearms, we will be wasting our effort about 99.9 percent of the time.

The Criminal Firearms Abuser

In line with this last point, advocates of gun control have tried to devise ways to distinguish between potential legitimate and illegitimate gun users in the hopes of hitting upon some way to regulate the one while leaving the other more or less untouched. For a period of time, attention was focused generally on handguns on the dual grounds that handguns had little or no legitimate sporting use and that handguns were the weapons of choice in the commission of crimes. Subsequent research (Wright et al., 1983, Ch. 3) has shown, however, that handguns are in fact used in all sorts of manifestly legitimate sporting ways by obviously legitimate gun owners who resent further restrictions on their prerogatives and activities. Furthermore, although the majority of gun crimes involves handguns, there is a fair-sized minority (15–30 percent) that involves shoulder weapons (see the studies reviewed in Wright et al., 1983, Ch. 9). In terms of types of weapons preferred, there appears to be a considerable overlap between legitimate and illegitimate users.

To keep guns out of the hands of illegitimate users means to regulate the sale and exchange of guns in order to interdict illegitimate users from obtaining weapons. In order to accomplish this properly, we have to have firm empirical knowledge about how the civilian weapons market works. Unfortunately, we know relatively little about this topic. We do know that a large fraction of all firearms transfers involves informal trading between private parties, does not involve retail brokers or merchants, and is therefore inherently very difficult to regulate (see, for example, Burr, 1977; Wright & Rossi, 1983). We also know that firearms are an important commodity on black markets in which stolen goods are bought and sold. The widespread theft of guns from private residences (about a quarter-million a year) and their subsequent sale in the black market tend to obliterate the distinctions between legitimate and illegitimate markets because any gun that can be acquired legitimately can be stolen from its legitimate owner and subsequently fall into criminal hands.

It is important to keep in mind that what we want to accomplish primarily with "gun control" is to lower the use of firearms in crimes. In order to do this, we obviously need to know why criminals carry guns in the first place, which, until recently, has been a virtually unresearched subject. In an attempt to uncover these motives, we have been interviewing convicted felons in state prisons throughout the nation, asking them about how they acquired their firearms and for what purposes such weapons are used (Wright & Rossi, 1983). Our preliminary tabulations strongly suggest that the primary motivation for carrying firearms is for self-protection and *not* specifically for use in committing crimes. The use of guns in ordinary crimes appears to be an almost incidental by-product of a strongly ingrained practice of carrying weapons as a means of surviving life on the streets.

Now the person who is habituated to being armed is a very different person than the criminal who arms himself for a specific criminal purpose. In the latter case, it may make some sense to think in terms of structuring sanctions so as to make the use of guns in such behavior too costly. But in the former (and, it appears, empirically more common) case, we would have to deal not only with the individual criminal but the entire environment of neighborhoods, and possibly with lifelong patterns of behavior whose roots may extend back into early childhood. Thus, the reasons why criminals carry guns—a topic now being researched for the first time—have immediate implications about how we might get them to stop it.

Mandatory Sentencing for Gun Abusers

Of course, it is sometimes argued that we should not try to prevent firearms abuse in advance, this being a largely hopeless enterprise, but rather should satisfy ourselves with punishing abuses after they occur. For this reason, several jurisdictions have recently enacted sentence enhancement measures that add one or two years on to a sentence if a firearm was used in the crime. Unfortunately, the appeal of this approach dissolves rather quickly: It is effective neither as a deterrent nor as a means of punishment.

First, as a before-the-fact deterrent, this approach faces the problem that most criminals do not expect to be caught in any case, a fairly common criminological finding. What might happen to them if they were caught therefore cannot be of much concern. Furthermore, most of the crimes that people commit with firearms already carry fairly stiff penalties. For example, a person charged with armed robbery faces a potential sentence of from 10 to 30 years. A one- or two-year add-on penalty may not significantly change the subjective magnitude of the sentence.

Second, research has also taught us that add-on penalties have a way of being assimilated into the sentencing practices of judges, who often reduce proportionately the sentence for the main charge, with the result that the total sentence for the main charge plus the add-on penalties remains the same. Judges, of course, are very much aware of the overcrowding of state prisons and appear to be reluctant to add to the ever-increasing burdens.

SUMMARY

Our main points can now be summarized: First, attempts to assess the impact of gun control legislation on crime have been fraught with specification errors. We do not yet know enough to model completely the use of guns in crime or to model the determinants of crime itself. Moreover, there is no reason to suspect that we *will* know enough to do so any time in the near future. Lacking this ability, our assessments of the impact of gun control legislation on crime cannot be completely credible. As in the case of public opinion on gun control issues, this lack of comprehensive knowledge about the uses of guns in crime makes it possible to obtain widely different results depending on the specification used. Also, as in the case of the polls, this again allows partisans to pick and choose a conveniently agreeable specification, a circumstance that turns research activity into partisan in-fighting.

Second, by piecing together fragments of knowledge about the elements that need to go into a correct specification of the problem, we have been able to show that the model-building issue is one of considerable complexity. Research assessing the impact of gun control legislation has shown inconclusive results mainly because of the problems involved in specifying a plausible and acceptable macromodel for crime rates or a micromodel for criminal behavior.

Third, we have shown that gun control legislation designed to affect the use of guns in crime has typically been developed without considering whether the legislation accords with any realistic understanding of how criminals acquire their guns and why guns are used in crime.

The fragmentary descriptions we have been able to put together imply that the roots of gun control legislation's ineffectiveness lie in the fact that criminals usually acquire their guns outside the legitimate, regulated gun market and carry guns mainly for reasons that have little to do with their criminal activities.

Social Science and Social Policy

As in most of the other political struggles of our times, advocates on both sides of the Great American Gun War have employed the findings of social science to add credibility to their political positions. Although some of the researchers in question may well resent the ensuing politicization of their work, there is little that can be done to prevent it. To publish one's results is to invite their political use—and misuse.

Not all social scientists try to keep their research findings out of the political arena; indeed, some enjoy and encourage it. Others insist on making their findings fully available to all partisans, acting on the principle that it is a researcher's responsibility to do so. Still others are themselves partisans and are particularly pleased when their findings bolster their own political positions. And then there are those whose talents are simply for hire, who are especially anxious to have their findings match the expectations of their clients.

There are few social scientists who are so above mundane concerns that they would actively prevent their findings from reaching lay audiences. Indeed, in these times, when the social science disciplines are scrambling to show their "relevance," the professions often reward those who find themselves in the limelight.

But, there are also very few—outside of the hired hands of social science—who have been completely happy with the political uses of their research. Subtleties tend to vanish when translated by journalists from even the best of the national media and suffer even more when lesser talents turn their hands to writing articles based on social science. Nor has social science research fared much better in the hands of the law. Many social scientists have had the experience of testifying in a court in which clever lawyers skillfully prevented them from doing complete justice to their research.

The coming together of social scientists and policymakers—hopefully for mutual benefit—is clearly problematic. It is easy to understand and discuss how political activists have misunderstood or misused the work of the social scientists, but there is another side to the story. What can we—the social scientists—possibly hope to contribute?

In the debate over gun control, as in most other political debates of equivalent duration and intensity, relatively little of what is at issue can, even in principle, be decided by more and better research. Partisans sometimes debate questions of fact, and, on such points, good research can sometimes be useful, especially in areas in which there is consensus over what are appropriate research procedures. But very often such "facts" are off on the periphery of a debate whose main terms center on value issues. The opponents and advocates of gun control are often debating world views, ideologies, and ways of life. On these usually far more important points, social science research at its best is mute. The best we can do is to make reasonable guesses at what might be the consequences of pursuing one or another policy innovation, but even here we are producing analyses that may be better than outright guesses, but perhaps only marginally so. And these days, the partisans are sufficiently sophisticated that the "iffy" nature of our conclusions will be quickly pointed out.

The major limitation of the social sciences in the policy arena stems from underdevelopment; simply put, we do not yet know enough to be able to predict with reasonable confidence what will be the consequences of pursuing one particular policy rather than another. Each of us has been asked to project the consequences of passing this or that piece of new legislation. For example, will a mandatory sentence enhancement reduce robbery rates? Usually, the best response we can give is, "Try it and we will see!" And even here, we will need long time series both before and after the legislation was passed, so by the time we have the answer, most policymakers will no longer care. In addition, we would need to carefully establish ceteris paribus conditions, an endeavor in which good theoretical understanding is needed on how crime rates are generated, a matter about which we have little knowledge.

If we want to be relevant and helpful, we might take our best shot, putting together the best measure we can find on the robbery rates and constructing reasonable models of crime rate generation that can make use of available data. We may then attempt several alternative specifications, picking the one that seems most reasonable to us, but still a judgment call. Being responsible social scientists, we may write up the results with pages and pages of caveats, disclaimers, and qualifications that are of little interest to anyone but fellow social scientists.

When the national media get their hands on the report, their accounts will likely contain few of the disclaimers and qualifications. The findings will also irritate one set of partisans and please another.

The irritated parties may hire a "methodological gun" to pick over the report and expose the flaws—flaws we felt were minor at the time, of course, but which, in the retelling, become major structural disorders.

Every piece of social science research is flawed to a lesser or greater degree and hence vulnerable to criticism. The spectacle of social scientists battling over whether particular defects are fatal or cosmetic cannot do anything but contribute to the image of social scientists as partisans whose skills are at the service of their values. Even in the best of circumstances, our ultimate input on policy formation will typically be modest.

Although it is undoubtably irritating to know that it is difficult for a social scientist to play a major role in the making of policy, this is, in fact, as it should be. A society in which social scientists play crucial policy roles through their research is a society in which human values have been subordinated to technocratic considerations, a world in which social scientists have become philosopher kings. In a truly democratic society, social science must be content with an advisory but not dominating role. Only the autocratic are confident enough in the righteousness of their own values to impose them on others. When policymakers ask of the social scientists, "Will it work?" we often have the skills, and therefore the obligation, to respond with the best research and analysis we can muster. But when they ask, "Is it just?" it is best if we leave the answer to others.

REFERENCES

Beha, J. A. (1977). "And nobody can get you out": The impact of a mandatory prison sentence for the illegal carrying of a firearm on the use of firearms and on the administration of criminal justice in Boston, Parts I and II. *Boston University Law Review, 57*(1), 96-146; and *57*(2), 289-333.

Brill, S. (1977). *Firearms abuse.* Washington, DC: The Police Foundation.

Bruce-Biggs, B. (1976). The Great American Gun War. *The Public Interest, 45,* 37-62.

Burr, D.E.S. (1977). *Handgun regulation.* Orlando, FL: Florida Bureau of Criminal Justice Planning and Assistance.

Cambridge Reports, Inc. (1978). *An analysis of public attitudes towards handgun control.* Cambridge, MA.

Cook, P. J., & Blose, J. (1981). State programs for screening handgun buyers. *Annals of the American Academy of Political and Social Sciences, 455,* 63-79.

Decision-Making Information, Inc. (1978). *Attitudes of the American electorate toward gun control.* Santa Ana, CA.

Deutsch, S. J., & Alt, F. B. (1977). The effect of Massachusetts gun control law on gun-related crimes in the city of Boston. *Evaluation Quarterly, 1,* 543-568.

Erskine, H. (1972). The polls: Gun control. *Public Opinion Quarterly, 36,* 455-469.

Geisel, M. S., Roll, R., & Wettick, R. S. (1969). The effectiveness of state and local regulation of handguns: a statistical analysis. *Duke University Law Journal, 4,* 647-676.

Hay, R., & McCleary, R. (1979). Box-Tiao time series models for impact assessment; A comment on the recent work of Deutsch and Alt. *Evaluation Quarterly, 3,* 277-314.

Jones, E., III (1981). The District of Columbia's "Firearms Control Regulations Act of 1975": The toughest handgun control law in the United States—or is it? *Annual of the American Academy of Political and Social Sciences, 455,* 138-149.

Loftin, C., & McDowell, D. (1981). "One with a gun gets you two": Mandatory sentencing and firearms violence in Detroit. *Annals of American Academy of Political and Social Sciences, 455,* 150-168.

Murray, D. R. (1975). Handguns, gun control laws, and firearms violence. *Social Problems, 23,* 81-93.

Pierce, G. H., & Bowers, W. J. (1979). *The impact of the Bartley-Fox Gun Law on crime in Massachusetts.* Unpublished paper, Northeastern University, Center for Applied Social Research, Boston, MA.

Rossi, P. H., & Wright, J. D. (in press). Evaluation research: An assessment. *Annual Review of Sociology.*

Wright, J. D., & Rossi, P. H. (1983, November). *The illicit firearms market: Preliminary results from a national survey.* Paper presented at the American Society of Criminology in Denver, CO.

Wright, J. D., Rossi, P. H., & Daly, K. (1983). *Under the gun: Weapons, crime, and violence in America.* New York: Aldine.

Zimring, F. E. (1975). Firearms and federal law: The Gun Control Act of 1968. *Journal of Legal Studies, 4,* 133-198.

PART III
Conclusions

14

Toward More Useful Social Science

MELVIN M. MARK
R. LANCE SHOTLAND

The relationship between social science and social policy is a complex and tenuous one, as the preceding chapters have indicated. In the present chapter, we examine some of the factors that influence the relationship between social science and social policy by reviewing and summarizing some of the major themes that appear in this volume. The present chapter is not simply a summary, however. In some cases, we integrate the perspectives offered in various preceding chapters. In a few cases, we offer critiques of positions put forward elsewhere in the volume. The primary goal of the chapter, however, is to offer suggestions for improving the relationship between social science and social policy.

The first four major sections of the chapter are organized around the four topics examined in Part I of the book: Measurement, implementation, the role of the social scientist as an actor in policy-making processes, and multiplism, respectively. In each of these sections we note relevant points from the chapters in Part II. Thus we identify much of the overlap between the "warp threads" and "weft threads" that constitute the "cloth" of the book.

In these sections, suggestions are offered for practices that may make social science more useful for policymaking. Of course, recommendations are of little value if they are not translated into practice. Thus, in the fifth section of the chapter we describe and advocate researchability assessment, a mechanism by which many of the recommendations could be instituted. The chapter ends with a brief conclusion.

MEASUREMENT

The central role of measurement in any scientific endeavor is apparent. A study can be no better than the measures it employs. It is not surprising, then, that several contributors to this volume discussed the role of measurement in the relationship between social science and social policy. In this section, we briefly discuss three measurement-related topics; the first two of these derive directly from ideas presented elsewhere in this volume.

(In)Adequacy of Government Statistics

Sechrest, Marsh, Taylor, and Tittle (all are authors in this volume) join other social scientists in suggesting that government statistics are frequently inadequate for addressing many policy-relevant research questions. This point, we believe, is worth reiterating. If promoting the common welfare is the "bottom line" of government, the "bookkeeping system" is in disrepair. Although there are many examples of the inadequacy of governmental statistics for policy research, for the sake of brevity we will provide just one.

As Rossi and Wright (this volume) illustrate, the private ownership of firearms is a hotly debated issue and a matter of substantial public concern. Given the importance of this topic, one may think that many social scientists would have investigated the relationship between the prevalence of firearms in a given jurisdiction and the incidence of homicides, armed robberies, and other violent crimes. It may seem reasonable that social scientists could at least provide an accurate estimate of the size of these relationships.

Only two things prevent this: (1) The questionable statistics on the incidence of crimes for most jurisdictions in this country and (2) the lack of good statistics on the number of handguns. The problems with the FBI's *Uniform Crime Report* (UCR) are well documented (e.g., Pepinsky, 1980), and the Victimization Surveys commissioned by the National Institute of Justice are extremely limited in their coverage of jurisdictions and have other flaws (Pepinsky, 1980). Estimating the number of firearms within a jurisdiction is even more problematic. Many jurisdictions keep no records at all of the number of guns. Further, in locales that attempt to monitor firearm purchases, these numbers may not be a valid indicator of the number of the firearms available to criminals (Bureau of Alcohol, Tobacco, and Firearms, 1976).[1]

Unfortunately, this example is hardly a rare exception. Government statistics are often inadequate for research on important, policy-relevant questions. Indicators may be of questionable validity, or may simply not exist. In some cases, researchers can overcome these problems. An investigator can: Collect primary data as a substitute (a costly and sometimes unfeasible task), collect data to assess the possible shortcomings of existing government statistics (see Marsh, this volume, for an example), or use proxy measures with their concomitant problems.

However, in many cases it is not feasible for an individual researcher to sufficiently overcome the inadequacy of government statistics. We offer two recommendations germane to this problem. First, social science research may benefit if social scientists increase their lobbying for more and better measures of policy-relevant variables. As Sechrest states, "social scientists and their organizations should bring and keep pressure on the executive branch and the legislature to provide funding and support for production of high quality government statistics" (this volume). Second, social scientists should critically examine the adequacy of available measures for the research task at hand and be willing to forego research if they are inadequate (Sechrest, this volume); we return to this point in our later discussion of Researchability Assessment.

The Proximal-Distal Distinction

The time frame in which policy-relevant research must be done often restricts one's ability to examine truly important, temporally distal outcome variables. St. Pierre (this volume), as well as Sechrest (this volume), discuss the proximal-distal dimension as it applies to outcome measures. (Belsky and Marsh make related points, without using the proximal-distal terminology.) As they note, practical constraints dictate that proximal rather than distal effects are generally studied, even though distal effects may be more socially important and more relevant to policy considerations.

An exclusively proximal focus is problematic in two ways. First, with respect to a given outcome, any effect may be temporally limited. Most notably, a program may have an immediate effect that diminishes over time. Second, what we would identify as relevant outcome variables may change over time. For example, an ideal evaluation of a compensatory education program might examine educational performance as a proximal indicator, but be concerned distally with such outcome variables as employment history and life satisfaction (Levin, 1977).

The basic point is that policy research that focuses exclusively on more proximal outcomes—or exclusively on distal outcomes—provides only part of the picture, and thus is less informative than it could be. Clearly it would be desirable for policy-relevant research to seek out a better balance between proximal and distal outcomes. Unfortunately, funding practices and the demand for "timely" information seem to make a greater focus on distal outcomes unlikely. However, three strategies exist for increasing the focus on more distal outcomes. One is for policy researchers to lobby, both individually and collectively, for the funding of more long-term research. A second, related strategy is to encourage independent follow-up studies when possible, even if these were not originally planned (e.g., McCord, 1978). A third strategy would be to use distinct methodologies in a single research program to examine proximal and distal outcomes. For example, both proximal and distal effects of an educational program could be assessed by combining a randomized experiment (that may provide strong evidence about proximal effects) with a causal model that estimates the causal linkage between treatment, proximal effects, and distal outcomes (see Kenny, 1980, and Shotland & Goodstein, 1983, for discussion and examples of combining randomized experiments with causal modeling). Perhaps by employing these and other strategies, the current underemphasis on distal outcomes could be reduced.

Construct Validity

Many of the measurement problems cited in this volume can be reduced, we believe, by placing greater emphasis on developing construct validity in policy research. Construct validity refers to the accuracy with which conclusions are made about abstract constructs, based on concrete research operations (Cook & Campbell, 1979). Several chapters in this book refer to construct validity problems (though generally not in these terms). For example, Levin (this volume) notes that in economic research relevant to employment policy "the research variables may be considerably different than the policy ones." Tittle (this volume) emphasizes that research operations designed to manipulate "deterrence" may in fact represent some other theoretical construct.

Our contention is that policy-relevant research can in general be improved by increased attention to construct validity: Construct validity is generally essential for interpretability. One example is the research Belsky (this volume) cites concerning the effects of day care on social development. As Belsky notes, measures of "social development" might reasonably be interpreted as representing any of several seemingly distinct constructs: Social skills, assertiveness, independence, or the frequency of interaction. Without greater construct validity, it is not possible to be confident about which construct the measures best represent, so interpretation of the research is difficult.

As another example, imagine two scenarios involving a hypothetical evaluation of the effects of the Medicare program. Such an evaluation could conceivably examine a number of outcome variables. First, imagine an evaluation that examined visits to a physician, prescriptions filled, and hospitalization rate as outcome variables. Further assume that there is consensus among policymakers and stakeholder groups that an increase in these measures would clearly represent a positive benefit of the program. In such a case, construct validity is of little importance. If the program is associated with increases in all or most of the measures, the policy implications will be perceived as straightforward, that is, the program has positive effects.

Now, imagine that the mortality rate is added to the set of outcome measures. Further assume that the evaluation takes place amid partisan debate about the worth of Medicare. If Medicare were found to affect the other outcome measures *but not mortality,* opponents of the program might argue that Medicare expenditures represent government waste because it does not affect the "ultimate outcome," mortality. Construct validity can help resolve partisan conflict in such a case, or at least aid in clarifying the value issues around which debate resolves.

In particular, construct validity leads one to consider the interrelationship among the various outcome measures. In doing so, it should be clear that medical treatment is related to mortality in some conditions but not others. For the sake of simplicity, we will focus on one outcome measure, prescription drug use, and examine its relationship to mortality. It seems likely that both no drug use and a high level of drug use can represent diverse health statuses. In the case of high levels of "drug use," some drugs counteract illness and prolong life, whereas other drugs, such as painkillers, do not extend life but rather may affect quality of life. Correspondingly, "no drug use" can mean that a person is healthy or that the person is neglecting ill health. Because both high and no drug use represent heterogenous sets of people, it would not be surprising that any relationship between prescription drug use and mortality would be modest at best. However, as the preceding analysis suggests, research that differentiated between *types* of drugs used (e.g., life prolonging versus painkilling drugs) should bring some clarification. That is, it should reveal if Medicare increases mortality by increasing the use of *some types* of drugs, but has no effect on mortality via its increase in the use of other drugs. Such a differentiated perspective, which a concern for construct validity would facilitate, would enlighten debate if there is partisan conflict with some partisans advocating mortality as the "ultimate" outcome.

Indeed, a concern for construct validity would likely improve the debate in another way. Researchers with such a concern would ask, "what theoretical constructs should Medicare affect?" Almost certainly, they would include the construct "quality of life," and would attempt to assess this construct, in part by assessing whether the use of various types of drugs represents the construct.

The Medicare example, although simplified, illustrates several points. First is the simple point that achieving construct validity is generally an important, and commonly underemphasized, component of policy-relevant research. Drawing reasonable interpretations of quantitative results requires understanding the constructs represented and confidence that measures are not unduly adulterated by extraneous factors (e.g., Shotland & Stebbins, 1983). Second, the example illustrates that construct validity is not equally important in all conditions. When consensus exists that change on a particular measure is to be valued in and of itself, construct validity is of little importance, at least in terms of perceived implications for policy. Finally, the example illustrates that construct validity problems are especially likely to occur when researchers uncritically use available archival measures measures that are likely to represent a hodgepodge of constructs (Cook & Campbell, 1979, p. 231).

Several changes in practice could increase construct validity in policy-relevant research. In evaluation, time and resources could be increased for the "front-end" work of validating measures. Also in program evaluations, an implementation assessment can enhance construct validity of the cause (see the section on implementation that follows). More generally, construct validity studies in policy-relevant research are sure to increase to the extent that funding agencies fund them and prestigious journals publish them. And, in general, the various methods of increasing construct validity (Cook & Campbell, 1979; Mark & Cook, 1984) can be applied in policy-relevant research.

Finally, we should note that the problems we have discussed here in terms of construct validity can be described in other terms, such as specification error in the theoretical model of a program (cf. Rossi & Wright, this volume; Chen & Rossi, 1983).

Summary

We have noted three general means of improving measurement in policy-relevant research: Lobbying for more and better government statistics, increasing the focus on distal outcomes, and placing greater emphasis on construct validity. In addition, other strategies exist for improving measurement in policy research, many of which are described by Sechrest (this volume).

THE STUDY OF IMPLEMENTATION

The importance of implementation processes is a theme that recurred in most chapters in this volume. Several possible ways in which the study of implementation can improve policy and policy research were noted, though these were not systematically differentiated. In the present section we describe various functions of conceptual and empirical work on implementation.

Implementation Theory

First, McLaughlin (this volume) and Marsh (this volume) argue that the development of *implementation theory*, that is, better conceptual understanding of implementation processes, should lead to the creation of more effective policy. In particular, a better understanding of implementation processes should lead to the development of more implementable and more effective programs, and to an understanding of the limits of intervention. Unfortunately, like most calls for theory advancement it is difficult to suggest specific means for attaining this goal (but see Marsh, this volume, for suggestions about a theory of the successful implementation of legal reform).

Implementation Assessment

Fortunately, research on implementation is useful even in the absence of a strong theory of implementation. One type of implementation study is related to what Wholey (1979, 1983) and Rutman (1980) have described as "evaluability assessment," in which one assesses the status of a program to determine whether it is adequately in place to be evaluated—or even whether the program exists in any identifiable form. In a similar fashion, Rossi and Wright, Tittle, Cook, Marsh, and St. Pierre, in this volume, point to the use of implementation analysis, as a precursor to impact assessment. This type of implementation study, which can be called *implementation assessment,* has as its goal assessing the extent to which, and the manner in which, a program or policy has been put into place. Thus implementation assessment concerns such questions as: Do judges actually give longer sentences after passage of a law that requires additional one- or two-year imprisonment for crimes involving guns?

Implementation assessment can serve two important functions as an adjunct to outcome evaluation. First, it is obviously inappropriate to expect a program to have any effects if the program is simply not in place. Therefore implementation assessment is a useful precursor to outcome evaluation to avoid the needless or premature application of outcome evaluation methodology. Second, implementation assessment enhances the "construct validity of the cause." That is, in an implementation assessment one obtains a description about the actual operation of a program, and such knowledge enhances understanding of the treatment and how it may lead to any observed effects.[2] In these two ways, implementation assessment is an important complement to outcome evaluation.

Implementation assessment studies are also of value in their own right, independent of any outcome evaluation. St. Pierre (this volume) notes that descriptive information on program implementation is itself often of considerable use to policymakers and funders. For example, an implementation assessment can provide useful descriptive information about what sorts of services are being delivered to what types of clients in what settings. In providing such information, implementation assessment can perform important monitoring functions, particularly in the case of large-scale social programs (see Wholey, 1983).

There is a developing literature that describes and evaluates methods for conducting implementation assessments (see, for example, Hall & Loucks, 1977; Leithwood & Montgomery, 1980; Rezmovic, 1984). Further development of such methodologies seems likely and will represent an important methodological development.

Variations in Implementation

The goal of implementation assessment is to describe the practice of a program or policy. Another type of implementation research exists that we can call research on *variations in implementation*. The purpose of such research is to guide practice by evaluating alternative implementation procedures in terms of their consequences, cost, efficiency, or some other criterion. As McLaughlin (this volume) notes in the context of education:

> For the foreseeable future, administrators are unlikely to be debating whether or not to adopt a new curriculum—that choice may be prohibited

by budgetary stringency—but deliberating about how to get better performance out of existing investments in people, materials and technologies. This, at its root, is an implementation question.

Thus, there often may be more latitude for modifying the implementation process (of existing programs) than for instituting new programs.

Other contributors to this volume also strongly advocate research on variations in implementation. Most notably, Crain and Carsrud's position that social scientists should focus on the "nuts and bolts" of desegregation policy is essentially an argument for research on variations in implementation. They argue that desegregation research should concern the question: What sort of implementation plan leads to more effective desegregation (where "implementation plan" involves such variables as busing plans, classroom arrangements, whether ninth graders are in senior or junior high, and so on)? Although Crain and Carsrud do not explicitly describe the research they advocate as implementation research, that is clearly what it is: Studies of the effects of alternative means of implementing desegregation.

Not only is it important to study variations in implementation, as McLaughlin, Crain and Carsrud, and others argue; also, such variations may generally be easier to study experimentally than are social programs in toto, and the results may be more useful to policymaking. This is the case for a number of reasons. Relative to entire social programs, many implementation variables will be more readily manipulated; more transferable to other sites; less likely to lead to problems such as differential attrition when studied experimentally; less value charged; and thus less susceptible to political debate and more likely to be useful to practitioners. For a variety of reasons, then, we believe that experimental evaluations of variations in implementation research are both feasible and desirable.

The Complexity/Interaction Problem

In her discussion of the lessons of implementation research, McLaughlin (this volume) highlights the importance of higher-order interactions as determinants of effectiveness. Local conditions may limit generalizability: "The causal and conditional statements associated with an evaluation in one setting are likely to have questionable relevance to program operations in another setting" (McLaughlin, this volume). Further, changes in contextual, institutional, and cultural variables across time may limit temporal generalizability. McLaughlin illustrates this point with the "It Works" example, in which compensatory education programs identified as exemplary at one time ("It Works") were not found to be effective at a later time. In a similar vein, Levin (this volume) notes that empirical results of studies of economic policies may not generalize across changes in economic conditions, labor markets, or phases of the business cycle. Tittle, in this volume, also emphasizes the possibility of interactions as a serious limit on the policy relevance of recommendations based on deterrence research.

The "interaction problem" has implications both for research practices and for the way research results are translated into policy. Concerning research practices, it is clearly important to employ methods that probe the limits of generalization. For example, one can deliberately sample for heterogeneity on important characteristics of respondents or sites and can examine whether the effect generalizes across diverse subgroups of persons and situations (Cook & Campbell, 1979; Mark & Cook, 1984). Another potentially important technique is meta-analysis, which can probe whether an effect generalizes across contextual or institutional variables, if these are measured.

Concerning translation into policy, the issue is whether research results are translated into mandates or into recommendations. Consider as an example research on variations in implementation in desegregation that might show that replacing desks with tables facilitates desegregation. Imagine that the replacement of desks with tables was then mandated; for example, federal funds could be made contingent on this change. However, if the desk versus table research did not thoroughly assess the limits of generalization, the change may be required in situations in which it is not effective or even harmful. Therefore, it may be more appropriate for research results to be offered as recommendations rather than as mandates, unless the limits of generalization have been throughly examined. As a recommendation, the policy or program can be invited to diffuse as its success warrants (Campbell, in press).

It should be noted that although we have discussed the "interaction problem" in the context of implementation research, it also applies more widely to other social science research.

Summary and Conclusion

In this section we have identified three forms of scholarly work on implementation processes: The development and application of implementation theory, the conduct of implementation assessment, and the study of variations in implementation. Our belief, consonant with that of nearly all the contributors to this volume, is that policy-related research will benefit by devoting increased attention and research to implementation processes.

Although we have not extensively discussed the methodology of research on implementation, it is worth noting that methodological multiplism is almost certainly warranted. For example, implementation assessment may best be served by a combination of quantitative (e.g., observational checklists, causal models) and qualitative (e.g., unstructured observations, open-ended interviews) methods. In the case of research on variations in implementation, it may be feasible to employ rigorous quantitative methods, such as randomized experiments, as we have noted. However, it may generally be desirable to precede such methods with more qualitative methods, such as interviews with "street-level bureaucrats" to glean practitioners wisdom, and with the strongest available correlational or quasi-experimental methods to identify promising and transferable implementation variables for experimental study. The point, as Cook, McLaughlin, and others suggest, is simply that implementation research is best furthered by multiple methodologies. Further, in light of McLaughlin's discussion of higher-order interactions, it seems that the methodologies employed will be the most useful if they probe the limits of generalizability; that is, if they are sensitive to the possibility that treatment effects may depend on contextual, institutional, or respondent characteristics.

THE ROLE OF SOCIAL SCIENTISTS
IN POLICYMAKING PROCESSES

Most of the contributors to this volume explicitly deal with their conception of the proper role of the social scientist and of social science research in policymaking processes. The opinions expressed ranged from righteous indignation about how politicians have failed to heed social science answers (Belsky) to the belief that if the social sciences can contribute to policy at all, it is simply by pointing out how complex policy issues are and how little we know (Tittle). Most contributors take a more moderate position, contending that the social sciences can contribute to policymaking processes—having at least some incremental impact much of the time. Let us examine the characteristics of this position in more detail.

First, "policymaking" is seen as a complex, political process with somewhat limited ability to be influenced by social science inputs.[3] Policymaking is viewed as often being incremental, evolutionary, and adaptive, rather than necessarily as the product of a major, discrete decision (see especially McLaughlin and Marsh, this volume). Further, policymaking is thought typically to involve the political accommodation of the interests of multiple stakeholder groups (Cook, this volume). And it is argued that values generally supercede information in policymaking. This image of policymaking that runs through most of this volume is thus consistent with other, recent portraits of policymaking (e.g., Cronbach et al., 1980; Weiss, 1982).

The characteristics of policymaking processes, and the relationship of the social sciences to such processes, are seen by most authors as placing limits on the impact of the social sciences. For example, some authors noted that complex processes sometimes determine whether social science information is considered, and, if it is, how it is interpreted. Pettigrew (this volume) emphasizes that the use of social science evidence is mediated by a variety of factors, including the media, funding agencies, and the receptiveness of the particular policymaking body. Belsky (this volume) provides an extreme example of the haphazard determinants of whether social science evidence is used. As he describes, the result of a social science study received greater attention in policy deliberations because a partisan (whose position was supported by the study) used his personal relationship with the wife of the White House Domestic Affairs Advisor to push the study's results into consideration. Other authors (e.g., Tittle) emphasize that it is reasonable for social science evidence to be discounted in policymaking when that evidence is so imperfect or incomplete that its utility as a guide for action is questionable.

Greatest emphasis was placed in this volume, however, on another chracteristic of the policymaking process that limits the impact of the social sciences: The role of values. The subservience of social science inputs to values was emphasized by several contributors to this volume, including Sechrest, Levin, Cain, Crain and Carsrud, Marsh, and Rossi and Wright. As most of these authors noted, however, the dominant role of values is not a flaw to be corrected; instead it is an inherent characteristic of democratic decision-making processes.

In this vein, it is worth noting the explicit criticism by Crain and Carsrud and Rossi and Wright of the "philosopher-king" model of the social scientist (which is concurred with implicitly by most of the other contributors to the volume). As these authors point out, many social scientists in the past seem to have operated under an implicit assumption that social science evidence should play a direct, determining, instrumental role in policymaking; that is, that social science research should be the primary, or even the sole, determinant of policy decisions. This notion has recently received wide, and we believe, well-deserved criticism (e.g., Cronbach et al., 1980; Lindblom & Cohen, 1979) that is echoed and expanded upon in this volume.

An Integrative Model of Social Science Tasks

If the philosopher-king is dead, what should the policy-oriented social scientist do to contribute to policy? Some clarification of the range of potential social science contributions emerges if we examine the various possible policy-related tasks of social scientists in terms of a more differentiated model of policymaking. A simple, but for our purposes, useful model suggests that policymaking processes consist of five possible phases: (1) *Problem identification,* which refers to the process by which an issue is defined and designated as requiring policy action; (2) *program or policy creation,* which refers to the specification by legislative, judicial, or other deliberations of the means by which the problem is to be addressed; (3) *implementation and monitoring,* by which we mean, first, the process of operationalizing the program or policy and, second, the inspection of the match between policy-as-planned and policy-as-implemented; (4) *evaluation,* which here refers to an analysis of the cost, efficiency, scope, and/or consequences of the policy or program relative to other alternatives; and (5) *adjustment,* which is included to acknowledge explicitly that the process is cyclical with feedback loops, that is, the activities of one phase may feed back into other phases (e.g., the results of evaluation can lead to adjustments in policy or in implementation, or even in problem identification).

This heuristic model of policymaking processes, which is represented diagramatically in Figure 14.1, is an idealized and simplified one: Policymaking generally does not proceed in discrete steps following one specific order. The model is offered not as an accurate description of policymaking, but simply as an aid in clarifying the potential roles of the social sciences in policymaking, particularly in showing that different contributions are appropriate at different stages of policymaking.

Another distinction can be made that helps clarify the various tasks that social scientists can perform to improve policymaking processes. It is the distinction, explicitly noted by Levin and Marsh (this volume), between (1) conceptual inputs, i.e., analytic or theoretical schemes that can provide improved understanding, and (2) empirical inputs, such as implementation assessments or evaluations of the effects of some policy or program. Although conceptual and empirical inputs are typically interrelated in practice, the distinction is helpful in clarifying alternative tasks for social scientists in policymaking.

What then does this distinction, along with the model of policymaking shown in Figure 14.1, tell us about the potential role of social scientists in policymaking processes? Consider first the problem identification phase. The considerable emphasis in this volume on the

Problem   Program or   Implementation
Identification → Policy Creation ——→ and ——————→ Evaluation ——→ Adjustment
                                                   Monitoring

Figure 14.1   A Simplified, Idealized Model of the Policymaking Process

limited role of the social sciences in determining matters of value refers
largely to the limitations of the social sciences in defining an issue
as one requiring policy action (i.e., problem identification). An example
is Sechrest's statement that from a public policy standpoint he has
"no interest in research on the bad effects of child abuse. Child abuse
is an evil and should be dealt with as effectively as possible." That
is, research is irrelevant to defining child abuse as a problem.

On the other hand, the importance of values in problem identification does not imply that social science data are useless at this stage.
Empirical social science research may be of value in documenting
the problem. For example, by estimating the severity and frequency
of child abuse and by probing its causes, social science research could
allow more informed discussion of the problem. Conceptual social
science inputs can also contribute to problem identification. Social
science theories or analytic frameworks can be applied to create one
or more conceptualizations of the problem (Saxe, 1983). These may
highlight factors that otherwise would be ignored, or they may expand
the perceived scope of the problem by emphasizing the interrelationship
of complex causal factors. As Weiss (1982) points out, conceptual
social science inputs to problem identification also include merely
providing a label that denotes a particular issue as a problem area
(e.g., "white flight").

Consider now the second phase in the policymaking model of Figure
14.1. Social science inputs to program or policy creation can be empirical, as in the case of research on the effects of group size in day
care (see Belsky, this volume). Alternatively, the social science input
may be conceptual, as when compensatory education programs are
based on an educational theory (as was attempted in "Follow Through";
St. Pierre, this volume). Of course, conceptual inputs do not require
a formal "theory," and conceptual and empirical inputs are likely to
be combined in practice (see, for example, Cain, this volume). As
an example, one of the authors recently argued against a "Good
Samaritan" law that criminalized failing to give help; the argument,

bolstered by both relevant (though indirect) research evidence and social science concepts, was that such laws could have the unintended result of reducing cooperation with the police.

Consider now the next two phases of our idealized model of policy-making. In the case of implementation and monitoring, conceptual contributions would include providing a conceptual framework to guide implementations and calling policymakers' attention to causal factors they have ignored. Empirical inputs would include implementation assessments and research on variations in implementation; such research is emphasized by McLaughlin, Marsh, Crain and Carsrud (in their advocacy of the "broker" or "social engineer" role), and others in the present volume. In the case of the evaluation phase, conceptual inputs would include the use of an analytic framework to identify possible unintended consequences of a program or to point out complex interrelationships among variables, and the construction of a "theory" of the program or policy. Empirical inputs would involve evaluations of program effectiveness, as advocated by Rossi and Wright, Levin, Marsh, and others in the present volume.

The final phase in Figure 14.1, adjustment, is used to acknowledge explicitly that one phase of the model may feed back into itself or into another phase. Levin's (this volume) "experimenting society" model of economic policy illustrates this process. In this model, continuing evaluation of the effects of economic policies on unemployment would feed back into policy creation, so that other policies would be instituted (and evaluated) as needed to maintain a desired level of employment (also see McLaughlin for further examples).

Theory as a Conceptual Input

In the distinction just drawn between empirical inputs and conceptual inputs, social science theory was cited as a major source of conceptual inputs. For example, *good* educational theory, it is frequently noted, should lead to good educational programs. Unfortunately, it is just as frequently noted that social science theories are usually not up to the task of providing good conceptual inputs into policy. For instance, Rossi and Wright state in this volume that one of the major reasons "why policies and programs tend to be ineffective or only marginally effective" is the inadequacy of the social science theories on which they are based.

One of the reasons social science theories tend to be inadequate for guiding policy is their lack of adequate specificity. In discussing the social reforms of the 1960s and 1970s Cook (this volume) points out that "many theories failed to specify the types of conditions under which a given relationship did and did not hold"; further, substantive theories are "not comprehensive enough to use as action blueprints." Tittle emphasizes the same point when he draws the analogy between deterrence theory and Etzioni's "rainmaker theory." Tittle's argument is that in terms of making predictions—about the conditions under which deterrence will work, the magnitude of the effect to be expected, and the duration between treatment and effect—deterrence theory is about as specific as the theory that a dance will produce rain. The consequence for research is that "because sanctioning theory is so weak [i.e., nonspecific], scholars cannot agree whether, in any test, the conditions for deterrence have been fulfilled; therefore, meaningful inferences cannot be drawn" (Tittle, this volume). A similar contention could be made concerning the application of social science theory to other policy areas.

One could conclude, then, that having a good theory that is highly specific would increase our ability to create useful programs and policies. Yet to say this is almost a truism and is of limited value given that we are not able to conjure up good, specific theory at will. On the other hand, it is possible to argue that applied social researchers have paid inadequate attention to theory (Chen & Rossi, 1983) and that greater attention to theory construction could lead to more useful and more applicable theories (cf. Heilman, 1983).

If attempts are made to construct more useful theories, a shift from the perspective of traditional social science theories may be helpful. That is, theorists might focus on the relationship between (1) variables that policymakers may conceivably be able to manipulate (at the "independent variable" end) and (2) particular, policy-relevant outcomes (at the "dependent variable" end). Concerning the former, the considerable use of economics by policymakers may reflect the policy-utilization advantage of theories that focus on variables that policymakers can change (Feurer, 1954; Lindblom, 1972; Scott & Shore, 1979; cf. Pettigrew, this volume, for another possible explanation). Concerning the "dependent variable" end of theories, theoretical frameworks that focus on particular outcomes of clear relevance to policy may be more useful—and more often used—than theories with a more general focus. For example, to policymakers concerned about raising the rate with which citizens report crime to the police, a theory focusing on that particular outcome may be of greater use than a theory concerned with why people help in general. We should note that, although a focus on manipulable causes and specific policy-relevant outcomes may lead to theory that is more usable in policymaking, an exclusive focus on such variables may entail a cost in terms of the comprehensiveness of theory (Mark & Bryant, 1984; Ravetz, 1971).[4]

Inputs Versus Uses

In this section we have distinguished between more empirical and more conceptual social science inputs to policymaking. It is important to differentiate these two forms of *inputs* to policymaking from the *use* made of social science inputs in policy processes. A growing literature on research utilization has emerged in the last decade (e.g., Rich, 1977; Weiss, 1978; for integrative reviews see Beyer & Trice, 1982; Leviton & Hughes, 1981).

An important distinction is made in that literature between instrumental and conceptual uses of social science inputs (e.g., Rich, 1977; see Lynn, 1978, and Weiss, 1978, for additional distinctions). Instrumental use involves basing specific decisions or actions on social science inputs; for example, basing funding levels or program continuance on the results of a program evaluation. Conceptual use involves changes in the way policymakers think about or define a policy area as a consequence of social inputs. Some contributors to this volume stress the importance of conceptual use. For instance, Taylor focuses on using social science analyses to raise the right questions to policymakers. Similarly, Tittle argues that social scientists may improve understanding of a problem if they simply describe its complexity and warn against simple solutions (cf. Cohen & Weiss, 1977, p. 79).

Other contributors provided examples of both conceptual and instrumental use within a particular policy area, sometimes even deriving from a single study. For instance, St. Pierre notes that the Follow Through evaluation helped to fuel the "back to basics" movement in education (a conceptual use), but was also used in the approval of local projects as "exemplary" by the Joint Dissemination Review Panel that, in turn, later affected funding decisions (instrumental use, though not temporally immediate). Cain (this volume) indicates that social science documentation of persistent inequalities helped "to shape public opinion and equity norms" toward greater acceptance of comparable worth approaches (a conceptual use); in addition, social scientists offered job evaluation methodology as a specific means to "diagnose and remedy sex discrimination," i.e., as a way to make pay decisions (an instrumental use, or perhaps misuse; see Cain). Numerous other examples of either instrumental or conceptual uses are given in this volume.

Inputs and uses may be related such that empirical inputs are more likely to lead to instrumental uses and conceptual inputs are more likely to result in conceptual uses. However, this relationship is probably not a strong one, as illustrated by the Follow Through evaluation having both instrumental and conceptual uses. Further, either type of social science input can be put to *no* use (see St. Pierre's distinction between useful and used, this volume), or to use as "political ammunition" (Belsky, this volume), that is, used not in an attempt to make better decisions but to validate one's preexisting position or to convince others (also see Pettigrew, and Cain, this volume).

The distinction between inputs and uses, and between the different forms of each, highlights a recommendation made recently by many social scientists, including several in the present volume. It is that social science inputs are more likely to be used if one assesses the information needs of potential users and the potential uses of social science inputs (see Cook, St. Pierre, and Marsh in the present volume). Such an assessment can then be used to guide the construction of social science inputs (e.g., the design of empirical research) so that they can be of greater value in policymaking processes. Assessing users' information needs and the uses of social science inputs is particularly important given that there exists a wide variety of possible instrumental uses.

Summary and Conclusions

Although a range of perspectives were presented in the present volume, most contributors contended that the social sciences can contribute to policymaking processes, that is, can at least make some useful contribution at least much of the time. In part, the effect of social science inputs are limited by characteristics of the process by which policy is made. In this volume, particular attention was given to the limited role that the social sciences can (and should) play in questions based on values.

Nevertheless, the social sciences can provide inputs of use in policymaking. A framework was presented that identified alternative kinds of social science contributions to policy. Social science inputs, we suggest, can be either empirical or conceptual, and can apply to any of five phases of policymaking. What is desirable, we believe, is a differentiated concept of the tasks that social scientists might perform that takes into account the nature of the policy issue and its "phase" in the model represented in Figure 14.1.

Unfortunately, social science theory is often inadequate to serve as a useful conceptual input to policy, primarily because such theories typically lack specificity. It was suggested that some improvement may occur if social scientists interested in policy attended more to theory construction, particularly if they focus on theory that relates policy manipulables to particular, policy-relevant outcomes. It was noted that the distinction between empirical and conceptual social science inputs does not imply distinct forms of use in policy; either form of input can be used instrumentally, conceptually, as political ammunition, or not at all. Increases in instrumental and conceptual use seem likely to occur if social scientists better assess policymakers' information needs and the potential uses to which social science inputs might be put.

MULTIPLISM

Cook (this volume) examines multiplism as an approach to applied social science research. Although Cook's concept of multiplism goes far beyond methodology to include multiplism of questions, values, and stakeholders, much of his focus is on methodological multiplism. Methodological multiplism (which we shall simply call multiplism for the remainder of this section) is based on the presumption that no single research methodology, measure, or manipulation is perfect; each has particular shortcomings. Further, multiplism posits that single studies involve many implicit assumptions based on idiosyncratic decisions (e.g., about the wording of a questionnaire item; see Campbell, in press).

Given the individual shortcomings and idiosyncrasies of single methodologies, multiplism suggests that it is difficult to place great confidence in the results of a single study or of several studies with a common methodology. Rather, multiplism indicates that it is appropriate to be confident in one's inferences if they are based on results that converge across different methodologies, across researchers with different values and assumptions, and therefore across different idiosyncracies in studies. This position is one long advocated by Don Campbell, who uses such terms as "triangulation," "multiple operationalism," and "heterogeneity of irrelevancies." Similar advocacy of multiple methods can be found elsewhere in this volume in the chapters by Rossi and Wright, Marsh, and McLaughlin. Belsky also invokes the logic of multiplism in that he places confidence in the results of day-care research because "despite limits in design and especially measurement, findings across studies are surprisingly consistent" (this volume).

Partisanship and Conflicting Theories

The outcome of methodological multiplism is generally presumed to be simple if results coverge across methods: One places greater confidence in the conclusions drawn. In contrast, if results do not converge, the outcome is less clear. Presumably, the true effect lies between the estimates provided by the different methods, or there is an interaction of some sort to be discovered. But if one method seems less biased, to what degree should it be taken as providing a better estimate? Partisans of multiplism are not completely directive about what sort of inference to draw in the absence of convergence, except to suggest that in the absence of convergence "an empirical puzzle is obtained that calls out for resolution" (Cook, this volume).

Many partisans of multiplism do, however, state that multiplism is useful for policy-relevant research even if convergence does not occur. Their argument is that if alternative methods lead to conflicting results, then appropriate caution will be exercised, and the conflicting social science results will lead policymakers to recognize that the issue at hand is not a simple one (e.g., Heath, Kendzierski, & Borgida, 1982). Unfortunately, research evidence indicates that contradictory results do not increase uncertainty among partisans. When partisans view a mixed body of evidence, both sides leave with strengthened certainty in their (opposing) beliefs (Lord, Ross, & Lepper, 1979; also see Wortman & Bryant, in press, for an apparent instance in a policy area). Thus, one assumption of multiplism—that the absence of convergence across methods leads to more cautious conclusions—may not hold for partisan policy issues. In addition, conflicting results may have another cost: Large bodies of contradictory results in a single policy area may reduce policymakers' confidence in the ability of social scientists to provide useful information in general.

Methods Biased in the Same Direction

This critical evaluation of multiplism (this volume) suggests that, despite its apparent promise, multiplism is not without limitations. One serious potential limit is the possibility that methods may be biased in the same direction. This is obviously a problem if studies in a given research area share a common threat to validity because they employ related designs (e.g., Director, 1979). However, even if two methodologies are clearly distinct and have *different* threats to validity, they may still be biased in the *same* direction. Thus, even if there is no true treatment effect, the design flaws of each methodology would bias the results in the same direction and lead to the same inaccurate conclusion. For example, it is conceivable that selection artifacts in a nonequivalent control group design and history effects in an interrupted time-series design would both create bias in the direction of a positive treatment effect. In such cases, methodological multiplism would lead to greater confidence in an incorrect inference. It was apparently such a possibility that led Tittle (this volume) to say that "it would be reassuring to find a variety of types of studies pointing in the same direction but it might mean only that they are all wrong in complementing ways. Without reliable information about the exact way the methodological problems . . . affect outcomes, concluding that the total body of evidence is somehow more correct than its separate defective parts is wishful thinking." Cook, Kendzierski, and Thomas (1983), and Cook (this volume) suggest that this problem of shared direction of bias *may* have occurred in research on the relationship between television and aggression. Cook suggests that the two distinct methodologies used widely to examine this relationship— experimental laboratory studies and cross-sectional correlational studies—may both be biased in the same direction, that is, toward showing a positive relationship between viewing TV violence and aggression.

In the case of laboratory experiments with normal children, researchers minimize internal and external inhibitions against aggression and amplify the treatment in order to maximize their ability to detect treatment effects. Although this may be appropriate for testing social learning theory, it does not mirror the typical conditions of TV viewing, which occurs at home where childen watch normal television faire and the normal sanctions and inhibitions against aggression operate. Hence, Cook suggests, laboratory studies may be biased in the direction of finding a positive relationship between television viewing and aggression.

In the case of cross-sectional studies, again a positive bias seems possible. These studies correlate viewing time with aggression and typically employ statistical procedures in an attempt to "partial out" background differences. As Cook (this volume; Cook et al., 1983) notes, attempts to control statistically for background factors involve the use of demographic proxies for the unknown psychological and social factors that affect exposure to violence, and some of the differences between heavy and light viewers are likely to remain due to "underadjustment" (Campbell & Boruch, 1975). As a result, the observed relationship between television viewing and aggression may be inflated. The point is not that "underadjustment" has definitely occurred, according to Cook, "it is only that a plausible case can be made that the bias may have operated" (Cook, this volume).

As this example illustrates, the benefits of multiplism require confidence that the different methods are not biased in the same direction. Unfortunately, such confidence can be much more difficult to obtain than it may initially appear. This is because we can often imagine a plausible bias to account for an observed treatment effect, *whatever the direction of the effect.* In other words, one plausible bias could be invoked to account for a positive relationship, and another bias to explain a negative effect. As an illustration, imagine that research on television and aggression supported the "catharsis" hypothesis; that is, that viewing televised violence produced less aggression. Assume that this effect (which is, in fact, not well supported by research) was found using the same methodology just discussed.

Given these assumptions, we could plausibly argue that in the experimental laboratory studies, the treatment group (that was exposed to TV violence) perceived a connection between the violent TV fare and the opportunity to aggress. Indeed, they may have been more likely than control group members to see the dependent variable as aggression. Thus, lower "aggression" in the treatment group could occur because of "evaluation apprehension," not catharsis. One could also contend that cross-sectional methodology is biased toward a negative relationship between TV and aggression. This bias could arise for either of two reasons. First, the use of proxy variables in statistical "control" may lead to overadjustment rather than underadjustment (Cronbach, Rogosa, Floden, & Price, 1977), providing artifactual support for a cathartic effect of TV viewing. This explanation would be plausible if the simple, zero-order correlation between TV viewing and aggression is positive and a negative relationship emerges only after statistical adjustment. A second explanation of bias could be invoked if a negative relationship was obtained both in simple zero-order correlations and after statistical controls were applied. This explanation would be that (1) TV violence watching and aggression are negatively correlated for reasons having nothing to do with the effects of television—for example, low levels of aggression might *cause* high levels of TV violence watching—as the catharsis hypotheses itself would predict; and (2) statistical control underadjusts for these differences between heavy and light viewers.

The point we are making is a simple one. Given the current state of methodological development, it is difficult to identify different methodologies (1) that can be applied to a given research question and (2) for which a plausible case cannot be made that the methods are biased in the same direction. One cannot be confident that methodologies are not biased in the same direction if, for each method, bias in either direction is plausible! In large part, this difficulty arises because of the ambiguity of "plausibility" as a criterion. Cook (this volume) states that "the likelihood of avoiding a constant direction of bias depends on identifying all the plausible sources of such bias." We would add that more is required to be confident that we have avoided this problem; not only must alternative sources of bias be identified, but also the likelihood and magnitude of each source of bias must be estimated.

Methods Examining Different Questions

There are further difficulties with a multiplistic approach. If we select methods that are quite different, in order to capitalize on the fact that they have different shortcomings, can we be sure that the different methods are actually focusing on the same question? In other words, do the methods examine the same variables, or study the same constructs, or probe the same process? If different methods are addressing different phenomena, we should not necessarily expect convergence; and if convergence occurs the implications are unclear. This point may seem obvious; yet with some frequency the different methods used to investigate "a" question in fact are addressing different questions.

Perhaps the best explicated example involves the differences between cross-sectional and longitudinal regression analyses, which are often used (or misused) to study the same question. Several investigators have noted that cross-sectional and longitudinal regression may provide different answers because the underlying causal structures differ (e.g., Lieberson & Hansen, 1974). Much of this literature is summarized by Firebaugh (1980), who presents four reasons for obtaining different results with cross-sectional and longitudinal data. Firebaugh also provides an example, involving the relationship between fertility and literacy in India. For each of eleven regional districts, a time-series regression analysis for an eleven-year period produces a *negative* correlation between fertility and literacy. In contrast, each of a series of cross-sectional regressions (one for each of the eleven years) finds a *positive* correlation between these variables. (See Firebaugh, 1980, for more detail and discussion of possible reasons for this discrepancy.)

In another example, Easterlin (1973) has examined the relationship between money and happiness. When money and happiness are correlated across people at any give time, a *positive* relationship is obtained (i.e., those people with more money are happier). In contrast, Easterlin reports that when aggregate data (e.g., national averages) are examined there is *no correlation* between money and happiness over time (i.e., higher average income in a given year is not associated with higher average happiness). Consider Easterlin's explanation as to why the two different methodologies provide such different findings. He posits that money is related to happiness by a social comparison process: Seeing that you are better off than others enhances happiness. Thus, cross-sectional analyses tap into social comparison (e.g., "John is rich, Tom is richer—boy, am I poor and miserable") and find a positive relationship between money and happiness. In contrast, time-series regressions of aggregate data (or individual data) do not tap into social comparison in that they track one unit over time (i.e., if average income in the country increases 5 percent this year, the income of each person *relative to others* will likely not increase, so that no increase in average happiness will occur if Easterlin's social comparison explanation is correct). Thus time-series regressions do not find a relationship between money and happiness.

Our examples may give rise to the idea that the problem we are discussing (i.e., different methods addressing different questions) is limited in some way. It may seem to occur only if weak methodologies are used. After all, the shortcomings of correlational methods are well known. Or it may seem to occur only if methods differ in terms of their temporal scope. After all, cross-sectional designs clearly do not focus on change across time whereas time series regressions do. We contend that this is not the case. The problem does not result simply from the use of weak methodologies or from methods that differ in their temporal focus (although this may exacerbate the problem).

To illustrate, consider two types of experimental studies that might be conducted to examine the relationship between money and happiness. Study 1 is a traditional, independent group design with random assignment of individuals. Study 2 is an interrupted time-series design with switching replications, with units (in this case, isolated towns) randomly assigned to receipt of the treatment. These are two of social science's strongest designs in terms of threats to "internal validity" (see Campbell & Stanley, 1966; Cook & Campbell, 1979), and both designs allow us to study change over time. In Study 1, we could randomly assign residents of one small town either to an "extra" money condition in which they are given an income supplement (e.g., $50 a week) or to a control group that receives no additional money. In Study 2, we could randomly assign isolated small towns to enter the extra money condition at different times, either early or late in our time series. If Easterlin is correct, we should obtain an effect in Study 1: People in the extra money condition should be happier than those in the control group because they experience a gratifying social comparison in terms of income. In contrast, no effect would be observed in Study 2, assuming no comparisons across towns, because receipt of extra money would *not* create an advantageous social comparison. Two methods—both strong in terms of internal validity, and both putatively examining the causal effect of money on happiness—would reach different results because they do not manipulate the same causal process.

This discrepancy can be understood in terms of differences between Study 1 and Study 2 in the unit of analysis or level of aggregation examined. But being able to explain the discrepancy does not undermine the point that strong designs, putatively examining the same question, may in fact examine different processes. The example also illustrates another point: Substantive understanding, itself largely the product of research, is needed to specify whether or not methods are probing the same process.

The inferential difficulty of multiplism can be better understood by considering simultaneously the problem of method bias and the problem of different methods exploring different questions. Table 14.1 presents a simplified illustration of the combination of these two problems. We emphasize that the table is a simplification; that is, it only presents a dichotomous distinction. Further, it represents only one of several possible conceptualizations that can be used to describe the inferential difficulties of multiplism. In particular, although we present the factors in Table 14.1 as two distinct problems, they can be conceptualized as alternative forms of the same general problem: A discrepancy between the inference the data allow and the inference the researcher intends (cf. Reichardt, 1983). However, because of its considerable value for understanding, we employ here the distinction between the two problems represented in Table 14.1.

The top two cells (1, 2) of the 2 × 2 table represent the conditions typically considered in discussions of multiplism. When multiple methods examine a single question and the two methods are not biased in the same direction (Cell 2), multiplism will lead to stronger conclusions when results converge. When the methods examine the same process but are biased in the same direction (Cell 1), multiplism does not enhance conclusions, as noted above.

The inferential challenge of multiplism becomes much more problematic when we recognize the possibility that distinct methods are

TABLE 14.1
**An Illustration of the Bias and Question Problems
in Methodological Multiplism**

		Are Methods Biased in the Same Direction?	
		YES	NO
Do methods examine the same questions?	Y E S	(1) A single question is studied but with methods that are biased in the same direction. Convergence of results across methods reflects the methods' shared direction of bias. "Pseudo-convergence" will result.	(2) A single question is studied, with methods that are not biased in the same direction. Convergence of results would lead to stronger, more accurate inferences. This cell represents the ideal case for multiplism.
	N O	(3) Two questions are studied, and estimates of each are biased in the same direction. Observed pattern of results depends on the size of the two processes and the magnitude of bias.	(4) Two questions are studied, with methods that are not biased in the same direction. Many patterns of results can occur (including "pseudo-convergence"), depending on the actual magnitude of each effect and the bias of each method.

examining different questions (Cells 3 and 4 of Table 14.1). No longer is it simply a matter of the direction of bias in each method, although this difficulty remains. In addition, the possibility that the methods are examining different questions, while at the same time each may be biased, leads to an inferential quagmire. If two methods have different results, is it because they are differently biased in addressing the same question (Cell 2) or because they are probing different processes (Cells 3 or 4)? If results converge, is it a success of multiplism (Cell 2)? Or is it because two processes, differing in magnitude, were studied using methods with biases of countervailing magnitudes (e.g., Process A is positive and was studied with a negatively biased method, whereas Process B is negative and studied with a positively biased method, resulting in converging no-effect results)?

Toward a More Successful Use of Multiplism

Clearly what is needed is a theory of multiplism that specifies when multiplism is needed, when two methods will be biased in the same direction, and when they will address the same research question. Although we cannot specify in full all of these issues, we can point toward approaches that we believe will move social scientists toward a more targeted theory of multiplism.

Most critically, it is important to develop our knowledge of the biases that affect particular methods, including some estimate of the magnitude of these biases. Because the operation of bias is typically context-specific, this development will probably have to be done separately for different research areas. Two empirical approaches can contribute to this development. Most notably, meta-analysis can be used to synthesize existing studies to evaluate differences between the results obtained with the methods. Of course, any observed differences must be thoughtfully considered in terms of whether they reflect (1) method bias or (2) the methods' focus on different questions—a judgment that will rely heavily on substantive understanding. In this and other ways, conceptual and analytic work should be stimulated that explicates the processes that different methods examine (cf. Firebaugh, 1980). A second empirical approach that may be useful in studying the magnitude of biases in specific policy areas (and that can supplement deliberations about the results of meta-analysis) is experimental: Those characteristics of research thought to induce bias can be deliberately varied to assess their effects. This experimental approach can be useful in assessing the possible direction of bias, but is highly limited in estimating its magnitude.

Ultimately, of course, the goal is to have planned multiplism where we are confident that convergence reflects the phenomenon studied. This will be facilitated by conscious planning of the use of multiple methods—in contrast with the unsystematic way in which the use of multiple methods currently arises. Successful planning of multiplism requires a "theory" of multiplism that guides the choice of methods in particular settings; the construction of such a theory, we believe, is among the central tasks for social science. And, of course, in any attempt to employ multiple methods, inferences will be enhanced to the extent that procedures are used to minimize the bias in each method (Cook & Campbell, 1979; Reichardt, 1983).

Our description of procedures to move toward a more successful use of multiplism has been brief, and Cook (this volume) provides additional suggestions for a targeted multiplism. We concur with Cook's assessment that the ultimate benefits of multiplism, which are "more incisive and comprehensive research questions as well as results that are more dependable . . . are not trivial expected gains, but they will be hard-won" (this volume).

Conclusions

The logic underlying methodological multiplism is an important component of contemporary social science practice. However, multiplism is not without limitations. In policy areas, the absence of convergence will probably not lead to cautious inference. Further, it is often difficult to interpret the results of multiple methods, in that (1) methods may be biased in the same direction and (2) they may, in fact, be examining different questions. These possibilities are especially troubling because the "plausibility" of bias is an ambiguous concept and we are typically unsure of the precise process(es) being investigated by any particular method. Suggestions were briefly offered that may move us toward a more targeted theory of multiplism.

Our criticisms of multiplism should not be taken as an overall attack on multiplistic approaches. Like Cook, what we are criticizing is the mindless, uncritical use of multiplism that is as likely to lead to greater confusion as to clarification. Futher, it is important to recognize that the use of a single method does not avoid the underlying problems we have discussed.

Finally, we should note that multiplism, in Cook's terminology, refers to more than methodology and includes multiplism of questions, values, and stakeholders. Of course, these issues are also critical (see Campbell, 1984, for a model of evaluation that incorporates multiplism of these various sorts).

RESEARCHABILITY ASSESSMENT

The preceding chapters in this volume highlighted numerous impediments to more effective use of the social sciences in policymaking processes. In the present chapter we have highlighted some of these impediments and have offered recommendations toward more usable social science. For example, we suggested that social science researchers focus more on distal measures and on construct validity; more frequently conduct implementation assessments and research on variations in implementation; and assess the possible uses of social science inputs.

To facilitate the implementation of many of our recommendations and, more generally, to aid in making social science research more useful, we suggest a mechanism for research planning that we call "researchability assessment." Researchability assessment can be seen as a generalization and extension to entire policy areas, such as day care, gun control, or deterrence, of the evaluability assessment methods developed by Wholey (1979, 1983), Rutman (1980), and others for specific programs.[5]

In this section we provide a brief sketch of researchability assessment, which we describe as being comprised of two phases: (1) Question formulation and appraisal, and (2) assessment of the feasibility of quality research. This dichotomy is a heuristic rather than descriptive one in that the two "phases" often overlap and finer distinctions can be made.

Question Formulation and Appraisal

This phase of researchability assessment involves the explication of the various research questions that might be asked about a policy area and the assessment of the degree to which each question is relevant for policy. In other words, in this phase one asks: What question *might* be investigated, and, further, which ones *should* be? A thoughtful, informed formulation and appraisal of research questions is needed to avoid three types of problems.

Problem 1: Investigating a research question that in general is not of high relevance to policy As Crain and Carsrud (this volume) state, "it is often the case in academic evaluations that a policymaker has one set of questions about a policy and the evaluator answers a different set. This is clearly what has happened in desegregation research." Crain and Carsrud go on to argue that the question, "Does desegregation work?" is irrelevant to policymakers because desegregation is not a policy choice—it is the law of the land. To local stakeholders—including superintendents, teachers, and parents—the critical question therefore is: "What things can we manipulate in implementing desegregation to make it most effective?" As this example illustrates, large bodies of purportedly policy-relevant research can develop, even though the research does not address the primary needs of potential research users.

Problem 2: Investigating a research question that in general is of high relevance to policy, but operationalizing it in ways that diminish policy relevance (Cronbach et al., 1980) For example, policymakers may be interested in an outcome evaluation of a program, but policy relevance would be diminished if the program is evaluated before it is fully operational and stable (Mark & Cook, 1984). As this example illustrates, not only must the general research question be of interest to policy, so too must the research question *as operationalized.*

Problem 3: Failing to address the range of research questions necessary to provide a reasonable answer to a policy-relevant question For example, policymakers may ask, "Does Program X affect Outcomes Y and Z?" It may appear that this question requires only methods of causal analysis, such as randomized experiments; however, a range of research must to conducted to provide a reasonable answer, including implementation assessment, description of contextual variables, and study of the process by which the program operates (Cook, Leviton, & Shadish, in press; Cronbach et al., 1980; Mark & Cook, 1984).

To avoid these problems, researchability assessment includes thoughtful critical analysis to specify the question or questions of greatest interest for policymaking. The methodology for this analysis is related to that described by Wholey (1979), Rutman (1980), and others (e.g., Cronbach et al., 1980) in discussions of evaluability assessment or evaluation planning and consists of several tasks. A critical task advocated by St. Pierre, Marsh, and Cook in the present volume is to hold discussions with policymakers and various stakeholder groups to prove their concerns. In addition, a model of policymaking processes for the policy area should be constructed to aid in the identification of leverage points; that is, places in the system in which change seems most possible (see Cook et al., 1983, for an example). The policy should be analyzed in terms of its location in the model presented in Figure 14.1, to identify research questions appropriate to the phase of the particular policy area. Additional insight into the possible range of policy questions may come from reviewing published and unpublished research in the policy area, any other documentation about the policy area, and relevant theory and research from related policy areas and basic social science. Through these various tasks, questions formulation should increase the likelihood that research will be targeted at important, policy-relevant questions.

Assessing the Feasibility of Quality Research

Given that policy-relevant questions have been identified, the question arises: To what extent can each be the subject of valid research, in light of existing methodological, measurement, resource, and other limitations? In short, can the policy questions of interest be addressed by research that meets contemporary standards of scientific validity? In addressing this question, a researchability assessment may specify a number of issues: (1) What sort of research is most likely to result in useful, high-quality information? (2) What assumptions underlie different research methods that might be used; and thus what sort of methodological multiplism is warranted, if any? (3) How should results be communicated to policymakers and interested stakeholder groups? (See especially Sechrest, this volume, on interpretable statistics.)

In considering the available research methods, a researchability assessment may conclude that a particular research question cannot currently be the subject of quality research. In such a case, the researchability assessment should identify what changes are necessary for quality research (e.g., the development and collection of some new indicator by the government); additionally, the researchability assessment should suggest means of making these changes (e.g., lobbying for better government statistics). Further, if a question cannot be adequately answered given existing constraints, a *suggestion* may be offered that the research community forego research on the question until the critical constraints are overcome.

Because a single researchability assessment will almost certainly deal with several research questions, very different conclusions may emerge. Question A may be readily amendable to quality research, whereas quality research on Question B may require changes such as the development of new measures.

Mechanisms

Researchability assessments could be conducted and staffed in a number of different ways. The actual procedure followed may depend on the sponsoring organization. For example, the National Academy of Science might choose to convene a "Blue Ribbon Panel." Government agencies might choose an RFP (Request for Proposal) approach. Social science organizations interested in social policy, such as the Evaluation Research Society (ERS) and the Society for the Psychological Study of Social Issues (SPSSI), could choose a number of different mechanisms. It is easy to imagine such organizations sponsoring a book or special issue of a journal to present the reports of multiple researchability assessment teams. The teams could be selected to represent divergent positions about the policy area to reduce the extent to which shared biases lead to a particular conclusion. Thus the robustness of conclusions across different value positions could be assessed.

Whatever its form, the researchability team or teams should provide a detailed description of its conclusions in the form of a book, special journal issues, etc. Before publication, it would be highly desirable for the researchability assessment team to present preliminary ideas at conferences or in draft form to solicit outside opinions. Indeed, if possible, systematic feedback should be obtained through surveys of the scientific community.

The conclusions of a researchability assessment should not be "cast in stone" either before or after publication. Other researchers should be encourged to make their own case that the team's conclusions are incorrect, or that they have overcome the problems cited in the researchability assessment. Open, thoughtful, critical debate in the scholarly community about what can be accomplished in a policy area and how is the most desirable outcome of researchability assessment.

Conclusion

Without experience it is difficult to estimate the payoff for researchability assessment. Nevertheless, we are optimistic that researchability assessment holds promise for improving the quality for policy research, for avoiding unresolvable debates based on low-quality research about currently intractable questions, and for enhancing the image of social scientists' ability to contribute to policy discussions. In this section, we have only briefly outlined the concept of researchability assessment. We have not even touched on some important concerns about this procedure that warrant discussion (e.g., scope of the assessment, timeliness of research, the ability to achieve consensus about research quality, and limitations in our ability to predict the future information needs of policymakers). In addition, further debate and consideration should be given to alternative mechanisms for conducting researchability assessments. Given its potential, we believe that researchability assessment is worthy of careful consideration by the social science community. We hope that, despite the brevity of our presentation, we have at least suggested the potential value of researchability assessment as a mechanism for planning research more useful to policy.

CONCLUSIONS

Like most contributors to this volume, we believe that social science research and theory can benefit policy. We also believe that despite some past successes, most policy-oriented social scientists would like their work to be even more useful.

Thoughtful social scientists do not wish to be the sole determiners of social policy, or to apply their value judgments in place of those of the democratic process. The social scientist as philosopher-king is dead. A less naive conception has emerged of the role of the policy-oriented social scientist that is more fitting of a democratic society. Social scientists seek to improve the conceptualizations of those involved in policymaking by widening and clarifying the range of policy choices, pointing out complexities that may be overlooked, and pro-

viding new perspectives on a policy issue. Social scientists also seek
to provide information that is useful in policymaking by documenting
problems, monitoring implementation, and evaluating policy alternatives.
To be more successful in our goal of contributing to policy, we
must try to clear our path of obstacles to such contributions. There
are no guarantees, and making social science more useful is not an
easy task, but it is certainly a worthwhile one. The potential payoff
for society is great—more effective and more just social policy.

NOTES

1. For example, most firearms used in crimes in New York City were not originally
purchased in New York; instead they were purchased in jurisdictions with less restrictive
gun laws (Bureau of Alcohol, Tobacco, and Firearms, 1976).

2. It is worth noting that implementation assessment should usually focus on the
"control group" as well as the treatment group. For example, studies of school desegregation are difficult to interpret without knowing the level and nature of desegregation
in the "control" schools. By focusing on the comparison group as well as the treatment
group, implementation assessment can increase understanding of the *contrast* that is
one's "independent variable" or "treament"; in this way, implementation assessment
can further increase the construct validity of the cause.

3. We use the term "policymaking" and related terms such as "policymakers" for
convenience's sake, even though they may imply a more rational, bounded process
than actually occurs in the creation of process (Weiss, 1982).

4. The comments in this section have dealt with *substantive* social science theory and
its use as a conceptual input into policymaking. The usefulness of social science research
for policymaking will also be enhanced—perhaps more so—by the development of strong
theories of *methodology*. We particularly have in mind the development of a strong theory
of methodological multiplism. As noted in the next section of this chapter, there is great
need for conceptual framework that identifies the conditions under which methodological
multiplism will be effective. Similarly, *implementation* theory may improve the effects of
social programs by leading to more effective institutionalization and dissemination, as
noted in the preceding section. Finally, the further development of theory about policymaking may lead to research that better addresses the information needs of potential
users.

5. Researchability assessment is an institutional mechanism for improving social
science inputs into policy. It joins other proposed institutional mechanisms that share
this goal, such as Cellarius and Platt's (1972) proposal for "Councils of Urgent Studies,"
Cronbach et al.'s (1980) proposal for "social problem study groups," and the "science
court" and "standing substantive committees" discussed by Hennigan, Flay, and Cook
(1980). We shall not here contrast researchability assessment in detail with these other
proposals, which it complements. Suffice it to say that relative to these other institutional
mechanisms, researchability assessment is generally more limited in scope; less expensive;
more amenable to a variety of sponsors; more oriented toward the planning of future
research; and less oriented to the conduct of research or the synthesis of past research.

REFERENCES

Beyer, J. M., & Trice, H. M. (1982). The utilization process: A conceptual framework and synthesis of empirical findings. *Administrative Science Quarterly, 27,* 591-622.

Bureau of Alcohol, Tobacco, and Firearms. (1976). *Project identification: A study of handguns used in crime* (ATFP 3310, 1, May). Washington, DC: Government Printing Office.

Campbell, D. T. (1984). Can we be scientific in applied social science? In R. Connor et al. (Eds.), *Evaluation studies review annual* (Vol. 9). Beverly Hills, CA: Sage.

Campbell, D. T., & Boruch, R. F (1975). Making the case for randomized assignment to treatment by considering the alternatives: Six ways in which quasi-experimental evaluations tend to underestimate effects. In C. A. Bennet & A. A. Lumsdaine (Eds.), *Evaluation and experience: Some critical issues in assessing social programs.* New York: Academic Press.

Campbell, D. T., & Stanley, J. C. (1966). *Experimental and quasi-experimental designs for research.* Chicago: Rand McNally.

Cellarius, R. A., & Platt, J. U. (1972). Councils of urgent studies. *Science, 177,* 670-676.

Chen, H., & Rossi, P. H. (1983). Evaluating with sense: The theory driven approach. *Evaluation Review, 7,* 238-302.

Cohen, D. K., & Weiss, J. A. (1977). Social science and social policy: Schools and race. In C. H. Weiss (Ed.), *Using social research in public policy making.* Lexington, MA: D. C. Heath.

Cook, T. D., & Campbell, D. T. (1979). *Quasi-experimentation: Design and analysis issues for field settings.* Chicago: Rand McNally.

Cook, T. D., Kendzierski, D. A., & Thomas, S. V. (1983). The implicit assumptions of television research: An analysis of the 1982 NIMH Report on "Television and Behavior." *Public Opinion Quarterly, 47,* 161-201.

Cook, T. D., Leviton, C. L., & Shadish, W., Jr. (in press). Program evaluation. In G. Lindzey & E. Aronson (Eds.), *Handbook of social psychology* (3rd ed.). Boston: Addison-Wesley.

Cronbach, L. J., Ambron, S. R., Dornbush, S. M., Hess, R. D., Hornik, R. C., Phillips, D. C., Walker, D. F., & Weiner, S. S. (1980). *Toward reform of program evaluation.* San Francisco, CA: Jossey-Bass.

Cronbach, L. J., Rogosa, D. R., Floden, R. E., & Price, G. G. (1977). *Analysis of covariance in nonrandomized experiments: Parameters affecting bias.* Occasional paper, Stanford Evaluation Consortium, Stanford University.

Director, S. M. (1979). Underadjustment bias in the evaluation of manpower training. *Evaluation Quarterly, 3,* 190-218.

Easterlin, R. (1973). Does money buy happiness? *The Public Interest, 30,* 3-10.

Feuer, L. S. (1954). Causality in social sciences. *Journal of Philosophy, 51,* 681-695.

Firebaugh, G. (1980). Cross-national versus historical regression models: Conditions of equivalence in comparative analysis. *Comparative Social Research, 3,* 333-344.

Hall, G. E., & Loucks, S. F. (1977). A developmental model for determining whether the treatment is actually implemented. *American Educational Research Journal, 14,* 263-276.

Heath, L., Kendzierski, D., & Borgida, E. (1982). Evaluation of social programs: A multimethodological approach combining a delayed treatment true experiment and multiple time series. *Evaluation Review, 6,* 233-246.

Heilman, J. G. (1983). Beyond the technical and bureaucratic theories of utilization: Some thoughts on synthesizing reviews and the knowledge base of the evaluation profession. *Evaluation Review, 7,* 707-728.

Hennigan, K. M., Flay, B. R., & Cook, T. D. (1980). "Give me the facts!": The use of social science evidence in formulating national policy. In R. F. Kidd & M. J. Saks (Eds.), *Advances in applied social psychology* (Vol. 1). Hillsdale, NJ: Erlbaum.

Kenny, D. (1980). *Correlation and causality.* New York: John Wiley.

Leithwood, K. A., & Montgomery, D. J. (1980). Evaluating program implementation. *Evaluation Review, 4,* 193-214.

Levin, H. M. (1977). A decade of policy development in improving education and training of low income populations. In R. Haveman (Ed.), *A decade of federal antipoverty programs: Achievements, failures and lessons.* New York: Academic Press.

Leviton, L. C., & Hughes, E.F.X. (1981). Research on the utilization of evaluations: A review and synthesis. *Evaluation Review, 5,* 525-548.

Lieberson, S., & Hansen, L. K. (1974). National development, mother tongue diversity, and the comparative study of nations. *American Sociological Review, 39,* 523-541.

Lindblom, C. E. (1972). Integration of economics and other social sciences through policy analysis. In J. C. Charlesworth (Ed.), *Integration of the social sciences through policy analysis.* Philadelphia: AAPSS.

Lindblom, C. E., & Cohen, D. K. (1979). *Usable knowledge: Social science and social problem solving.* New Haven, CT: Yale University Press.

Lord, C. G., Ross, L., & Lepper, M. (1979). Biased assimilation and attitude polarization: The effects of prior theories on subsequently considered evidence. *Journal of Personality and Social Psychology, 37,* 2098-2109.

Lynn, L. E., Jr. (Ed.). (1978). *Knowledge and policy: The uncertain connection* (Study Project on Social Research and Development, Vol. 5). Washington, DC: National Academy of Sciences.

Mark, M. M., & Bryant, F. B. (1984). Potential pitfalls of a more applied social psychology: Review and recommendations. *Basic and Applied Social Psychology, 5,* 231-251.

Mark, M. M., & Cook, T. D. (1984). Randomized and quasi-experimental research design. In L. Rutman (Ed.), *Evaluation methods: A basic guide* (2nd ed.). Beverly Hills, CA: Sage.

McCord, J. (1978). A thirty-year follow-up of treatment effects. *American Psychologist, 33,* 284-289.

Pepinsky, H. E. (1980). *Crime control strategies: An introduction to the study of crime.* New York: Oxford University Press.

Ravetz, J. R. (1971). *Scientific knowledge and its social problems.* New York: Oxford University Press.

Reichardt, C. S. (1983). *On the logic and practice of assessing cause.* Paper presented at the annual meeting of the American Educational Research Association, Toronto, Canada.

Rezmovic, E. L. (1984). Assessing treatment implementation amid the slings and arrows of reality. *Evaluation Review, 8,* 187-204.

Rich, R. F. (1977). Uses of social science information by federal bureaucrats: Knowledge for action vs. knowledge for understanding. In C. H. Weiss (Ed.), *Using social research in public policy making.* Lexington, MA: D. C. Heath.

Rutman, L. (1980). *Planning useful evaluations: Evaluability assessment.* Beverly Hills, CA: Sage.

Saxe, L. (1983). The perspective of social psychology: Toward a viable model for application. In R. F. Kidd & M. J. Saks (Eds.), *Advances in applied social psychology* (Vol. 2). Hillsdale, NJ: Erlbaum.

Scott, R. L., & Shore, A. R. (1979). *Why sociology does not apply.* New York: Elsevier.

Shotland, R. L., & Goodstein, L. (1983). Just because she doesn't want to doesn't mean it's rape: An experimentally based causal model of the perception of rape in a dating situation. *Social Psychology Quarterly, 46,* 220-232.

Shotland, R. L., & Stebbins, C. A. (1983). Emergency and costs as determinants of helping behavior and the slow accumulation of social psychological knowledge. *Social Psychology Quarterly, 46,* 36-46.

Stromsdorfer, E. W., & Farkas, G. (Ed.). (1980). *Evaluation studies review annual* (Vol. 5). Beverly Hills, CA: Sage.

Weiss, C. H. (Ed.). (1977). *Using social research in public policy making.* Lexington, MA: D. C. Heath.

Weiss, C. H. (1978). Improving the linkage between social research and public policy. In L. E. Lynn, Jr. (Ed.), *Knowledge and policy: The uncertain connection* (Study Project on Social Research and Development, Vol. 5). Washington, DC: National Academy of Sciences.

Weiss, C. H. (1982). Policy research in the context of diffuse decision making. In R. C. Rist (Ed.), *Policy studies review annual* (Vol. 6). Beverly Hills, CA: Sage.

Wholey, J. S. (1979). *Evaluation: Promise and performance.* Washington, DC: The Urban Institute.

Wholey, J. S. (1983). *Evaluation and effective public management.* Boston: Little, Brown.

Wortman, P. M., & Bryant, F. B. (in press). School desegregation and black achievement: An intergrative review. *Sociological Methods and Research.*

About the Authors

R. Lance Shotland is a Professor of Psychology at The Pennsylvania State University. His interests include the interphase between social science and social policy, methodology, evaluation research, bystander behavior, and crime control. In addition to his other publications he is co-author of *Television and Antisocial Behavior* (with Stanley Milgram) and author of *University Communications Networks: The Small World Method.*

Melvin M. Mark is an Assistant Professor of Psychology at The Pennsylvania State University. He is co-editor of *Evaluation Studies Review Annual,* Volume 3, and author of several chapters and articles on methodological issues in evaluation and applied social science. In addition to his interests in the use of social science theory and research in policy processes, Dr. Mark's research focuses on relative deprivation and the social psychology of justice.

Leigh S. Shaffer (born 1947) is an Associate Professor of Psychology at West Chester University in West Chester, Pennsylvania. Dr. Shaffer studied with Carolyn W. Sherif at the Pennsylvania State University, completing his doctorate in 1974. His research interests include the impact of social norms and beliefs upon behavior and social problems. His publications include "The Golden Fleece: Anti-Intellectualism and Social Science" (in the *American Psychologist*), "The Growth and Limits of Recipe Knowledge," and "Toward Pepitone's Vision of a Normative Social Psychology: What is a Social Norm?" (both in *The Journal of Mind and Behavior*). He has also written several articles for the forthcoming *Baker's Encyclopedia of Psychology.*

Stephanie A. Shields received her Ph.D. from the Pennsylvania State University. She is an Assistant Professor of Psychology and Director of the Women's Studies Program at the University of California, Davis. Her research is concerned with the impact of socialization on individual emotional experience. She has also done extensive work on the history of the scientific study of gender.

Thomas D. Cook is a Professor of Psychology and Education at Northwestern University where he is also a Faculty Research Associate at the Center for Urban Affairs and Public Policy. He is interested in metascience, policy research in general and program evaluation in particular, social psychology, and communication research. Although he yearns for the peace and quiet in which to try to relate these interests to each other, he despairs of ever climbing off the treadmill for overcommitted academic junkies who, if they did not write so much, would probably end up dreaming each day away or organizing academic programs that probably need benign neglect more than reorganization. In 1982 he received the Myrdal Prize for Science of the Evaluation Research Society. It had to be the prize for science; the other relevant prize is for service!

Lee Sechrest has recently moved to the University of Arizona where he is Professor and Head of the Department of Psychology. Prior to that he was Director of the Center for Research on the Utilization of Scientific Knowledge, The Institute for Social Research, The University of Michigan. Even earlier, he taught at Florida State University, Northwestern University, and Pennsylvania State University. Ever since receiving his Ph.D. at Ohio State, he has been fascinated by problems in research methods in the social sciences.

Milbrey Wallin McLaughlin is an Associate Professor of Education, Associate Director of the Institute for Research on Educational Finance and Governance, and Chair of the Evaluation Training Program at Stanford's School of Education. Prior to joining Stanford, McLaughlin was a Senior Social Scientist at the Rand Corporation. Her areas of specialization include education change and development, policy implementation, and evaluation of programs in the public sector. Most recently, she has been involved in studies of teacher evaluation and a national study of state and local responses to the Reagan Administration's Education Consolidation and Improvement Act.

Thomas F. Pettigrew is a Professor of Social Psychology at the University of California, Santa Cruz. He is a former president of the Society for the Psychological Study of Social Issues (1967-1968) and Council Member of the American Sociological Association (1979-1982). His books include *Profile of the Negro American (1964), Racially Separate or Together?* (1971), *Racial Discrimination in the United States* (1975), and *The Sociology of Race Relations: Reflection and Reform* (1980).

Marylee C. Taylor is an Associate Professor of Sociology at the Pennsylvania State University. A social psychologist interested in methodological issues, she has recently authored a meta-analysis of research on psychological androgyny and an application of latent class analysis to longitudinal attitude data. Her primary substantive interest is race relations, and her current research focuses on the structure of white racial attitudes.

Pamela Stone Cain is Associate Professor of Sociology at Hunter College of the City University of New York. She received her Ph.D. from Johns Hopkins University in 1979 and her B. A. from Duke University in 1973. She has published several articles on job analysis, job segregation by sex, and comparable worth. She is currently studying the career histories of women and their husbands over the family life cycle in order to better understand some of the factors contributing to the maintenance of sex segregation.

Henry M. Levin is a Professor in the School of Education and Department of Economics, and is the Director of the Institute for Research on Educational Finance and Governance at Stanford University. He is a former Fellow at the Center for Advanced Study in the Behavioral Sciences. Prior to his arrival at Stanford in 1968, he was a Research Associate in the Economic Studies Division of the Brookings Institution. He has also served on the faculties of Rutgers and New York Universities. He has been a consultant to many state and federal agencies on issues in public finance, the economics of education, and cost-effectiveness analysis, and he is presently a consultant to the World Bank. He is the author of over 100 scholarly articles and the author or co-author of eight books. He was the President of the Evaluation Research Society in 1982.

Robert G. St. Pierre is a Vice President at Abt Associates Inc. where he has been principal investigator or co-principal investigator for several national evaluation studies in areas such as agriculture, nutrition, and education. He is currently directing a congressionally mandated evaluation of alternatives to the donation of agricultural commodities in the National School Lunch Program. Dr. St. Pierre has published over 30 articles in technical and substantive journals and has an ongoing interest in the management of evaluations.

Robert L. Crain's most recent study of exemplary high schools, *Making Desegregation Work* (with Rita Mahard and Ruth Narot), is his fourth book on schools and race. His review of the effect of desegregation on black achievement in *American Sociological Review* has been widely reprinted, and he has done several studies of the effects of desegregation on minority college success, employment, and personal adjustment. Most recently he has co-authored with Diana Pearce and Reynolds Farley a study of the way school desegregation encourages desegregation of housing. A sociologist, his other research fields are research methods, education, and urban politics.

Karen Banks Carsrud is a Planning, Evaluation, and Program Adult Specialist for the Governor's Office in Austin, Texas. She received her Ph.D. in quantitative methods from the Educational Psychology Department at the University of Texas at Austin. Previously, she has served as Lecturer in Mathematics at St. Edward's University and as Evaluator of the Austin Independent School District. She has written or co-authored numerous articles and reports of research in applied settings, primarily focusing on institutionalized clients, educational programs for disadvantages students, and desegregation.

Jay Belsky received his Ph.D. in Human Development and Family Studies from Cornell University in 1978 and is currently an Associate Professor of Human Development in the Department of Individual and Family Studies at Penn State University. He presently directs a three-cohort longitudinal study of infant and family development and recently published a volume entitled *The Child in the Family* (Addison-Welsey, 1984).

Charles R. Tittle is a Professor of Sociology and Chairman of the Department of Sociology and Social Psychology, Florida Atlantic University, Boca Raton, Florida. He received his Ph.D. in Sociology from the University of Texas, Austin, in 1965 and has served on the faculty of Indiana University at Bloomington. His interests have included the sociology of corrections, social control, social status and crime, and criminological theory. He is the author of two books (*Society of Subordinates* and *Sanctions and Social Deviance*) as well as numerous journal articles.

Jeanne C. Marsh is an Associate Professor at the School of Social Service Administration at the University of Chicago. She has teaching and research interests in the areas of program and policy evaluation with special emphasis on the utilization of evaluative information for program management and policy development. She has been involved in evaluations in the areas of substance abuse, mental health, and sexual assault, and is co-author with Alison Geist and Nathan Caplan of *Rape and the Limits of Law Reform* (Auburn House, 1982).

Peter H. Rossi is a Professor of Sociology at the University of Massachusetts and Past President of the American Sociological Association. He has written more than 20 books and 125 scholarly papers on topics ranging from political sociology to applied social research. Among the most distinguished of American social scientists, Rossi's recent publications include four books on natural hazards and environmental risk management, the volume (with James Wright) on weapons and violent crime, and *Measuring Social Judgments* (with Steve Nock).

James D. Wright is the Director of the Social and Demographic Research Institute at the University of Massachusetts. He is author or co-author of seven books and over 50 scholarly articles, including *The Dissent of the Governed* (1976) and, most recently, *Under the Gun: Weapons, Crime, and Violence in America* (co-authored with Peter Rossi).